Democratic Justice

THE INSTITUTION FOR SOCIAL AND POLICY STUDIES AT YALE UNIVERSITY

THE YALE ISPS SERIES

Democratic Justice

Ian Shapiro

Yale University Press • *New Haven & London*

Designed by Rebecca Gibb. Set in Janson type by Tseng Informations Systems, Inc. Printed in the United States of America.

Library of Congress Catalog Card Number 98–55976

ISBN 0-300-08908-2 (pbk. : alk. paper)

A catalogue record for this book is available from the British Library.

The paper in this book meets the guidelines for permanence and durability of the Committee on Production Guidelines for Book Longevity of the Council on Library Resources.

10 9 8 7 6 5 4 3 2

For Judy, Xan, and Yani

There are those who grow
gardens in their heads
paths that lead from their hair
to sunny and white cities

it's easy for them to write
they close their eyes
immediately schools of images
stream down from their foreheads

my imagination
is a piece of board
my sole instrument
is a wooden stick

I strike the board
it answers me
yes—yes
no—no

Zbigniew Herbert

Contents

Acknowledgments

MANY HANDS, THEY SAY, make light work. This book, which began struggling for life more than a decade ago, has not been light work. Still, it would have been immeasurably heavier but for the obliging assistance of dozens of students, research assistants, colleagues, and friends. Drafts of all its chapters have been discussed in so many seminars, conferences, and workshops that it would be impossible to catalogue the names of everyone who helped improve it along the way. That I do not try to do so here does not mean that I am ungrateful for any of the advice I have received, whether or not I have been wise enough to heed it.

A number of people should nonetheless be singled out for notably helpful discussions, or for commenting on parts or all of earlier drafts. Bruce Ackerman, Dick Arneson, Mark Barenberg, Brian Barry, David Benatar, Bob Dahl, John Dunn, André Du Toit, David Dyzenhaus, John Ferejohn, Michael Graetz, Casiano Hacker-Cordón, Jeff Isaac, John Kane, Bob Lane, Ed Lindblom, Ted Marmor, Jerry Mashaw, Nicoli Nattrass, Susan Okin, David Plotke, Adam Przeworski, Doug Rae, Jeremy Seekings, Marion Smiley, Steve Smith, Shannon Stimson, Norma Thompson, Philippe van Parijs, Steve Wizner, and Iris Young have all left their marks on the final product, as have two remarkably helpful anonymous readers for Yale University Press. Graham Duncan, Matthew Funk, Clarissa Hayward, Ji Yun Kim, and Joshua Kleinfeld performed valiant service as research assistants. Duncan and Hayward far transcended this role; both have my gratitude for exceedingly useful suggestions.

Three people deserve more particular thanks. Jim Scott was ready with sage advice at several critical junctures. His concept of mētis is a second cousin of the notion of insider's wisdom deployed in these pages. It should be said by reference to both ideas that Scott is the consummate author's author. Adolph Reed Jr. and Rogers Smith have lived with the project from its most formative and least coherent stages through to an end that would have been more bitter than sweet without their extensive assistance. Reed's uncanny ability to keep his eye on the ball through welters of chattering literature has saved me from irrelevance more often than is comfortable to recall. Smith's combination of acuteness, intellectual range, and generosity of spirit is unparalleled in my experience. He insists, modestly, that he is not a political theorist. No one who has dealt with him on a sustained basis can believe that. The effort he has put into helping me improve this book outstrips any reasonable interpretation of the collegial call of duty. The prospect of repaying such debts is daunting.

I began writing, with the help of a much appreciated Guggenheim, at the Center for Advanced Study in the Behavioral Sciences in Palo Alto in 1988. I finished a decade later at the University of Cape Town, thanks to generous support from its Department of Political Studies. It is difficult to imagine more inspiring circumstances in which to live and write about politics. In the interim, visiting fellowships at New York University Law School in 1991–92 and Nuffield College, Oxford, in 1995 provided stimulating environments from which this work derived edification. Yale University should also be given its due for generous sabbatical leave and research support policies. Its Institution for Social and Policy Studies, led by Don Green, sustains a Political Theory Workshop that is the best forum I know of in which to try out arguments and get constructive criticism. Most of these pages have been put through its wringer at one time or another, and at least some of them have been improved. I am deeply grateful for all this help, as well as for Kellianne Farnham's sterling secretarial assistance and boundless good humor. Many hands, indeed.

Material in the first two chapters was first published as "Three Ways to Be a Democrat" in *Political Theory*, vol. 22, no. 1 (February 1994), pp. 124–51. An earlier version of Chapter 3 appeared as "Elements of Democratic Justice" in *Political Theory*, vol. 24, no. 4 (November 1996), pp. 579–619, and some arguments now reworked in Chapter 6 appeared in "Resources, Capacities, and Ownership: The Workmanship Ideal and Distributive Justice," *Political Theory*, vol. 19, no. 1 (February 1991), pp. 28–46. They are copyright © 1994, 1996, and 1991, respectively, by Sage Publications and drawn on by permission here. Thanks are also due to Ecco Press for permission to reprint from "A Knocker," published in *Selected Poems* by Zbigniew Herbert, translated by Czeslaw Milosz and Peter Dale Scott in the United States. Copyright © 1968 by Zbigniew Herbert. Translation copyright © Czeslaw Milosz and Peter Dale Scott, 1968 in the United States. Thanks are due to Penguin Books Ltd. for permission to reproduce this material elsewhere in the world.

John Covell of Yale University Press has my appreciation for his confidence in the project from the beginning, and for talking his colleagues into offering me an advance contract on the basis of a pretty miserable first draft. And Judy, Xan, and Yani Shapiro all deserve much, much more than the usual "thanks-to-family" for their many indulgences over the years during which I labored to improve its spirits.

Democratic Justice

Why Democratic Justice?

HOW COMFORTABLY DO OUR COMMITMENTS TO DEMOCRACY fit with our convictions about social justice? This question is rooted in two observations about our circumstances. First, in spite of democracy's unexpected triumph in much of the world since the 1980s, little attention has been paid to democracy's rightful place in a just social order, or even to what democracy is and what it requires. Perhaps this is inevitable. Those who fight for democracy often define their goals reactively. Sure as they are about the fine details of what they are against, they are less clear about the texture of what they hope to create. The French revolutionaries had a good sense of why *l'ancien régime* should be destroyed; they knew little of what a world in which *liberté, égalité, et fraternité* reigned supreme might actually be like. Their American counterparts discoursed with alacrity on imperial injustice, but they and their successors argued for decades—even fought a civil war— over how their indigenous democratic institutions should be structured. The Russian revolutionaries in 1917 may have thought they had a blueprint for utopian people's democracy; but they were wrong. Efficacious as the dictatorship of the proletariat was at destroying czarist Russia, it quickly atrophied into the dictatorship to the proletariat by the Vanguard Party.

In our own era democratic ideals have also been forged out of opposition ideologies. In the revolutions since 1989, demands for democracy had little to do with well-thought-out plans for the future political order. More often they have been placeholders for what people believed they have hitherto been denied. In South Africa, for instance, those who fought for democracy identified it in the first instance with apartheid's abolition. What it might mean beyond that began to come dimly into view only as the old order was displaced; in many respects it remains an open question a decade after the National Party regime began crumbling. Likewise with the momentous events surrounding the collapse of communism. Before the Soviet Union's demise, the main opposition movements there and in Eastern Europe all identified themselves as democratic. Yet many Westerners who traveled behind the remnants of the iron curtain in the early 1990s found themselves taken aback by how little grasp of democracy its advocates there actually seemed to have. We ought not to have been surprised. No living generation in the Soviet Union in the 1990s had any prior experience of democratic politics, and in Eastern Europe the experience was partial and in any case confined to those old enough to have adult recollections predating 1939. Despite the appeals to democracy, then, what the revolutionaries of 1989 really shared in common was hostility to communism. The imperative to get rid of it inevitably shaped their perceptions of what democracy is about.[1] In short, John Dewey's comment on older democratic revolutions rings equally true of our own: they aimed less to implement an abstract democratic ideal than "to remedy evils experienced in consequence of prior political institutions."[2]

Because democratic ideals are forged out of reactive struggles, we should not be surprised that, on ascending to power, democratic oppositions bear the antithetical traces of the orders they replace. The fanatical egalitarianism of the French and Russian revolutionaries was partly a response to the absolutist character of the French monarchy before 1789 and czarist Russia before 1917. American obsessions with representation at every level and in every forum of government are partly an affirmation of what the British had denied the colonies. The strongly unitary new South Africa, with its hostility to all claims for subgroup autonomy or secession, stands as a repudiation of the separate-development philosophy that upheld apartheid. Most striking in this regard is the degree to which the public rhetoric spawned by the anticommunist revolutions has identified democracy with communism's historical archantagonist: unregulated market capitalism. From the beginning the democratic and market revolutions were widely seen as, if not synonymous, intimately linked. Indeed, where communists have survived or reinvented themselves as viable parties, as in Lithuania, they have had to run on strongly promarket platforms. Even in Russia, the communists in parliament have sought mainly to slow the pace of market reform, not to scuttle it.

Although the pursuit of democracy is typically a reactive endeavor, intellectual reflection about it is meant to be less so. Much Western commentary on the recent wave of democratization, however, is itself reactive in its own way. As the tendency to equate democracy and freedom with markets and capitalism has gathered momentum in the East, many in the West who are persuaded of the defects of centrally planned economies but troubled by the ecological and human costs of unregulated capitalism express worry at the implications. There is a disconcerting possibility that failed socialist systems drawn to regimes of private accumulation might end up with the worst of both worlds, and that the reduced legitimacy of socialism in the East will weaken the hands of those in the West who hope to diminish defects in their own institutions. Yet a sense of unease is not an argument, and those who resist the unthinking identification of democracy with either socialism or capitalism are bound to take up the burden of rethinking democracy's nature and its place in a just social order. That aspiration motivates this book.

The second observation prompting my initial question is that there is a disjunction between most of the writing on democratic theory since the 1950s and the voluminous literature on distributive justice spawned by John Rawls's *A Theory of Justice*, published in 1971. It would be going too far to say that theoreticians of democracy and justice speak past one another, but there has been little systematic attention by political theorists to the ways in which considerations about democracy and justice are or should be mutually related.[3] This relative inattention seems partly to have sprung from optimism among many justice theorists about what armchair reflection should be expected to deliver, a driving conviction that what is just in the distribution of social goods can be settled as a matter of speculative theory. Their arguments often appear to take it for granted that there is a correct answer to the question what principles of justice we ought to affirm; that Rawls, Ronald Dworkin, Robert Nozick, Amartya Sen, or someone else will eventually get it right. On this understanding of the enterprise, tensions between proffered accounts of justice and the requirements of democratic politics can comfortably be thought of as problems of implementation to be worried about later or by others.[4]

The tendency to speculate about the nature of a just social order without attention to democratic considerations has been reinforced by democratic theory's apparently moribund condition. Joseph Schumpeter and the empirical theorists of democracy offered formidable arguments that its traditional aspirations could not be realized in the modern world of continental nation-states and market economies, yet their attempts to redefine the democratic ethos by reference to the prevailing practices of advanced capitalist countries prompted understandable criticism that they had stripped democracy of much of what makes it morally attractive.[5] In 1979 John Dunn underscored the impasse thus created by noting that democratic theory oscillates between two variants, "one dismally ideological and the other blatantly utopian."[6] Compounding democratic theory's troubles was a plethora of analytical work on the logic of decision rules, much of which purported to show that democracy generates perverse results such as arbitrary and manipulated outcomes, logrolling politics, and continuous unplanned increases in the size of the public sector.[7] These and related findings reinforced traditional fears about democracy: that it courts the possibility of majority tyranny and contains an ever-present potential to ride roughshod over whatever justice might be thought to require.

Yet the hiatus between academic commentary on democracy and on justice is surprising. Despite the rationalist temper of much of the substantive writing on justice in recent years, there are few self-styled Platonists today. Democratic intuitions play a role in most everyday conceptions of social justice, and theories of justice frequently involve reliance on those intuitions, as we shall see.[8] Most people would balk at the suggestion that there is a right answer to the question *what is just?* in the same way that there is an answer to the question *what is the sum of the interior angles of a triangle?* Likewise, most people—including those who fear unbridled democratic politics—are unnerved by the idea of philosopher kings. Even if one theory of justice is better than the others, there is something disconcerting to the suggestion that it ought for that reason to be imposed on the world. One naïve undergraduate reading Rawls learned this from the cynical titter of his peers when he asked why, "now that the difference principle has been established," the Constitution had not been changed to incorporate it. Yet a titter is not an argument, and the question what should be the relations between the demands of justice and the practices of a democratic polity remains remarkably unexplored.

This book is an attempt to explore it and to formulate one answer to it. I advance the claim that a suitably developed account of democracy offers the most attractive political basis for ordering social relations justly. I develop and defend this account partly in general terms and partly by exploring its implications for the governance of particular aspects of human interaction relating to childhood, domestic life, work, old age, and dying. In this way, the general argument for democratic justice is developed, adapted, and modified as it is pursued through major phases of the human life cycle. The motivation for this life-cycle approach is taken up in Chapter 2. Here I describe the understanding of politics that informs the enterprise, and explain why developing a democratic account of justice is worthwhile.

My dual pursuit of abstract argument and particular case reflects the fact that democratic justice is a semicontextual ideal. It engenders certain constraints on and possibilities for human interaction, but these work themselves out differently in different domains of human activity, depending on peoples' beliefs and aspirations, the causal impact of activities in one domain for others, the availability of resources within domains, and a variety of related contingent factors. Exploring the implications of democratic justice for the governance of different domains thus serves the dual purpose of providing test cases for the general argument as well as vehicles for its elaboration.

Broad Versus Narrow Conceptions of Politics

Where do the domains of politics begin, and where do they end? This is the primary question for any theory of social justice. Arguments about competing principles of political organization are bound to be parasitic on assumptions and convictions about it. If we think of politics as limited to what usually goes on in Congress, statehouse, and town hall, one class of possibilities will seem appropriate; if we regard institutions like the family or the workplace as political, then different possibilities will seem attractive. In the Western tradition of political theory there have been two principal strategies for getting at the nature of the political, one focusing on its boundaries, the other on its essence.

The first strategy is one of negation; its proponents try to nail down what politics is by establishing what it is not. Their central question is: which domains of human life are beyond politics, immune from arguments about social justice? Despite an impressive variety of attempts by first-class theoretical minds to answer this question, it has never been settled definitively and no answer to it commands wide agreement. The reason is that no domain of human interaction is beyond politics. Proponents of negationist strategies deny this, yet in doing so they typically commit one or another of two antipolitical fallacies. By unmasking these fallacies we can negate negationist strategies, opening the way to defending the first substantive claim on which the argument of democratic justice depends: that the question should never be allowed to be whether or not arguments about social justice are relevant to particular domains of human interaction, but always about how they are relevant.

The first antipolitical fallacy—putting boundaries on the political realm —derives from the characteristic liberal view that there is or ought to be a private sphere beyond the reach of politics. Historically this view emanates from the natural-rights tradition, whose proponents insisted on the existence of prepolitical rights; indeed, they often thought of political institutions as being geared to the protection of those rights. Thus Locke argued that human beings create political institutions in order to preserve their natural rights and that the authority vested in those institutions is always limited by this motivating purpose.[9] It is sometimes said that the difficulties such arguments confront derive from the secularization of the natural-rights tradition, that once rights are no longer seen as theologically based we cannot be surprised that there is so little agreement on their origin and content. Yet such claims ignore the fact that throughout its history the natural-rights tradition has been marked by enduring disagreement over which natural rights there are, how they are to be discovered in and related to natural law, how disagreements about their nature and content are to be resolved, and what they entail concerning the relations among individuals, groups, and the state.[10] Jeremy Bentham's declaration, in the late eighteenth century, that there are no rights without enforcement and no enforcement without government merely transposed these controversies into a secular key.[11] The question now became: what rights must it be rational to treat as beyond the power of the state?

Grappling with Bentham's question has set the terms of debate around which much modern liberalism revolves. In the utilitarian tradition he founded it was dealt with in consequentialist terms: what distribution of rights will maximize utility, wealth, or preferences? Even on Bentham's account there had been no unambiguous answer, for it depended on controversial and ideologically loaded counterfactuals about the relation between the prevailing system of rights and the production and distribution of the means to utility.[12] Partly for this reason, liberal theorists have committed plenty of ink to the search for a nonconsequentialist basis for a private sphere beyond politics. To many, the most promising vehicle has seemed the idea of autonomy, affirmed either for reasons that are second and third cousins of Kant's ethics or via a mixture of intuitions—as in the justification of Mill's harm principle—supporting the thought that autonomous self-development is the supreme moral value.

But this strategy has also resulted in indeterminate controversy. For instance, when Mill insists that to justify interfering with the actions of another, "the conduct from which it is desired to deter him must be calculated to produce evil in someone else," the term *calculated* is pregnant with ambiguity.[13] If it is interpreted to mean *intended*, the harm principle seems unacceptably weak: although our intuitions may require something like malevolent intent or *mens rea* in areas we designate as criminal, there are many walks of life where something less demanding seems appropriate to legitimate collective action. If, on the other hand, *calculated* is interpreted as referring to probable effects, the principle seems unacceptably strong and has the potential to destroy the entire private-regarding sphere. Accordingly, most liberals seek some kind of middle ground. But it is notoriously difficult to pin down, as has been revealed in heated debates over the past few decades between proponents of *de facto* and *de jure* standards for antidiscrimination remedies, and between defenders of strict liability and those who favor negligence tests in tort law.[14] Similarly, people who defend private rights by appeal to Kant find themselves unable to agree on what system of private rights, if any, the categorical imperative can be argued to entail.[15] Because the boundaries to the private sphere are themselves politically constituted and change over time, no argument for an a priori distinction between public and private can be sustained.

The second antipolitical fallacy involves depoliticizing politics. It also depends on wrongheaded assumptions about privacy. Variants of the fallacy rest on appeals to idealized pictures of traditional communities, contemporary private life, communitarian utopias yet to be created. All such appeals share in common political ideals that are alleged to be beyond what Michael Sandel describes as "the limits of justice." [16] But Sandel's view, that justice belongs characteristically to the world of "strangers" reified in the deontological vision he rejects, both misdescribes the private communities we inhabit and relies on expectations from politics that cannot withstand scrutiny. In the family—that paradigm of the private community held together in the communitarian ideal by bonds of intimacy and affection—justice and the sense of it play indispensable roles. The abused wife, or the child who knows herself to be loved or respected less than her siblings, will bring to bear notions of injustice, because she will feel that the pertinent principles of love and affection have been violated. As this example illustrates, the language of justice comes into play whenever there is conflict over the goods valued in a community. [17]

Appeals to apolitical communities of the past or the future run into analogous difficulties. Although most contemporary communitarians appear not to have noticed, sociologists and historical anthropologists have been waging war on the idealization of "traditional society" for decades; it is now undeniable that the search for historical communities that were immune to political conflict is vain. [18] Equally unpromising are arguments about the possibility of creating such communities in the future, as in Marx's claim that under genuine communism politics will be displaced by administration. It is sometimes said that such a view could be persuasive if a theory of needs could be developed that distinguished them from wants: wants might be infinite, as the bourgeois economists argued, and scarcity with respect to them inevitable, but needs are not. On this view a well-developed theory of needs might generate an Archimedian point for transcending the induced wants of the market. Yet these formulations assume a static and unrealistic (not to say surprisingly un-Marxist) view of human needs. AIDS and cancer research, dialysis machines, and other forms of medical innovation satisfy needs, not wants, yet the potential for investment in them is limitless. Once innovation is taken into account, human needs are potentially infinite, scarcity inevitable, and distributive conflict inescapable. [19]

What communitarians think of as the limits of justice are really limits to the politicization of social life. By declaring a sphere of action to be beyond politics, part of the private sphere, we render it immune from political criticism and action. Yet the accepted boundaries of politics shift constantly as the result of political struggles. When the law changes from denying by conclusive presumption the possibility of marital rape to creating such a crime by statute, a significant movement of this kind has occurred. The public-private dichotomy in this and other prevalent formulations misses such poignant complexities. Those who invoke the idea of justice in traditionally private realms like the family are generally those on the short end of power or distributive relationships within them. The general rule (to which there are, doubtless, exceptions) is that the dominated try to politicize to delegitimize, whereas the dominators try to depoliticize to legitimize. In sum, negationist strategies fail. No social practice can be declared to be beyond politics, and therefore beyond the possibility of political regulation. Indeed, the term *regulation* is often misleading because it implies that absence of visible action by government is an indicator of the absence of politics.

Many who sense the conceptual vulnerabilities of strategies for delimiting the political realm are nonetheless left uncomfortable by the thought that politics are everywhere. Some aspects of life seem at most trivially political, others momentously so; the suggestion that everything is politics threatens to obscure such distinctions in the name of a conceptual clarity that verges on the self-defeating. Partly for this reason, many have pursued an alternative strategy of trying to specify a domain of human interaction that is in some sense basic or essential to politics, in which fundamental conflicts are fought out and social possibilities determined. Religious theorists have sometimes thought in such reductive terms about the domain of spiritual life, Marxists about work, feminists about gender relations, liberals and fascists— from different standpoints—about the state. Strategies of this kind are conceptually tempting because they appear to make arguments about social justice manageable. Once the essential realm has been adequately identified and understood, everything else can be thought about derivatively, as epiphenomenal. Reductive strategies of this kind are also politically tempting; they hold out the joint possibility of focusing our energies on what really matters—spiritual life, work, gender, civil society, institutions—and of placing limits on the demands that might be made of us in a world in which everything was politicized. No decisive case has ever been made, however, for such a reductive view. The paucity of the explanatory power of these strategies, as well as their unpredictable programmatic consequences, routinely belie their pretensions. The troubled history of Marxism is a vivid illustration of this state of affairs, but in this respect it is scarcely unique. Hobbesian, Freudian, sociobiological, and other ambitious reductionisms have all been consigned to similar fates. By the end of the twentieth century there are good grounds for skepticism toward every essentialist venture of this sort.[20]

Rather than join a vain search for the true essence or site of politics, the account of justice developed here rests on the view that politics are both no-where and everywhere. They are nowhere in the sense that there is no speci-fiable political realm—not religious practice, not buildings in Washington, not modes of production, not gender relations, not any bounded domain of social life. Politics are everywhere, however, because no realm of social life is immune from relations of conflict and power. The significance of this truth will vary, to be sure, with time and circumstance, and even from person to person. Yet the appropriate constitution of any aspect of collective life is always open to dispute; people benefit and are harmed in different ways by prevailing practices, and there is the ever-present possibility that these might be ordered differently than they are. Politics conditions everything we do, yet it is never simply what we do.

The broad view of politics just sketched is perhaps most commonly as-sociated with the name of Michel Foucault, yet it has progenitors in the Western tradition as distant as Plato and as unalike as Aristotle, Hobbes, and Marx, who agreed—for all their differences—that politics permeates every facet of human interaction. That they disagreed so much on so many ques-tions signals how little of normative significance flows, by itself, from affirm-ing a broad conception of politics. It indicates something about the terrain and sets some of the terms of the problem, but no more. It tells us noth-ing about what facets of human interaction can be understood, controlled, or shaped, or even about what is possible and desirable in organization of social life. That politics is ubiquitous to human interaction is neither good nor bad; it is part of the reality from which we are bound to begin.[21]

Justice in Multiple Domains

Inevitably and appropriately, arguments about justice track conceptions of politics. Embracing a broad view of politics thus commits us to a correspondingly wide-ranging account of justice. It also opens the way to affirming a second substantive claim on which the argument of democratic justice rests: that there is no single underlying metric or unit-of-account of social justice that applies throughout social life. If the requirements of justice are conceived so broadly as to range over every aspect of human interaction, it seems inevitable that they must be pertinent to different walks of life in different ways. Family life, religion, education, leisure, and work revolve around activities that differ greatly from one another; any plausible account of justice is bound to consider this fact.

Few political theorists have denied this.[22] Rawls treats liberties, opportunities, income and wealth, and the "social bases of self-respect" as at least partly pertinent to different domains and governed by different distributive principles.[23] Michael Walzer and Alasdair MacIntyre push analogous reasoning further. Whereas Rawls embraces a system of lexical rankings to settle conflicts among the principles for distributing different goods in different ways, Walzer and MacIntyre relativize the process. Goods are defined internally, by reference to the logic of the relevant sphere or practice, and the challenge for achieving social justice is understood as preserving the integrity of spheres and practices. This is achieved for Walzer by the argument that no good pertinent to conduct in one sphere should "dominate" conduct in another sphere, and for MacIntyre by the comparable claim that social practices function well when participants in them act by reference to the goods "internal" to those practices, eschewing the pursuit of "external goods." Thus if political office or familial affection can be bought for money, dominance in Walzer's sense is occurring, and if I win a game of chess by cheating when my opponent is distracted, rather than playing by the rules, I am engaging in the pursuit of external goods in MacIntyre's sense.[24]

Both strategies confront difficulties. It has long been a stock critique of Rawls that his characterizations and orderings of human goods are idiosyncratic, and that they rely on controversial assumptions about human psychology—particularly the propensity toward risk.[25] The early Rawls dealt with this partly by denying that the argument relied on "special" attitudes

toward risk and partly by insisting that his assumptions about human motivation were uncontroversial "laws" of economics and psychology. More
recently, perhaps partly in response to the skepticism both these claims engendered, he has shifted his ground to the claim that they rest on beliefs that
are widely shared so as to form an "overlapping consensus."[26] Yet the difficulty remains that we do not all share the same intuitions about the human
propensity toward risk. Rawls's assumptions about human motivation will
convince those who share his intuitions on this matter, but to others they are
bound to seem arbitrary.[27]

The relativizing strategy confronts different difficulties. The intuition informing it is that the goods governing social practices are and should be
internally defined. Part of what makes the norms internal to practices is that
they are governed by what I will refer to as insider's wisdom. The activities
are learned from other participants, and it is the judgments of those others
that are often decisive, for a given individual, to the meaning and satisfaction derived from a given practice. An author will want to be valued by a
critic whose capacities she has come to value. There will be nuances to every
activity from child rearing to cabinet building that can be fully appreciated
only by others who have learned to excel at those same practices. "He's a
pitcher's pitcher" is a commendation we can intuitively grasp as an appeal
to insider's wisdom. Such examples seem to lend support to the contention
that defining the goods pertinent to different practices, even defining the
practices themselves, should be left to the participants. By the same token,
however, appeals to insider's wisdom appear to render outsiders impotent to
judge the justness of the practices in question.

The routes that contextualists like MacIntyre and Walzer have sought
out of this difficulty are less than satisfactory. MacIntyre declares by defini-
tional fiat that certain activities are not practices, whereas Walzer's attempts
to pin down the limits to his plural spheres and the nature of the goods internal to them have provoked charges that his argument rests on an illicit
Rawlsian move of simply asserting that one controversial account of these
matters is correct.[28] In short, although the relativizing strategies embraced
by Walzer and MacIntyre rest on an attractive resistance to the use of armchair reflection to choose the values underlying justice, making this move
creates a dilemma: it appears either to require us to allow as just practices
that many would regard as unjust in the name of preserving the integrity of

spheres or practices, or to rest implicitly on exactly the kind of move that makes the Rawlsian strategy objectionable.

A Place for Democratic Moral Intuitions

A principled commitment to democracy offers a way out of this bind that protagonists on both sides of the debate appear not to have noticed. This assertion might provoke initial skepticism as to its novelty; after all, both the Rawlsians and the anti-Rawlsians rest their arguments on appeals to democratic moral intuitions. Although the early Rawls did not discuss his foundational democratic commitments at any length in *A Theory of Justice*, they might be argued to enter with the requirement of unanimity in the original position.[29] The Kantian claim that everyone should be respected as an end which motivates the requirement suggests a commitment to the basic moral equality of persons that most democrats would affirm. But to treat a requirement of unanimity as an interpretation of the democratic ethos confuses unanimity qua decision rule with unanimity qua state of affairs because of the former's propensity to privilege the status quo.

Perhaps partly for this reason, in later work Rawls appeals directly to consensus as a state of affairs, replacing the foundational appeal to unanimity with a contextual justification. He now claims that his argument is supported by an overlapping consensus that includes "all the opposing philosophical and religious doctrines likely to persist and gain adherents in a more or less just constitutional democratic society."[30] Similarly, a contextualist like Walzer appeals to consensually held norms as part of a democratically inspired resistance to armchair speculation about just distribution, even as he concedes that interpretations of these norms are bound to be contentious.[31] The complaint against such strategies that one philosopher's speculations about prevailing norms differ from another's is a symptom of how little democratic ice is cut by this kind of appeal to consensual norms. Certainly none of these appealers to consensus has engaged in what a social scientist would regard as empirical study of the values in question.

It is true that the contextualists do not appeal exclusively to conventional meanings. Walzer argues for resisting "dominance": conventional meanings should reign within their appropriate spheres but may legitimately be prevented from infiltrating other spheres. MacIntyre's argument against the pursuit of "external goods" rests on the analogous anti-imperial view that goods germane to one practice ought not to imperialize into others.[32] Walzer and MacIntyre both argue that such domination is illicit, and these arguments appear not to be derived exclusively from conventional meanings, for they are applied to conventional meanings in a critical way; they are seen as independently justified.[33]

Whatever the status of such anti-imperial claims, as an interpretation of the democratic ethos they are too weak to be satisfying, intellectually or morally. In their stead I argue, in the next two chapters, for a more robust view that favors bringing democratic considerations to bear on conduct within spheres and practices as well as on the relations among them. It turns on the suggestion that people should always be free to decide for themselves, within an evolving framework of democratic constraints, on the conduct of their activities. Explaining the rationale for this suggestion brings us to a third substantive claim on which the argument of democratic justice depends: that in every walk of social life there is room for disagreement about how it is appropriately governed.

Whereas contextualists often see their appeals to consensus as flowing from democratic moral intuitions, my foundational appeal to democracy rests on the contrary intuition that dissensus is an essential ingredient to the just ordering of any domain of human interaction. Almost every social practice exhibits disagreement among participants as to its goals and how best to achieve them, and in the rare cases when we encounter practices unencumbered by internal dissensus, there are usually good reasons to be skeptical of their authenticity: one person's consensus is often another's hegemony. Most people recognize this; they know that agreement can mask all kinds of things from acts of cultish following to strategic behavior of various kinds to plain ignorance of interests and of how to protect them. The great premium that academic contextualists so often place on consensus is thus belied by much everyday life. Their attempts to come up with consensual ideals speak past too many of its realities.[34]

Contextualists are too quick either to wish disagreement away or to pursue minimalist strategies of deriving principles of social justice from the lowest common denominator of what they claim we agree on or can be brought to agree on, at least in principle. For all their differences, Rawls's aspiration to ground his argument in overlapping consensus, Walzer's attempts to divine the moral imperatives that "really" flow from our prevailing norms, Mac-Intyre's desire to re-create the conditions under which agreement about ends allegedly was possible, and Habermas's project of specifying the abstract conditions under which uncoerced agreement can be achieved share commitments to consensus as the ultimate court of appeal in arguments about social justice.[35] Even Amy Gutmann and Dennis Thompson, who concede the inevitability of a degree of dissensus in politics, propose a deliberative model that is intended to minimize it.[36] In contrast to such ventures, I develop the claim that the reality of dissensus in social life should play a central role in our thinking about ordering social practices justly. When appropriately managed institutionally, its presence is a sign of health and vitality, not of the valueless anomie about which philosophers and political moralists frequently complain.[37] They hope for a wider range of social agreement than is available or desirable.

Democratic Justice: Compared to What?

We all countenance some foundational political commitments, whether rooted in our convictions or our actions. As a result, decisions about which commitments to endorse are unavoidably comparative; we have to be committed to something, and the most plausible way to think critically about its merits is by reference to the conceivable alternatives. As a first step toward exhibiting the comparative advantages of a democratic conception of social justice, notice how its assumptions about political reality differentiate it from the conventional liberal and communitarian alternatives. Most liberals accept my claim that disagreement is endemic to social life, but they see this as a reason for escaping the political, or at least minimizing its reach via "gag rules"—constitutional constraints on the range of decisions that legislatures should be free to enact.[38] Whether defended in contractarian or utilitarian idiom, all such attempts to fly from politics are chimerical, as we have seen. They rest on implausible assumptions about precollective or perfectly private states of affairs, and as a result they depend on misleading views of political reality. By contrast, communitarians usually agree with me in affirming the ubiquity of politics, and they share this indictment of liberalism's unrealism. Yet we have seen that they make implausible assumptions on another score: about the possibility and desirability of consensus. Moral disagreement is conceived of as a condition that can and should be changed, a view that reasonably makes liberals nervous; it conjures up images of creeping mediocrity at best, and more often of intimidating Big Brotherism shrouded in fraternal communitarian rhetoric.[39]

Enough has now been said to open the way for the argument of democratic justice as a third way between liberal and communitarian views, for the critical side of each is evidently right about the other. Neither the assumption that moral disagreement is endemic nor the recognition that politics is ubiquitous can plausibly be denied; it is with their joint affirmation that we are bound to begin. This affirmation is not by itself an argument for democracy of any sort. Liberals can be expected to respond to what has been said so far with the claim that democracy may be threatening to individual autonomy just as totalitarianism is, and many traditionalist communitarians see democracy as fostering an insufficiently robust sense of communal purpose and public-spiritedness. The sentiments that motivate such fears are often well founded. Any credible defense of a foundational commitment to democracy is bound to speak to them, and a good part of the argument of succeeding chapters is devoted to that goal. As we move into the constructive argument, it should be reiterated that the possibilities and risks of democratic justice should be evaluated not against some unspecified ideal of a perfect social order but against the alternative feasible systems of ordering social relations. As Dewey noted so perspicaciously in his own defense of democratic politics: "All intelligent social criticism is comparative. It deals not with all-or-none situations, but with practical alternatives; an absolutistic indiscriminate attitude, whether in praise or blame, testifies to the heat of feeling rather than the light of thought."[40]

• 2 •

Preliminaries

LIKE *JUSTICE*, THE TERM *DEMOCRACY* MEANS different things to different
people. Sometimes it is identified with a particular decision rule; at other
times it conjures up the spirit of an age. Democracy can be defined by reference to lists of criteria (such as regular elections, competitive parties, and
a universal franchise), yet sometimes it is a comparative idea: the Athenian
polis exemplified few characteristics on which most contemporary democrats
would insist, but it was relatively democratic by comparison with other ancient Greek city-states. Many people conceive of democratic government in
procedural terms; others insist that it requires substantive—usually egalitarian—distributive arrangements. In some circumstances democracy connotes
little more than an oppositional ethic; in others it is taken to require robust
republican self-government. And whereas some commentators insist that
collective deliberation is the high point of democratic politics, for others deliberation is an occupational hazard of democracy, best minimized.[1] Given
this multitude of meanings, any argument that appeals to the adjective *democratic* to help discriminate among the multifarious meanings of *justice* will
require an elaboration and defense of the preferred interpretation of democracy. That task is deferred to Chapter 3. Here I attend to the aspiration for
democratic justice.

Democracy and justice are different values that can operate at logger-heads with one another, yet in the popular mind they are often seen as going together. Academic commentators are wont to dismiss this as indicative of a confused propensity, given democracy's current hegemonic legitimacy, to identify it with all good things.[2] My view, by contrast, is that we should rise to the challenge implicit in the popular identification. This involves defending an account of justice that accords a central place to democratic ways of doing things, and a conception of democracy that can be justice-promoting rather than justice-undermining. To this end, my contention is that we should think of democracy as a subordinate foundational good, de-signed to shape the power dimensions of collective activities without sub-verting their legitimate purposes.

Democracy and Justice

Why is it that in the lived world of actual politics, the promise of democ-racy and the demands of justice are often seen as intimately linked? This is due partly to the reactive character of movements for democratic change, the fact that their moral authority so frequently derives from the hope they hold out of displacing unjust social arrangements. One has only to recall the ways in which the lack of democracy and the presence of social injustice were fused in the ideologies of opposition to communism in the Soviet bloc or to apartheid in South Africa to be reminded that people often blame social in-justice on democracy's absence and assume that democracy is an important weapon in the battle to replace unjust social relations with less unjust ones.

Yet this popular expectation is often frustrated in practice, because achieving political democracy does not guarantee broad advances toward greater social justice. In countries where the basic democratic institutions of popularly elected governments based on universal franchise prevail, wealth may or may not be redistributed in justice-promoting ways, minorities may or may not be respected, opportunities may or may not be open to all, and religious dissent may or may not be tolerated. Far from promoting justice, then, democracy can actually undermine it. Indeed, some political scientists suggest that it is prudent, for this reason, to sever the link between democ-racy and expectations about justice as much as possible. The danger, they suggest, is that otherwise when democracies fail to deliver on the justice front their legitimacy will erode—undermining their capacity to survive.[3]

Prudential considerations cut both ways, however, because it may often be impossible to sever the links in popular expectations between democracy and justice. If those who were oppressed by the injustices of apartheid or communism discern no improvement in the successor democratic regimes, then their allegiance to the democratic order may indeed be expected to atrophy. Why would it not? The more prudent moral for democrats to draw in the face of that likelihood is that they should work for variants of democracy that can be justice-promoting. To be sure, not every form of democracy is of this sort. But some are likely to be. The creative challenge is to discover which they are, and how to move things in their direction.

Wise as this course can be argued to be on prudential grounds, my motivation in arguing for it is more than expedient. It reflects an underlying conviction that the popular expectation is in fact warranted, and that consequently it is worthwhile to try to deliver on it by arguing for forms of democracy that can be valued by those who care about justice. On my account, the ideals of democracy and justice are indeed mutually implicating in ways that have been undernoticed in the academic literature. This is true for two related reasons. One has to do with the multitude of competing theories of justice on offer, and no decisive reason to choose among them. The other reflects the endemic reality that people have a better developed sense of what is unjust in their circumstances than of what fully just circumstances would be like.

To start with justice's indeterminacy, notice how it nudges us in democratic directions. Once we grant that what justice requires is, and is likely to remain, debatable, some sort of procedural tack inevitably forces itself onto the agenda. We are no longer in a position to take the view that democracy should reign only within the ambit of justice, that its logic should operate so long as this does not violate what justice requires. We need guidelines for proceeding in the face of our differences and uncertainties about what justice does require. Given the difficulties with appeals to consensus alluded to in Chapter 1, it is hard to see what the alternative to a democratic procedure might be. Indeed, as I suggested there, theorists of justice appeal to democratic moral intuitions in their justificatory arguments partly because they know that democracy confers legitimacy on institutional arrangements.

This is reflected in the real world no less than in academic argument. Constitutions often constrain democracy in the name of justice (via such devices as supermajoritarian requirements and bills of rights enforced through judicial review). Yet constitutions are themselves usually both legitimated and alterable through democratic processes such as constitutional conventions and amendment procedures. Even exceptions to this generalization tend to underscore the proposition that democracy is a wellspring of political legitimation. In Germany the Basic Law entrenched after the Second World War was put in place to prevent a repetition of the abandonment of democracy for fascism.[4] Likewise, the constitutional principles that were entrenched in South Africa in 1993 were designed in part to ensure that no future constitution could abrogate the basic elements of a democratic system of government: universal franchise, regular elections, a multiparty system, and one class of citizenship for all.[5] Given the nature of the predecessor regimes, one cannot be surprised by such aspirations to entrench democracy as the underlying font of political legitimacy.

There is, second, an internal relationship between democracy and justice, captured in the popular expectation. Among the reasons why people turn to democracy in the quest for justice is that injustice is so often experienced as arbitrary domination.[6] Democracy appeals because of its principled hostility to this. Perhaps systems of domination displace one another ad infinitum in social life as Foucault has suggested.[7] If so, democratization will be powerless to forestall or even mitigate these endless cycles. But there is no reason to assume this to be so. Sometimes democratizing unjust practices will indeed fail to alleviate the injustices in question. In some cases it might even lead to worse injustices. When this happens, democratic justice fails to meet its challenge and the task becomes to try again: to come up with alternative modes of democratization that are better suited to achieving the goal in the context at hand. No doubt there will be circumstances where no form of democratization is compatible with reducing injustice, prompting an impulse to turn to nondemocratic methods instead. In extreme circumstances this might be defensible. But given the dangers that accompany all proposed blueprints for social justice, not to mention the kinds of people who characteristically promote them, these should always be seen as strategies of last resort.

The conventional academic opposition between democracy and justice misses the reality that that no account of one that undermines one's moral intuitions about the other is likely to be judged satisfactory for long. This does not mean that the two are no more than different aspects of the same idea. Rather, it suggests that although democracy is not sufficient for social justice, usually it is necessary, and that where democracy leads to injustice it will likely lose legitimacy. Perhaps this is why Rawls includes rights of democratic participation among those features of his theory of justice that are protected by his first principle, thus according them lexical priority over many of justice's other demands.[8] He, at least, seems aware that it is possible for democracy and justice to pull in opposing directions, but that it is important to discover forms of the two that can pull together. That is the dual aspiration here: to articulate a conception of justice that accords a central place to democratizing social life, and a view of democracy that can be justice-promoting rather than justice-undermining.

A Subordinate Foundational Good

Think of the relations between a foundational political commitment and the rest of our lives as roughly akin to the relations between the foundations of buildings and the structures and activities they support. One feature of foundational commitments brought out by this comparison is that although they are essential, by their nature they are incomplete and open-ended. Every house needs a foundation lest it fall over, yet a foundation is not to be confused with a house, much less with the lives of its inhabitants. In the spirit of avoiding analogous conflations, my claim is that we should resist every suggestion that just because democracy is a foundational good, it is the only good for human beings, it is the highest human good, or it should dominate the activities we engage in. Democracy operates best when it facilitates our activities, not when it displaces them.

By using the term *foundational* here I do not mean to signal a position in debates about the nature of knowledge and existence.[9] In describing democracy as a foundational good I mean only to maintain that no prior or more basic institutional commitment rightly commands our allegiance. It should be said, however, that, similar to Rawls in his "political, not metaphysical" mode, my account is developed as independently as possible of claims about the metaphysical validity of contending world views.[10] This is not to say that my argument aspires to be philosophically neutral. It rests on skepticism of

absolutist epistemologies and ontologies, such as those embraced by fundamentalists, classical Marxists, or Platonists. This skepticism is political, not
metaphysical, in the sense that I take no position on whether or not such
views are valid (perhaps one is), only on whether or not it is wise to let any
of them achieve hegemony in a world populated by a plurality of contending views of the good life. Evidently, partisans of such absolutist views will
find their political aspirations frustrated by the politics I am advocating in
ways that many philosophical fallabilists, pragmatists, empiricists, realists,
and some (but not all) philosophical antifoundationalists will not.[11] My argument, then, is not that philosophical neutrality is desirable; indeed, I do not
believe it to be available. Rather, my claim is no more and no less than this:
when compared with the going alternatives, the democratic view of justice
elaborated here is the most attractive foundational political commitment.

Democracy as I argue for it here is also a subordinate good. It operates
best when it shapes the terms of our common interactions without thereby
determining their course. Most of the things that human beings value can
be sought after in a variety of ways. The challenge is to get people to pursue
them—even to want to pursue them—in ways that are more rather than less
democratic. The goal should be for democracy to be omnipresent, in that
it appropriately shapes the pursuit of all goals in which power relations are
implicated, but democracy should not be omnipotent. Finding ways to do
things more rather than less democratically is valuable, but it should rarely,
if ever, be the point of the exercise. Accordingly, people should be pressed to
pursue their goals democratically without sacrificing those goals *to* democracy. Democratic justice succeeds as an enterprise to the extent that people
engage successfully with the challenges this presents.

Let me characterize my claim a little more fully by pursuing its contrasts
with the principal alternatives. Conventional liberals and communitarian
democrats reify politics by conceiving of it as a distinctive activity. As we
saw in Chapter 1, whereas liberals often denigrate what they think of as the
political realm, communitarian democrats bemoan either what they take to
be its passing or its recalcitrance in coming into being. The view developed
here shares something with each of these views while resisting their joint
preoccupation with the costs and benefits of political participation. With
the communitarians, I agree that politics ranges into all walks of life and
cannot be walled into a thing or place called a public realm. With the lib-

erals, however, I resist the idea that communitarian democrats routinely take for granted: that participation is the highest human good.

Communitarian democrats make wrongheaded assumptions both about the nature of democracy and about its appropriate place in everyday life. On the first score they take too reductionist a view of democracy, equating it with participation. This move has had the doubly unfortunate consequence of making democracy seem more vulnerable than it actually is to findings in the public choice literature about difficulties in the logic of participatory politics, and of diverting attention away from significant dimensions of democratic politics other than participation. As an alternative, my claim is that participation plays a necessary but circumscribed role in ordering social relations justly. Valuable as democratic participation is in managing the power dimensions of collective activities, it is not the point of the exercise. The activities themselves—the superordinate goods—are ultimately more important, and schemes for promoting democratic participation should always be designed bearing this in mind. In circumstances when democratic participation does become the point of the exercise, this should be diagnosed as a failure of institutional design.

This is not to say that democracy is purely of instrumental value. Democracy has intrinsic value as a subordinate good, but this value is only realized in conjunction with superordinate goods. Collective goals are better pursued democratically than not, and better pursued more democratically than less democratically. In this sense doing things democratically should be thought of as inherently valuable. By the same token, however, I want to insist that valuable as democracy is as a conditioning good, it is wrongheaded to expect much from it in the way of spiritual enrichment or edification. This is not intended as a denial of the value of democratic participation or even of the claim that such participation may have beneficial effects on participants, though the evidence on this question is mixed.[12] It is intended, rather, to emphasize that democracy should be our servant, not our master. To the extent that the reverse becomes true democracy will impoverish our lives, not enrich them.

To be sure, there will always be those—political junkies—for whom participation in collective decision making *is* the most fulfilling thing they do. We should not seek to deny them their fulfillment. By the same token, however, they should not be able to force others to participate more than is needed to condition social relations democratically. Beyond this, participation should be thought of as a consumption good. Consenting adults should be free to commit themselves to as much of it as they like, without obliging the rest of us. Whether by running for political office, participating in political organizing, or spending their free time sustaining civic clubs and associations, people should be free to pursue political lives in these senses as little or as much as they desire. For some of them democratic participation may indeed become a superordinate good, supplying a source of meaning and purpose to their lives. This is not the dimension of democracy's value that is of central interest here. My focus is on the value of subordinate democratic constraints, which are fairly regarded as obligatory on all.[13]

Participation, as Oscar Wilde's quip that socialism takes up too many evenings underscores, can be tedious. Even communitarian democrats have begun to concede that too much participation can be counterproductive, and that the inescapable scarcity of time entails at a minimum that we are bound to confront choices among which kinds of participation most matter in our lives. Hence Carmen Sirianni's "paradox of participatory pluralism." It derives from the fact that once politics is broadly conceived, enhanced participation in one sphere, such as the town meeting, may be argued to diminish participation in others, such as the family. Sirianni makes a compelling case that this paradox raises serious difficulties for conventional participatory theory. Yet he continues to reify participation by seeking to rescue it as a final good. To this end, he advances arguments to distinguish participation itself from participating in decisions about participation and from participating in discussions about decisions about participation—arguments reminiscent of the debates among act- and rule-utilitarians some decades ago.[14] In contrast, the view developed here is that the ongoing challenge for democrats is to find ways of democratizing the multiple domains that structure social life while retaining democracy in a subordinate or conditioning role.

Semicontextualism and the Life Cycle

Earlier I described democratic justice as a semicontextual ideal. To spell out my meaning more fully, consider again the comparison with physical foundations. They all share properties in common (which enable them to support the buildings constructed on them), but they also vary with the type of edifice that is planned, its intended uses, the available construction materials, and the terrain on which it is to be built. This is the kind of mix that I hope to capture with the term *semicontextual.*

In Chapter 3 I elaborate on two general constraints on human interaction that democratic justice requires. Thereafter I explore the implications of these constraints for the power relations that structure different parts of the human life cycle, in light of their contextual particularities. Some modification and refinement of the general constraints occurs in the course of these applications, but they do not lose their general or subordinate character. Rather, the modifications and refinements are needed to vindicate the general argument's purpose, given this or that contextual particularity. The enterprise is thus cosmopolitan in motivation, but its persuasiveness turns partly on its plausibility as applied. People cannot evaluate the serviceability of a building's foundations without knowing whether the structure it supports seems attractive and worth inhabiting.

By adopting this stance I take up a middle ground between those who seek to derive principles of justice from abstract argument and those who appeal to the contingencies of context and history as the source of normative ideals. I agree with Walzer and MacIntyre that an attractive conception of justice should be flexible and context-sensitive in two respects. First, different walks of social life can be justly ordered only in ways that remain faithful to their distinctive logics and purposes. As a result, the requirements of democratic justice differ partly as a consequence of the goals around which these activities are organized. Second, the demands of a plausible theory of justice must be sensitive to the contingencies of historical circumstance. Even within a single domain, the requirements of democratic justice may vary depending on different objective possibilities, cultural priorities, and other contingent factors. A little reflection on the obstacles to, and possibilities for, democratization of family life in India, Japan, sub-Saharan Africa, and the United States should make this plain. Yet in the end the argument is only *semi*contextual. Flexible as democratic justice must be, it properly conditions the power dimensions of all human interaction. Just as physical foundations share structural properties, democratic justice generates subordinate constraints that recur across domains, cultures, and time.

A different feature of semicontextualism has to do with my life-cycle approach to social justice, because justice requires different things at different points in the life cycle. This is partly because our activities change but also because the power relations among us change as we evolve from being our parents' children to being our children's parents, then to being our parents' parents, and eventually to being our children's children. Human young are dependent creatures for longer than is the case with most species. Yet as they mature, people can develop capacities for considerable independence concerning how to organize their lives, meet their needs to survive and thrive, and shape their dealings with one another. Dependence on others usually increases again in the later phases of the life cycle, as illness and frailty begin taking their toll and younger adults gain in status and authority. Because the power relations that structure different phases of the life cycle vary, the questions presented about justice change as well. Justice responds to them differently.

Attending to justice over the life cycle also raises questions about how its different phases fit together and affect one another. These vary, within limits, and we need to be sensitive to the possibilities and limitations in a given set of circumstances. In our own era, both childhood and old age have become comparatively extended throughout the developed West. The full legal incidents of adulthood are not acquired before the age of eighteen, or even twenty-one in some countries, and advances in medical technology have combined with other causes of longevity to produce growing dependent elderly populations. Consequential justice questions arise out of the human choices that shape these developments and are shaped by them. The argument for democratic justice seeks to take account of what is at stake in these choices. Here, too, it supplies different answers in different circumstances, rooted in the available contextual possibilities.

Democratic justice's concern with power relations also has implications for semicontextualism. Authors like Walzer and MacIntyre, who develop contextual arguments about justice, focus on zones of activity—"spheres" or "practices"—as the primary objects of analysis. Democratic justice does not suggest that we dismiss such categories. They encapsulate the inherited meanings that constitute much social life; as such they should make partial claims on our allegiance. As I explain in Chapter 3, democratic justice is seldom about institutional design; usually it is about institutional *re*design. We are born into ongoing complexes of institutions and practices. The task is to democratize them as we reproduce them, not to design them anew.

This means granting conditional legitimacy to inherited practices but also subjecting them to critical scrutiny through the lens of democratic justice. Doing this involves attending to the power relations that structure particular activities.

Power relations are not, however, coterminous with the sorts of domains that Walzer and MacIntyre identify as spheres and practices. Sometimes power relations transcend those boundaries, as when the police become involved in domestic violence or when public officials exert authority over children against their parents' wishes. Sometimes single spheres or practices contain multiple power relations, such as those in the family between parents and minor children, adult children and aging parents, and married or cohabiting adults. Sometimes power is exercised as an external effect of how a sphere or practice is organized, as when homosexuals or polygamists find themselves disadvantaged by the marital regime in contemporary America. The concern here is with democratizing the power relations that structure social life. We must therefore take account of accepted conceptions of how it is organized without reifying them in ways that obscure power relations. The life-cycle approach facilitates this by focusing attention on the changing ways in which people deal with one another as they move through various causally linked practices and spheres.

A word should be said about what has been excluded. The noncontextual part of the argument for democratic justice is fully general. It can be brought to bear wherever power relations are involved in human affairs, in the service of helping them operate more justly. By writing a book about democratic justice in the life cycle I have thus carved out only a small piece of a large potential terrain. Other books could be written pursuing the argument through different parts of the social landscape. Moreover, because this book's main empirical focus is on the contemporary United States, issues and policy debates have been taken up that would arise differently in other contexts if they arose at all. Considering them does involve some comparative reference to how things have been done elsewhere, but exploring democratic justice through the life cycle would be different were the central focus another part of the world or historical period. The questions that remain constant have to do with the ways in which power relations structure the life cycle. But contingencies concerning economic organization, religious practices, medical technologies, and many other matters have to be taken into account in answering these questions in different circumstances.

The subjects explored through the life cycle here could also be tackled from other points of view. For instance, my treatment of education is mainly concerned with its role in developing the skills people need to live together in a democratic political order and the wherewithal to survive in the economy as it is likely to operate over the course of their lifetimes. One could, however, bring the argument for democratic justice centrally to bear on education as a domain of social life. This would involve a more extensive investigation of the organization and governance of education, and its relations with other social and political arrangements, than I undertake here.[15] Likewise, although I have a good deal to say about governmental institutions in the course of developing the general argument for democratic justice and exploring it through the life cycle, I do not subject them to the kind of scrutiny that a full treatment in their own right would warrant. This is not to say that one approach is necessarily preferable. We focus on the world from one perspective at a time, but reality is invariably more complex than any single perspective on it reveals. A life-cycle focus highlights some aspects of human relations; others inevitably recede into the shadows. Hopefully, the insights gleaned from delimiting the field of inquiry in this way make up for the corresponding limitations.

· *3* ·

The General Argument

ANY FOUNDATIONAL DEFENSE OF DEMOCRACY will reasonably make
level-headed people nervous, yet my argument for it is intended partly to
quell—and even draw on—understandable fears of the organized power of
others, of the potential for politics to undermine many values people cherish,
and of the workability of all blueprints for social justice.[1] The suggestion that
these claims can be squared with a foundational democratic commitment
will raise skeptical eyebrows, at least in the absence of further clarification. I
hope to show that such skepticism is misplaced and that, properly construed,
democracy both speaks better than other foundational political commitments to reasonable political fears and contains uniquely attractive features.

Two Dimensions of Democratic Justice

Democrats are committed to rule by the people. They insist that no aristo-
crat, monarch, philosopher, bureaucrat, expert, or religious leader has the
right, in virtue of such status, to force people to accept a particular conception of their proper common life. People should decide for themselves, via
appropriate procedures of collective decision, what their collective business

should be. They may reasonably be required to consult and take account of one another, and of others affected by their actions, but beyond this no one may legitimately tell them what to do. The people are sovereign; in all matters of collective life they rule over themselves.

Although this is less often commented on in the academic literature, democracy is as much about opposition to the arbitrary exercise of power as it is about collective self-government. In this connection Barrington Moore remarks that historically democracy has been a weapon "of the poor and the many against the few and the well-to-do." Those who have actively fought for democracy in organized political movements "have wanted it as a device to increase their share in political rule and weaken the power and authority of those who actually rule."[2] Rooted in the remnants of feudal and absolutist regimes and shaped by the vicissitudes of conquest and chance, the political arrangements in eighteenth- and nineteenth-century Europe and North America seemed to the dispossessed to personify arbitrary hierarchy and domination. This reality, as much as anything else, motivated working-class and other democratic movements. The English philosophic radicals, the French and American revolutionaries, the nineteenth-century Chartists, and the anticolonial movements in the third world after the Second World War all wanted to free their supporters from hierarchical orders for which they could see no rationale or justification. It was also to this oppositional dimension of the democratic ideal that Nelson Mandela appealed at his sentencing for treason by a South African court in 1961. Conceding that he had disobeyed the law by inciting resistance to the government, he nonetheless wondered whether "the responsibility does not lie on the shoulders of the government which promulgated that law, knowing that my people, who constitute the majority of the population of this country, were opposed to that law, and knowing further that every legal means of demonstrating that opposition had been closed to them by prior legislation, and by government administrative action."[3]

Mandela's formulation might be taken to embody the conventional view that democracy is primarily about collective self-government and only secondarily about opposition. Part of his claim, after all, is that he should not be bound by "a law which neither I nor any of my people had any say in preparing."[4] But he insisted also that the law lacks legitimacy because every avenue of legal opposition to it had been sealed off. In a world of ideal political institutions a derivative view of the place of opposition in democratic politics might be sustainable. But in the actual world, where social orders come to be what they are in morally arbitrary ways, and where all procedures of government turn out on close inspection to be flawed, opposition must enjoy a more independent and exalted status in a persuasive account of just democratic politics. Or so I argue below; but first let us attend to the governance side of the equation.

COLLECTIVE SELF-GOVERNMENT

If democracy is understood to require the people to be sovereign over their collective activities, it exhibits considerable overlap with liberalism as a political ideology. Both are rooted in antivanguardist conceptions of the good; their proponents resist the idea that values should be imposed on people against their wishes in the name of some greater social good. The reasons for affirming this antivanguardist stance vary: they range from commitments to variants of philosophical skepticism, pragmatism, and antifoundationalism to beliefs in the psychological value of critical reflection and contested authority, to the conviction that a degree of pluralism about values is sociologically or politically desirable. Liberals and democrats do not divide predictably over these foundational matters, but for most of both some combination of these reasons leads to resistance of moral vanguardism.[5]

Liberals and democrats do divide predictably, however, over the institutional implications that they draw from their moral antivanguardism. Liberals, who typically regard individual freedom as the greatest good, usually focus on devices to protect the individual from the realm of collective action. Democrats, by contrast, try to structure collective action appropriately to embody the preferences of the governed. Liberals characteristically resist this logic on the grounds that no procedure can fairly embody the preferences of all the governed. For liberals, democratic decision rules all too readily become devices by which phantom majorities—sometimes even manipulative minorities—tyrannize over individuals.[6]

Although there is merit to the liberal argument, it rests on flawed assumptions about the nature of politics and about the limits of collective action. Concerning the first, the characteristic liberal mistake is to focus on the forms of tyranny performed by and through government as the only—certainly the principal—kind of tyranny that should worry political theorists.

Liberal commitments to negative freedom, conventional constructions of public-private dichotomies, and arguments for limited government are all shaped by this governmentalist view of politics. As I note in Chapter 1, this view is not sustainable. Governmental power is one potential site of domination, but there are many others that permeate different domains of "private" life. Government can be an instrument for mitigating domination as well as a source of its generation. As a result, the choices and trade-offs that can minimize domination throughout society will likely defy such simplifying formulas as "the government that governs least governs best."

The liberal view is flawed also because its proponents tend to think that whether or not our lives should be governed by collective institutions is an intelligible question about politics. Hence Robert Nozick's remark that the fundamental question of political theory "is whether there should be any state at all."[7] This view is misleading because the institutions of private property, contract, and public monopoly of coercive force that liberals characteristically favor were created and are sustained by the state and are partly financed by implicit taxes on those who would prefer an alternative system.[8] In the modern world, Nozick's assertion makes as much sense as would a claim that the fundamental question of astronomy is whether or not there ought to be planets. A characteristic liberal sleight of hand involves trying to naturalize or otherwise obscure liberal institutional arrangements in order to disguise the particular regime of public institutions that they favor. Such subterfuges have received more attention than they deserve in the recent history of political theory; they cannot any longer detain us.[9]

This is not to say that the liberal fear of majority rule is groundless. It is to say that we need a different response to it than the conventional liberal one. We can begin this by noting that there is no reason to think that there is one best rule of collective decision. Different rules will be appropriate for different activities, depending on the nature of the activity in question, the importance of the decision to participants, the potential costs of decisions to third parties, and related contingent factors. Such a plural attitude toward decision rules flows naturally out of the view that civil society is made up of activities that differ qualitatively from one another.

Few liberals would deny this last claim, but they usually regard unanimity rule as the best default option, the decision rule most likely to protect individuals against violations of their rights. This is at least partly why liberals so often find markets attractive. Markets embody unanimity rule in the sense that every transaction requires the consent of both parties. On this view, classically advocated in *The Calculus of Consent*, it is always departures from unanimity that stand in presumptive need of justification, whether on efficiency or other grounds.[10] This story is intuitively plausible only if we take seriously the contractualist metaphor on which it rests, assuming a prepolitical status quo where there is no collective action and then a series of consensual moves that lead to the creation of what we know as political society. But as Brian Barry, Douglas Rae, and others have pointed out, once this assumption is jettisoned there is no particular reason to regard unanimity rule as the most appropriate default decision rule.[11] In the real world of ongoing politics, if I assume that I am as likely to oppose a given policy as to support it regardless of whether it is the status quo, then majority rule or something close to it is the logical rule to prefer. Once we move from majority toward unanimity rule, we begin to privilege the status quo. This will rightly seem arbitrary in a world that has not evolved cooperatively from a precollective condition. In short, other things being equal, tyranny of the majority is something that people should rationally fear, but not as much as they should fear tyranny of the minority.[12]

The preceding discussion reinforces the suggestion that there is no single best decision rule for democratic governance. In domains of social life where relations really do tend to approximate the contractualist story—in that they are both created ex nihilo by the participants and are basically cooperative in character—a presumptive commitment to unanimity rule is defensible. One might think of marriage in contemporary America as a paradigm case. It is created consensually, usually with the expectation that in important matters day-to-day governance will also be consensual. (Indeed, with the advent of no-fault divorce in the 1970s, we have seen an unusually strong form of the unanimity requirement at work. In most American states either spouse can unilaterally insist—subject to a brief waiting period—on a divorce, so that marriage continues only so long as both parties agree. Far from privileging the status quo, this variant of unanimity rule makes it perpetually vulnerable, for the rule is defined not by reference to the status quo but by in effect re-creating the conditions antecedent to it at the wish of either party.)[13]

Few social relations fully exemplify the contractualist ideal. Most of them are not created ex nihilo in the sense that contemporary American marriages usually are, and they are to a high degree structured by forces other than the wills of the participants. Even childless marriages involve the generation of reliances and externalities that can undermine their exclusively consensual character. These are questions of degree. Social relations are often not contractualist to anything like the extent that marriage is, even when such reliances are taken into account. Most obviously, think of parent-child relations. Constitutional political arrangements are often pointed to as presumptively contractualist because of their foundational character and their place in the social contract tradition. Such arrangements might once have been consented to by the relevant parties, although even in the American founding a narrowly circumscribed class agreed in fact—and then not unanimously. Generations later, whatever contractualist element these arrangements once exhibited has receded into the mists of time. In such circumstances (and no doubt there are others) there is no evident reason to regard unanimity rule as best on the grounds that it embodies the consent of the governed.

Nor are there good reasons to think that some alternative decision rule should appropriately govern all relations where a contractualist element is either missing or overdetermined by other factors. As the examples just mentioned indicate, this is a heterogeneous class. In some domains, the sort that Barry and Rae evidently have in mind, majority rule is prima facie the best decision rule. These include relations typically characterized by arms-length transactions, where substantial aspects of the collective action in question are competitive rather than cooperative, where all parties will be bound by outcomes, and where there are no obvious reasons to countenance paternalistic decision making. They are also often circumstances in which either people are born into structural relations that cannot easily be escaped or, if there is a contractualist element to their participation, it is accompanied by a good deal of what Marxists like to think of as "structural coercion." Whatever the surface appearances, the relations in question are not substantially voluntary. Arguments for workplace democracy in which majority rule plays a substantial role generally appeal to some combination of these characteristics in justifying their appeal; the Barry-Rae logic supplies us with reasons for accepting them.[14]

Not every noncontractualist or minimally contractualist form of association should be governed by majority rule, however. Both Buchanan and Tullock's stance and the Barry-Rae reasoning take it for granted that decision-making costs should be minimized, for which they have sometimes been criticized by participatory democrats.[15] Rather than follow the participatory democrat's reasoning (which creates difficulties of its own, as I note in Chapter 2), the argument here is that participation must itself be thought about in a context-sensitive way. In some circumstances participation is no more than a cost to be minimized, subject to achieving or preventing a particular outcome. Anyone who has sat through enough faculty meetings recognizes at least one of those circumstances. In other situations, institutions may reasonably be structured to maximize participation. Juries are an obvious example. Unanimity is generally required because it forces discussion and joint deliberation, which, in turn, are presumed most likely to lead to discovery of the truth in trial courts, and that is the point of the exercise. Parent-child relations are also noncontractualist relations (because the child does not ask to be born, let alone to be born to the parent in question) that do not lend themselves to governance by majority rule, at least not on many questions. In these relations more flexibility is necessary in delineating the appropriate scope for participation by different parties, because they include the total dependence of young children on their parents, relations among more-or-less equal adults, and relations between adults and their aging parents. And because human beings are developmental creatures for whom decision making has to be learned over time, there has to be space for regimes of domestic governance to adapt to people's changing capacities and dependencies. To be appropriate, the decision rules governing domestic relations must be responsive to this complex reality.

Taking note of such complexities lends credence to the suggestion that when they can be discovered and made to work, local solutions to local problems are to be preferred. This is the thought embodied in the principle of subsidiarity, meant to structure decision making in the European Union, which endorses moves toward more central authority only when more local administrative structures are ineffective.[16] Such a presumption often makes sense from the standpoint of democratic justice. The kinds of knowledge that are pertinent to democratizing an activity involve the hands-on experience that comes with insider's wisdom. And because those with insider's wisdom are often disproportionately able to derail projects of democratization imposed from above, securing their active commitment to the enterprise is often essential to its success.[17] In this respect the argument for democratic justice is compatible with the aspirations of many who think of themselves as communitarians.

Notice, however, that this should not commit us to an across-the-board endorsement of localism. There are circumstances in which no local decision rule can be made to work effectively from the standpoint of democratic justice, the most obvious being when the obstacles to exit are insuperable for some yet easily overcome by others. The American history of white flight from inner-city school districts since the 1960s stands as eloquent testimony to that fact. Whether the substantially white middle-class population opts out of the public school system or moves out of the inner city (or both, to avoid both using and paying for the inner-city schools), its capacity to leave undermines democracy in local educational provision. In this type of circumstance, the reality that different players are differently bound by collective decisions suggests that constraints other than choosing one local decision rule over another should come into play.

The decision rules appropriate to different walks of life vary, then, with the activity in question and the purposes around which it is organized. Yet to say this is to solve one problem by introducing another, because these activities and purposes are never fixed and there is usually, perhaps endemically, disagreement about them.[18] How can we say that the nature of the activity in question makes one decision rule more appropriate than another, having conceded that those purposes and activities are inevitably in contention? Whereas most liberals would say that all social relations should be redesigned to approximate the contractualist ideal as much as possible (regardless of how they are currently organized), the subordinate character of the democratic commitment in the argument for democratic justice precludes my defending an analogous claim. Instead it recommends a more pragmatic and antivanguardist approach, because we should neither accept things as they have evolved nor aspire to redesign them from scratch. The goal is to take social relations as we find them and discover ways to democratize them as we reproduce them. Democratic justice thus has a Burkean dimension, but this is tempered by the aspiration to create a more democratic world over time. Prevailing ways of doing things reasonably make a partial claim on our allegiance, but this claim is conditional and always subject to revision in democratic ways. The inertial legitimacy of existing ways of doing things can never achieve a status greater than that of a rebuttable presumption. The creative challenge is to devise methods of governance that both condition inherited activities democratically and open the way to their reevaluation over time.

Although there is no best decision rule for the governance of different domains of civil society, a general constraint for thinking about decision rules follows from what has been said so far: everyone affected by the operation of a particular domain of civil society should be presumed to have a say in its governance. This follows from the root democratic idea that the people appropriately rule over themselves. To require that everyone affected should have a say is not to require that this presumption be conclusive, or that every say should necessarily be of equal weight. There are often, though not always, good reasons for granting outsiders to a domain (who may be subject to external effects of decisions made within it) less of a say than insiders concerning its governance. Even within a domain there may be compelling reasons to distribute governing authority unequally, and perhaps even to disenfranchise some participants in some circumstances. In subsequent chapters I make the case that those whose basic interests are most vitally affected by a particular decision have the strongest claim to a say in its making. This constraint justifies limits on the general presumption in favor of universal inclusion, and it is often well served by a rule of thumb that tells us to look first to the principle of subsidiarity in determining the appropriate demos for a given decision. As the example of white flight indicates, however, this is not always appropriate.

Generally we can say that proposals to undermine inclusion reasonably prompt suspicion, whatever their source. In the limiting case, if someone sells herself into slavery, her agreement should be regarded as void *ab initio*. Most incursions on inclusion are considerably less radical than selling oneself into slavery is. As a consequence, evaluating policies and practices that limit the nature and extent of the governed's participation in decisions that affect them is more difficult and controversial from the standpoint of democratic justice than is the case of slavery. In the ongoing world of everyday politics there are often circumstances in which rights to be included are reasonably traded off against other imperatives. But the general argument counsels suspicion of these trade-offs; the burden of persuasion lies with those who advocate them.

Although the requirements of universal inclusion vary with circumstances, it is possible to defend in general terms at least one constraint on it that goes beyond the limiting case of slavery: participation by one individual or group in ways that render the participation of other legitimate participants meaningless is unacceptable. For instance, it is estimated that in the United States the health-care and medical-insurance establishments spent some fifty million dollars in 1993–94 on advertising and lobbying to derail the Clinton administration's proposed health-care reform legislation, and that they would presumably have spent whatever was necessary to achieve this result.[19] Granting, *arguendo*, this account of the facts, we can say that an understanding of participation that permits such a result goes too far. It gives one set of interests affected by the proposal the power to obliterate the participation of others and to determine the result more or less unilaterally.[20] To be sure, this does not tell us which types of limitations on lobbying and political speech are appropriate, but it sets an outer constraint on the debate.

Notice that this account of collective self-government rests on a causally based principle of legitimation: the idea of affected interest. The right to participate comes from one's having an interest that can be expected to be affected by the particular collective action in question. In this respect the argument for democratic justice differs from liberal and communitarian views, both of which tend to regard membership in the relevant community as a trump (liberals by assumption, communitarians by express argument).[21] Once the contractualist way of thinking has been dethroned, it is difficult to see any principled basis for regarding membership as primary. On the view advanced here, the structure of decision rules should follow the contours of power relations, not those of memberships. The principle of affected interest should thus figure centrally in thinking about appropriate decision rules in different circumstances.

It will be objected that major difficulties arise in establishing who is affected how much by a particular decision and who is to determine which claims about being affected should be accepted. These are serious difficulties, to be sure, but two points should be noted in mitigation. First, although who is affected by a decision is bound to be controversial, this fact scarcely distinguishes causally based arguments from membership-based arguments about social justice. Who decides membership, and by what authority, is as fraught with conceptual and ideological baggage as who decides, and by what authority, the causal effects of a particular collective decision. These difficulties should not therefore count as decisive against the causally based view if the membership-based view is seen as the alternative. Second, there is considerable experience with causally based arguments in tort law. Although tort actions are often concerned with the causal effects of individual rather than collective decisions, courts have developed mechanisms for determining whose claims should be heard, for sorting genuine claims from frivolous ones, and for distinguishing weaker from stronger claims to have been adversely affected by an action and shaping remedies accordingly. This is not an argument for turning politics into tort law; the point of the comparison is rather to illustrate that in other areas of social life institutional mechanisms have been developed to assess and manage conflicting claims of being causally affected by actions. They may be imperfect mechanisms, but they should be evaluated by reference to the other imperfect mechanisms of collective decision making that actually prevail in the world, not by comparison with an ideal that prevails nowhere.[22]

INSTITUTIONALIZING OPPOSITION

Barrington Moore singles out "the existence of a legitimate and, to some extent effective, opposition" as the defining criterion of democracy. One need not go all the way with him to be persuaded that institutions fostering "loyal" opposition are essential to democratic life.[23] This is true for several related reasons. First, opposition institutions perform the functional role of providing sites for potential alternative leaderships to organize themselves, making possible periodic turnovers of power that are necessary—though not sufficient—for democratic governance. Second, opposition institutions help stabilize democracy by attracting social dissent toward antigovernment forces within the regime, rather than directing it at the regime's foundations. Anger and disaffection can thus be directed at particular power holders, without endangering the democratic order's legitimacy. Third, opposition institutions serve the public interest by ensuring that there are groups and individuals who have incentives to ask awkward questions, shine light in dark corners, and expose abuses of power. These considerations are buttressed by a more basic reason why the possibility of effective opposition is an essential requirement of democratic justice. Unless people can challenge prevailing norms and rules with the realistic hope of altering them, the requirement that the inherited past not bind us unalterably would be empty. The Burkean dimension of democratic justice could not be tempered in the ways that democratic justice requires.

Because there are no perfect decision rules, the products of even the best democratic procedures will leave some people justifiably aggrieved. Libertarian writers draw from this the implication that it is better to have as little collective action as possible, but in a world of ubiquitous power relations that option is neither satisfying nor plausible. To point this out is not to deny that democratic decision rules can lead to the imposition of outcomes on one group by another, or that the classical justification for those impositions—that they embody a "general will"—is unavailable.[24] Rather, it leads to the suggestion that procedures for expressing opposition should be thought valuable no matter what the prevailing mechanisms of collective decision-making. Recognizing that life goes on and decisions have to be made, we should seek the most appropriate rules of democratic governance for every circumstance. But people should nonetheless be able to oppose what has been decided, and to try to change it.

To require that meaningful opposition be tolerated is frequently to require more than dominant groups want to accept, for it can weaken their control of collective values and purposes. Accordingly, they often resist opposition or seek to render it ineffective. Part of the challenge of democratic justice is to institutionalize ways to stop them, and it seems safe to assume that procedural guarantees of the freedom to oppose will not, on their own, secure this goal. Democratic theorists who value effective opposition have long recognized that unless procedural guarantees are backed up by permissive civil and political freedoms of speech, press, assembly, and organization, they are all too easily rendered meaningless.[25] This is not to deny their importance. The history of sham democracies during the communist era illustrates what can happen when permissive freedoms are not honored. Democrats would be unwise ever to think them dispensable.

Unless permissive freedoms are accompanied by other measures, they can actually undermine the possibility of challenging the status quo, as we saw in the case of the proposed Clinton health-care reform. Inequalities in control over the resources needed to transform permissive freedoms into the service of effective opposition can mean that strategically powerful groups, when committed to prevailing arrangements, may be able to block all attempts to alter them. Thus, although permissive freedoms are reasonably deemed valuable for their propensity to permit and even foster opposition, they are not a panacea. When those committed to the status quo have unmatched access to information, wealth, and organizational resources, they may actually be able to use permissive freedoms to cement their advantages.

Awareness of the combined impact of imperfect decision rules and differential control over political resources has led some commentators to defend "substantive" conceptions of democracy over "procedural" ones, usually by appeal to some variant of Justice Stone's celebrated fourth footnote in *United States v. Carolene Products Co.* Noting that well-functioning democratic processes might lead to the domination of "discrete and insular minorities," he countenanced the possibility that their operation might reasonably be limited when this occurs. Stone dealt with a circumscribed class of cases.[26] But others have employed his reasoning more expansively. For instance, John Hart Ely defended much of the judicial activism of the Warren Court by reference to *Carolene Products* reasoning.[27] Likewise, Charles Beitz has pressed similar considerations into an argument that the quantitative fairness of equal voting power will never ensure substantively democratic outcomes.[28] In Beitz's view, a truly democratic system of "qualitative fairness" requires a prior system of "just legislation," because mere equal voting power can never be relied upon to produce fair outcomes.[29]

Substantively democratic views merely have to be stated for the difficulty with them to be plain: How can Ely know what democratic processes ought to have achieved had they not been corrupted by the *Carolene* problem? Whence the theory of just legislation against which Beitz will evaluate the results of voting procedures? Writers like Ely and Beitz have little to say to those who are unpersuaded by their respective conceptions of "equal concern and respect" and "qualitative fairness." If, as I maintain, there is no criterion for justice that is entirely independent of what democracy generates, this should not be surprising. To say this is not, however, to respond to the difficulty that motivates *Carolene*-type reasoning: There are no perfect decision rules and those who are better placed to translate permissive freedoms into political power should be expected, *ceteris paribus*, to get their way. The problem is real but the proffered solutions overreach, suggesting the desirability of finding a middle ground.[30] "More than process, less than substance" might be an appropriate slogan.

My suggestion is that we stake out the middle ground with the proposition that hierarchies should be presumed suspect. The reason is that although hierarchies can exist for many legitimate purposes, by definition they contain both power inequalities and truncated opportunities for opposition. Power, as Lord Acton said, tends to corrupt. Even when they acquire it legitimately, power holders all too easily convince themselves that their authority should expand in space and time, that critics are ignorant or irresponsible, and that subordinates lack the requisite ability to ascend from inferior roles. The allure of power can thus divert power holders within hierarchies from their legitimate goals, leading to the reduction of hierarchies to their power dimensions. The limited scope for opposition within hierarchies makes it difficult to block or check their atrophy into systems of domination. Indeed, as they atrophy the possibilities for opposition are likely to be increasingly constrained. It is for this reason that democrats should cast a skeptical eye on all hierarchical arrangements, placing the burden of justification on their defenders. Power need not be abused, but it often is, and it is wise for democrats to guard against that possibility.

These observations do not imply that all hierarchies should be eliminated.[31] Rather they suggest that there are good grounds for prima facie suspicion of them, even when they result from democratic collective decisions. Too often avoidable hierarchies masquerade as unavoidable ones, involuntary subordination is shrouded in the language of agreement, unnecessary hierarchies are held to be essential to the pursuit of common goals, and fixed hierarchies are cloaked in myths about their fluidity. Democratic justice suggests mistrust of prevailing hierarchies; it invites us to look for institutional and other structuring devices to limit them and to mitigate their unnecessary and corrosive effects. Such devices may be thought of as contributing to the evolving frameworks of democratic constraints within which people should be free to negotiate and renegotiate the terms of their cooperation and conflict.

To say that hierarchies should be presumed suspect is not to say anything about what is to count as sufficient to rebut the presumption. Nor is it to say anything about what kinds of constraints on hierarchies should be employed in different circumstances, or about how these constraints should be enforced. By itself, the general argument cannot answer these questions. But it does generate a series of appropriate queries about hierarchies, ways of probing them in the name of democratic justice.

The first concerns the degree to which a given hierarchy is inevitable. Consider the differences between adult domestic relations and parent-child relations. Both have taken a multiplicity of forms, even in the recent history of the West, yet almost all of these have been explicitly hierarchical in character. It is evident, however, that parent-child relations are inevitably hierarchical in ways that adult domestic relations are not. If a relationship is not inevitably hierarchical, the first question that arises is why should it be hierarchical at all? There may be justifiable reasons for a particular inessential hierarchy (that it is comparatively efficient, that it has been chosen, that the relevant people like it, or some other), but from the standpoint of democratic justice the presumption is against hierarchy, and the proponent of such reasons should shoulder the burden of persuasion.

When relations are inevitably hierarchical, a different class of considerations becomes relevant. We begin by asking: is it necessary that the relations in question be maintained at all? Parent-child relations of some kind must exist, but not all inevitably hierarchical relations are of this sort. To consider a limiting case once again, history has shown that the institution of slavery need not exist. If an inescapably hierarchical relationship is unnecessary, it immediately becomes suspect from the standpoint of democratic justice. Slavery thus fares badly from this standpoint quite apart from its incompatibility with the presumption of universal inclusion.

A second class of appropriate inquiries about hierarchies concerns their pertinence to the activity at hand: are the hierarchical relations that exist appropriately hierarchical? Parent-child relations, for example, may be more hierarchical than they need to be in many instances, and they may include unnecessary kinds of hierarchical authority. They may also be maintained for a variety of reasons—ranging from the convenience of parents to their desires to dominate—that have nothing to do with the interests of their charges. Of alterable hierarchies we should thus always inquire: in whose interests are they maintained? Those who would sustain a hierarchy of a particular kind, or sustain it for longer than necessary, take on the burden of establishing that this operates in the interests of those who are subjected to the relevant hierarchy. For this reason one would be unmoved by the argument advanced by Amish parents in the *Wisconsin v. Yoder* litigation— namely, that they should be free not to send their teenage children to school because experience had taught them that this induced in the teenagers the desire to leave the Amish community, which, they contended, interfered with the parents' rights of free religious exercise.[32]

Democratic justice also bids us to attend to the degree to which hierarchies are ossified or fluid. We should distinguish self-liquidating hierarchies, as when children become adults or students graduate, from non-self-liquidating hierarchies, such as caste systems and hierarchies constituted by hereditary transmissions of wealth and power. We should also distinguish hierarchical orders in which anyone can in principle ascend to the top from those where that is not so. No woman can aspire to become pope, a fact that makes the Roman Catholic religion less attractive than some others from the standpoint of democratic justice on this score. In general, the argument tells us to prefer fluid hierarchies over ossified ones, other things being equal. Fluid hierarchies may not engender permanently subordinated classes, whereas ossified hierarchies do. Of course, other things seldom are equal; nonetheless, the requirement is a useful starting point. It tells us what the presumption is and by whom the burden of persuasion should be carried.

Similarly, asymmetrical hierarchies are questionable, whereas symmetrical ones are not necessarily so. Polygynous marriages are asymmetrical, for example, and as such are suspect from the standpoint of democratic justice: a husband can have many wives but a wife cannot have many husbands.[33] If these regimes were symmetrical, or had their members practiced "complex marriage," as the nineteenth-century Oneida perfectionist community was supposed to have done (so that any number of men could marry any number of women), they would not be questionable by reference to this aspect of the argument for democratic justice. Again, there may be other reasons rooted in democratic justice for objecting to such arrangements, but their symmetry would count in their favor.[34]

Closely related to questions about the relative fluidity and symmetry of hierarchies are questions about the degree to which they are imposed. Did the people who are subjected to them elect to be thus subjected? What were their other realistic options at the time? Whether or not they chose to enter, what degree of freedom to exit now exists? Generally, nonimposed hierarchies fare better than imposed ones, and less imposed hierarchies fare better than more imposed ones. If someone chose to participate at the bottom of a hierarchical relationship when she had alternative nonhierarchical (or less hierarchical) options in front of her, the fact of her choice confers some presumptive legitimacy on the state of affairs. Analogously, if someone remains in a hierarchical order when we are fairly confident that she has the resources to leave, we have less reason to be troubled from the standpoint of democratic justice than when this is not the case.

Finally, the general argument for democratic justice directs us to attend to the relative insularity of hierarchies. To what extent do they consist of self-contained groups of people minding their own business, who want to be left alone by outsiders? Withdrawing sects like the Old Order Amish, or migrating groups like the Mormons who went to Utah in the nineteenth century to escape persecution in the East, have at least prima facie valid claims that they should be able to set the terms of their association unimpeded. Such groups do not proselytize or seek to shape the world outside their communities (as religious fundamentalists, for example, often do). Hierarchical and undemocratic as these groups might be in their internal organization, they are of little consequence to the outside world. By contrast, a hierarchical established church whose influence on outsiders could not be escaped without substantial cost would not enjoy the same prima facie claim to be left alone. Relatively insular groups may be objectionable from the standpoint of democratic justice on some of the other grounds just discussed, but the fact of their insularity diminishes any externality-based claim by outsiders to restructure or abolish them.

Some Difficulties Considered

The preceding elaboration of the two central dimensions of democratic justice raises many questions. The most fundamental of these have to do with the complex character of democratic justice, tensions between it and other goods, and the appropriate role for the state that is implied by the general argument. Other questions, relating to the mechanics of implementation in particular cases, are deferred to subsequent chapters.

CONFLICTS INTERNAL TO DEMOCRATIC JUSTICE

Any argument for an internally complex set of principles must confront the possibility that they cannot be satisfied simultaneously. The question then arises: how are conflicts among the different injunctions to be resolved? One response to this question is to come up with a system of metarules for resolving conflicts when they occur. For instance, Rawls's theory of justice consists of a number of principles that, he argues, should be lexically ranked: in the case of conflicts the principles that are higher in his lexical ordering trump those that are lower.[35]

It is evident that democratic justice exhibits an analogous potential for internal conflict. What the general argument recommends as the appropriate system of governance in a domain may conflict with the presumptive suspicion of hierarchy. People might choose to create a hierarchy by voluntary action or majority rule. Likewise, the various injunctions against hierarchy might produce contradictory prescriptions as far as a particular practice is concerned. The insular character of withdrawing sects, such as the Amish, counsels leaving them alone, yet their internally hierarchical practices prompt suspicion from the standpoint of democratic justice. How should conflicts of this kind be resolved?

The two alternatives here are either to try to come up with a system of metaprinciples analogous to Rawls's lexical rules or, as I propose, to supply a principled defense of a more underdetermined view. To try to come up with a complete system of metaprinciples that would resolve every possible tension that could arise out of the complexities of the general argument seems an all but impossible task.[36] The range of circumstances that can arise is exceedingly large, if not infinite, and the complexity of the social world is such that there will always be challenges to the logic internal to democratic justice. Yet this is less troubling than might at first appear. For one thing, the lack of a complete system of metaprinciples does not silence democratic justice in every circumstance. We can still say, for example, that a practice that runs up against a great many of the presumptions of democratic justice is correspondingly more suspect for that reason. Slavery is an easy case for democratic justice just because this is so. It violates basic principles of collective self-governance, and it is on the wrong side of every presumption about hierarchy that I have discussed: it is unnecessary, it is not usually entered into voluntarily, it is hard or impossible to escape, it is both asymmetrical and non-self-liquidating, and it has external effects that permeate through the social world. By the same token a practice that turns out to be on the right side of every presumption will be equally easy to deal with.

The more difficult and interesting cases are less clear-cut. In many of these instances it may be possible to find accommodations among conflicting injunctions. In the case of the Amish, for instance, one might take the view that the withdrawing character of the group and the absence of a threat posed by it to the rest of society counsel against any attempt to interfere with its existence, but that the state should nonetheless insist that Amish children be educated so that they have the capacity to function outside the Amish community in the event that they decide to leave. On this view not all Amish educational practices would be tolerated, but in other respects the group would be left alone.[37] Likewise, although the ossified and non-self-liquidating hierarchies in the Catholic Church contravene some of the presumptions of democratic justice, the history of domination that has accompanied attempts by the state to control religion might also counsel that there is wisdom in an especially wide latitude of tolerance as far as religious matters are concerned. A government guided by the principles of democratic justice might nonetheless attach some costs to religions that contravene them, such as denying tax-exempt status to those in which some offices are reserved for men, persons of a particular race, or any other group that is defined in a morally arbitrary way. The governing body of the religion in question would then be free to decide whether to live with the sanctions in question or to adjust its practices to avoid them.[38]

As these examples illustrate, once we recognize that there is a range of possible sanctions and of feasible responses to them, apparently conflicting imperatives can be managed in a variety of ways that can, over time, be expected to encourage civil institutions to evolve in comparatively democratic directions.[39] The examples also underscore the fact that when we have multiple commitments, we must either live with resulting tensions or find creative solutions. This is no less true of the world in which we actually live than it would be in a world in which democratic justice furnished the basic principles of governance. The imperatives that follow from the constituent parts of the United States Constitution and its amendments generate many such tensions, and just as courts and legislatures have to order, rank, and accommodate them in particular contexts, so the same would have to be done in a world governed by considerations derived from the argument for democratic justice. Admittedly, to say this is not to resolve any specific tensions, but it does perhaps indicate the limits of what it is reasonable to expect from a general statement of principles.

A different objection is that democratic justice is unnecessarily complex.

My contention is that the freedom to oppose collective outcomes is not derivative of rights to inclusive participation. This might be granted, but if this freedom is valued regardless of whether decisions were made democratically, then why value democratic decision making? Is not democracy, on my account, reducible to opposition? My answer is that although inclusive participation and freedom to oppose are independently valuable, the ways in which they are exercised are not without implications for one another. In particular, I propose the following injunction: the more democratically those who win in battles over collective decisions conduct themselves in victory, the stronger is the obligation on the defeated to ensure that their opposition be loyal rather than disloyal—and vice versa. Processes of inclusive consultation, meaningful hearings, good-faith consideration of how to mitigate external effects of decisions, and willingness to consider alternatives all build legitimacy for democratic decision making, and they should. No less appropriately, their opposites breed cynicism and mistrust on the part of losers, which erode democracy's legitimacy in predictable ways. By linking the obligation to make opposition loyal to how democratically those in power conduct themselves, protagonists on all sides are reminded of the imperfection of the rules that give current winners their victories and losers their losses. In addition, if the two are linked, both winners and losers have incentives to search for mechanisms that can diminish the distances that divide them.

TRADE-OFFS BETWEEN DEMOCRATIC JUSTICE AND OTHER GOODS

Additional sources of tension arise because my argument is premised on the notion that democracy is a conditioning good—subordinate to the activities whose pursuit it regulates. This means that there can and most likely will be tensions between the requirements of democratic justice and the activities it is intended to condition. In the limiting case, there are activities that operate in flat contradiction with the principles I have described. Apart from the case of parent-child relations, to which systematic attention is devoted in Chapter 4, there are football teams, armies, and many other organizational forms whose purposes seem to defy democratic governance. No doubt one can always challenge the proposition that such organizational forms must necessarily be undemocratic, and as the rich literature on the governance of the firm indicates, we should always be open to creative possibilities for the democratic management of institutions that seem inherently undemocratic.

Yet one has to confront the possibility that there will be circumstances in which there are inescapable trade-offs between democratic control and the pursuit of a particular good, be it the gathering of military intelligence, the running of a professional sports team, or other valuable activity.

One response is to deal with these trade-offs in the same way that tensions internal to democratic justice are handled: recognize that when we value more than one thing we may have to choose among them. But this should be the last response, not the first. Although there is never a guarantee that trade-offs between democratic justice and other goods can be avoided, the argument for democratic justice bids us to try to find ways to avoid them. Consider the two examples just mentioned. Congress has devised oversight mechanisms which, however imperfectly, ensure some democratic accountability of intelligence agencies consistent with their secret purposes. No doubt we pay a price for them and they could be improved upon, but the outcome of the Cold War scarcely suggests that our system fared worse than the Soviet system, in which there was virtually no democratic accountability of any sort, or indeed that it fared less well than other systems in the West that until recently have had little or no democratic oversight.[40] The situation in professional sports, too, is less clear-cut than might first appear. Although one would not want everyone on the team calling plays, there are many areas where a measure of democratic control can be achieved without compromise of athletic purpose. Pay and working conditions are the most obvious areas; no doubt there are others. To reiterate, the general point is that the presumption is against undemocratic ways of doing things. It is only a presumption and it can be overcome, but reasons should be demanded and the burden of persuasion should always lie with those who would limit democracy's operation.

COMPETING DEMANDS OF DIFFERENT DOMAINS

Still other potential tensions arise for democratic justice out of the fact that it is simultaneously concerned with many domains of civil society. It may be the case that pursuing democratic justice in one domain makes it more difficult, perhaps even impossible, to pursue it in other domains. For instance, participation in governance is part of what democratic justice requires. Yet there are limits to how much time people have available, so that increased participatory involvement in one domain, like school board meetings, may mean diminished participation in others, like the family. Hence Sirianni's paradox of participatory pluralism, which arises for anyone who both values democratic participation and embraces a view of politics that ranges throughout civil society. We cannot maximize participation over all domains simultaneously.

The paradox is inescapable for participatory democrats like Sirianni, but the argument for democratic justice suggests avenues for dealing with it. Participation is not valuable for its own sake. It is valuable when pursued in conjunction with the goods that it conditions. Collective self-governance is important in every domain of civil society, but it is never the most important thing; adherents of democratic justice should thus always be open to time saving and other novel devices to conserve participatory resources. Since the 1970s, for instance, a number of writers have explored the use of so-called "citizen juries" and "deliberative polls," randomly selected groups that are paid to debate public issues from the selection of presidential candidates to the governance of school districts.[41] Experience with these devices suggests that they may be useful both for exerting democratic control and for solving the difficulty, pointed to by Sartori and others, that "knowledge— cognitive competence and control—becomes more and more the problem as politics becomes more and more complicated."[42] Randomly selected lay groups, whose members have no particular vested interest in the outcome in a given area, can invest the time and energy needed to make informed decisions. Such groups can gather data and listen to expert witnesses, making use of esoteric knowledge without being held hostage to it. The decisions that they render might be merely advisory or perhaps even binding, at least for certain matters. From the standpoint of democratic justice, the possibilities they offer are worth exploring because they provide a potential way out of Sirianni's paradox: they combine citizen control with the possibility of sophisticated decision making in a complex world, and they do it in a way that takes account of the economy of time.[43]

Earlier I suggested that participation should be seen neither in purely instrumental terms nor as the point of the exercise in politics. Deliberative polls and citizen juries are attractive as a creative institutional response to the goal of trying to occupy a middle ground between these two views. Everyone might be expected to participate in some citizen juries, just as everyone is expected to sit on some conventional juries. Everyone would know that in the juries they are not involved in, other randomly selected groups were sitting with no particular agendas or interest groups driving the outcome. Everyone would also know that no matter how complex and technical decisions were becoming, a meaningful element of lay control would nonetheless be present in all collective decision making. This is essential for democratic justice.

Role for the State

Apart from the extremes of limiting cases like slavery, the general argument for democratic justice does not provide conclusive assessments of particular decision rules or mechanisms of opposition. Instead, as we have seen, it generates presumptions and distributes burdens of persuasion in various ways. That is as it should be. Because the general argument is semicontextual, particularities of context are needed to decide when burdens have been appropriately carried and when presumptions have been rebutted. Democratic justice generates determinate conclusions in particular contexts only.

To say this is not, however, to deliver on everything that should reasonably be expected of the general argument. Invoking the language of presumptions and burdens of persuasion immediately raises the question, Who is to judge when burdens have been carried and presumptions rebutted? Because the evidence is often inconclusive and opinion about it must be expected often to be divided, just where decision-making authority should be located is, and is bound to remain, an important general question. The answer is also partly contextual; different authorities are appropriate in different kinds of circumstances. But the answer is only partly contextual; some general considerations apply.

ANTIVANGUARDISM AND ITS LIMITS

Whenever anyone claims to know how to get to democracy undemocratically, skepticism is in order for two reasons. One is practical and one is normative. The practical reason is that it is doubtful whether the person making the claim can know that he or she is right. Because democratic reforms, reacting to particular evils, chart new courses into an unknown future, it is usually difficult to know what their full consequences will be or what new problems the reforms will create. For instance, the changes in American family law that made marriage more a contract and less a status were motivated by a desire to undermine the patriarchal family. But one effect of these changes has been to render women increasingly vulnerable to the greater economic power of men in marriage. As the implications of this become clear, creative democratic responses will be sought, and new experiments tried that will give rise to new difficulties. So the process will continue. Likewise with the debate on democracy in the workplace, there is considerable disagreement about the most effective approach in undermining alienating hierarchy: strategies of worker self-management, plans for employee ownership or part-ownership that leave the structure of management comparatively untouched, or various other devices. Different possibilities have been tried in different industries. It seems certain that no single model will turn out to be generally applicable, and that new possibilities are yet to be tried.

To take an example from the realm of institutional governance, during the nineteenth century reasonable salaries and working conditions for politicians were rightly seen as essential to undermining a system in which government was a part-time activity for the wealthy. But these improvements have brought with them new brands of ossified power in the form of professional politicians with lifetime career aspirations in government. In the United States, political elites often manage to maintain themselves in positions of power for decades in ways that are at odds with democracy's hostility toward entrenched hierarchy.[44] As a response to this, new democratic reforms are being called for, geared toward limiting the number of terms politicians can serve and better regulating the role of money in electoral politics.[45]

It defies credulity to suppose that in these instances democratic reformers could have understood social processes profoundly enough, or seen sufficiently far into the future, to have anticipated all the problems and possibilities that lay ahead. Yet these cases are not exceptional. The fabric of social life and the dynamics of historical change are complex and little understood; that is the reality with which we have to live. Designing democratic institutional constraints is thus bound to be a pragmatic business, best pursued in context-sensitive and incremental ways. New activities come into being, and technological change, experience, and the evolution of other causally linked activities present fresh problems and generate novel possibilities for democratic governance. There are good reasons to be skeptical of those who deny this, whether they harbor a hidden agenda that is being obscured by their vanguardist pretensions or they are acting out of misplaced faith in their own prescient abilities.

Means-ends dichotomies are also suspect for the normative reason that they undermine the spirit of democratic justice. Although I have argued that we should resist the contention that participation is valuable for its own sake, we should be no less wary of purely instrumental conceptions of democracy. Democratic means are never the point of the exercise, but they are usually of more than mere instrumental value. There is value to doing things democratically, and there is value to struggling with how to do things democratically while still achieving one's other goals. Democratic habits of self-restraint and attention to the needs and aspirations of others have to be learned through democratic practice; succumbing to the authoritarianism inherent in means-ends dichotomies should be expected to undermine it. In this connection, Dewey penned the right maxim for democratic justice more than half a century ago: "Our first defense is to realize that democracy can be served only by the slow day by day adoption and contagious diffusion in every phase of our common life of methods that are identical with the ends to be reached."[46]

The principled refusal to impose solutions from above can provoke the argument that they will not then be implemented at all, and there are, indeed, at least four important classes of exceptions to the initial presumption against vanguardism. One has already been mentioned: substantial differences in exit costs, which render democracy at the local level infeasible. As we have seen, when power dynamics are thus structured, no local decision rule will be effective in diminishing injustice. This amounts to saying that policies will have to be imposed from above if an impact is to be made on the problem. Aspects of decision making should be centralized in this type of circumstance, though not necessarily all aspects. Such remedial policies as desegregation remedies may have to be imposed, whether by courts or other state or federal institutions.[47] Other components of ongoing governance may have to be centralized as well. Moving toward greater statewide or even national financing of public education, for instance, would ameliorate the white flight that financing out of local property taxes invites. But this need not mean doing away with robust local control of curricular and other matters.[48] Subsidiarity suggests moving toward more centralized control only of those dimensions of decision making that produce perverse consequences at the local level. Funding out of taxes raised at what is effectively the sub-urban level brings the system of financing into conflict with the principle of affected interest, due to differences in capacities for exit. In areas where the effects of these differences is most marked, the case for moving away from local control is strongest.

A different class of exceptions to the presumption against vanguardism concerns the provision of public goods. Public goods, typically things like clean air, can be provided only for entire populations. As a result, they must be supplied collectively, and it is impractical to exclude some individuals or subgroups from consuming them.[49] Unless the costs of providing pub-lic goods are imposed on everyone, some can be expected to opt out of, and perhaps even oppose, their provision. The public-goods exception is more easily defended in principle than in practice, because whether some-thing is a public good is often contentious politically. Proponents of "shock therapy" in the transition from communism to capitalism, for instance, made a public-goods argument in support of their vanguardism. Thus Adam Przeworski argued that during the move from authoritarianism to democ-racy, unless economic reforms are rammed through from above, those who are adversely affected by them will mobilize their opposition through the democratic process, scuttling the reforms. Fledgling democratic govern-ments "face the choice of either involving a broad range of political forces in the shaping of reforms, thus compromising their economic soundness, or trying to undermine all opposition to the [reform] program." Consequently, any government "that is resolute must proceed in spite of the clamor of voices that call for softening or slowing down the reform program." Be-cause reformers "know what is good," all political conflicts become no more than a waste of time. Przeworski went on to point out that every instance of successful market reform during democratic transitions then on record was implemented by executive decree, remarking that "this potential is inherent in the very conception of market reforms."[50]

The critical question is whether the reformers really do "know what is good" and pursue it in fact. Much of what is presented by technocratic re-formers as desirable is controversial, and many economic reforms that are described as public goods do not meet the technical criteria, which require both joint supply and nonexcludability. Whether the sorts of privatization and stabilization policies that such political economists as Przeworski, Janos

Kornai, Jeffrey Sachs, and others advocated lead to the supply of public goods in this sense is debatable.[51] No doubt parts of what is provided are public goods, but other aspects of these policies may amount to little more than mechanisms for strategically well-placed groups to raid public treasuries, generating little or no benefit for anyone else. In such instances, the pursuit of private benefit may be cloaked in the language of public goods, and opposition to them that is really a reflection of zero-sum distributive conflict masquerades as a collective-action problem. What are billed as solutions to it are actually partisan policies that help some sectors and hurt others. Democrats who suspect that this is the case with substantial parts of postcommunist privatizations are bound to find themselves ambivalent, at least, about "bitter pill" strategies, which depend on "initial brutality, on proceeding as quickly as possible with the most radical measures," and implementing reforms either by administrative fiat or forcing them through legislatures.[52]

In circumstances where one does not doubt that a public good is being supplied, one's democratic moral intuitions may not be troubled by decisive action from above. In the South African constitutional negotiations that led up to the April 1994 elections, for instance, it gradually became clear that, desirable as multiparty roundtable negotiations sounded, they were not going to produce an agreement on a democratic constitution. Too many groups had too many incentives to pursue private agendas at the expense of ensuring that the public good was provided. Consequently, it became evident that if a democratic political order was to be put in place, it would have to be hammered out as an elite pact and then imposed on the society. This is what transpired in fact, and democrats the world over applauded as opponents to the transition were so effectively either marginalized or co-opted because almost no one doubted that what the elites proposed to impose—a democratic constitutional order—is in fact a public good.[53]

Distinguishing the provision of genuine public goods from spurious ones is a difficult and controversial business. Often the two are mixed, making the distinction even more difficult, as is almost certainly the case with most privatization plans. Even in the case of the South African constitution it seems clear that the elites who committed themselves to providing the public good in question sprinkled in benefits for themselves—notably a system of electoral and parliamentary rules that greatly weakens backbenchers vis-à-vis leaderships—as well as bribes to particular interest groups to insulate them from the new political order.[54]

The extent to which policies may legitimately be imposed from above via a public-goods logic varies with the degree to which genuine public goods are being provided. This question is often hotly disputed and ideologically charged, not least because there are those who have an interest in obscuring the matter. It may also be genuinely unclear in certain circumstances. When either of these conditions applies, what we witness is not a failure in the argument for democratic justice. Rather, it is a failure in understanding of, or agreement about, whether or not something constitutes a public good. This is not to diminish the normative importance of the matter. It is only to say that it would be to expect the wrong kind of thing from any political theory to ask that it resolve or avoid such contentious empirical questions of political economy. The argument for democratic justice can be expected to counsel what to do when a certain fact pattern obtains; it cannot be expected to tell us whether or not the fact pattern really does obtain.

The argument does, however, counsel us to harbor suspicion of claims to be providing public goods. Because of the attendant dangers, it would be wise to subject them to what lawyers think of as "strict scrutiny." American courts typically subject legislative action to this most demanding level of constitutional scrutiny when the proposed action interferes with a "fundamental" liberty, usually a freedom protected by the Bill of Rights. Strict scrutiny requires a showing that the governmental objective is unusually important—that a "compelling" state interest is at stake—and that it cannot be accomplished in a less intrusive way. (This is contrasted with "intermediate" scrutiny, which requires only the showing of a "substantial relationship" between the proposed policy and an "important government objective," and "minimal" scrutiny, which merely requires demonstration of a "rational relationship" to legitimate governmental objective.)[55] By analogy, we might say that the imposition of a public good is justified only when the good in question is essential to the operation of a democratic order and cannot be attained in any other way. Because those who claim to provide public goods may have ulterior motives, and because private goods can often masquerade as public goods, the strong presumption should always be against their imposition from above.

A third class of exceptions to the antivanguardist presumption arises when illegitimate hierarchies have been maintained by the state. For example, in the West the disadvantaged status of women in family life was for centuries sustained by the common law and other active policies of the state. One dramatic legacy of this history is that as recently as the 1950s throughout the United States a husband could not be prosecuted for raping his wife. By the end of the 1980s, marital rape was a prosecutable felony in forty-two states, in the District of Columbia, and on all federal land. This change was the product of a concerted feminist campaign in state legislatures and courts. It would have been impossible for such changes to have come about without the state's active involvement, for the policies of the state were at the root of the injustice in question.[56] Likewise, it took the passage of the married women's property acts (the first wave of which began in the 1840s) to expunge the common-law rule that had given the husband control, and sometimes title, to the wife's property and possessions during marriage.

In such circumstances it is necessary, and justifiable from the standpoint of democratic justice, for the state to be centrally involved in dismantling the unjust system that it has created. Women would have been morally misguided as well as politically shortsighted had they not sought to enlist public institutions in this struggle to refashion the terms of their domestic association. Because the unjust hierarchies to which they had been subjected were sustained by the legal order, it was reasonable to require the state to play an active role in dismantling the injustices in question. Likewise, the effects of the Group Areas Act in South Africa, which led to the forced removals of millions of blacks from viable communities to desolate deserts, are properly responded to by remedial action from a democratic South African state.[57] The general point here is that the more antidemocratic practices have been underwritten by the state, the more powerful is the case for the involvement of state institutions in remedying the unjust status quo.

A fourth class of exceptions arises when domination within a domain is not a direct product of state action, but it is nonetheless sustained by forces external to that domain that can be removed only by state action. This is what Walzer describes as dominance, the transfer of power in one domain of social life where it may be legitimate into another where it is not. Walzer contends, for instance, that economic inequality is not objectionable as such and that it may be justified in the sphere of production for its incentive and other efficiency effects. What is objectionable is that disparities in income and wealth are all too easily translatable into disparities in the political domain, the domestic domain, the educational domain, and other areas where they have no evident rationale.[58] This happens because the resources necessary to exercise power tend to be fungible across domains, and Walzer sees it as one of the appropriate tasks of a democratic state to limit this fungibility. On this view, laws against buying and selling votes can be defended, for example, even though such laws are inefficient in the economist's sense. Similarly, refusals by courts to enforce antenuptial agreements that leave divorcing spouses destitute amount to a refusal by the state to allow economic disparities that may be justifiable outside the domestic domain to set the terms of life within it.

Walzer's intuition about this class of cases is defensible, if for different reasons from those that he supplies. His argument for trying to prevent domination within a sphere by those who control goods external to it appeals to shared meanings. For democratic justice the justification is rooted in considerations drawn from the political economy of power. Again, the shape of decision rules should follow the contours of power relations, not those of memberships. It follows that when obstacles to democracy within a domain are externally sustained, state power is appropriately used to remove such obstacles. To deny this would amount to abandoning democratic justice in particular domains to those who have hegemonic control of fungible resources. In short—pace Walzer—because causal effects, not shared membership within a domain, are decisive in legitimating a right to democratic control, it follows that state action that crosses the boundaries of domains can be justified when this is necessary to achieve democratic justice within a domain.

Action by the state to advance democratic reform can be justified, then, but not as part of any missionary quest on behalf of democratic justice. There is no secular analog to "Christianizing the infidels" to justify such action, whether by courts, legislatures, or invading armies. Rather, external involvement can be justified by four main classes of reasons. First, when wide differences in capacities to escape the effects of decisions undermine the principle of affected interest, then the logic of subsidiarity justifies action from above. Second, when the provision of a public good is at stake, imposed solutions may be justifiable, subject to the caveats I have mentioned. Third, the state may often have an affirmative obligation to help foster democratic reform flowing from its historical culpability in creating and sustaining injustice. Last, when external sources of domination within a domain can be removed only by state action, this can be justified by reference to the argument from causal legitimacy.

The aspiration to avoid imposed solutions suggests that the presumption should generally be in favor of doing things through representative institutions rather than courts or other agencies, because legislatures are more democratically accountable. Even when action from above is warranted in accordance with the logic of subsidiarity, it is generally better for this action to be by elected legislatures rather than by appointed judiciaries or administrative authorities. Some exceptions to this general stance are explored in subsequent chapters. Notice, for now, that it is the exceptions that stand in need of justification. In this connection the argument for democratic justice exhibits an elective affinity with the approaches to constitutional adjudication that have been defended in recent years by Ruth Bader Ginsburg and Robert Burt, and it will be useful to end this statement of the general argument with some discussion of their views.

Burt conceives of a constitutional democracy as inescapably committed to two principles—majority rule and equal self-determination—that have the potential to conflict with one another. If majoritarian processes are employed to promote domination of some by others, the contradiction latent in democratic politics becomes manifest. In such circumstances democracy goes to war with itself, and an institutional mechanism is needed to resolve the conflict. This is supplied, on Burt's account, by judicial review, understood as "a coercive instrument extrinsic to the disputants" in a political struggle. Burt sees judicial review as a "logical response to an internal contradiction between majority rule and equal self-determination. It is not a deviation from that theory."[59]

If the court's legitimate role in a democracy is rooted in this logic of preventing domination through democratic process, then it follows for Burt that its activities should be limited to dealing with the consequences of the democratic contradiction. And because preventing domination is the goal, it also follows that courts should generally avoid imposing solutions of their own when democracy has wrought domination. Rather, they should declare the domination that has emerged from the democratic process unacceptable and insist that the parties try anew to find an accommodation. Thus in contrast to what many have seen as the altogether too timid approach taken by the U.S. Supreme Court in the school desegregation cases of the 1950s and after, on Burt's view the Court took the right stand. In *Brown v. Board of Education* the justices declared the doctrine of "separate but equal" to be an unconstitutional violation of the Equal Protection Clause, but they did not describe schooling conditions that would be acceptable.[60] Rather, they turned the problem back to southern state legislatures, requiring them to fashion acceptable remedies themselves.[61] These remedies came before the Court as a result of subsequent litigation, were evaluated when they did, and were often found to be wanting.[62] But the Court avoided designing the remedy itself, and thus avoided the charge that it was usurping the legislative function.

Ginsburg, too, has made the case that when courts try to step beyond a reactive role, they undermine their legitimacy in a democracy. Although she thinks that it is sometimes necessary for the court to step "ahead" of the political process to achieve reforms that the Constitution requires, if it gets too far ahead, it can produce a backlash and provoke charges that it is overreaching its appropriate place in a democratic constitutional order.[63] She and Burt both think that the sort of approach adopted by Justice Blackmun in *Roe v. Wade* exemplifies this danger.[64] In contrast to the *Brown* approach, in *Roe* the Court did a good deal more than strike down a Texas abortion statute. The majority opinion laid out a detailed test to determine the conditions under which any abortion statute could be expected to pass muster. In effect, Justice Blackmun authored a federal abortion statute of his own. As Ginsburg put it, the Court "invited no dialogue with legislators. Instead, it seemed entirely to remove the ball from the legislators' court" by wiping out virtually every form of abortion regulation then in existence.[65]

On the Ginsburg-Burt view, the sweeping holding in *Roe* diminished the Court's democratic legitimacy at the same time as it polarized opinion about abortion and put paid to various schemes to liberalize abortion laws that were under way in different states. Between 1967 and 1973 statutes were passed in nineteen states liberalizing the permissible grounds for abortion. Many feminists had been dissatisfied with the pace and extent of this reform. This is why they mounted the campaign that resulted in *Roe*. Burt concedes that in 1973 it was "not clear whether the recently enacted state laws signified the beginning of a national trend toward abolishing all abortion restrictions or even whether in the so-called liberalized states, the new enactments would significantly increase access to abortion for anyone." Nonetheless, he points out that "the abortion issue was openly, avidly, controverted in a substantial number of public forums, and unlike the regimen extant as recently as 1967, it was no longer clear who was winning the battle."[66] Following the *Brown* model, the Court might have struck down the Texas abortion statute in *Roe* and remanded the matter for further action at the state level, thereby setting limits on what legislatures might do in the matter of regulating abortion without involving the Court directly in designing that regulation. On the Ginsburg-Burt view, this would have left space for democratic resolution of the conflict, ensuring the survival of the right to abortion while at the same time preserving the legitimacy of the Court's role in a democracy.[67]

Although the tensions that arise within democratic justice differ from those that motivate Burt and Ginsburg, in three important respects their view of the appropriate role for courts in a democratic order fits comfortably within the general argument developed here. First, they articulate an appropriate institutional response to the injunction that rather than impose democracy on collective activities, the goal should be to try to structure those activities so that people will find ways to democratize things for themselves. By placing courts in a nay-saying stance of ruling out practices as unacceptable when they violate the strictures of democratic justice, courts can force legislatures and the conflicting parties they represent to seek creative democratic solutions to their conflicts that can pass constitutional muster. Second, the Ginsburg-Burt view is attractive because it is reactive but directed; it exemplifies the creative pragmatism that motivates democratic justice. It involves accepting that there is an important—if circumscribed— role for courts in a democracy, yet it does not make the unmanageable and undemocratic administrative demands on courts that accompany more proactive views of adjudication. On this view a court might reasonably hold that a given policy should be rejected without stating (indeed, perhaps without having decided) what policy would pass muster. "This is unacceptable for reasons *a*, *b*, *c* . . . ; find a better way" is seen as an appropriate stance for a constitutional court. Finally, by recognizing the relatively greater legitimacy of legislatures and treating courts as institutional mechanisms for coping with legislative failure, the Ginsburg-Burt view takes account of the fact that no decision-making mechanism is flawless. Yet it does so in a way that is rooted in the idea that democratic procedures should be made to operate as well as possible, and when they fail, remedies should be no more intrusive on the democratic process than is necessary to repair them.

Some will object to this as too minimal a role for reviewing courts, but democrats have to concern themselves not only with courts that aspire to advance the cause of democratic justice, as they might reasonably be thought to have done in *Brown* and *Roe*, but also with courts that do not, as was the case in *Dred Scott*, the *Civil Rights Cases*, and *Lochner v. New York*.[68] Insulated from any further review, and lacking, at least in the American context, in democratic accountability, courts can put decisions of this kind in place that may not be reversed for decades or even generations. Although it may thus be wise from the standpoint of democratic justice to embrace an activist role for a constitutional court, it is equally wise to limit courts to a circumscribed and negationist activism.

The Path to Application

My aim here has been to state the general case for a democratic conception of social justice. This I have sought to do by building on the popular view, in which considerations of democracy and justice are intimately linked, rather than conventional academic views of them as fundamentally distinct and mutually antagonistic. The account that I offer rests on the twin commitments to government and opposition in democratic theory, suggesting that there should always be opportunities for those affected by the operation of a collective practice both to participate in its governance and to oppose its results when they are so inclined. These two injunctions should reasonably be expected to have different implications in different cultures, and, within the same culture, to evolve over time and play themselves out differently in different circumstances. They are best thought of as conditioning constraints, designed to democratize social relations as they are reproduced, rather than as blueprints for social justice.

This view contains internal tensions, to be sure, but I have tried to show that these come with the territory in reflecting about the justness of social arrangements, and to indicate something about how these tensions might best be coped with consistent with the spirit of the general argument. Beyond this, I have sought to point out the main outlines of a view of the state that follows from my view, and to develop some of its implications for the state's role in responding to structural and inherited injustice, providing public goods, and advancing the cause of democratic justice more generally. I have sketched the basic principles that should guide state action, as well as the fitting nature and place for judicial review in the argument for democratic justice. No doubt I have raised as many questions as I have settled, but I hope, nonetheless, that I have characterized the central argument and its motivation sufficiently fully to cast it in an attractive light.

In 1918 Dewey remarked that any philosophy animated by the striving to achieve democracy "will construe liberty as meaning a universe in which there is real uncertainty and contingency, a world which is not all in, and never will be, a world which in some respects is incomplete and in the making, and which in these respects may be made this way or that according as men judge, prize, love and labor. To such a philosophy any notion of a perfect or complete reality, finished, existing always the same without regard to the vicissitudes of time, will be abhorrent."[69] Democratic justice is conceived of in a similar contingent and pragmatic spirit. Just as there are no blueprints, there are no final destinations. Social practices evolve, as do technologies of government and opposition, often presenting fresh injustices and novel possibilities for dealing with them. The challenge is to confront the injustices and take advantage of the possibilities in a principled and satisfying way. Democratic justice is intended to help in that endeavor. Exploring its implications for the human life cycle is the task I turn to next.

· 4 ·

Governing Children

WE FIRST CONFRONT POWER RELATIONS as children. It is logical, therefore, to start pursuing democratic justice through the life cycle by developing its account of governing children. This also provides a good initial test
of my claim that the general argument for democratic justice can usefully
be tailored to power relations of all kinds. Dependent children, particularly
in their early years, are not much capable of meaningful decision making or
effective opposition to the power relations that structure their lives. Nor, on
many conceptions of the matter, ought they to be. Given the centrality of
inclusive participation and meaningful opposition to the general argument
developed in Chapter 3, the question therefore arises: what can it contribute
to thinking about the justice of children's circumstances? Responding to the
challenge implicit in that question is the task taken up here.

It might seem artificial to consider adult-child relations independently of
adult domestic relations, as I do, because most children live in forms of association that are intimately bound up with their parents' relations with one
another. This is true, yet the ensemble of relations out of which families
are composed differ from one another in ways that matter for democratic
justice. Moreover, many children live in domestic arrangements that are un-

conventional when measured by the yardstick of the late twentieth-century Western nuclear family. At least in the United States, children often have no parents, one parent, unmarried parents, stepparents, or divorced parents.[1] Our account must speak to these various circumstances without loading the dice by treating them from the outset as deviant from some "normal" case.

Origins of America's Dual-Regime System

Just as the suspension of the wife's legal identity during marriage was never complete in common-law systems, so the child was never unqualifiedly subject to the father's power. In contrast with children's status in Roman law — where the *paterfamilias* had total power over all members of his family — at common law the father's right to restrict his child's liberty ended once the child reached twenty-one. Even before this age was reached, the law placed various constraints on the father that Roman law never recognized. He could not kill his children or sell them into slavery, although it seems that custody could be sold to another for the balance of the child's minority, that girls could be sold into "apprenticeship" to be raised as prostitutes and boys to work in many circumstances, and that the law could not compel a father to supply children with food, shelter, and the other wherewithal necessary for survival.[2]

The inherited system of legal constraints on parental authority was bound to be reshaped with the move to a wage-labor economy. The industrial revolution brought increased demand for unskilled and semiskilled labor, pulling children into the workforce at early ages and subjecting them to market forces as apprentices and, later, factory workers. Starting at least at the time of Henry VIII, any child over the age of five could be apprenticed if the parents were in poverty. Similar practices were common in England's American colonies. In Virginia, for instance, county commissioners were ordered by a 1646 statute to send seven- and eight-year-old children to work in public flax factories.[3] Parents began to find that they had legal obligations to raise productive children, and the realities of a wage-labor economy meant that children could become both liabilities and assets to their families in new ways.[4] They could be drains on a worker's income during their dependent years but sources of family income once they could work outside the home. Over the course of the nineteenth century, however, as the opportunities for child labor diminished and the costs of child rearing increased, children became increasingly expensive liabilities.[5]

In such a context, the notion that government should protect children both from unscrupulous employers and exploitative or inept parents could gain in credibility, feeding the rise of what has been described as the therapeutic state.[6] Factory acts and child-labor legislation set limits on how children could be used in the workforce, but they were accompanied by a widespread expansion of governmental authority over children. In the name of *parens patriae*, educators, social workers, judges, and other public officials carved out roles for themselves in governing many aspects of children's lives. Laura Nader might overstate her case when she describes the preindustrial American family as self-sufficient, but she is surely correct that industrialization was accompanied by a circumstance in which parents, "who earlier had both power and responsibility for their children, found their legal responsibility increasing at a time when their power over the intimate home environment was declining."[7]

Imperatives for involvement by the state in children's lives were reinforced by the general expansion of its reach into civil society that began in the late nineteenth century and accelerated through the New Deal. This involved government's assumption of explicit responsibility for dimensions of the general welfare that had previously been left to other social institutions. Through such measures as public health statutes, unemployment legislation, and regulation of commerce and trade unions, the state had an indirect impact on many aspects of children's lives.[8] But the state also had an increased direct impact, via such measures as the enactment of compulsory school legislation and the creation of the juvenile justice system. In virtually every aspect of their lives, if as a consequence of different and sometimes conflicting forces, children found themselves subjected not only to the authority of their parents but also to that of teachers, judges, bureaucrats, social workers, and other public officials. Much of the expansion of public authority over children was motivated by a concern for their welfare, but, perhaps predictably, its effects were mixed. In some areas at least, it produced new forms of subjugation.[9]

The expansion of state authority over children was not always at the expense of parental authority. The modes of state subordination of children that had been inherited from the colonial era had at least partly been designed to augment and reinforce parental authority. The notorious stubborn children laws of colonial New England—which authorized local magistrates to enforce the death penalty on teenagers for disobedience to their parents—stand as an extreme illustration. Although the death penalty appears never to have been carried out as authorized in these statutes, their existence underscores the fact that the law guaranteed, with considerable vengeance, the status of children as wards of their parents. Puritan ideology had justified this subjection on religious grounds. Indeed, like the state, the church reinforced the patriarchal order, sustaining a system of overlapping authority structures that must often have seemed indistinguishable to the children who lived within them.[10]

Yet the potential always existed for church, state, and parental hierarchies to compete with one another for authority over children, and compete they did. The passage of the Constitution and the Bill of Rights diminished the authority that the Church could wield over children with the backing of coercive state power.[11] However, the practice of allowing private religious schools to deliver compulsory education, constitutionally validated by the Supreme Court in 1925, ensured that religious institutions would continue to have a substantial impact on many children.[12] This is buttressed by the structure of the First Amendment, which protects the religious institutions it disestablishes, as well as a variety of policies—notably tax deductions for charitable contributions and tax-free status of charitable institutions—which support religious institutions. But the authority of religious schools over children is now firmly subordinate to parents and the state. Parents, who speak for their children in most religious matters, have the decisive say over whether their children will attend religious schools, subject to some secular limitations. The state regulates religious delivery of instruction insofar as it sets minimal curricular standards and licenses and accredits all schools. States and parents have thus emerged as the two principal sources of authority over dependent children. Partly competing, partly mutually reinforcing, they structure the basic terms of children's existence into adolescence and beyond.[13]

Parents and Children: Alternative Models

The central challenge that adult-child relations pose for democratic justice is that they are inevitably hierarchical and inegalitarian. But the challenge changes. Children evolve from conditions of utter dependence on adults, to circumstances where equality is possible, to reversed conditions, where once-independent adults become increasingly feeble and dependent—sometimes on their adult children, sometimes on others. This evolving reality has substantial implications for both the governance and opposition dimensions of democratic justice.

GOVERNANCE AND OPPOSITION FROM
THE STANDPOINT OF CHILDREN

On the governance side of the equation, young children find themselves in circumstances that they did not choose to enter, and in which initially they can play no governing role.[14] The principal questions for democratic justice concern when and how children should start to participate in the decisions that affect their lives, and what model of governance should prevail before the ages of emancipation arrive. I use the plural form here because the capacities needed to participate in some kinds of decisions may develop later than those needed to participate in others. And the answer should indeed be capacity-dependent: democratic justice requires that mechanisms of collective self-governance be as inclusive as possible, limited by necessity only.[15]

This requirement immediately raises questions, because the historical trend in the West over the past century and a half has been to lengthen the status of childhood. Whereas children used to be treated as miniature adults from their earliest years, childhood is now widely regarded as a distinct developmental phase. The status "adolescence" is also a comparatively recent Western creation, and although its precise terminus in most countries is unclear, it is a status that—with notable exceptions, usually caused by wars—has also steadily been lengthening. The major views of human psychology that have been fashionable since the nineteenth century differ from one another concerning many particulars, but they share assumptions about the gradual character of human learning and maturation that have reinforced this tendency.[16]

Democratic justice invites us to view such developments with suspicion.

There may be justifications for them, but these need to be supplied. It may be, for instance, that learning what is needed to function in our high-technology, information-based world takes longer than was the case in the mid-nineteenth century, justifying a longer period of paternalism. It may also be that before the advent of widespread democratic aspirations, the great majority did not achieve much of their potential partly because of the early age at which adult expectations and responsibilities were foisted upon them. Preparing people for life in a democracy, rather than a system in which futures are determined by class, caste, or gender, may thus require expansion of the preadult phases of life. If occupations and rewards are determined more by aspirations tempered by capacities and less by luck or accidents of birth, people need the time and resources to discover and develop their capacities.[17] That this may be more complex, and take longer, than preparing the young peasant for life on the land, the coal miner's son for life down a mine shaft, and the gentleman's second son for a military career, should not be surprising.[18]

Such arguments might reasonably persuade us to delay some incidents of adulthood, but by themselves they do not justify excluding the young from a governing role in the institutions that control them; participation in governance by those whose interests are significantly affected should be limited by incapacity only. When relevant capacities develop and are learned, therefore, structures of power should be required to be receptive to them, suggesting the appropriateness of a developmental attitude toward youthful inclusion. The young should begin to participate in governance as soon as they are able, and to the extent that the capacity to participate needs to be taught this should be done sooner rather than later.[19]

What of the opposition dimension of democratic justice? The dependent character of children limits their capacity for effective opposition, and such opposition as they are able to muster is often inappropriate, given their immaturity and lack of responsibility. To say this is to say that hierarchical relations between adults and children are inevitable and appropriate. Recognizing this does not justify any particular hierarchy, however. The considerations adduced in Chapter 3 suggest that adult-child hierarchies should not be unnecessarily prolonged or more hierarchical than necessary, they should be hierarchical only in ways that are pertinent to their legitimate purposes, they should be constrained to operate in the interests of the children on whom they are imposed, they should be designed to prepare children to leave them in a timely fashion, and, where possible, they should be structured so as to reinforce—and certainly not to undermine—democratic practices in the broader polity.

According to the OED, a fiduciary is "one who holds anything in trust; a trustee." The term derives from the Roman law *fiducia*, which denoted "the transfer of a right to a person subject to the obligation to transfer it again at some future time or on some future condition being fulfilled."[20] A fiduciary acts on behalf of someone else, usually because of that person's temporary or permanent incapacity. Fiduciaries do not pursue their own interests; indeed, to do so would generally be seen as an abuse of the fiduciary role. Rather, fiduciaries are bound to pursue the interests that have been committed to their trust. A fiduciary understanding of adult-child relations is thus attractive from the standpoint of both dimensions of democratic justice: as fiduciaries, parents represent the interests of their charges until they are able to do this for themselves, and when they exercise authority over children, this must be done in the interests of the children over whom it is exercised.

In thinking about the advantages of a fiduciary model, it is helpful to locate it on a continuum of possibilities. At one end, children may be conceived of as utterly dependent subjects, morally indistinguishable from objects over which one may exercise complete and exclusive dominion. This approximates the Roman law view already alluded to, as well as that embraced in at least some variants of English absolutist ideology of the sixteenth and seventeenth centuries that I take up below. Anchoring the other end of the continuum is a conception of children as miniature adults, indistinguishable from grown-ups in virtue of their youthful status. The miniature-adults view has informed some variants of the children's-rights movements, as well as such experimental systems of education as A. S. Neill's Summerhill, a progressive school in England famous for its lack of rules and requirements.[21]

That democratic justice rules out regimes at the dependent-subjects end of the continuum should be self-evident. By their terms such regimes deny participation of children in parental decisions and declare all opposition to parental authority illegitimate.[22] Regimes toward the miniature-adults end of the continuum merit more serious attention. They acknowledge the moral independence of children and prompt many of the kinds of queries of authority that democratic justice endorses. For at least two reasons we should, nonetheless, be suspicious of regimes that embody the miniature-adults view. First, they rest on a quixotic denial of the reality that for lengthy periods human young are dependent creatures who have to learn a great deal of what they need to survive and thrive.[23] In this connection it should be said that such experiments as Summerhill can be misleading because they occur in artificially protected contexts, where second chances are available to children who make inappropriate choices for themselves, and the costs of error are therefore small. Contrast this with the "adult" choices that quickly intrude on the lives of inner-city children, where the costs of a single imprudent decision can be permanent and devastating. There the miniature-adults model is cast in a less sanguine, but more revealing, light.[24] Children may need to learn by making their own mistakes, but they also need protected space in which to make them. This cannot be provided if their very childhood is denied.

Second, those in the vanguard of the children's-rights movements tend to be at the anarcho-libertarian end of the political spectrum, not primarily concerned (perhaps not concerned at all) with rearing children who can survive and thrive in a democracy. Having established in Chapters 1 and 3 the inferiority to democratic justice of the libertarian approach for organizing collective life, it would be a mistake now to treat this view as on a par with the requirements of democratic justice. Here our central concern must be with what democratic justice requires for all children; the claims of anarcho-libertarians, like any other claims, must be evaluated from that standpoint.

The capabilities people need to develop may differ in different political systems, but to make democratic justice real, people must learn both how to develop and pursue their own interests as independent adults and how to take account of the relevant concerns of others. A fiduciary understanding of adult-child relations captures the focused yet open-ended transformation this requires. Like the dependent-subjects view, it assumes that young children have to learn what is needed for adult life. Like the miniature-adults view, the fiduciary model recognizes that children are independent moral creatures from the beginning. Proponents of fiduciary views also assume, however, that authority will have to be exercised over children during their immaturity. Such a view presupposes something of an Aristotelian philosophical psychology, but it is quite minimal: human beings are thought of as developmental creatures, for whom gradual acculturation is an inescapable part of maturation. It is not assumed that there is only one form that this can take, or even that one form is best. The implications of this constrained pluralism are spelled out below in the course of distinguishing basic from best interests. First, it is necessary to explore the idea of fiduciary responsibility for children, and its political implications, more fully.

Locke's View: Advantages and Limitations

In most countries in the modern world, at least some dimensions of authority over children are understood in fiduciary terms. To recognize that, however, is not to resolve many pressing questions that fiduciary views inevitably confront: Who should set the limits of authority over children? Should this authority be divided? If so, who should divide it and what criteria should they employ? Under what conditions should responsibility for children be terminated or transferred? By whom and to whom? What are the rights of parents in conflicts with children, or with other parents or other fiduciaries? Should those who raise children be paid? If so, how much and by whom? What, if any, are the obligations of children to their fiduciaries? What mechanisms of enforcement should accompany authority over children? What constraints should there be on that enforcement, enforced by whom?

When debates about the appropriate size of tax exemptions for dependents, the wisdom of public assistance to the children of poor parents, and the revival of orphanages are all on the political agenda, such questions cannot be escaped. But they cannot be addressed in a principled and satisfying way without a fully fleshed out account of the nature and purposes of fiduciary authority over children. It is surprising, perhaps, that there has been no sustained attempt at such an account in the contemporary literature, which is dominated on the one hand by debates about the nature and status of "the family" and on the other by ad hoc responses to particular policy issues.[25] To find a fully reasoned defense of a fiduciary model one has to go back to Locke's critique of Filmer's patriarchalism in the *First Treatise*.

LOCKE'S FIDUCIARY MODEL

Locke's general discussion of rights and obligations did not obviously lend itself to thinking about parent-child relations. He conceived of rights over objects as rooted in their production, whereas obligations among persons were based on mutual consent. He thought that natural law constrains both rights and obligations in a variety of ways. Before discussing those constraints, it is useful to note that although Locke's views concerning production and consent did not provide an adequate foundation for thinking about parenthood, they did influence his decision to conceive of parents as fiduciaries and his account of the purposes of, and limits to, parental authority.

On Locke's view of ownership, making a thing is the ultimate source of rights over it. This found expression in his labor theory of value and in the famous theory of property defended in chapter 5 of the *Second Treatise*. At bottom this was a theological view for Locke; his "workmanship" ideal was derived from what he took to be God's right over his creation.[26] God owns everything in the universe because he made it; that is the source of his natural-law authority. Human rights of ownership are derived, for Locke, from an analogous model. We are unique among God's creations because he gave us the capacity to make things—to act, as James Tully puts it, in a godlike fashion. So long as our exercise of that capacity does not violate natural law (which is literally God's natural right over his creation), we stand in the same relation to the objects we create as God stands in relation to us. We own them just as he owns us.[27]

Although for Locke, making entailed ownership, he refused to countenance the suggestion that parental authority is makers' authority. Indeed, his central preoccupation in the *First Treatise* was to refute defenses of absolutism that appealed to Adam's "Right of Dominion over his Children."[28] Conventional defenders of absolutism, such as Filmer, had insisted "that Fathers, by begetting them, come to an Absolute power over their children."[29] Locke insisted, by contrast, that God makes children and uses their parents for that purpose. Parents are "but occasions for [children's] being, and when they design and wish to beget them, do little more towards their making, than *Ducalion* and his Wife in the Fable did towards the making of Mankind, by throwing Pebbles over their heads."[30] If parents were the givers of life, Locke conceded, they might have some sort of quasi-ownership claim, but he insisted that they are not.[31] To give life "is to frame and make a living Creature, fashion the parts, and mold and suit them to their uses, and having proportion'd and fitted them together, to put into them a living Soul."[32] Human beings are God's workmanship.[33]

If Locke's understanding of workmanship limited parental authority, so did his view that legitimate obligations among humans are rooted in mutual consent. Relations between parents and children cannot be thought about in consensual terms because the child does not agree to be born, let alone to the parent in question. Consequently, Locke concluded that children are placed in their parents' trust, and also that the resulting parental authority is limited to the period of the child's temporary incapacity. Not to limit it thus would be to acknowledge a basis for human obligation other than free consent or natural law. This Locke was unwilling to do. As a result, he conceived of parental authority as self-liquidating. Children are not born in a "state of *Equality*, though they are born to it." Parents have "a sort of Rule and Jurisdiction over them when they come into the World, and for some time after, but 'tis but a temporary one." The bonds of children's subjection "are like the Swadling Cloths they are wrapt up in, and supported by, in the weakness of their Infancy." Developing age and reason loosen these bonds, "till at length they drop quite off, and leave a Man at his own free Disposal."[34] The power to command "ends with nonage." Thereafter, although "*honour* and respect, support and defense, and whatsoever gratitude can oblige a Man to the highest benefits he is naturally capable of, be always due from a Son to his Parents; yet all this puts no Scepter into the Father's hand, no Sovereign Power of Commanding."[35] The only legitimate sanction at the parent's disposal is the power to withhold inheritance, or "to bestow it with a more sparing or liberal hand, according as the Behavior of this or that Child hath comported with his Will and Humor."[36]

Locke argued that parental authority should be limited in scope as well as by time. Parents may not employ capital punishments, for that is the "proper power of the magistrate, of which the Father hath not so much as the shadow." His command over his children "reaches not their Life or Property." The power of parents over children is "very far from a power to make Laws, and enforcing them with Penalties that may reach Estate, Liberty, Limbs and Life."[37] Although a parent's obligations continue until his children "are out of danger of perishing from want, yet *his power* extends not to the Lives or Goods, which either their own industry, or anothers bounty has made theirs; nor to their Liberty neither, when they are once arrived to the infranchisement of the years of discretion." The parent's authority is rooted exclusively in the child's incapacity, which dictates both its extent and duration.[38]

LIMITATIONS OF LOCKE'S ACCOUNT

Much in Locke's analysis is useful from the standpoint of democratic justice. His rejection of every variant of the idea that children belong to their parents, and his account of parental authority as limited by children's incapacity, both fit comfortably with the idea that regimes of governance should be as inclusive as possible while taking account of children's inherent limitations as far as self-government is concerned. Locke's discussion of the limited and self-liquidating character of parental authority is consistent with the opposition injunctions of democratic justice, which require that inevitable hierarchies be pertinent to the activity at hand, that they be no more hierarchical than necessary, that they operate in the interests of those on whom they are imposed, and that they prepare those who are subject to them to leave the hierarchy in question and function independently. To build usefully on Locke's discussion, however, we must disentangle it from his theological commitments and look more systematically than Locke did at its implications for the distribution of authority over children between parents and various agents of the state.

On Locke's account, natural law supplies both the foundation for and the limits to parents' fiduciary authority. In a secular formulation, therefore, different foundations and limits must be articulated. In this regard it is useful to note, first, that Locke's critique of the Filmerian idea of parental ownership is easily rescued from his natural-law formulations. The negative argument that parents do not "make" their children in the sense of giving them life, designing them, or fashioning them can stand independently of Locke's theological commitments.[39] It may be true, as Nozick suggests, that Locke's argument on this point proves too much because it can be applied to many things other than children that Locke thought could be owned, indeed perhaps to everything that human beings believe that they "make" for themselves.[40] Whether the workmanship theory fails only in the case of the human production of children, as Locke believed, or whether it fails more generally, is of no consequence here.[41] In neither case can the Filmerian view survive. This point is worth stressing: although few parents today would defend the proposition that they own their children, many defend claims about their rights as parents that seem to rest on something close to an ownership-based claim. The appropriate secular analogue of Locke's view that children are God's property is thus the view that children are no one's property.

What of Locke's justification for his fiduciary model? He had little to say about the precise role of natural law in child rearing beyond noting that parents may never exceed the bounds of their fiduciary authority.[42] If anything (and fortunately, from my point of view), his account is remarkable for how little practical force it gives natural law. For instance, although Locke notes that children have a natural-law obligation to honor their parents, he is careful to say that this should not be enforceable. "After all I've done for you! . . ." can operate as a moral exhortation on a parent's part in a Lockean world, nothing more. For Locke, this is because enforceable obligations always require mutual consent, which is conspicuously lacking in parent-child relations. The discussion on this point parallels Locke's demolition of the Filmerian argument that parents have makers' authority over their children: enforceable obligations require relevant consent; children do not consent in the relevant ways; ergo children cannot be required to act on reciprocal obligations to parents. Should we be persuaded by this claim?

The argument of Chapter 3 suggests that not all enforceable obligations need be rooted in consent, but the idea that an obligation should be owed by children to their parents, in return for being begotten and raised, is not a promising candidate to be backed by the state's coercive power. A little reflection on the difficulties of identifying the appropriate metric or unit of account, not to mention mechanisms of enforcement, moral hazards, and potential conflicts of interest, should suffice to establish the impracticality of any such proposal. Practical considerations aside, notice that a parent might foist all kinds of things on a child that, in retrospect, the adult child would prefer not to have been given—let alone held to account for. Binding children in advance would limit their ability to participate as adults in decisions about the relations between them and their now elderly parents.[43] Locke's fiduciary model is attractive from the standpoint of democratic justice partly because it avoids this result. Fiduciary relations are by their terms antithetical to contracts between the fiduciary and the charge; indeed, the perceived need for them derives from the impossibility, or inappropriateness, of contracts in this type of circumstance.[44]

Locke's natural-law formulations lack practical bite in this area for the same reasons that they do elsewhere: although the state is supposed not to violate natural law, the only available enforcement mechanism is consent of the governed as expressed through majority rule. In the state of nature *"every one has the Executive Power* of the Law of Nature," but this right is given up at the formation of civil society.[45] Thereafter, "it being necessary to that which is one body to move one way; it is necessary the Body should move that way whither the greater force carries it, which is the *consent of the majority:* or else it is impossible it should act or continue one Body, *one Community,* which the consent of every individual that united into it, agreed that it should; and so everyone is bound by that to be concluded by the *majority."*[46] Locke thus defends a default presumption in favor of majority rule "in Assemblies impowered to act by positive Laws where no number is set by that positive Law that empowers them." Majority rule thus has "by the Law of Nature and Reason, the power of the whole."[47] Unless a substantial majority comes to agree that abuse has occurred, the opposition of the individual, while legitimate, will have no practical effect.[48] Opposition may otherwise be legitimate, but even when it is to an action that is life threatening, an individual or minority might have to wait for vindication until the next life.[49] In practice, in this world, natural law constrains the actions of governments only to the extent that a majority discerns it and acts on it.[50]

I argue in Chapter 3 that there is a wide class of circumstances in which a default commitment to majority rule is defensible, if on different grounds from those proposed by Locke. With respect to the governance of children, however, mere majority rule is insufficient to regulate the state's actions.[51] This is because the state exercises power directly over children, not only over parents or over children through parents. Because children cannot participate in the constraining mechanisms that majority rule makes available in other circumstances, additional constraints on the state's exercise of power over children are in order. In short, the state—no less than a parent— is properly conceived of as a fiduciary in this context. In both instances an inescapable hierarchy exists that cannot be legitimated by consent, and in both instances democratic justice should therefore lead us, via comparable considerations, to comparable conclusions. Parents and governments should thus be conceived of as parallel fiduciaries with similar kinds of authority over children, subject to similar constraints. Locke appears not to have confronted this fact, perhaps a by-product of his central focus on the dynamics of revolutionary politics and concomitant inattention to the nature of ordinary politics in nonrevolutionary circumstances.[52]

A MODIFIED LOCKEAN ACCOUNT

There is much to recommend a view of parents and state officials as parallel fiduciaries from the standpoint of democratic justice. In significant part democratic justice is about the management of power relations that are nested in collective activities, and in this context the conventional liberal and democratic mechanisms to limit the arbitrary exercise of power—allowing those who are affected a say through representative or participatory control—are unavailable. Accordingly, the republican idea, that power should be controlled by being divided, is especially attractive in this area if it can be made to work. This republican view stands in contrast to a competing conventional wisdom. It rests on the Hobbesian view that power is by its nature indivisible, and that the only remedy available to those who fear its unbridled exercise is to try to limit its range.[53] Republicans, by contrast, have always maintained that power is divisible, and that regimes that institutionalize competition among power holders are more likely to insulate society from arbitrary or corrupt exercises of power than those that do not. This was the view that prevailed among the American founders and that shaped the divided authority regime they sought to embed in the new nation.[54]

If the republican view can be sustained in this area, it is attractive not only for the reasons just mentioned but also because more than one type of competence is required for child rearing, and there is reason to believe that public officials and parents might appropriately exhibit different relevant competencies. When President Clinton opined in his 1995 State of the Union speech that "governments do not raise children, people do," he was noting that in this culture much of what children need—love and affection, the caring use of authority, and the fostering of valued purposes—is provided, if at all, in the intensely personal context of the parent-child relationship.[55] This is not to deny that there may be viable alternatives. To underscore this possibility, one might point to such examples, among others, as Israeli kibbutzim, Plato's *Republic*, or the notably impersonal childhoods of the upper classes in Victorian England.[56] Democratic justice does not assume, however, that existing ways of doing things are best, or, indeed, that there is one best way of doing many things. It assumes, rather, that existing practices make prima facie claims on our allegiance, subject always to criticism and reexamination to shape their future evolution in better directions. Conventional American attitudes about the intensely personal nature of child rearing, which reflect what Richard Brodhead has described as "a strategic relocation of authority relations in the realm of emotion," should be seen in this light.[57] They set the initial terms of discussion, but no more.

Thus construed, President Clinton's remark captures a significant part of the normative terrain. Yet it overreaches. In the occidental world government has long been responsible for certain aspects of child rearing, ranging from ensuring the physical security of children to insisting that certain capacities be developed that are needed if they are to function as adults. With a few exceptions such as the New England stubborn-child statutes discussed earlier—most notable, perhaps, as exceptions in this regard—the state's responsibility has been to protect children as well as adults by means of the criminal law, and to ensure that certain basic essentials for survival are provided. Locke's insistence that parental authority may not reach into those areas reserved for the magistrate fits as comfortably into modern Western practice as it does into the presumptions of democratic justice.

Reflecting on the assertion that "governments do not raise children, people do" helps fix intuitions in another useful way. Although I have suggested that government is properly sovereign over certain aspects of children's lives and that it rightly retains some—as yet unspecified—final authority over parents qua parents, it would be a mistake to think of parents as mere agents of the state, a species of civil servant. Intuitions might grate against that notion for a variety of reasons. Two are most important from the standpoint of democratic justice: one concerns the lack of any decisive check on the governmental authority that the analogy throws into sharp relief; the other springs from the sense that aspects of child rearing involve types of local knowledge, intimacy, and commitment—insider's wisdom— that are unlikely to be forthcoming from those who sees their primary allegiance as due to the polity at large rather than the child.

The civil-servant analogy is frighteningly Orwellian because it conjures up the possibility that parental authority could be altered, perhaps even terminated, by official whim. The parallel-fiduciaries conception avoids this result by placing two kinds of limitations on state power. First, although fiduciaries are generally accountable to a third party in the exercise of their authority, theirs is not an agency relationship. Rather it involves a weaker kind of oversight, usually confined to responding to the breakdown or abuse of fiduciary responsibility. If a court finds that a fiduciary has abused authority, it may have the power to terminate the fiduciary's authority, but usually this will involve replacing one fiduciary with another. Assuming the role of fiduciary directly is a last resort, taken on temporarily by the court if at all. This is compatible with the notion that public officials can be expected to lack the relevant insider's wisdom to perform the fiduciary role in question. Generally a relative or foster parent is appointed guardian if there is no functioning parent; only if no such solution is available will a court commit a child to an orphanage or comparable state institution.

A second limitation on state authority built into my modified Lockean account flows from the fact that the state, no less than the parent, is seen as a fiduciary in its dealings with children. In contrast to Locke's view, this interpretation strengthens the state's hand in one way and weakens it in another. It strengthens the state's hand because it includes a presumption that the state has some relevant insider's wisdom as well, and that such wisdom merits deference. Just what that particular kind of insider's wisdom should be assumed to consist in is taken up below; note here that the parallel-fiduciaries conception does set aside a class of questions about child rearing as an appropriate concern of government. My account weakens the state's hand, though, in the sense that if governments, no less than parents, are fiduciaries when they exercise authority over children, then they too should be answerable to a third party if they fail in, or abuse, their fiduciary responsibilities. The logical candidate here—most likely to care about failure or abuse of the state's fiduciary responsibilities and to be relevantly informed—is the parent.

Thinking about the appropriate place of insider's wisdom involves qualitative questions, not merely agency problems and economies of smallness.[58] In Chapter 1 I make the case that although Walzer and MacIntyre go too far in deferring to insider's wisdom, they are nonetheless right to insist on its distinctive value. Because insider's wisdom can be abused and appeals to it may provide smoke screens for domination, it should be limited by the requirements of democratic justice. Insider's wisdom should not, however, be displaced by those requirements. Rather, we should seek to use insider's wisdom appropriately while constraining it by the requirements of democratic justice. Conceiving of parents as mere agents of the state goes beyond the idea of conditioning insider's wisdom democratically, devaluing it to the point of obliteration. The idea of parallel fiduciaries avoids this result. It involves recognizing that different relevant competencies are involved, and reserving to governments and parents appropriate ranges of responsibility.

Parents and public officials can be thought of as checking one another's authority in two ways. First, because the two sets of fiduciaries have different provinces of legitimate authority over the same children, there are bound to be border disputes in which both sides will demand reason-giving justifications of the other, and where there are unavoidable conflicts, each side will pressure the other to exercise authority in ways that are as unobtrusive as possible on the authority of the first. As I elaborate below, in this scheme public officials are seen as primary custodians of children's basic interests and secondary custodians of their best interests. This allocation of authority is mirrored by that of parents, who are primary custodians of children's best interests and secondary custodians of their basic interests. The role of the fail-safe custodian is essentially a second-guessing one. In the limiting case fail-safe custodians are obliged to pick up the pieces when primary custodians utterly fail to carry out their fiduciary responsibilities. But in less extreme circumstances, detailed below, fail-safe custodians can play important roles in keeping primary custodians honest and forestalling—if not responding to—their failures.

POWER ASYMMETRIES AND THEIR IMPLICATIONS

Attractive as the analytical symmetry of the parallel-fiduciaries view might be, it is reasonable to ask how it can work in practice, given the great asymmetries of power between parents, on the one hand, and officials who wield the instruments of public coercion, on the other. Stephen Wizner has reminded us with respect to the juvenile justice system that governments act under the auspices of their police power as well as their *parens patriae* power, and it is all too easy for the two roles to be conflated.[59] In this light it might be said that parents' standing to challenge state action will often be hollow, and that by the same token the state's second-guessing role could be dangerously great. After all, the state is inevitably the final arbiter in finding the existence of parental transgressions and deciding what to do about them. Given parents' lack of an equivalent sanctioning power, no parallel force exists to back up their role in this particular separation of powers.[60]

The more "the state" approaches being a unitary actor, the greater is the cause for concern. To conceive of the state in these terms is always misleading, however, particularly in countries like the United States, where there is an explicit separation of powers among governmental institutions. In such systems, the typical conflict is not between parents and the state in the person of single-minded bureaucratic power. Rather, the parent challenges the actions of one state actor (perhaps a social worker or other public official), but the challenge occurs in a different forum, such as a court. In a federal system, it may be the decisions of a state court or legislature that are challenged in a federal court.[61] Parents may thus try to vindicate their claims against the state by employing the resources made available through one public institution to challenge another. This can occur in circumstances when parents—concerned to preserve the integrity of their own fiduciary authority—perceive an encroachment into their domain of legitimate authority by public officials, or when they discern failures by public officials to meet *their* obligations to children, triggering parents' fail-safe fiduciary responsibilities. For these reasons, although basic interests inevitably enjoy a lexical priority over best interests, it is too simple to say that the former will invariably vanquish the latter.[62]

The nature of the power asymmetry in this context suggests that some separation of powers is desirable. Indeed, parents' hands might reasonably be strengthened, relatively, by giving them legal standing to challenge public officials who fail to protect children's basic interests. Further, when a parent's understanding of a child's best interests is at stake, we might require something like the heightened American constitutional standard of "intermediate" scrutiny of governmental action (which demands that a "substantial relationship" be shown between the proposed policy and an "important government objective"). Upon a prima facie showing by a parent that a public official's method of protecting a child's basic interests threatens a parent's understanding of the child's best interests, the burden would fall to the public official to demonstrate that the proposed method of protecting basic interests meets the intermediate-scrutiny requirement.

Why, it might be asked, only intermediate scrutiny, given my earlier defense of a strict scrutiny requirement for public-goods arguments? There is a significant difference between the two cases. The public-goods argument turns on the claim that by their nature democratic politics fail to provide certain types of goods on which democracy is critically reliant. It is the political analogue of a market-failure argument. The stakes are especially high in that type of circumstance, because the remedy involves bypassing or otherwise actively subverting democratic processes and accepting unchecked authority as far as the provision of the public good in question is concerned. Such a course threatens the foundational requirements of democratic justice and is not to be embarked upon lightly; hence the strict-scrutiny requirement. With children the situation differs in that religious parents who object, for example, to an educational curriculum on the grounds that it interferes with their understanding of their children's best interests, have a number of remedial options to which they can turn. Most relevantly, the curriculum's adoption does not abrogate their rights as democratic citizens to try to get it changed through the political process.[63] Accordingly, although considerations relating to power asymmetries suggest that some tilting in parents' direction is warranted, these considerations fall short of embracing a standard of constitutional scrutiny that little legislation could survive.

Notice that the argument in support of a role for courts in adjudicating conflicts between parents and public officials is unrelated to the debatable liberal constitutionalist claim that courts are better protectors of individual liberties than are democratic legislatures. Dahl and other critics of judicial review might be right that as a general matter courts have not been shown to be comparatively more effective in this regard.[64] Here, however, conventional majoritarian politics is not the relevant alternative to making space for a role for courts. It is, after all, the inability of the child to participate in relevant decision making that marks off this area as distinctive. When a public official interferes with the proper exercise of parental authority, it is not the unhappiness of the parent but rather the resulting harm to the child that should be our principal concern. Likewise, when a public official fails in a fiduciary responsibility to a child, the parent is best thought of as a kind of *amicus curiae*, whose job is to draw attention to the failure and try to get other powerful institutions to set matters aright.

If "the state" should not be thought of as a unitary actor, neither should "parents" or adults in other "communities of nurture," who may disagree with one another about aspects of their joint child-rearing responsibilities. This leads to some conclusions that are analogous to those that emerged from the preceding discussion of the state, but the parallel is only partial. On the one hand, it suggests, *ceteris paribus*, that two parents may often be better than one.[65] They can act as checks on one another in the same way that different branches of government can: they can hold one another to their responsibilities and talk things through that will often need to be talked through. Much of the literature on the distribution of authority over children seems to assume that everyone involved knows what they believe should be done and the problem is how to reconcile conflicting views of the matter. As anyone who has raised children will know, the reality involves learning as one goes along, often under conditions of meager resources and considerable stress. Parents often need sounding boards, a degree of second-guessing, and relief and reinforcement to cope with the demands of child rearing. A second parent can perform all these roles, and, in the limiting case, act as a whistle blower on the child's behalf if there is failure or abuse of fiduciary responsibility by the other parent. Locke was thus correct to note, at the start of his discussion of parental authority, that the mere existence of a second parent tends to undermine absolute patriarchal power.[66]

On the other hand, no parallel is evident here for the separation-of-powers logic that led to the suggestion that parents should be able to draw on divisions internal to state institutions to vindicate children's interests when these appear to them to be threatened. That argument found its basis in the power asymmetries between parents and the state. It was defended as a means by which parents, lacking other resources for the purpose, might reasonably function as watchdogs over the state qua fiduciary. The state, by contrast, has many resources at its disposal when it acts in its second-guessing and fail-safe capacity; as a result, analogous reasoning does not apply. Given the other considerations, adduced in Chapter 5, in support of the view that the state should not seek out involvement in disagreements in ongoing marriages (as opposed to those that have broken down), there is a strong case for the presumption that the state should employ different mechanisms to vindicate its responsibilities and play its fail-safe role here.

Basic and Best Interests of Children

Just as President Clinton's maxim conflates different types of responsibility for child-rearing, so does much of the academic literature. Joseph Goldstein, Anna Freud, and Albert Solnit, for instance, postulate that children have a trumping interest in continuity that should override other considerations except in instances of extreme abuse and neglect.[67] There is much to commend their conclusions because, consistent with the argument here, these authors insist that children's interests, rather than the rights or aspirations of parents, should be the criterion by which authority over children is allocated.[68] But Goldstein, Freud, and Solnit make no attempt to distinguish among different kinds of children's interests. In contrast, the view pressed here is that state officials should recognize their incapacity to determine children's best interests and should insist, in a "political, not metaphysical" spirit, on protecting what they determine to be children's basic interests. Public officials should not affirm one controversial psychology, as Goldstein, Freud, and Solnit propose that they do.[69] Rather, they should evaluate claims about the psychological importance of continuity to children from the standpoint of children's basic interests. Claims for continuity that do not threaten basic interests merit respect from public officials. When there is a threat to basic interests, however, the state's fiduciary responsibilities are triggered, trumping competing claims about the value of continuity.[70]

BASIC INTERESTS

Basic interests concern the security, nutrition, health, and education required for children to develop into normal adults. Every account of them is controversial. Resourcist views of the sort defended here are sometimes said to be vulnerable when they are coupled with the claim that they do not presuppose contestable conceptions of the good, or with a denial that they load the dice against some conceptions.[71] Because democratic justice rests on no such claim, this version of the controversiality objection has no force. The view of "normal" adults implicit in my—or any—formulation can be challenged, and indeed I argue below that it should always be open to challenges of a certain sort. But child rearing invariably proceeds on some assumptions about development toward normal adulthood; pointing out that they are controversial scarcely alters this reality. To insist on this is not to deny that what falls within the ambit of basic interests may at least partly be "socially constructed," or that it may vary with time and circumstance.

The conception of basic interests embraced here is comparatively minimal, somewhat diminishing the controversiality problem.[72] It is thinner, for example, than Sen's account. I agree with Sen that in evaluating people's circumstances it makes more sense to focus on the good that they derive from a resource rather than either the amount of the resource that they own or the subjective satisfaction they derive from consuming it. In the area of nutrition, for instance, better to ask how well-nourished a person is than how much food she has or how much utility she derives from eating it.[73] However, my account of basic interests does not require a full account of human flourishing, or "functionings," to use Sen's term.[74] In this respect the neo-Aristotelian philosophical psychology presumed valid by democratic justice is more minimal that Sen's. By remaining agnostic about whether there is one best set of human functionings and by explicitly limiting the state's authority to determining what is in children's basic interests, it does not require governments to make judgments about what is needed for the full development of every—or indeed any—child's potential.

Children's basic interests are not limited, on this account, to the realm of their physiological needs. In addition to meeting these, children may also be said to have a basic interest in developing the capacities required to function adequately and responsibly in the prevailing economic, technological, and institutional system, governed as a democracy, over the course of their lives. *Adequately* here refers to a person's ability to comprehend, shape, and pursue his or her individual interests. Adequate pursuit of interests depends on being able to evaluate different lifetime aspirations critically, and being able to understand—at least as well as others generally do—the costs and benefits of different courses of action. By contrast, the idea of *responsible* pursuit of interests is other-regarding; it has to do with the expectations that people may reasonably entertain about the ways in which others pursue their interests.

Notice that by linking the definition of basic interests to adequate and responsible participation in the existing order, democratic justice does not underwrite that order as just. Accepted ways of doing things may be unjust, and people may reasonably aspire to change them or opt out of them. Indeed, as I note below, it is doubtful whether government can deliver on its basic obligations to children in the contemporary United States without re-structuring social and economic arrangements to a degree. Recall that, from the standpoint of the general argument, existing ways of doing things make provisional claims on our allegiance, but these claims are always subject to critical evaluation from the standpoint of democratic justice. Democratic justice is intended to militate against the tabula rasa reevaluation of all social institutions, characteristic of much political philosophy at least since Rawls, from the perspective of every individual who is on the hypothetical thresh-old of entering them. Human beings seldom design institutions afresh, and they never design all their institutions afresh. They redesign institutions, and the argument here is that things should be structured so as to incline people to redesign them in more, not less, democratic ways. Doing this well requires the insider's wisdom necessary for intelligent redesign, and teach-ing people to function adequately in the existing system is in turn required to develop the relevant insider's wisdom. Thus, whether or not existing con-ditions stand in need of reform from the standpoint of democratic justice (they almost invariably do), adequate pursuit of interests requires that people develop the appropriate skills and resources to survive within them.

This in turn suggests a general constraint for thinking about basic inter-ests: that people be nurtured and educated so that they can become compe-tent adults within the evolving system of institutions. We may amplify this by saying that if society holds people responsible as adults not to become a net drain on its resources, then they must be able to develop the where-withal to achieve the relative self-sufficiency that this mandate implies. "Be able to develop" has implications both for the capacities people are able to develop and for the contexts in which they must use them. With regard to the former, it suggests that as well as meeting essential needs of nutrition, health, and physical security, society has an obligation to develop in children the salable skills and capacities—human capital—that the children are going to require, given prevailing economic and technological circumstances, in order not to become a net drain on society's resources.[75] With regard to the latter, it means that a structure of employment opportunity should be provided in which it is possible for people to vindicate their basic interests. We cannot justly deny people the opportunities for survival in the system into which they have been born and then castigate them for being depen-dent on others. Blaming the victim in that way is what gives much of the public debate about dependency and the welfare state its disingenuous air.[76] Democratic justice recognizes that a condition for requiring certain levels of functioning from people includes not only that they be enabled to develop the resources to function at the specified levels but also that the opportunities exist for them to function as required.[77]

There is a significant sense in which the notion of adequacy discussed here, though often not met, is minimal. People should have the essentials to survive in the world as it can reasonably be expected to be for the course of their lifetime. However, invoking a standard of what is essential in the way of physical security, material resources, education, prudent medical care, employment opportunities, and human capital does not entail that someone whose basic interests are adequately met will be happy or fulfilled. People reasonably aspire to lives that are more than merely adequate. Democratic justice recognizes this fact, but under the heading of best interests rather than basic. The state's primary fiduciary responsibility children is to protect their basic interests, a duty that all states fail to discharge for some of their citizens, and many with respect to most of their citizens. Developing in children both the aspirations and the wherewithal to achieve fulfilling lives is a task that falls in the first instance to parents.

Whereas the idea of adequate pursuit of interests refers to the freedoms and resources that people need to live their lives, that of responsible pursuit of interests directs attention to what they may reasonably require of one another. At a minimum this includes the expectation that people be sufficiently committed to the democratic order so as to refrain from pursuing their interests in ways that can be expected to destroy it.[78] Some have contended that worrying about the democratic commitments of citizens is either unnecessary or pointless. Adam Przeworski, for example, defines democracy as a system of spontaneous or self-reinforcing compliance that operates successfully only when self-interested players who fail to get their way calculate that, rather than destroy the system, it is to their advantage to accept defeat and wait for the next chance to prevail within the rules. When the system works, normative commitments to democracy, while sometimes present, are "not necessary to generate compliance with democratic outcomes." The strategic calculation by anyone who has the power to destroy the system that it is in her interest not to do so is sufficient, and likely necessary as well, for the system to survive. Otherwise the "commitment problem," as game theorists since Thomas Schelling have labeled it, cannot be solved.[79] If Przeworski is right, trying to induce normative commitments to democracy in people is a waste of time. In the circumstances where they are needed to prevent breakdown they will probably not produce that result, and where breakdown does not threaten they are redundant.[80]

Przeworski's conclusions are insufficiently attentive both to the fragility of democratic institutions and to the role of beliefs in sustaining them. He himself notes the existence of a counterexample to his discussion of necessity, and there appear to be other instances where groups whose instrumental interests are harmed by democratic processes have nonetheless supported them.[81] Others have questioned whether even pure self-interest is sufficient, arguing that normative commitments to democracy are often necessary as well, whether on the part of elites or in the broader political culture as well.[82] It is too simple, in any case, to say that a certain structure of preferences (such as one that the pluralists referred to as a system of cross-cutting cleavages) will lead to self-sustaining democratic institutions while others will not.[83] Preferences are not primordial givens; they are shaped, partly by education and acculturation, and partly in response to institutional arrangements.[84]

Because self-interest alone will often not sustain democratic institutions, it seems wise to try to structure things so that people will reflect on their goals from the standpoint of the reasonable demands of others, and be prepared to modify the ways in which they pursue them so as not to undermine democracy. This means that losers must come to accept the legitimacy of present defeats and sometimes even try to play constructive roles in implementing policies they oppose, while winners should appreciate the wisdom of not exploiting every dimension of their current strategic advantage. They should see the wisdom of tolerating—even valuing—continuing opposition, even if this limits the degree to which their goals can be maximized in a given situation. In short, it is prudent to assume that if democracy is to survive people will have to be persuaded to value it for more than its short-term instrumental benefits.[85]

Democratic justice gives us a second reason for regarding Przeworski's account as inadequate: because of its pure procedural character. As we have seen, Przeworski takes preferences as given and treats democracy as a device for managing disagreement. Democratic justice, by contrast, is a more-than-procedural view. It is concerned with reshaping civil arrangements to ensure that those affected by collective decisions have a say in them, and wherever possible to diminish the domination they facilitate. Because this is a creative endeavor for which there are no blueprints, people have to be committed to the goal of discovering and inventing the best ways of shaping their interactions democratically. Otherwise they will have no motivation to engage in the creative endeavor at all. Democratic mechanisms must continually be refashioned as they are seen to work more or less well. This depends on developing in the people the conviction that doing things more rather than less democratically is a good thing, and that sometimes they should be prepared to modify their preferences in order to achieve this result. It is therefore reasonable to hold that the responsible pursuit of interests requires people to be taught the value of democratic government, to appreciate the costs of its breakdown, and to have a due regard for the interests of others.

It might nonetheless be asked why people should be said to have an interest of any kind, let alone a basic interest, in engaging in what I have described as responsible behavior. No doubt third parties who are affected by a person's behavior have an interest in her behaving responsibly, but why might she be said to have an interest in so behaving? In addition to the third-party interest, children themselves have a basic interest in developing the capacities for the responsible behavior, whether or not they or their parents appreciate it. Once it has been concluded, as it was from my earlier discussion of Przeworski, that behavior of a certain kind should be presumed essential to democracy's survival, it is but a short step to this conclusion. Because at this point in the argument I take it as established that everyone has an interest in the survival of the democratic order; it follows a fortiori that each person has an interest in developing capacities that are needed to ensure this result. Someone might, of course, resist my contention that the survival of democracy should be presumed to be in everyone's interest, but for this person I have failed in describing the relative advantages of a democratic conception of justice over the going alternatives in earlier chapters. Nothing I can say here is likely to be more persuasive.

BEST INTERESTS

If basic interests are conceived as emerging out of the minimum conditions for satisfactory interaction, best interests have to do with the full development of human potential. There are two reasons why best interests, unlike basic interests, should be understood in a pluralistic fashion. There appears, first, to be an irreducible plurality of human personalities that forces us to go at least part of the way with Hobbes's critique of Aristotle and recognize that what is good for one person may not be good for the next.[86] Second, even if the Hobbesian view could ultimately be shown to rest on a misreading of human nature, it would remain true that disagreement about the good life is endemic.[87] Democratic justice supplies no reasons to prefer some conceptions over others. It rests, indeed, on agnosticism over whether anyone really knows what the best life is, and the conviction that rather than impose one conception it is better to structure matters so that people can grapple with this issue for themselves. It rules out certain modes of grappling, to be sure, and to that extent it necessarily loads the dice in favor of some views over others. Every approach does that. Given the corrigibility of human knowledge in general and the Orwellian dangers of permitting partisans of one view to impose what they take their knowledge to be, it is better to opt for a system that permits considerable latitude in developing one's best potential but requires that this be done in ways that sustain, rather than undermine, democratic modes of interaction.[88]

The general argument does place two types of constraint on interpersonal judgments about children's interests. The first is symmetrical: except in the uncommon circumstances where fail-safe roles are activated (discussed below), guardians of basic interests and best interests are not deemed competent to second-guess the other within their appropriate domain. The second is not symmetrical: Anyone may legitimately try to influence the state's operational understanding of basic interests through the political process, just as anyone is free to try to influence public policy on other questions in this way. This freedom—which attaches to parents and nonparents of voting age—has no corresponding parallel, however, for the definition of best interests. Third parties might take a dim view of the way in which some people raise children, but there is no forum in which they have standing to do anything about it. This naturally follows from a pluralist understanding of best interests. Others might think that you are misguided about your children's best interests and how to vindicate them, but if you are not interfering with their basic interests, then others are bound to acknowledge that they have no justification to try to make you act differently.

WHY THE STATE SHOULD BE PRIMARY CUSTODIAN
OF CHILDREN'S BASIC INTERESTS

Primary responsibility for basic interests appropriately falls to the state rather than to parents for three reasons. First, thinking about what is needed to sustain democracy involves attending to the externalities of people's actions, the reasonable claims of third parties, and the nature of the divisions of interest within a society generally. In short, it involves attending to the society's macropolitical dynamics. This is not to deny that rearing children involves reliance on insider's wisdom. It does, but there is more than one kind of insider's wisdom. Ensuring that children develop the capabilities to function in a democracy involves insider's wisdom that comes with attention to, and responsibility for, the health of the polity at large.

Now there may often be good reasons for the state to delegate aspects of its responsibility concerning children's basic interests to parents, but when this is done the relations between state officials and parents remains an agency one, over which the state does not relinquish final authority. (This contrasts with circumstances in which parents are acting as custodians of children's best interests where, I have argued, no such agency relationship exists.) Although the state will, for instance, reasonably require that children be educated to the minimum necessary level and provide schools at public expense for this purpose, it might nonetheless permit parents to purchase or provide the relevant minimal education in other ways. This course might be defended on grounds of economies of smallness, or on the grounds that schools are sites where children are educated in ways that are relevant to their best interests, of which parents are primary custodians, as well as ways that are relevant to their basic interests, of which parents are not primary custodians. In such circumstances, the state appropriately retains the right to ensure that what it regards as the minimal curriculum for the vindication of basic interests is taught, perhaps by inspecting private schooling arrangements, licensing teachers, and adopting comparable measures.

Delegation of this kind can create other difficulties, whose resolution remains a responsibility of government. Differences in capacities to exit the public schools system rooted in the different resources of parents would not matter, for instance, from the standpoint of protecting children's basic interests, if the education provided to the children who must remain were adequate. If there is a causal impact of exit, however, as when essential funding leaves with the children of wealthier parents, then the externalities of their actions are not properly ignored by government. When acting as fiduciaries of their child's best interests, parents need not pay particular heed to the interests of other children. When parents act as delegates of government in the protection of basic interests, however, attention to third-party effects is obligatory. This suggests that voucher schemes should be looked upon with considerable suspicion. Such schemes may operate well for their direct beneficiaries, though the evidence on this question is inconclusive.[89] Even if it turns out that they do, the external effects of voucher schemes may well be devastating. If publicly funded vouchers can be used in private schools, the quality of public schools can be expected to deteriorate, perhaps below levels required to vindicate children's basic interests. Thus, although private schools are tolerable from the standpoint of democratic justice, privatization of public education raises more serious difficulties. Perhaps it could be made viable, from the standpoint of democratic justice, by linking the right to privatize to the existence of an education that meets the basic-interests criterion throughout a school district. Any such possibility is considerably in advance of current American practice.[90]

With respect to physical safety, nutrition and medical care, no less than with education, children have a basic interest in receiving what they need to develop into normal adults. As a result, the state has final responsibility—which may be extinguished only by a child's coming of age—to ensure that these goods are supplied. Nonetheless, as with the education required by basic interests, day-to-day responsibility for children's health and nutrition may, for a variety of reasons, reasonably fall to parents. However, if parents lack the resources to supply adequate nutrition or medical care, or if they refuse to do so, then the state remains obliged to supply the relevant resources itself or to intervene in other ways to ensure that the resources are supplied. Public authorities who refuse to intervene in families to prevent physical abuse on the grounds that this disrupts "family integrity" are properly criticized from the standpoint of democratic justice. It is not an issue over which the writ of family integrity should run.[91]

For analogous reasons, we should not be troubled when the preferences of Christian Scientists to withhold essential medical care from children are overridden by courts.[92] These are instances where parents' conception of a child's best interests lead to a violation of the child's basic interests. For this reason the parents' conception must give way. Parents might perhaps take the view in such circumstances that there is no other way to vindicate the child's best interests (in this case spiritual salvation), and for all anyone knows they might be right. The state can respect such claims, however, only to the extent that they do not interfere with its responsibility for children's basic interests as these are understood by the appropriate public authority. Beyond this, the state is bound to adopt a "political, not metaphysical" attitude to the parents'—in this case religious—arguments.

The state should bear primary responsibility for children's basic interests, second, because parents are generally predisposed to give great weight to what they perceive as best for their children and to press this when it conflicts with the interests of others. There is nothing wrong with this stance; fostering and defending their children's best interests is what democratic justice expects of parents. Just because this is so, however, parents qua parents are not always well-placed to think about what democracy requires of the way in which their children develop their potential and pursue their goals. Particularly when there are tensions between what democracy requires and parents' perceptions of their children's best interests, it would be reasonable to expect parental impulses to tend in the direction of sacrificing the former to the latter. Public officials, responsible for maintaining the democratic vitality of the society at large, will, no doubt, take the contrary view. Although in the last analysis parents will lose when the state's interpretation of children's basic interests is at stake, it should be recalled that the separation-of-powers argument advanced earlier is intended to stave off the last analysis as long as possible, to force conflicting custodians on both sides of the divide to seek creative solutions to the difficulties that their respective fiduciary responsibilities create for one another.[93]

A third reason why the state should hold fiduciary responsibility for children's basic interests is that parents may lack the resources needed to ensure that they are protected. The state, by contrast, disperses these costs through the tax system so that the child's basic interests need not be compromised due to accidents of birth. This raises the thorny question of whether and to what degree governments may reasonably aspire to regulate the number of children who are born. Surely they may. Children whose basic interests will be violated should not be born, and social policies designed to limit rates of reproduction in order to achieve this goal are defensible within the framework of democratic justice. In Chapter 5 I argue that questions about the sexual mores and practices of consenting adults are reasonably judged their exclusive business, but this is not true of all matters relating to reproduction. Deciding whether or not to have children, and deciding how many to have, has substantial consequences for others. The most obvious consequences are for the children themselves. But there are also consequences for those who may be required to bear costs, through the tax system, of vindicating children's basic interests and of supporting them indefinitely if their basic interests cannot be met once they become adults. Democratic justice suggests that we be "pro-choice" in the sense that no one should be required to have unwanted children but not in the sense of recognizing an unconditional right to have children whatever the circumstances. Devising policies that can link population growth to the minimally acceptable quality of life encapsulated in the notion of basic interests may, indeed, be one of the more important tasks for governments in the twenty-first century.[94] The goal should be to maximize the proportion of children born whose basic interests will be vindicated.

There are good reasons for insisting, however, that governments should limit themselves to indirect forms of regulation in pursuit of this goal. One has only to mention the specter of bureaucrats ordering forced sterilizations, and perhaps even abortions, in individual cases for alarm bells reasonably to begin ringing. The difficulty here does not stem from interference with an unconditional right to procreate, for there is no reason to think any such right should be recognized. Rather it has to do with the possibilities for domination raised by direct state intervention in women's lives in order to limit rates of their reproduction. Indeed, it is difficult to see how direct regulation of this kind could be carried out without subjecting women to domination. Creating unnecessary possibilities for domination is always unwelcome from the standpoint of democratic justice. This is particularly unwelcome in circumstances where power will be exercised disproportionately over a subset of the population, in this case women. Given these dangers, the better course for governments is to try to influence reproductive rates indirectly, by adopting measures that can be predicted to influence incentives in the direction judged desirable.

This is not to say which indirect means of regulation are most likely to be effective. The evidence suggests, for instance, that such policy measures as cutting welfare benefits and other transfer payments have, at best, no effect on the rates at which poor people produce children. If this is so, such measures amount to no more than gratuitous punishment of poor children for the accidents of their birth. In general, rates of childbirth appear to increase rather than decrease as people fall into poverty.[95] Important as limiting the rate of population growth might be in many circumstances, forcing poor parents more deeply into poverty is thus unlikely to achieve that goal. More likely to be effective are policies that reduce poverty and expand educational opportunity, factors that have been positively associated with reduction in family size.[96]

In developed countries such as the United States, the characteristic governmental concern is less to limit the absolute number of children, and more to limit the number of children that the state will be obliged to support through transfer payments. To some degree this concern is artificial, because the system of tax exemptions for dependents effectively (and appropriately) involves government in subsidizing all child rearing. Calls to limit the number of children who are reliant on transfer payments thus all too easily become smoke screens for illegitimate judgments, such as that poor people—or some subset of them—are inappropriate guardians of children's best interests. Nonetheless, limiting the number of children in light of ecological considerations, the competing fiscal demands on governments, and other factors is a legitimate subject for collective democratic decision. Democratic justice has nothing to say about what the number should be. It requires only that governments not absolve themselves from final responsibility for the basic interests of those children who are created in the territories under their control.

WHY PARENTS SHOULD BE PRIMARY CUSTODIANS OF CHILDREN'S BEST INTERESTS

It might be asked, in light of the preceding discussion, why should the parents to whom children are born be the custodians of their best interests? One thought-provoking answer is Coasean in inspiration: other things being equal, it is simply more efficient to leave children with the parents who beget them than it would be to try to distribute them after their birth in accordance with some yet-to-be-specified criterion. Merely entertaining the suggestion that the state might engage in redistribution of this kind is unnerving, for reasons already mentioned. In this area there are not the conventional democratic checks on governmental authority by those whose interests are most affected by it, and certainly no possibility of children's opposing the government's decisions. Moreover, given the power imbalances that flow from the state's position as final arbiter of disputed claims with parents, assigning parents to whom a child is born the status of custodian of the child's best interest is a valuable limitation on state power. To this it should be added that because the state is not well positioned to determine best interests to begin with, it follows a fortiori that it is not well equipped to choose one potential parent over another as a better custodian of a child's best interests. No doubt there will be circumstances in which the state is forced into this role. Parents who wish to give up custody and divorcing parents who cannot agree on custody arrangements are obvious cases in point; they trigger the state's fail-safe responsibility. In the conventional case, however, the state's authority over children's best interests is appropriately limited by denying it the power of initial assignment of children to parents, and deferring instead to the assignments that result from accidents of birth.[97] This is one reason to resist the—perhaps disingenuous, given what would be the immense cost— calls by the Republican Congressional leadership in 1994 and 1995 to create state-run orphanages for the children of poor women. They wrongly assume that public officials are appropriately placed to make judgments about the best interests of children, or at least of the children of groups who are stigmatized in the orphanage debate.

The preceding considerations aside, there are dimensions to fostering best interests that suggest that, other things being equal, they are best left to parents. Parents can be expected to know about their children's proclivities and idiosyncrasies, their strengths and limitations, better than anyone else. Parents are also more likely than anyone else to care about their children unconditionally, to want what is good for them, and to try continually to translate that desire into efficacious action. Democratic justice bids us to defer to insider's wisdom, within limits, and this is no exception. It is true that the bonds of birth can be overrated, as parents who have adopted children will attest. Giving birth is not always necessary or sufficient to foster the relevant personal caring, though sometimes it is necessary and often it is sufficient. No doubt, not every birth parent will care in the relevant ways, care as much as one might want, or have the resources to develop a child's capacities as well as possible. For these and other reasons, it makes sense to anticipate that there will be inequalities among children with respect to how close they come to vindicating their best interests.

These particular inequalities are not, however, among those that government should aspire to redress. Trying to do so makes ontological demands that not only are beyond the state's capacity; they are beyond anyone's capacity. As I have argued, once basic interests are taken out of the equation, the realm of disagreements about best interests is appropriately seen as one where interpersonal judgments should not be attempted by anyone other than parents. Some might resist the thought that inequality with respect to vindicating best interests has to be accepted, suggesting instead, perhaps, that the appropriate imperative should be that the full vindication of every child's best interests be a condition for the full vindication of each child's best interests. But democratic justice is not in the business of embracing principles that cannot be implemented.[98] This issue is cast in appropriate perspective below, when I take up the matter of how dramatically the state is failing at its primary fiduciary responsibilities with respect to children. Seen against that backdrop, politicians and other public officials who make political capital by bemoaning the moral decay of the family and the decline of "family values" are revealed at best to be focusing on the wrong questions, and at worst to be diverting public attention from their own failings as guardians of children's basic interests.

The Relative Importance of Basic and Best Interests

Are basic interests more important than best interests? To say that one thing is more important than another might be taken to imply the existence of a metric along which they can be ordered. Part of the point of distinguishing basic from best interests is to deny that any such metric can be identified. Although the ways in which they are dealt with have consequences for one another, basic and best interests are linked to different dimensions of children's lives and involve different kinds of insider's wisdom. Democratic justice recognizes this by limiting the fiduciary authority of parents and public officials to their respective domains of competence, except in the—unfortunately all too common—circumstances when there is a failure of fiduciary authority and fail-safe roles are activated. These circumstances are seen as second-best just because they require fiduciaries to act outside their domains of distinctive competence.

Basic interests are more important than best interests, however, in two senses from the standpoint of democratic justice. First, on a great many interpretations of best interests that are likely to prevail in a democracy, basic interests will be seen as necessary preconditions. Most parents can be expected to affirm the importance of basic interests, given that they include the necessities for physical survival, the development in children of sufficient human capital that they will not become a net drain on social resources, and the minimal wherewithal to live cooperatively as adults in a democracy. There might well be disagreements on how best to vindicate basic interests, but few are likely to resist them as a matter of principle. There will be some parents, to be sure, who will resist, perhaps because their views of their children's best interests are flatly incompatible with one or more dimension of basic interests. To concede this is to acknowledge the reality that democratic justice is not neutral among all defensible conceptions of the good life. My account of basic interests does, however, fall into the family of resourcist views of justice—defended by such theorists as Rawls, Sen, and Dworkin— that are intended to be as pluralistic as possible in facilitating the pursuit of different conceptions of the good life that are compatible with their foundational requirements.[99]

Basic interests are treated as more important than best interests in practice for reasons having to do with the state's police power. In spite of my earlier discussions of divided authority and creative solutions to tensions between parents and public officials, when conflict is inescapable some duly authorized public officials have the final say. A public official (though not necessarily the fiduciary—perhaps a judge rather than a schools superintendent) decides whether the last analysis has been reached, and if so what compromises must be made by whom.[100] This is not to deny that the relevant officials may compromise best interests unnecessarily or make other mistakes for which they cannot, ultimately, be held to account. It is merely to face up to and make explicit the implications of requiring that the state's view of parental interpretation of children's best interests be political, not metaphysical.

America's Dual-Regime System Reconsidered

The dual-regime structure of authority over children that has evolved in the United States and elsewhere since the nineteenth century is attractive from the standpoint of democratic justice, though there is manifest room for improvement in the ways in which the different fiduciaries interpret and exercise their responsibilities. Before attending to some of these, a prior question arises: if division of authority over children has so many benefits, why not multiply sources of authority over them yet further?[101]

WHY NOT A TRIPLE REGIME?

Republican theory, to which I appealed to justify the dual-regime system, conventionally divides authority three ways. This is notable in the present context, in view of the fact that until comparatively recently children were directly subject to religious authority as well as that of governments and parents. It raises the question whether—given the oft-recognized failures of governments and parents to vindicate children's interests—religious or other civil associations might not once again exercise independent authority over children. Such a view might gain credence from some recent academic commentary on democracy, motivated by a sense—perhaps more often asserted than argued for or even persuasively explained—that democracy needs a "strong" civil society and that American civil society is in a condition of precipitous decay. Joshua Cohen and Joel Rogers, for instance, argue that democratic states should transfer some of their traditional responsibilities to civil associations as a way of both multiplying centers of authority and delivering services more effectively.[102] Such accounts might be thought to support a brief, consistent with the spirit of democratic justice, for reallocating some authority over children from parents and public officials to intermediate civil associations.

No doubt such a view can seem attractive, particularly when one contrasts the failures of governments and parents, on the one hand, with the apparent achievements of churches, charities, and other civil associations in picking up the slack, on the other. But just as there were grounds for skepticism of George Bush's appeals to his thousand points of light, so one is bound to wonder here whether the cure might not be worse than the disease. Proposing it may have more to do with abdicating responsibility or pursuing other agendas than with protecting the interests of children. The question is not what some church or Cub Scout group does well by contrast with some poorly performing governmental agency or parent with respect to a particular child. Rather, it is whether a regime which transferred significant authority over children to intermediate associations should in general be expected to perform better than the dual-regime system. There are at least three sets of reasons for suspecting that it would not.

The first has to do with externalities. It arises principally when government functions are transferred to civil associations. Those who run civil associations may care more or less intensely about their members, but they need have little regard for the interests of nonmembers. The voluntary character of civil associations, in the eyes of the law at least, makes this a permanent possibility. Although turning certain responsibilities for children from the state to civil associations may improve conditions for some children, this can come at the price of worsening conditions for others, by giving public officials new excuses to ignore their obligations and further diminishing weak institutional capacities. We saw earlier that education is a case in point. It may be true, as New York City mayor Rudolph Giuliani alleged in August 1995, that Catholic and parochial schools do a better job of educating children, on virtually every measure, than do the New York City public schools.[103] Arguendo let us concede that this is so. But as my discussion of voucher systems and white flight revealed, variation in resources to exit from the public school system is arguably a principal source of public school weakness and may be resisted on these grounds.[104]

Second is the problem of first allegiances; it has to do with the devolution of parental authority to civil associations. An attractive feature of the proposition that parents should be primary custodians of best interests, I have argued, is that they can be expected to care intensely about their children's welfare and want what is best for them unconditionally. No doubt some parents fail to meet this standard, but nothing in their role as parents gives them incentives to do so. This is not so with civil associations, which generally do have ulterior interests—at a minimum, in sustaining themselves as organizations and in building membership. As a result, those who run them may indeed face incentives to view their commitments in instrumental, rather than unconditional, terms, or at least to confuse the two. Such confusion was well illustrated in the arguments put forward by Amish elders in the *Wisconsin v. Yoder* litigation in 1972. In support of their contention that Amish children should be exempted from some compulsory education requirements, they conflated claims about what was in the children's interests with what they believed would be the impact of denying the exemption on the Amish community's capacity to survive.[105] No doubt, this is a question of degree. One's perception of one's responsibilities as a parent are invariably colored to some degree by one's civil commitments, but the two are nonetheless distinguishable. The more parental authority is devolved to civil institutions, the greater the likelihood that children will be subjected to fiduciaries whose first allegiance is to the civil institution in question rather than to the child.[106]

The specter of devolving authority over children from parents or public officials to civil institutions raises a third set of difficulties having to do with appropriate limits to the authority of those institutions. Part of the attraction of the dual-regime system is that it provides for checks and mutual accountability on what would otherwise be complete freedom by parents or public officials to tyrannize children. Once civil associations enter the picture as independent potential sources of authority over children, the questions arise: how will their activities be policed, and by whom? The concern here is not with general issues concerning institutional monitoring. Courts could presumably play the same kind of mediating role here that they do in conflicts between parents and public officials. The concern, rather, is that the likeliest candidates for an expanded role are religious institutions, and there are good reasons—independent of issues concerning children—for avoiding state regulation of their activities.

The conventional reasons for embracing both disestablishment and wide religious toleration—which find American expression in the establishment clause of the First Amendment—militate against giving religious institutions direct authority over children. Whether such authority is concerned with basic interests or best interests, if it is to be genuinely independent then conflicts are bound to arise that involve the state in regulating religious institutions. From this vantage point, it is preferable to allow the parent to speak for the child in religious matters and to hold the parent rather than the church responsible if religious practice compromises basic interests. In addition to requiring parents to discern a distinction between their own religious affiliations and their responsibilities as parents, it helps insulate religious institutions from stronger forms of state supervision that might otherwise be justifiable to protect children's basic interests or to mediate conflicts among religious and other fiduciaries. In sum, the policing problem reinforces considerations about first allegiances and externalities that favor the dual-regime system.

THE CONTEMPORARY CONDITION OF CHILDREN'S BEST INTERESTS

To embrace an authority structure is not to suggest that its operation is optimal. The question remains to be confronted whether children's interests are generally being vindicated as well as possible within the present dual-regime system and, if not, what might be done to improve matters. With respect to best interests, the inquiry is necessarily limited by the plural understanding of them endorsed earlier. One may be appalled, as a matter of personal judgment, by the way in which a parent comprehends a child's best interests, but if no threat to a basic interest is involved, then there is no basis for third-party interference. Not only should the state keep out, it has an affirmative duty to proscribe other coercive third-party interference. There is no basis for knowing that the judgments on which such proposed interference rests are valid, and those who would impose one view of the question are reasonably to be feared more than those who would not.

There are, however, three areas in which democratic justice should not fall entirely silent on the subject of vindicating children's best interests in practice. The first has already been mentioned: when parents interpret best interests so as to compromise the state's reading of basic interests, or when they believe that best interests are basic interests, their claims must give way as the lexical priority of basic interests takes effect. Institutional devices that can make the assertion of this priority a solution of last resort rather than one of first resort are desirable, as are substantial burdens of proof on governments as discussed earlier. But at the end of the day some conflicts of this kind will be inescapable, and parents properly lose them. In their roles as ordinary participants in the democratic process, parents can try to influence the state's reading of basic interests, but as parents they have no additional claim or recourse. Thus if the appropriate governmental entity determines that compulsory education to a given age is necessary to vindicate children's basic interests, then parents who see this as inimical to their children's best interests appropriately lose even though the parents may in fact be right.

Second, although the state's reading of children's basic interests trumps parents' reading of their best interests, if governments seek to interfere with children's best interests where a basic interest is not at stake, they are appropriately resisted. This claim may ring hollow if an official insists that a basic interest is at stake when in fact it is not, but it is notable that often this is not so. The temptation for politicians to make hay out of moralizing denunciations of the values of stigmatized minorities is ever present in pluralist cultures.[107] In the United States it is illustrated by the strand of political commentary that stretches from the Moynihan Report through the 1990s utterances by many politicians of both political parties about the moral decay of "family values," with poignant illustrations drawn disproportionately from groups who lack healthy bank balances, white faces, or round eyes.[108] Scant pretense is typically made of deference to different values; indeed, excessive deference to difference is often pilloried as the problem. Democratic justice suggests turning these arguments back on their proponents in light of the distinction between basic and best interests: insisting—with a substantial burden of persuasion—that a link be established between the criticized value and a threat to a basic interest. If this burden is not met, courts should enforce parents' claims against those of public officials.

Third, the state's fail-safe responsibilities for best interests merit brief comment. These come into play when a child has no parent or an unwilling parent, and therefore affect the state's role in procreation and adoption. I have already mentioned that governments may reasonably try to regulate population growth to numbers whose basic interests can be met. By the same token, as fail-safe fiduciaries of best interests, governments have the duty to try to prevent the creation of children for whom no willing parent will be available. This suggests a permissive policy with respect to contraception, as well as a combination of abortion and adoption policies designed to ensure that every child who is born will be wanted by parents. By itself this does not amount to an argument for permissive policies toward abortion, though it does suggest that abortion should be available when adoption is not. As with basic interests, better that a child not be born at all than be born with no one to watch out for its best interests.[109]

With respect to adoption policy, in its fail-safe role the state appropriately oversees and regulates transfers of parental authority and obligation. Governments should therefore resist privatization of adoption and "rent-a-womb" surrogate parenting arrangements. Because parents in no sense "own" their charges, they may not sell them. Nor may they buy or sell their parental rights and responsibilities. This is generally the case with fiduciary authority: although it involves latitude for independent judgment, its basic terms may not be altered unilaterally by the fiduciary, and it may be given up but not sold. When fiduciary authority is given up, it reverts either to the original grantor or, if this is not possible or appropriate (as is the case with parents), to a court or other agency that is empowered to appoint a new fiduciary.

This is not to say that giving up fiduciary authority should be costless. A fiduciary who has abused authority may owe damages or restitution.[110] Alternatively, a fiduciary may be deemed to have assumed costly responsibilities that are not extinguished by the decision to abandon fiduciary authority. This is what happens, for example, when a parent is held financially responsible for a child even if he or she makes no claim for custody. The question whether and to what degree parents should be held responsible for producing offspring is independent of the question whether they are willing to raise them. As I argue below, democratic justice is not offended by garnishing delinquent parents' paychecks in the aggressive pursuit of "deadbeat dads."

THE CONTEMPORARY CONDITION OF
CHILDREN'S BASIC INTERESTS

Few if any governments in the world today can rest content with the job they are doing of protecting the basic interests of children for whom they are responsible. In many countries the state's capacity is severely constrained by conditions of general poverty and lack of resources, but even in such wealthy countries as the United States, governments have exhibited a checkered record at best in meeting these obligations. In 1992 some 14.6 million children in the United States were living in poverty, more than in any year since 1965. In the 1960s child poverty rates had been close to those of working-age adults (and somewhat lower than those of the elderly). By 1992, however, the poverty rate stood at 12.9 percent for the elderly (over 65) and 14.5 percent for the total U.S. population, yet for children under eighteen it was 21.9 percent. By 1994 the poverty rate for children under six was double the 1973 figure, standing at 24.6 percent. Minority children and those living with single parents are especially likely to be poor. In 1994, 43.8 percent of black children and 41.5 percent of Latino children—compared with 16.9 percent of white children—lived below the poverty line. Children in female-headed families are five times as likely to be poor as those in two-parent families, so that more than half of all children in families headed by women live in poverty. Bad as this problem might be, it would be a mistake to think that child poverty is limited to single-parent families. In 1989 almost five million poor children lived in married-couple families, so that even if there were no female-headed households, the United States would have one of the highest child-poverty rates in the industrial world.[111]

The picture concerning children's physical security, nutrition, and health is scarcely more encouraging. Three million instances of harm to children are reported in the United States annually, involving neglect, physical and sexual abuse, and severe emotional maltreatment. More than a third of these are substantiated.[112] As recently as 1993 the United States ranked twenty-second among industrial countries in controlling infant deaths, behind Japan, Singapore, Germany, and the Scandinavian countries.[113] In 1992 as few as 55.3 percent of two-year-olds had been fully immunized against preventable childhood diseases.[114] In 1990 infant mortality rates in the United States were 7.7 per thousand live births for white children, 17 per thousand for blacks, and 7.8 per thousand for Hispanics.[115] Although this represented a mild improvement since the mid-1980s due to improvements in medical technology, by 1992 the United States still had one of the highest mortality rates in the industrial world: 8.5 infant deaths per thousand live births.[116] Low-birth-weight children suffer two to three times as much from blindness, deafness, mental retardation, learning disorders, and hyperactivity as normal-birth-weight children. In 1992, 7.1 percent of births in the United States were considered low (less than 2,500 grams), up from 6.8 percent in 1985. The figures among minorities and the poor were significantly higher.[117] No doubt a considerable part of the explanation for this is that poor women lack the resources for adequate prenatal care. In 1989, one in four American mothers and 40 percent of black mothers received no first-trimester prenatal care at all.[118]

Democratic justice does not require particularly robust civic education, yet minimal literacy surely is needed for people to function successfully in a democracy. As Amy Gutmann put it in her 1987 study *Democratic Education*, people in a democracy do need "the intellectual skills and the information that enable them to think about democratic politics and to develop their deliberative skills and their knowledge through practical experience."[119] She noted that in the United States at least 15 percent of adults (more than 23 million people) did not meet this criterion, being insufficiently literate to read and understand a newspaper.[120] Bemoaning the declining quality of education is a perennial theme of American politics, often exaggerated by politicians and others with particular axes to grind, but it seems clear that rates of functional illiteracy have worsened, if anything, since Gutmann wrote.[121] In 1992, 9.3 percent of American teenagers were high school dropouts, and in 1993 almost a fifth of Americans aged 25 and up lacked high school diplomas.[122] Indeed, the percentage of students graduating from high school has been declining, from 76.7 in 1985 to 73.4 in 1990 for white teenagers and from 62.8 to 60.7 for blacks.[123] Although the nationwide level of dropouts aged 16 to 19 has fallen slightly, from 11 percent in 1985 to 9.3 percent in 1992, the rate increased during that period in fourteen American states. The prospects for the next generation are scarcely more encouraging: in 1992, 43 percent of fourth-grade children were scoring below basic reading level and 41 percent below basic math level.[124] This is to say nothing of the reality that underinvesting in the human capital of the next generation is immensely costly to the economy at large and has potentially devastating implications for the care of the dependent old, as I discuss in Chapter 7.[125]

In such circumstances, the state's failure to protect the basic interests of vast numbers of children is beyond dispute. Whereas people may debate the responsibility that is, or should be, borne by adults for their own poverty (a subject taken up in Chapter 6), children manifestly bear no responsibility at all for this condition. This suggests the desirability of directing substantial subsidies to children through the tax code, perhaps of the sort suggested by the Rockefeller Commission in 1991.[126] To the extent that they are to be targeted on children in poverty, however, they should be more steeply progressive than the 1995 congressional proposal ($500 per child exemption up to family incomes of $110,000), and it should in any case be stressed that such a proposal will not begin to get at the worst of the problem. Children of parents who lack sufficient income to make use of the exemption will not derive relevant benefit unless it is refundable. Tax benefits are also subject to the criticism sometimes leveled at AFDC mothers: that benefits given to parents for children may or may not make their way to the children. As some economists have noted, policies targeted more directly at children — such as funding quality child care of working mothers — avoid both difficulties. Expensive as they might be, they are not unthinkably so, and such benefits can be channeled directly to the children who need them most.[127]

Targeted policies of this sort seem to be the most cost-effective way of funding what Bergmann describes as a "basic needs budget," which may be thought of as a rough proxy for the economic dimensions of a child's basic interests.[128] Yet in the 1990s they were not part of the public political debate in the United States. Rather than attend to the dire condition of so many American children's basic interests, the Clinton administration chose to join the Republicans in moralizing denunciations of parental failure, calling "character conferences" in the White House and advocating "character education" programs in public schools to make up for children's perceived moral deficiencies and what Amitai Etzioni has referred to as the "parenting deficit."[129] One commentator on these developments half-jokingly suggested that the administration's aspiration was to create "virtuecrats," a description that neatly captures the hypocrisy of government's failure to meet its responsibilities at the same time as it insists that it can do a better job than parents of meeting theirs.[130] As a result of this shift, the principal child-policy disagreement between Democrats and Republicans was no longer whether to increase the flow of benefits from government to poor children, but rather how much to reduce it.

In closing, something must be said about parents as fail-safe fiduciaries of children's basic interests. Earlier I argued that when governments fail to protect children's basic interests, parents have a responsibility to step into the breach if they can. It should be emphasized that when acting in this capacity, the concern for their child should not be exclusive; the fail-safe fiduciary should be trying to deliver what government is not delivering in the protection of basic interests. This includes attending to the appropriate expectations of third parties and the externalities of their own actions. If one's child is in a hopeless urban school where the education for basic interests is not being provided and illiterate children are routinely graduating, for instance, a parent's first impulse may be to move to a different school district, go to a private school if this can be afforded, or embark on a program of home education. But for a fail-safe fiduciary these should be seen as solutions of last resort, because of their propensity to make the situation worse for those children who remain in the failing public school. Better to try to improve the system, whether through local activism or class-action lawsuits, designed to ensure that a public education is provided that does meet the basic-interest criterion.

To be sure, there are profound collective-action problems here. Parents who opt for voice instead of exit may expend much energy to little effect, and their children might be adversely affected for life as a result. It is difficult, in these circumstances, to blame parents for choosing what I have characterized as fail-safe solutions of last resort. To recognize this, however, is merely to acknowledge the devastating consequences of institutional failure. The presence of serious externalities and collective-action problems are significant components of the state's mandate to protect children's basic interests to begin with. As a result, we can scarcely be surprised that these difficulties run rampant when government fails to do its job.

• 5 •

Consenting Adults

MARRIAGE HAS USUALLY BEEN UNDEMOCRATIC, but this need not be the case. Marriages can be governed by agreement in all significant particulars, and those involved in them can oppose aspects of married life that they find unsatisfactory—either to modify or end them. Nor is this merely a theoretical possibility. In many countries marriage has become dramatically less hierarchical over the past several decades, at least as a matter of law. The ready availability of divorce, enactment of various egalitarian measures to re-structure marriage, and a growing willingness in many countries to consider legalizing unconventional forms of domestic partnership all underscore the reality that in the adult domestic arena we live in an era of evolving possibilities and considerable flux.

The rivers of history seldom all flow in a single direction, however, and many powerful contemporary forces press against these developments. Where marital relations have become more formally egalitarian, economic realities often sustain—and even increase—the possibilities for domination within marriage. The availability of divorce on demand is not much of an equalizing device if both parties know that it is more costly, as it generally is, to women than to men; it remains a debated question whether this has been a net benefit for married women.[1] Nor is it clear that those advocating recognition for unorthodox domestic partnerships have won the day. Despite extensions of such conventional benefits of marriage as health insurance to same-sex partners in many places, there is also formidable resistance. In the United States, the Supreme Court's 1986 decision in *Bowers v. Hardwick* permits state governments to continue outlawing homosexuality, and Congress's 1996 Defense of Marriage Act enables them to abjure Hawaii's decision to legalize single-sex marriage.[2] In many non-Western countries exploitative forms of domestic association—most obviously state-enforced patriarchialism and polygyny—are deeply embedded in legal orders, sometimes more securely than a few decades ago due to the resurgence of Islamic fundamentalism. Our task begins, then, not with an evaluation of any uniform trend of evolution but rather with an appreciation of multidimensional change and of open possibilities.

Patriarchy's Legacy

The system of family law that seventeenth- and eighteenth-century Americans inherited grew out of the broader patriarchy of English society, traceable to feudalism and strengthened by the rise of absolutism in the sixteenth century. The common law reinforced this system by sustaining doctrines in which wives verged on being property of husbands no less than children did of fathers. On the western side of the Atlantic, patriarchialism was detached from some of its English ideological moorings in natural-law justifications of absolute power. But it continued to be nourished in the legal order that Americans adapted from the English, and by other social forces. The American colonists justified their social arrangements by appeal to religious ideologies that were explicit about the need to subjugate women, along with children and slaves.[3] Nor did the democratic aspirations of the American revolutionaries extend to undoing women's subordinate status inside or outside of marriage. Women remained second-class citizens, until comparatively recently denied even the right to vote. They were obliged to live in a man's world on substantially male terms.[4]

No doubt this history partly accounts for why marriage so long remained a paradigm of antidemocracy. Although the shape of the family has evolved considerably since colonial times, recent scholarship on the cult of domesticity reveals that patriarchialism persisted, if in subtler forms, throughout the nineteenth century and well into the twentieth. To be sure, there was also some variability. Polygamous and other heterodox arrangements were always present, and blacks and other ethnic groups lived in domestic arrangements that were often little understood, or even much known about, in establishment circles. Nonetheless, in the mainstream of American domestic life married women occupied a distinctly subordinate status, which was reinforced by the political, legal, and social systems in interdependent ways. Married women had to pursue their goals indirectly—as underscored by the aphorisms about "power behind the throne" and "the hand that rocks the cradle"—and generally to defer in situations where interests conflicted. The costs of exit, for them, were high, usually prohibitively so. To the degree that democratic practices existed in marriage, they did so on sufferance from husbands whose needs and aspirations set the basic terms of matrimonial association. This state of affairs did not begin to erode significantly until after World War II.[5]

In the past half-century it is doubtful that any piece of the American social fabric has changed more dramatically than adult domestic life. In 1965 the Moynihan Report sounded alarm at the discovery that a quarter of urban black marriages ended in divorce.[6] By 1990 the national divorce rate was double this figure, with professional and lay opinion sharply divided over its social and moral significance. The percentage of the adult population who are married declined from 71.7 percent in 1970 to 62.7 percent by 1988. Over the same period the number of unmarried cohabiting households leapt fivefold from about five hundred thousand to more than two and a half million. Whereas during the 1950s some 60 percent of all families consisted of a breadwinner husband and a stay-at-home wife who cared for children full-time, by 1990 only 7 percent of households conformed to this pattern. Married women have moved into the paid workforce in large numbers during the past three decades, so that well over half of married women now work outside the home. Women continue to do the lion's share of domestic work, but more often than not this is in addition to working in the money economy rather than instead of it.[7]

Today it would not be difficult to elicit a broad American consensus against the kind of patriarchialism in which the wife was a chattel of the husband, yet subtler defenses of patriarchal arrangements remain influential.

The power in electoral politics of code terms like "profamily" and "family values" attests to this reality. Sometimes the appeal is frankly religious, but secular defenses of "traditional" or "normal" family arrangements have been no less efficacious in shaping American public debate and social policy. In both conservative and liberal circles, it is common to blame the decline of the "traditional" family for a host of social problems in urban America. This view was taken for granted in the Moynihan Report, which blamed the troubles of poor black Americans on what its author believed was the matriarchal structure of the traditional black family.

Moynihan relied bluntly on medical metaphors, declaring matriarchy to be a pathology that must be treated so that blacks of both genders could be made more accepting of male-led households.[8] Similar arguments were made in the 1960s by commentators like Oscar Lewis, who sought to link a "culture of poverty" among the urban poor to deviations from white middle-class family norms.[9] Although such arguments are often criticized for ideological bias, they have never been driven from the field. They can readily be discerned in the 1980s and 1990s debates on pathologies of the underclass initiated by William Julius Wilson and others that set much of the social policy agenda of the Reagan, Bush, and Clinton administrations.[10] Commentators from William Galston to Charles Murray continue to garner public attention by blaming "the decline of the family" for antisocial behavior, welfare dependency, and other assorted social ills.

Some have contended that marital arrangements subordinating women have been sustained even by those who intended liberation. For instance, Carole Pateman notes that partial attempts to turn marriage into a conventional private-law contract lend the gloss of authentic contractarian choice to participation in an externally defined status that continues to subordinate women in many ways. Pateman believes this state of affairs to be insuperable on the grounds that the notion of the individual required by the idea of contract inherently subordinates women, so that "the final victory of contract over status is not the end of patriarchy, but the consolidation of the modern form."[11] I disagree with this contention below, but Pateman is surely right that marriage remains a quasi-public status in which women are less than equal partners in many respects. Developments such as the Married Women's Property Acts which began in the 1840s, the abolition of the marital rape exception in many jurisdictions since the 1970s, and increased willingness by courts to enforce prenuptial agreements since that time have eroded traditional marriage only partly. The freedom of husbands to dominate wives through violence continues to be shielded by old laws and half-hearted enforcement of new ones. The distribution of economic and decision-making power often remains substantially unequal, as does the actual freedom to leave. Quips about "the march from status to contract" notwithstanding, marriage continues as a publicly defined status, many essential features of which are not alterable by contract.[12]

Pateman is not alone in contending that would-be liberators of women from patriarchy have sometimes contributed to their subjugation. Observers of the family from Jacques Donzelot to Christopher Lasch have argued that patriarchy has been displaced, in much of the West, by a different sort of domination. On these accounts, whereas nineteenth-century patriarchialism subjected women—as "objects of matrimonial exchange"—to arranged marriages, humiliating double standards in sexual mores, and generally subordinated lives, the system of companionate marriage that has come to replace it subjects them to subtler mechanisms of control. Lasch describes the reform of marriage as part and parcel of the rise of the "therapeutic state." By siding with the wives against patriarchal authority, medical doctors, psychiatrists, psychologists, and therapists of various kinds sought to make women agents of a new medical morality, just as under the old regime they had been ambassadoresses of patriarchal culture. In Donzelot's formulation, the rejection of patriarchialism "replaced a government of families with a government through the family," in which ideologically loaded definitions of normalcy neutralized potentially aberrant and destabilizing behavior, made people more docile and accepting of technical authority, and reduced of the scope of their actual freedom.[13]

Donzelot sees the medicalization of family life as fitting into a larger historical pattern of the increasingly subtle control of all kinds of human behavior by a variety of institutional mechanisms, some more visible than others. (The market and the state worked in tandem more than in opposition in this regard, he argues.) As early as the beginning of the nineteenth century in Europe, doctors and civil servants had begun to argue that unconventional unions among the poor produced illegitimacy, incest, and other immoral behavior, trapping them in conditions of chronic demoralization, preventing their becoming industrious workers, and making them dependent on public charity. Prefiguring today's culture-of-poverty theorists, they insisted that promoting orderly habits of domesticity would make workers sober and self-supporting and that projects of family reform should be geared toward that end. Donzelot argues that this kind of normalization was a characteristic liberal way of producing the armies of obedient workers that industrial society requires. Liberal reformers in countries like France looked for a middle way between conservatives—who upheld the family as the backbone of the social order, not to be trifled with if society was to survive uncorrupted—and socialists who sought the destruction of traditional families and their replacement by direct state supervision. The resulting pattern that he detects in France is discerned by Lasch in America: liberal reformers "outflanked their adversaries by creating a therapeutic state which left the family more or less intact yet subjected it to nonstop supervision." [14]

The Donzelot-Lasch thesis owes much to Michel Foucault's portrayal of the post-eighteenth-century history of liberalism, and in particular to his focus on how utilitarian and other scientistic ideologies of progress facilitated the production of order among modern mass citizenries.[15] One may reasonably harbor skepticism about many aspects of these claims. Yet the picture of the family that Donzelot and Lasch paint has to be taken seriously as a possibility from the standpoint of democratic justice, if only because of the degree to which therapeutic arguments dominate so much of the terrain of public debate about family policy. This is not to deny that expertise may have a role to play in democratizing adult domestic life. But it is important to devise mechanisms through which people can take advantage of expertise without being held hostage to it, better to manage their own social relations in more rather than less democratic ways.

Reforming the Marriage Status

Democratic justice bids us to find ways to condition social relations so as to encourage democratic governance and opposition within them. Facilitating democratic governance means promoting inclusive decision making, with those whose interests are centrally at stake—usually the participants in an activity—enjoying a particularly strong claim. Advancing the cause of democratic opposition means insisting on viable avenues for people to resist, and to try to change, conditions that affect them adversely. It, too, is constrained by the centrality of the interest at stake. Those whose basic interests might be compromised by a particular decision have a stronger claim that their opposition be taken into account than those who have a disinterested opinion about it. How do these general presumptions play themselves out here?

DISPATCHING PATRIARCHY'S REMNANTS

One easily rendered judgment is that pressure should be kept on the institutions shaping adult domestic life to evolve away from the vestiges of patriarchal marriage. An externally defined hierarchical status of this kind is radically at odds with both the governance and opposition dimensions of democratic justice. On the governance side, it is hard to see a justification for imposing such a system on people without consulting them, so that their only choice is to opt in or out. Many other possibilities are available in both principle and practice, and by limiting the choice in this way society effectively disenfranchises participants in a practice from central aspects of its governance.[16]

Some will raise the possibility that an elected legislature might enact elements of patriarchy in the available marriage status, either explicitly (as with affirming a marital rape exception) or implicitly (as with refusing to legitimate nonpatriarchal domestic unions). Is that not democratic governance by the relevant citizenry? This suggestion should be rejected. Democratic justice bids us defer to insider's wisdom and local decision making unless compelling reasons can be given for not so doing. Because issues concerning public goods and free riding are not at stake in this area, there is no reason in principle to countenance solutions imposed from outside.[17] The continuing effects of historical injustice do suggest an appropriate role for the state in restructuring the terms of adult domestic life, but as I shall argue below, this must be linked to undermining patriarchy. Beyond this, in deciding what constitutes the appropriate demos for governing adult domestic life, small is beautiful. Those whose are centrally affected by the results should be able to define, or at any rate redefine, the rules governing their common association.[18]

On the opposition front, patriarchal marriage runs afoul of every presumption against hierarchy discussed in Chapter 3. It is evidently unnecessary, as demonstrated by the existence of a gamut of alternatives. It is pertinent only to one conception of family life, which many people reject. Its hierarchy is asymmetrical: matriarchy is not only unavailable, but frowned on in patriarchal cultures, as I have noted. Nor is patriarchy self-liquidating, for the subordination it involves is typically expected to be permanent. It can be said to be chosen only in the highly constrained sense that people can opt for it or not, often knowing that the latter choice will come at a considerable economic and social price. Nor is patriarchal marriage an insulated hierarchy. As a publicly defined status, it is imposed throughout the society. Indeed, the burden falls to those who reject it to devise ways of insulating themselves from its effects. This is not to prejudge the question whether some people might not reasonably choose patriarchal domestic arrangements for themselves. It is only to insist that the dice should not be loaded in favor of patriarchy.

AN EGALITARIAN STATUS?

Democratic justice disposes swiftly of patriarchy's legitimacy as an imposed form of marriage, but the issue becomes more complex once we consider what should be affirmed in its stead. One possibility, proposed by Okin, is to move toward an egalitarian status. She makes a powerful case that replacing patriarchy's remnants with genuinely egalitarian marriage would require more than getting rid of inegalitarian laws and changing attitudes about the traditional division of labor within the family. Given the degree to which women's "subordination by marriage" is underwritten by economic disadvantages inside and outside marriage, major economic changes are needed as well. Women have moved into the labor force in large numbers over the past several decades, but their earning power remains substantially below that of men. Moreover, domestic work and child rearing continue to be performed predominantly by women, even when they also work outside the home. In many ways wives continue as "dependents," whose domestic contribution to the economic well-being of families is either undervalued or ignored.[19]

In these circumstances, Okin thinks it necessary to go beyond echoing the calls of other feminists for gender equality in career opportunities, equal pay for equal work, and better economic protections for women at divorce. Action is also needed within marriage to equalize the costs and benefits associated with domestic tasks and child rearing. Okin's proposed remedy is simple and radical: the state should mandate equal splitting of wages between husbands and wives, requiring employers to send half of an employee's paycheck to his or her spouse. This step, she argues, would have a direct impact on the problem by preventing the invisible exploitation of those who do domestic work. It would also help facilitate the changes in hearts, minds, and behavior that egalitarian marriage requires. Mandatory wage splitting would place explicit value in the public legal culture on domestic work, thus undermining the widespread practice of disvaluing or ignoring it. Wage splitting would also achieve the economic empowerment of homemakers without forcing them into the labor market, where some do not want to be and where many who worry about the decline of conventional family life do not want them to be forced to go.[20]

At first sight Okin's suggestion might seem attractive from the standpoint of democratic justice. My earlier discussion buttresses the thought that those who are vulnerable within marriage need empowerment, not moralizing models of "normal" family life imposed on them from the outside. Okin's is a resourcist view that speaks directly to this requirement. It is geared to empowering the disempowered through basic equalization of a major resource—arguably now *the* major resource—that sustains domestic domination. True, her proposal is at odds with democratic justice's presumption against vanguardism, but it fits comfortably within the ambit of exceptions to that presumption. Women's subordination by marriage was enforced by state action historically, suggesting that comparable action will be required to undo its lingering effects. Moreover, this subordination is a clear instance of Walzerian domination: men's greater economic power in the marketplace reinforces their economic dominance within marriage. As such, Okin argues, it calls for a Walzerian solution. Wage splitting would require domestic labor to be valued, but not to be bought and sold in the labor market. As a result, it could equalize economic resources within marriage without introducing the cash nexus into personal relationships, a worthy pluralist goal in Walzer's sense.[21] Democratic justice bids us recognize that Walzerian domination can warrant remedial state action. Should it not, then, lead us to embrace Okin's wage-splitting proposal?

No. Close inspection reveals that wage splitting would achieve neither of the Walzerian goals Okin claims for it. On the one hand, it would not prevent translation of inequalities in the labor market into the domestic realm. Far from insulating family life from market relations, it would achieve gender equality within individual marriages at the price of reinforcing inequalities among homemaking spouses along class lines. Different homemakers would be differently rewarded for their homeworking services based on nothing other than their wage-earning spouse's place in the labor market.[22] On the other hand, wage splitting would not keep the cash nexus out of personal relationships. Assuming it to be mandated by the state and not modifiable by the parties (via such devices as prenuptial agreements), the proposal would still preclude only some kinds of bargaining over the distribution of family income by the participants, and then only in an artificial fashion. The reality that one person's income varied with how much, and how successfully, the other chose to work would never be far below the surface in their dealings with one another. They would also confront serious potential moral hazards which become evident if one reflects on the gains available to a spouse who might decline to do any domestic work, preferring to watch television all day instead. Realistically, there is no way to keep the cash nexus out of personal relationships if economic inequality within marriage is identified as a source of injustice that stands in need of remedy.

These difficulties aside, Okin's appeal to Walzer begs the more important question why an egalitarian marriage status should be judged desirable. We saw in Chapter 1 that although the basic idea behind Walzer's pluralist view of civil society is attractive, his claim to know which values are appropriate to which spheres is unpersuasive. It rests either on an unconvincing appeal to shared understandings or on implicitly carving up the domains of civil society by reference to an undefended metric of value. Whether or not the difficulties attending Walzer's appeal to shared understandings can ultimately be resolved, surely it cannot generate a justification for mandatory wage splitting in contemporary America, as Okin is aware.[23] Accordingly, an independent justification is needed to sustain the claim that the egalitarian marriage status implicit in wage splitting is desirable.

In fact, Okin's justification is Rawlsian. Embracing Rawls's idea that we should reason about the justice of society's basic structure from behind the veil of ignorance, she argues that his mistake lay in failing to realize that this should include family relations.[24] She believes that, appropriately modified, his approach can be brought to bear on the economics of domestic life in support of her argument. The Rawlsian method asks us to evaluate elements of society's basic structure from the standpoint of the worst-off representative individual affected by their operation. Someone potentially engaging in unpaid domestic work would seem to fit the relevant bill, and wage splitting would presumably be attractive to her or him. Hence, justice requires us to support it.

This reasoning is less than compelling. People in the original position know that even under conditions of moderate scarcity there is likely to be substantial inequality, and that the absolute condition of those at the bottom may well be dire. "Grave risks," as Rawls says, are associated with being the worst-off.[25] Hence their risk-aversion which carries so much freight in Rawls's justification of the difference principle. In the present context, the question thus becomes: would it be reasonable to embrace wage splitting, assuming that one was going to be the penniless homemaking spouse of the worst-paid person in the workforce?[26] If this is the question, why would someone choose a fifty-fifty distributive maxim that might leave them at the point of starvation? Even if literal starvation did not result, affirming wage splitting might involve acquiescence in an exploitative arrangement within the family: half the most poorly paid worker's wage would presumably be less, on most plausible measures, than the actual value of the work done by the homemaking spouse.[27]

The Rawlsian thought experiment is comparative: deciding whether a proposal would be chosen depends on assessing it against an alternative from the standpoint of the worst-off. The implicit alternative that apparently drives Okin's argument is the more or less laissez-faire regime that currently prevails concerning the distribution of income within marriage. But why is that the relevant alternative? Even if one were to grant that wage splitting might be chosen over laissez-faire, it is far from obvious that it would be chosen if the alternative were, say, a universal social wage or a minimum wage for certain types of domestic work—particularly if this took the form of a refundable tax credit for child rearing of the kind proposed by the Rockefeller Commission in 1991. Okin never considers how such alternative candidates might fare from her modified Rawlsian point of view, yet mere mention of them is sufficient to underscore the fact that various possibilities might be judged superior to mandatory wage splitting from the standpoint of the worst-off in domestic circumstances. Trying to discriminate among such possibilities in a Rawlsian way is not a course pursued here, however. As I have noted, when Rawlsian speculation is fed sufficient information to produce determinate results, it generally relies on so much that is contestable about human psychology that it is unlikely to persuade skeptics.

Democratic justice suggests instead that we evaluate Okin's proposal by reference to the twin injunctions to promote inclusive self-government and meaningful opposition. Focusing on the latter first, mandatory wage splitting might indeed go a significant distance toward empowering many homemakers and diminishing the prospects of their domination within marriage. True, it might also generate new possibilities for domination in some settings, as my observations about Okin's Walzerian gloss on her account suggest. But there is arguably no principle that will not lend itself to domination in some situations, so that the realistic issue is whether Okin's proposal is plausibly more likely to reduce domination within marriage than the going alternatives.

There might be settings in which democratic justice should lead us to endorse mandatory wage splitting. The promising candidates that come to mind are those where divorce is either impossible or prohibitively costly for homemakers. Consider a Catholic country with entrenched proscription of divorce, or orthodox Jewish sects in which divorced women are shunned in dehumanizing ways. If such practices are judged unalterable, then trying to make the marriage status more egalitarian would make sense as the best available path for diminishing domination within it. Indeed, passage of the Married Women's Property Acts in the nineteenth century could plausibly be viewed in just that light: a way of equalizing an important aspect of marriage's power dimensions when its permanence as a status could not be called into question. Wage splitting might be defended as an analogous move in circumstances where economic power in marriage has come to revolve less around inherited wealth or the lack of it, and more around labor-market participation.[28]

The plausibility of this reasoning is tied to the high costs, for a vulnerable homemaker, of leaving a marriage. As a result, it naturally prompts the question: why should marriage be a publicly imposed status at all? The alternative is to endorse, and press further, the march from status toward contract in this area. This option naturally suggests itself once we focus on the self-governance dimension of democratic justice. As I have noted, because the marriage status is not a public good and there is a variety of competing conceptions of what an appropriate marriage is, the only good reason to impose a particular conception is to prevent injustice. Otherwise, subsidiarity considerations support the presumption that small is beautiful when deciding on the appropriate demos for governing a marriage. Disenfranchisement requires necessity, and adults are generally presumed competent judges of their own interests. Accordingly, no government should aspire to govern a marriage for the participants. Governments do better, rather, to enable consenting adults to design and operate their own domestic arrangements in ways that do not undermine the possibility of effective opposition. When our presumptions about both governance and opposition are borne in mind, that is the more attractive course.

Alternatives to the Marriage Status

We should not mourn the fact that the widespread rejection of patriarchy has not led to consensus around an alternative family form. In Chapter 1 I argue that the search for agreement about the values structuring different domains of civil life is unrealistic, and that in any case it is unattractive from the standpoint of democratic justice. But how much pluralism should there be? Which, if any, domestic arrangements should government proscribe? Should some be discouraged without being proscribed? Should some be encouraged through the tax system or other collectively financed incentives?

LIBERTARIAN CONSIDERATIONS

One logical point of departure is libertarian. If people should generally be free to establish the terms of their own association, why place any restrictions on them at all? Why not simply abolish all obligatory dimensions to the marriage status, leaving the shape of adult domestic arrangements up to those who live in them? The pure libertarian stance runs into difficulties from the standpoint of democratic justice, as we will see. Yet there is something to be said for taking it as a point of departure, and then adding conditioning constraints as further reflection warrants.

Adopting the libertarian stance disposes of the objection frequently advanced that marriage arbitrarily privileges conventional mores by excluding the unorthodox. Democratic justice attaches prima facie importance to such claims because domination is often achieved by exclusion. Proscribing gay and lesbian marriage reinforces stigmatization of homosexuality in the dominant culture. It also relegates those who practice it to second-class status by limiting their accessibility to a variety of tax, employment, and health benefits that are attached to marriage—not to mention protections built into inheritance laws such as the rules of intestate succession.[29] Like gays and lesbians, some Mormons have argued that proscribing polygamy discriminates against them, buttressing these claims with arguments about free religious exercise. And when interracial marriages have been outlawed, they, too, have been subject to criticism on analogous grounds.[30] Excluded groups will inevitably be disprivileged by a dominant marriage status. Embracing the libertarian stance responds to their concerns.

Comparing Mormon polygamists with proponents of gay and lesbian marriage illustrates the fact that unorthodox marriages can be proscribed on two different types of grounds. Homosexual unions are outlawed because they are seen as morally objectionable in the dominant culture. Homosexuality is still widely thought to be both unnatural and wrong, and until recently characteristic homosexual practices were outlawed in the criminal statutes of all American states.[31] Polygamy is also frowned on in much of the public culture, and arguments for outlawing it also generally refer to the state's interest in protecting public morals. But because the predominant form of polygamy in the history of the United States has been polygyny, independent arguments are usually advanced as well that have to do with the protection of women. Both kinds of arguments were endorsed, for instance, in *Reynolds v. United States*, the 1878 Supreme Court decision that outlawed polygamy.[32] Appeals to orthodox public morality should always be rejected in this type of context; majority disapproval of an adult domestic practice is never sufficient to justify proscribing it. The protection argument merits attention from democratic justice, however, particularly when asymmetrical hierarchies of the kind generally involved in polygamy are at issue.

Endorsing the libertarian stance need not entail pressing for the abolition of marriage. Default arrangements, geared to minimizing the costs of drawing up marriage contracts, would be defensible, provided those who did not like them could change them by agreement. The only costs imposed on anyone would then be the inconvenience involved in varying the default institutions.[33] These costs would fall disproportionately on the unorthodox, to be sure, but for efficiency reasons rather than any collective judgment about the ethics of heterodox lifestyles. Perhaps a pure private-law regime—

in which every future aspect of every marriage was explicitly negotiated by the parties—would avoid this result, but this is at most a philosophical possibility. The long-term and open-ended nature of marriagelike commitments means that some eventualities will not be foreseen by the parties in many instances, so that some default regime is bound to prevail. Moreover, because few of those who marry make prenuptial agreements, we should anticipate that in any case the system of default institutions will continue to govern the great majority of marital unions for the foreseeable future.

LIBERTARIANISM'S LIMITS

Here as elsewhere, libertarianism's attractiveness founders on the realities of power. There are differences between a person who chooses to marry because of a desire to commit herself and one who does so to avoid ostracism from her father's family. Likewise, there are differences between someone who stays in a marriage because of a continuing desire to be there, and another who makes the same choice only out of fear of physical violence or a predictable decline into poverty. In the end these may sometimes be differences of degree, but, even when this is so, the distances matter. To get at the ways in which they matter, democratic justice directs us not to take the choices people make at face value. Rather, we should evaluate them in the power contexts within which they actually arise.

Earlier I argued, against Okin's proposal, that meaningful self-governance of domestic life is as important as preventing domination within it. This suggests the desirability of some sort of quasi-contractual regime. It should not be a pure private-law regime, however, because that all too easily presses apparent self-governance into the service of domination. The historical shift from a world in which prenuptial agreements were held void as against public policy to one in which many such agreements are enforceable by courts is instructive in this regard.[34] This change dramatically expanded the possibilities for self-governance, by allowing the parties to create designer marriages rather than accept statuses imposed by law. By the same token, however, once enforcing the husband's support as permanent ceased to be public policy, women began to lose protections (such as for alimony at divorce) that had traditionally been built into family law to compensate for their comparatively vulnerable status. Contractual agreements tend to reflect and replicate disparities in the power of the contracting agents, so that the more parties are able to negotiate individually, the more structural disparities in their power are likely to be replicated in the marriage relationship.[35]

Given this reality of widely disparate power relations surrounding the domestic domain, democratic justice suggests that freedom of contract over the terms of domestic life should be regulated. But what should the content of such regulation be, and how should it be enforced? How does one defend a particular regulatory regime without falling prey to the kind of criticism I leveled at Okin—namely, that the regime imposes a contestable conception of how to order family life on people who may reject it? To avoid this result, the law should sustain people's capacities to agree on their own terms of domestic association, but it should also load the dice against features of such agreements that can facilitate domination. Although such a policy would not be neutral among all possible domestic arrangements, it would sustain a pluralism of legitimate marriage forms.[36]

Before exploring the constraints to the marriage contract that flow from democratic justice, we should attend to Pateman's contention that such contracts inherently subordinate women. Her argument proceeds differently from my focus on the external power contexts within which contracts are made, though she agrees that these contexts contribute to the injustice within marriage.[37] Instead, Pateman argues that the very act of contracting to marry subordinates women. Most of what she actually says about marriage, however, concerns the euphemistic description of it as a contract, when really it is a status. Marriage contracts are not drawn up by the parties, and historically they have mandated practices such as obedience of wives to husbands, loss of legal protections of person and property, and even diminished legal status as persons for women. Although many exploitative features of the marriage contract have been abolished or ameliorated, in some respects it remains an externally defined status that contributes to women's subordination.[38] Granting this argument, it entails only that an exploitative status disguised as a contract merits no allegiance. It says nothing about the infirmity of contract as such.

Pateman's objections to contract run deeper, however. Defenders of the social-contract tradition since Hobbes have underwritten patriarchy, she argues, by assuming the contracting agents in their theories to be male heads of households with patriarchal authority over women. As a result, they have "incorporated conjugal right into their theories and, in so doing, transformed the law of male sex-right into its modern contractarian form."[39] Even contemporary contractarians like Rawls make this move implicitly by treating the contracting agents in the original position as "heads of families."[40] The result, on Pateman's telling, is a conception of the individual at the core of social-contract theory that subjugates women.[41]

Because democratic justice is no more sympathetic to the social-contract tradition than is Pateman, we need not take up her general assault on it here. She overreaches, however, in claiming that it sustains a rejection of contractual marriage in the contemporary world. Contractual marriage can be defended on a variety of grounds, and Pateman establishes no necessary link between it and the social contract tradition. Moreover, we can agree with her that contractual marriage has sustained modern patriarchy without being persuaded that contracting must lead to sexual oppression, or that there is a viable alternative to it if one's goal is to diminish the injustices wrought by patriarchy. Certainly Pateman does not propose one.[42] For democratic justice, as for Pateman, fake contracts are to be resisted, and so are contracts that replicate power disparities outside the domestic realm. But we part company with her by arguing that achieving this requires pressing toward a regulated contractual regime, one that is geared to heading off the ways in which marriage contracts atrophy into the service of domination.

A Regulated No-Fault Regime

An essential constraint on marriage concerns the freedom to end it. Unless people are free to leave circumstances in which their power is unequal, we cannot have much confidence that they are not being coerced into remaining when they do. Accordingly, we should endorse the move toward no-fault divorce in the system of default institutions, and oppose the enforceability of prenuptial agreements designed to limit or waive it. In effect, this means underwriting as inalienable a universal right to unilateral divorce. Before characterizing the implications of this constraint more fully, it will be useful to take up three possible objections to it.

ANTICIPATING LIKELY OBJECTIONS

The first objection, a contractarian one, is that this is a clear limitation on people's freedom of choice. If they want to bind themselves "for better and for worse, until death do us part," why stack public policy and the legal system against them? This objection cannot be treated lightly, given the reality that many people conceive of marriage as a lifetime commitment. Notice, however, that defending no-fault divorce does not mean endorsing the view that marriage commitments should not be permanent. People might reasonably believe—perhaps, but not necessarily, for religious reasons—that their marriages are irrevocable. Democratic justice need not deny them the freedom to hold or act on such beliefs, or challenge the veracity of such beliefs as matters of theology or domestic ethics. It merely requires that the state should not enforce commitments to beliefs about the irrevocability of marriage, whatever their source. People have a basic interest in developing and retaining the wherewithal to govern themselves democratically. As I argue in connection with the disenfranchisement of children, this is fairly compromised by necessity only, and then only by as much, and for as long, as necessity requires. People may choose to disenfranchise themselves in various circumstances, but this is not generally a choice that government should enforce.

The wisdom of this stance is reinforced by considering other agreements in which people risk disenfranchising themselves. We comfortably distinguish between enforcing wage-labor agreements and refusing to enforce contracts in which people indenture themselves into long-term servitude or sell themselves into slavery. If the goal is to underwrite people's freedom to govern themselves, enforcing agreements marked by such finality and extreme loss of autonomy is self-defeating. Only on a rigidly proceduralist view of the justness of contractual arrangements would one adopt the contrary view. Rejecting such a view is consistent with the search under democratic justice for a middle ground between procedural and substantive decision rules.

A second, traditionalist objection to the claim that marriages should be terminable unilaterally rests on appeal to the importance of stability in family relations. It leads observers like Lasch to object to the rise of no-fault divorce, arguing that divorce should be made more difficult, perhaps even impossible, to obtain.[43] Most commentators on the decline of "the family" and the need to reverse that decline focus almost exclusively on the costs of family instability for children. I have already discussed this in Chapter 4, arguing that although stability is a value in parent-child relations, it is not the only or most important one, and that it should give way when children's basic interests are threatened. As far as adult domestic relations are concerned, the state has no defensible interest in preserving domestic unions against the wishes of the relevant parties. Subsidiarity considerations suggest, rather, that it should keep out. There is a Burkean element to democratic justice, to be sure, but it is a tempered Burkeanism. The goal is to democratize social relations as we reproduce them, not to insist on preserving them unchanged merely because they exist.

A third, feminist objection is that divorce on demand enhances the bargaining power of the stronger parties in marriages, typically men. Noting that the women's movement is often unfairly accounted responsible for the move to no-fault divorce, commentators like Okin and Leonore Weitzman argue that the shift has actually weakened the position of women at divorce. Having lost the common-law protections that went with wives' traditional subordinate status in marriage, divorcing women often confront substantial and long-term economic decline.[44] In practice this creates a situation where the incentives are analogous to the problem of white flight mentioned in Chapter 3: different capacities for exit operate to the systematic advantage of those who are the stronger position.

Feminists are right to point out that the move to no-fault divorce was not the product of their political agenda, and that in some respects it may have worked to women's disadvantage.[45] It would be shortsighted, however, to oppose it for that reason. Ready access to divorce provides an avenue of escape for women who are subjected to forms of physical and psychological abuse in marriage that would often be impossible to establish in court, given the difficulty of litigation, burdens of proof, and the common problem of lack of witnesses. Moreover, there is no compelling reason to require women to satisfy a third party that they have legitimate reasons to end a marriage if that is what they want to do. Resisting no-fault divorce because of feminists' legitimate economic concerns is to conflate matters about the grounds for divorce with those relating to the terms of divorce. Because of the differences in capacities for exit, democratic justice legitimates regulation of the latter. But it would be unwise to give up on the meaningful possibility of exit as a device for promoting democratic justice within marriage.

Would it make better sense to treat the sexes differently, allowing wives, as the "structurally weaker" party, freedom to leave unilaterally, but denying this right to husbands?[46] Some might think of the employment context as suggestive here, noting that employers' exit options are sometimes more constrained, legally, than those of workers to counter the power disparities.[47] In Chapter 6 I defend such an asymmetry, arguing for a link between employers' relative freedom in this regard and the vulnerability of workers to the consequences of their decisions. Marriage warrants different treatment, however. It is not forced on people in the way that employment generally is in a market economy. Moreover, whereas equality of power between employer and worker is often unavailable (making some form of hierarchy inescapable), this need not be true of marriage. There, the aspiration to move toward a world in which people deal with one another as sovereign equals is realistic. Accordingly, a regulatory regime that makes sense for a system of enduring power inequality is inappropriate.

Most important, however, employment relations involve arms-length transactions that are often substantially competitive. Adult domestic relations differ by being intimate, and they can operate without domination only if they are basically cooperative in character. Unanimity rule generally recommends itself for cooperative social relations, and no-fault divorce is an extreme form of unanimity rule designed not to privilege the status quo. This makes sense when one reflects on the fact that the affective dimensions of adult domestic commitments cannot be forced on, or revived in, people against their wishes. Allowing one party an effective veto on divorce (which is what no-fault for wives only would amount to) ignores this reality. It makes more sense to give the veto power to whoever would end the marriage, as conventional no-fault does, and then manage the potential for domination engendered by that regime by regulating the terms of divorce.

FOCUSING ON OBSTACLES TO EXIT

Those who are vulnerable to domination within marriage often will not leave if they perceive the costs to be unacceptably high, as they frequently do. They remain partly as a result of resource disparities but also because of vulnerabilities that are embedded in the residues of patriarchialism. Millions of women continue to live in abusive relationships marked by degradation and physical violence, knowing the likelihood of successfully holding violent husbands to account is low.[48] For them, the legal freedom to leave is not enough. If the conditioning constraints of democratic justice are to be realized in their lives, husbands' remaining domestic immunities from the criminal law should be rooted out of the legal system and prevented from reentering through the back door of contractual marriage.

Insisting on the genuine possibility of exit provides a device for evaluating the legitimacy of different marital practices from the standpoint of democratic justice. This can be particularly helpful when considering hierarchical family forms, as can be seen by returning to the case of Mormon polygamy. Earlier I noted that in addition to objecting to polygamous unions on the spurious grounds of their being offensive to public morals, in *Reynolds v. United States* the Supreme Court also upheld Congress's right to proscribe them in order to prevent the injury of Mormon women, whom the trial court had described as "innocent victims of this delusion."[49]

Asymmetrical hierarchies should be presumed suspect, but this presumption is not conclusive. If people choose to enter them, or to stay in them when they could leave, this fact is often sufficient to rebut the presumption. Polygamous marriage might be part of a larger hierarchical social order and sustained by the legal system, as in some Islamic countries, severely limiting the exit options for women. Alternatively, it might be the spontaneous creation of a particular group or religious community that does not seek to impose it on others or to retain its adherents by force. The latter kind of polygamy fares notably better than the former by the standards of democratic justice, because we have reasons to think that women's continuing presence in optional polygamous marriages reflects their authentic desires. There is always the possibility that they have been brainwashed, of course, and arguments to this effect cannot be dismissed out of hand. But their proponents will have to come to grips with the eloquently reasoned denials of this by some Mormon women who insist, for instance, that polygamy "is good for feminism" on the grounds that it makes it easier for women to have both a career and a family.[50]

One might reasonably be skeptical of such a claim without doubting the sincerity or sanity of those who accept and act on it; if so, the argument for democratic justice suggests that their polygamy should be tolerated. No doubt there will be disagreements in particular cases over the whether women genuinely have the wherewithal to leave, but this difficulty is not unique to polygamy. Nor does the fact that there are bound to be disagreements over such questions undermine the general claim that policies geared toward preserving the possibility of exit can be expected to diminish the degree to which hierarchical marriage forms are imposed on those who do not want to be governed by them.[51]

COERCION

Traditionally, many actions by husbands toward wives and their property that would be criminal or tortious in other circumstances could not be prosecuted.[52] Husbands never enjoyed blanket immunity from criminal prosecution (for murder, say), but they enjoyed great latitude to beat and otherwise abuse their wives with virtual impunity. This liberty has eroded in recent decades, as is signaled by the move toward abolishing the marital rape exception. The doctrine of interspousal tort immunity has also been fading, partly via evolution of common law and partly by such statutes as Congress's Violence Against Women Act of 1994.[53] Increasingly, courts will entertain actions between spouses concerning damage or destruction of property, battery, defamation, infliction of emotional distress, and other criminal and noncriminal harms. This trend toward wholesale abolition of interspousal tort immunity is likely to be more or less complete throughout the United States by the end of the century.[54]

Proponents of democratic justice should welcome these changes and argue for their acceleration. There is no defensible reason to shield husbands from liability for what would otherwise be criminal or tortious conduct. To the extent that marriage should survive as a status at all, it should not generate any such immunities. As I have argued, from the state's point of view marriage should constitute nothing more than a convenient system of default institutions, regulated with an eye to undermining the characteristic ways in which consensual governance is liable either to break down or to foster domination. Publicly enforced constraints on marriage are necessary for that purpose, but they should exclude policies that outstrip this subordinate or conditioning mandate.

An important class of necessary constraints on marriage concerns agreements to limit liability for harmful acts. Just as the system of default institutions should not immunize people from liability for what would otherwise be crimes or torts, so designer marriages and prenuptial agreements should shield perpetrators only to the extent that this would be possible outside the marriage context. People cannot generally waive most forms of criminal liability through contractual arrangements. Accordingly, agreements to achieve this result among those who marry should be unenforceable.[55] Likewise with such criminal torts as assault and battery.[56] People should be no more able to give up the law's protections by contract in marriage than in other walks of life.[57] All remaining patriarchal protections from liability for rape, assault and battery, and other forms of domination and abuse within marriage ought to be abolished, and it should be impossible to re-create these protections by contract.

RESOURCES

Deferring to insider's wisdom often conflicts with the conditioning demands of democratic justice. The tension is particularly acute in the adult domestic arena. On the one hand, people comprehend their personal involvements in intensely private ways, and they reasonably resist prying eyes. Intimacy defies inspection. Recognizing this supplies part of the rationale for defending a robust form of localism in thinking about the shaping and operation of marital institutions. On the other hand, perpetrators of spousal abuse also resist third-party inspection. They often appeal to the sanctity of intimacy to evade being called to account for their actions. All too frequently they are successful, as the data on domestic violence reveal.[58]

As different as intimacy and domination may be from one another, they can be hard to tell apart in practice. As a result, respecting intimacy while preventing secret domination presents formidable challenges. In the limiting case, consenting adults who engage in sadomasochistic sex may live worlds apart from battered and abused women who are immobilized by fear from trying to leave abusive circumstances.[59] But that does not mean we can easily devise institutions to prevent the latter without interfering with the former. Only a small minority engages in consensual sadomasochism, to be sure, but the example highlights the difficulty of distinguishing the cases where interference is warranted from those where it is not. Proponents of democratic justice should, in any case, be skeptical of moving toward a world in which government inspectors check on the daily conduct of ongoing marriages. Such zeal to stamp out injustice would subvert genuine intimacy. Instead, the search should be for better subordinate constraints that can prevent injustice without undermining authentic consensual intimacy.

An indirect approach is better in these circumstances, geared to empowering those at risk of suffering abuse and domination to avoid it for themselves. In addition to freedom from fear for their physical safety if they remain in a relationship, people need the resources to survive once they have left, and to make new lives for themselves. This suggests a dual approach: better strategies are needed to encourage victims to blow whistles on abusers, but attention must also be paid to the external context. In the immediate term people need safe havens to escape in crisis situations; in the longer term they need to know that leaving is not a life sentence to grinding poverty.[60]

Part of what is required is for government to go beyond lip service in enforcing the criminal law in domestic contexts. If everyone knows that authorities will prosecute credible charges of spousal rape and assault, battered and abused wives will be more likely to pursue them in the relevant circumstances than if, as all too often remains the case, nominal enforcement is the most that can be expected. When abusers are ignored by the police, restraining orders are not enforced, and apprehension and conviction are routinely followed by warnings and minimal sentences, a culture of expectations is sustained in which domestic violence is not seen as "real" crime.[61] Perpetrators feel free to continue their abuse, and victims all too rationally perceive that trying to alter their circumstances may actually make them worse. Unless that culture is replaced by one of predictable law enforcement, cycles of domestic violence are unlikely to be broken.[62]

Important as legal resources are, often they are not enough to assure victims the wherewithal to break cycles of spousal abuse. At critical moments many also need centers for battered women and counseling help, notwithstanding the claims of Lasch and others that well-intentioned plans to assist married women who are victims of oppression can foster dependence on social workers and the helping professions. Those are dangers to be guarded against, to be sure. But the alternative is worse in a world in which extended families have diminished as networks of support and abused spouses are often decisively dependent for financial and other forms of security on their abusers. The hidden and unchecked power of the spouse batterer must surely be judged more dangerous than the public authority of those who operate shelters and who counsel victims of domestic abuse.

Unless people know that they can generate the resources to survive outside their relationships, their continuing presence within those relationships cannot be judged consensual. This suggests that they should be able to know that they could vindicate their basic interests were they to leave. What this requires in practice depends partly on the local facts of particular marriages, but only partly. It also depends on the external context—the constraints and opportunities those contemplating life outside of existing marriages must confront. In the contemporary United States, where resources ranging from health insurance to retirement benefits may be tied to a spouse's employment, the costs of leaving can be substantial and the possibility of people remaining in marriages they would otherwise leave is correspondingly strong. This likelihood of structural coercion within marriage is lower in countries where the social wage is more robust. The universal availability of health insurance, unemployment compensation, and pensions detaches the needs they serve from the power dynamics of marriage. It avoids situations in which a spouse who stands to lose the benefits in question may be in the control of one who does not. Accordingly, there are fewer grounds, in such circumstances, for suspicion that people might become trapped in marriages that they would otherwise leave.

Government's obligation to regulate the terms of divorce becomes stronger as such suspicions grow, with a result that initially might seem paradoxical: the more people's basic interests are socialized or otherwise underwritten by the state, the more laissez-faire it should be in regulating the economic terms of domestic life. In fact, this is not paradoxical at all. The closer the social wage comes to ensuring that people can protect their basic interests, the less scope there is for others to dominate them by taking advantage of their necessity. In Chapter 6 I develop this line of thinking more generally, arguing that governments in market economies should be obliged to underwrite basic interests that are not vindicated through employment as a means of promoting democratic justice within the firm. Without rehearsing that larger thesis, it suffices to note here that although democratic justice recommends a robust social wage approach as preferable, failure to take this path legitimates—indeed, requires—a more interventionist regime in structuring divorce settlements.

A question that courts should always ask of proposed settlements is whether, given the prevailing needs and the external context, they provide resources adequate to protect the basic interests of all concerned once the marriage is dissolved. In the economic context, this means keeping people out of poverty in the short term and ensuring that they can develop the assets and human capital, given the prevailing structure of opportunities, to remain out of it in the longer term. Recall that it is not only the parties themselves who fairly expect to be able to vindicate their basic interests; third parties reasonably expect this of them as well. Accordingly, courts should reject settlements that avoidably threaten either party's basic interests, and provisions in prenuptial contracts that would have this effect for either party should not be enforced.

What if poverty following divorce is unavoidable? There are two relevant cases here: when the parties are in poverty already, and when the breakup of the family unit would push some or all of them into poverty. In the first case there is obviously no answer linked to the divorce settlement. The state is already failing in its underwriting responsibilities as I argue for them in Chapter 6, and nothing in a settlement will alter that reality. In the second case, some might suggest that couples should be forced to stay together to avoid poverty, either directly by a court's refusing to enter a divorce decree, or indirectly, as Galston and others have proposed, by terminating certain income-support benefits to people who divorce.[63] Democratic justice bids us reject all proposals of this kind. The dangers of removing exit options for those at risk for abuse and domination have already been dealt with in the course of defending no-fault divorce. Public policy should be moving in the contrary direction, removing obstacles to exit rather than creating new ones.[64] Third-party attempts to force disaffected couples to remain together are in any case unrealistic. The authentic intimacy and cooperative living characteristic of viable adult domestic partnerships in a modern democracy cannot be forced on people.

Children should be considered in the same way, at divorce, as others dependent on the family budget. Government's fiduciary responsibility to them is unaffected by the parents' decision to separate. It is, indeed, a time for particular vigilance with respect to that responsibility, given the upheavals and antagonisms often associated with divorce. Courts should evaluate proposed divorce settlements from the perspective of how well they are likely to serve children's basic interests, as I argue in Chapter 4.[65] And just as courts and other public agencies should not be able to force adults to stay together as a condition for underwriting their basic interests, nor should they be free to use their fiduciary responsibility for children to achieve this result. Policies such as denying child-support payments to those who divorce is doubly illegitimate from the standpoint of democratic justice. There is no justification for the goal, and children who cannot affect the outcome bear the costs.

Once basic interests have been guaranteed as well as possible at divorce, courts should be less interventionist in dealing with disputes among divorcing parties and the enforceability of their prenuptial agreements. We have already seen that democratic justice takes no position on how child-custody disputes should be settled other than seeing to it that children's basic interests not be threatened.[66] With adults, the state's concern to underwrite basic interests has different roots: in guaranteeing a continuing freedom to exit for the weaker party, and minimizing the proportion of the population whose basic interests may be violated. Once this has been done, democratic justice suggests that the state's interest in the financial and other arrangements surrounding divorce should diminish. Courts should deal with it like other long-term contractual arrangements that break down.

DIVISION OF ASSETS AT DIVORCE

The Married Women's Property Acts eventually destroyed the common-law rule that had given the husband control, and sometimes title, to the wife's property and possessions during marriage. Yet the regime that has replaced it is far from settled, as is reflected in the fact that division of property is second only to custody disputes as the most litigated aspect of divorce proceedings.[67] That the law of property division is replacing alimony as the main device for adjusting the financial relationships of the spouses makes sense from the standpoint of democratic justice. Traditionally, alimony was a subsistence payment from the husband or his estate to the wife, a consequence of his duty to support which came with the marriage dowry and was enshrined in his marriage vows. The justification for alimony was rooted in the fiction that the marriage did not actually terminate.[68] By its terms alimony treated the wife as a dependent creature, so that his obligation to support ceased only with her death or remarriage. This doctrine is anachronistic in a world in which neither party loses independence of personhood as a consequence of marriage, let alone in a world of no-fault divorce. It is unsurprising, therefore, that alimony is seldom affirmed in its traditional form by American courts.[69] Increasingly alimony is awarded for a fixed term and a defined purpose only. Usually it is "rehabilitative alimony," wherein a spouse who has been a homemaker is supported for sufficient time and to a sufficient degree to attain the needed skills and qualifications to make the transition back into the labor market.[70] This makes sense in light of my earlier analysis, provided that the rehabilitative alimony is adequate for recipients to develop the wherewithal to vindicate their basic interests outside the marriage.

The old system of marital property has been replaced by two regimes in America. Some "community property" states have passed statutes that make property acquired during the marriage, and sometimes before it, jointly owned and susceptible to equal division at divorce. The other "common-law property" states treat each spouse as owning his or her own property individually. Courts in these states are now generally guided by an equitable rule at divorce. This provision is geared to achieving fairness, given calculations about the relevant counterfactuals, the duration of the marriage and what the parties did during it, and other contingent factors.[71]

The argument for democratic justice does not supply us with decisive reasons to choose between these regimes, or between the distributive principles that guide them. There is merit to the flexibility inherent in the common-law approach, which allows courts to arrive at an equitable division taking all factors into account. Yet it gives great discretionary power to judges who tend to be white, male, conservative, and upper middle class; their prejudices may be systematically biased. The very flexibility of the common-law approach (and the lack of predictability that entails) may also promote litigation, with both sides having incentives to gamble on the benefits of going to trial rather than reaching a settlement. Opting for a community property regime with equal division avoids some of these difficulties. But as my earlier discussion of Okin revealed, this comes at the price of creating injustice in particular cases (where equity suggests that a spouse does not have a credible claim to half of the community resources). Various hybrids of these systems can also, perhaps, be defended.[72] Just what the advantages and pitfalls of the different systems will be can be discovered only as they operate on the ground, and it is one of the advantages of a federal system that various systems can be experimented with simultaneously.[73]

More controversial and interesting from the standpoint of democratic justice is the definition of property itself. Okin and others have pointed out that equal and equitable rules of division systematically undervalue domestic work, so that even when property is formally divided equally or equitably

at divorce, systematic gender disparities in earnings power are often exacer-
bated by the difficulties for women of reentering the workforce after years
of absence from it. This is partly why divorcing women generally face both
absolute declines in their standards of living and growing disparities between
their incomes and standards of living and those of their ex-husbands.[74]

These problems are not insurmountable, and some courts have begun to
explore ways of grappling with them. One revealing illustration of the possibilities occurred in 1985 in New York (not a community-property state) in
O'Brien v. O'Brien, a contested division of property, when a husband's license
to practice medicine was held to be marital property on the grounds that "the
contributions of one spouse to the other's profession or career . . . represent
investments in the economic partnership of the marriage and the product of
the parties' joint efforts." The divorcing wife was awarded 40 percent of the
estimated value of the license, to be paid over eleven years, and the divorcing husband was ordered to maintain a life insurance policy for the unpaid
balance of the award, with the divorcing wife named as the beneficiary.[75]

The logic behind the trial court's allocation in this case was not entirely
clear. It rested on some unexplained commitment to the virtue of propor-
tionality of rewards for work, and an interpretation of the totality of relevant
facts about the marriage that emerged from the divorce litigation. Had the
judge decided on a fifty-fifty or a seventy-thirty split of the interest in the
medical license, however, it would be difficult to know whether this better
reflected the parties' relative contributions. In any case, it would likely have
been affirmed on appeal on the grounds that—unless there was evidence that
discretion below has been abused—the trier of fact is presumed to be in the
best position to settle questions of this kind. This might sound like rough
justice to political theorists, but in practice it may be the best that can be
done in such circumstances.

The *O'Brien* outcome is defensible from the perspective of democratic
justice. Whether an equal rule or an equitable rule is to be applied when a
marriage dissolves, the results may be systematically biased against those who
perform unpaid domestic labor, contributing to the feminization of poverty
and the systematic subordination of divorced women to ex-husbands with
whom they may have to maintain economic ties for many years.[76] Likewise,
democratic justice should lead us to endorse the approaches of courts that
regard such items as retirement benefits and intangible business assets (such

as business goodwill) as marital or community property for the purposes of apportionment at divorce. Such moves strengthen the position of the economically weaker party, minimizing the likelihood of divorce settlements that foster domination.[77] Incorporating them into the system of default institutions would therefore be an advance for democratic justice.

ENFORCING PRENUPTIAL AGREEMENTS

Whatever the system of default institutions, democratic justice does require that for the most part people should be free to modify it by contract. In a world of evolving experimental regimes, where we do not expect everyone to want the same arrangements, there is no reason to deny them this freedom. So long as their freedom to exit is not jeopardized by the economic and other arrangements they choose to make, there is no good reason to force arrangements on people that they do not want.

Most states now recognize prenuptial agreements as legitimate, but they differ on what aspects of the domestic partnership may be governed by them and on what principles should be employed in interpreting them. On the former, courts have generally (but not universally) shied away from enforcing aspects of prenuptial agreements that would involve them in an ongoing marriage, such as attempts to enforce an agreement to raise children in a certain religious faith.[78] Courts have preferred to keep out unless and until marriages are actually breaking down. On the question of interpretation, they have divided over whether to interpret prenuptial agreements by contract-law principles, in which case the principal concern is whether they were fair at the time they were made (that is, they met the statute of frauds and were not unconscionable), or by family-law principles, in which case the principal concern is whether they are fair at the time they are implemented (usually divorce or the death of one of the parties). The latter approach is more paternalistic in that it questions the inherent ability of people to foresee their future wishes over long periods of time and protects them from the folly of trying to do so.[79]

On the interpretive question, democratic justice suggests a hybrid approach. So far as preserving the capacity to leave is concerned, the situation at the time of dissolution is what is relevant, and no agreement should be enforced that avoidably violates the basic interests of an affected party. The freedom to leave cannot be contracted away, so whatever is judged necessary to preserve that capacity at the time of dissolution should trump the contents of any prenuptial agreement. This consideration apart, there would seem to be no good reason for the state to take a paternalistic stance toward prenuptial agreements, and generally they should be enforced like any other contract, as written. Within the constraints just mentioned, if people want to take the risks inherent in departing from the protections built into the system of default institutions, there is no good reason to prevent their so doing.[80]

On the question whether courts should avoid getting involved to enforce agreements in ongoing marriages (as opposed to marriages that are breaking down), there is no general reason consistent with the argument of democratic justice why they should not. There may be provisions in these agreements that are impossible to enforce, or too costly for the parties continuously to litigate, but that does not differentiate prenuptial agreements from other contracts. Courts have ways of discouraging frivolous lawsuits; beyond this, if a couple wants to waste all its resources taking one another to court, the state should not prevent their doing this. Individuals and corporations do it in other contexts all the time. Why treat married people differently? True, taking one another to court over disagreements scarcely exemplifies the intimacy and cooperation that I have described as characteristic of modern marriage. However, in noncriminal settings, deciding whether or not litigation is compatible with an ongoing marriage should be up to the parties, not outsiders.[81]

SPECIAL PRIVILEGES OF MARRIAGE

Evaluating special privileges that historically have gone with marriage presents democratic justice with different complexities. These privileges have included such things as tax advantages, employment and health insurance benefits, procedural privileges in legal proceedings, and related perquisites. When, if ever, can these be justified?[82]

Members of some unorthodox groups have argued that they should receive all privileges that currently attach to the marriage status. The cases that prompt such demands reveal that great injustices can be done when this extension of privileges is denied, as when lifetime cohabitants discover that they cannot inherit as spouses, or some other benefit of the marriage status is denied them. Cohabitants have successfully altered some aspects of these exclusions in recent years. Courts have begun to recognize their standing to bring actions for loss of consortium, for instance.[83] There is no reason to bar such actions from the standpoint of democratic justice, but it is less clear that other special privileges of the marriage status should be extended to unorthodox and cohabiting couples. Consider the fact that in some American jurisdictions in recent decades the marital rape exception has been extended to cohabiting couples.[84] This example reminds us that special privileges can be vestiges of the patriarchialism we should be seeking to undermine. Privileges that permit or foster domination within marriage should be abolished, not extended to achieve equal treatment of marriage and unconventional domestic unions.

But what of privileges that lack this character? What of different tax treatment for married couples, better employment, health and insurance benefits, and the rights of testimonial privilege that limit the testimony spouses can be compelled (and in some circumstances permitted) to give against one another in court? In general, the answer is that privileges that go beyond the transactions–cost minimizing logic discussed earlier—in that they are geared to promoting and subsidizing a particular marital form—should be presumed suspect. Perhaps some such privileges can be justified consistent with the argument for democratic justice. This should have to be established on a case-by-case basis, however, with the burden of persuasion falling on the defender of the privilege in question. The traditional justification for barring testimony by spouses against one another in court, for instance, was linked to the common-law suspension of the wife's legal identity during marriage. Once that suspension was abandoned, so, too, was the rationale, and the bar began to disappear. It has now been almost universally abandoned, partly because spouses could scarcely be prosecuted for crimes and torts against one another if injured plaintiffs could not testify. This is a welcome development for democratic justice, because the common-law justification for the rule, and the fiction from which it was derived, are indefensible.

This does not mean that every aspect of the law of testimonial privilege should be abandoned, however. Many jurisdictions retain some variant of the rule that spouses cannot be compelled to testify against one another. There may be justifications for retaining this rule that do not appeal to the old common-law status of wives. It may be likened to the attorney-client privilege, the doctor-patient privilege, or the sanctity of confessions to a priest. These analogies suggest that there may be wisdom in protecting the privacy of spousal communications when both parties desire this, given the nature of the relationships in question and the intimate character of much that goes on within them. Such a justification for retaining a ban on compelled spousal testimony need not run afoul the argument of democratic justice, although for reasons already mentioned it would not allow us to endorse the suppression of testimony by one spouse at the request of the other.[85]

Issues like employment benefits and health insurance present different complexities. They are taken up more fully later. Here I conclude that when benefits essential to basic interests are linked to spouses' employment, there is no principled justification for not extending the same links to cohabiting and other unorthodox couples. It is difficult to see what principled justification could be given, consistent with democratic justice, for preferential treatment of orthodox couples in such contexts.[86] Indeed, we should go further and argue, as I do in Chapter 6, that if the state underwrites a system in which benefits essential to basic interests are tied to a spouse's employment, government should be bound, also, to find ways to extend comparable benefits to unemployed and single people who may not be reached through employment-related mechanisms of this kind.[87]

· 6 ·

Controlling Work

WORK PRESENTS DEMOCRATIC JUSTICE with challenges and possibilities that differ from those discussed in the preceding two chapters, though there is some overlap with each. Like the adult domestic realm, work in market-based industrial societies generally involves fully competent adults who are presumed sovereign over their interests.[1] Also in parallel with the adult domestic realm, work revolves around voluntary individual transactions that take place in larger, more or less coercive, contexts. Like adult-child relations, on the other hand, much work involves unequally distributed knowledge and expertise, hierarchical organization, and substantial exercises of power. True, the organization of work is not inevitably hierarchical in many of the ways in which adult-child relations are, and partly for this reason there is now an extensive literature on the democratic control of the firm. But at least in many circumstances there are tensions between the productive efficiency of firms, however measured, and the democratic control of work. As a result, questions arise for democratic justice that are analogous to those discussed in Chapter 4. What constraints should there be on hierarchies within firms? How should these constraints be decided on and who should police them? Generally, what scope is there for democratic justice to condition labor relations while retaining its hallmark subordinate status?

The realm of work also presents democratic justice with distinctive challenges arising from its complexity. Employers and employees are perhaps the most visible players in modern industrial and postindustrial economies, but other pertinent actors and institutions must be taken into account as well. The separation of ownership from control of many corporations raises questions about the nature and role of stockholders. Power, in the world of work, is also exercised by, over, and within trade unions. Then there are those, most obviously domestic workers, who work outside the money economy but are nonetheless dependent on it. Nor should we forget the unemployed, significant not only for the difficulties they face in having to survive without work but also because of their role in shaping the power context in which management deals with labor. Attending to this power context raises additional questions about the more or less visible realm of global corporations and investors, central banks, and international financial institutions. In varying degrees—though increasingly for many countries—international capital, credit, and currency markets shape the context of employment relations within countries. Finally, every modern industrial economy is to some degree a mixed economy. This means that governments are not mere regulatory players. Even after more than a decade and a half of more or less aggressive privatization in most OECD countries, their governments continue to be large employers, accounting for between 6.7 percent (Japan) and 27.7 percent (Norway) of all employment.[2] The percentages are greater in much of the developing world, and despite the collapse of communism and concomitant growth of private sectors in the east, many postcommunist governments continue as large employers, if not the largest, in their countries.[3]

The Inherited Context: Workmanship Suffused by the Market

Market relations are the main forces shaping the control of work in the world we have inherited. How and why this came to be so are much-debated subjects that need not concern us in detail. True, things might perhaps have developed differently, and unearthing a system's origins can be a useful corrective to the impulse to reify current arrangements as inescapable. But this can be overdone. The path-dependence of historical change often rules out the possibility of reviving the status quo ante; even if viable nonmarket orders have or might have existed, evolving toward them from current circumstances might be impossible. Such counterfactual speculations are — in any case — antithetical to the spirit of democratic justice, whose purpose is to find viable ways of democratizing existing social relations. Returning us to an idealized past is no more part of its agenda than is crafting blueprints for a perfect future. Our concern with institutional redesign does require us to keep an eye on how inherited constraints may shape the possibilities as we move into the future, but it is where we are now that sets the terms of the enterprise.

THE DUAL-MARKET DYNAMIC

Market relations shape work in two related ways in today's world. Goods and services produced by human work are traded in markets, but so is the capacity to work itself. The first type of market has existed for many centuries. The second is more recent; it interacts with the first, resulting in capitalist labor relations.[4] These are relations in which most people sell their capacities to work for a given time to others, then use the proceeds of that sale to buy goods and services that they consume. Some of this consumption is optional, but much of it is essential to human survival. This reality creates the foundational power dynamic of capitalist labor relations: most people must work for others in order to survive. No doubt, even when they are not driven by survival needs, people in capitalist systems may often choose to work, even to work for others. This complicates the issue, raising subsidiary questions for democratic justice. But the most important issues involve interactions between the dual-market dynamic and constraints of human necessity.

Conventional justifications of the dual-market dynamic combine the allure of utilitarian efficiency with affirmations of individual rights. On the efficiency front, markets facilitate advances in the division of labor, which is, as Adam Smith noted, the single most important engine of productivity yet devised.[5] Markets also cope with the information problems of complex production more efficiently than any planned system yet conceived. They give investors and producers focused incentives to discover — and respond to — consumers' desires, and to remain at the cutting edge of innovative technologies. It is no accident that modern utilitarianism has developed in tandem with neoclassical market theory; their joint preoccupation with efficiency often leads to mutually reinforcing prescriptions.

Markets in productive capacities affirm individual rights by legitimating the idea of self-ownership. If people did not own themselves they would not, after all, be in a position to sell the use of *their* productive capacities. Indeed, market-based wage labor differs from slavery because the slave can be owned by another, whereas the employee cannot. She sells the use of her productive capacities for a given time and under specified conditions but continues to own both what she earns from selling the use of those capacities and the capacities themselves. Hence the appeal of the term *human capital;* it connotes that every human is sovereign over a productive self.[6] By making available the use of her human capital at the market-clearing rate, the individual appears to retain sovereignty over herself while at the same time contributing to overall efficiency.

The synthesis of rights and utility as expressed through the dual-market dynamic has great ideological power partly because it takes account of the value that human beings place on work. Most people spend more than a third of their conscious lives working.[7] This is partly rooted in necessity, and people often chafe at the arduous and constraining dimensions of laboring as a result. Yet despite what economists might say, few see work exclusively as "alienated" labor, at least in principle, or as something that, if feasible, a rational person would rather avoid in favor of "leisure." People might object to what their work currently demands of them, to the pay or status that goes with it, or to the manner in which it is organized. But for many people in many circumstances the vocational dimensions to work surpass its roots in the necessities of survival. Whether in the world of work as they now know it or as they would like it to be, people look to work to satisfy ambition, to transform environments, to realize creative impulses, and to open up new frontiers of human endeavor.[8] Marx and Engels might have overstated things by identifying productive work as *the* defining feature of the human condition.[9] Yet they were surely right that it is *a* central feature.

LOCKEAN WORKMANSHIP AND THE RIGHTS-UTILITY SYNTHESIS

Two centuries before Marx and Engels wrote, Locke offered a version of the rights-utility synthesis that repays attention from the standpoint of democratic justice. The extent of Locke's influence is not always fully appreciated, yet aspects of his formulations continue to shape modern arguments in support of the dual-market dynamic. Although, as will become apparent, Locke's account of the rights-utility synthesis is more seriously flawed than his discussion of adult-child relations that launched our investigation in Chapter 4, significant aspects of it usefully survive critical scrutiny, and his failures are themselves illuminating for democratic justice. Pursuing their implications provides a powerful rationale for insisting on the priority of employees' basic interests over the demands of efficiency in the workplace, as well as grounds for a political defense of a robust social wage. More fundamentally, the arguments I develop here to expose the limitations of neo-Lockean views buttress my own overall case: that if the dual-market dynamic is plausibly to be defended by appeal to the rights-utility synthesis, this dynamic should be constrained by the requirements of democratic justice.

Locke's account of the rights and obligations surrounding work is elegant, coherent, and—if one embraces all the premises to which he was committed —compelling. He saw natural resources as comprising a minor part of the value of produced goods and services, the great majority of which resulted from human work.[10] Against Filmer (who had maintained that God gave the world to Adam and his heirs via a system of primogeniture), Locke insisted that God gave the world to mankind in common, subject to the provisos that it not be wasted, and that "enough, and as good" remain available to others to use in common.[11] The rights and obligations surrounding work were thus intimately bound up, in Locke's account, with his natural-law commitments.

Making, for Locke, entails ownership. In the first instance, this is why humans are constrained by God's natural law. As created beings, they are "the Workmanship of one Omnipotent, and infinitely wise Maker. . . . They are his Property, whose Workmanship they are, made to last during his, not one another's pleasure."[12] But they are unique among God's creations, for Locke, because he gave them capacities to make, and thus to create ownership rights of their own. Natural law dictates that humans are subject to divine imperatives to live in certain ways, but within the limits set by natural law they act—as Tully notes—in a Godlike fashion: "Man as maker . . . has analogous maker's knowledge of, and a natural right in his intentional actions." In contrast to the situation with children (where God is the creator and humans mere instruments), human makers are sovereign over produced goods and services. So long as they do not violate natural law, they stand in the same relation to the objects they create as God stands in to them; people own what they make just as God owns them.[13]

Within the constraints of natural law, Locke saw the rights and obligations surrounding human work as substantially determined by market arrangements. Indeed, he was convinced that the productivity effects of the dual-market dynamic could justify a wage-labor regime.[14] This conviction led to his famous insistence that "the turfs my servant has cut . . . become my property" and his endorsement of a state of affairs in which "a free man makes himself a servant to another, by selling him for a certain time, the service he undertakes to do, in exchange for wages he is to receive."[15] Locke believed that the dual-market dynamic enhances productivity so much that it also justifies the enclosure—effectively the privatization—of common land, the natural-law proviso protecting universal access to the common notwithstanding. For "he who appropriates land to himself by his labour, does not lessen but increase the common stock of mankind." The goods produced on an acre of enclosed land are at least ten—more like a hundred—times more than those "yielded by an acre of Land, of an equal richnesse, lyeing wast in common." As a result, someone who encloses ten acres "may truly be said, to give ninety acres to Mankind," at least.[16] Locke saw these productivity increases as buttressed by the move to a money economy, which, for all practical purposes, rendered the natural-law proscription of waste obsolete.[17]

Impressed by the productivity effects of the dual-market dynamic, Locke thus believed the emerging economic order capacious enough to give legitimate expression to our God-given creative capacities within the constraints of natural law. Yet Locke's endorsement of the dynamic was contingent all the way down: if the market failed to have the predicted effects for all, then the natural-law constraints must again come into play.[18] The right to preservation guaranteed a starving person a right to another's plenty and the able-bodied poor the right to work (albeit in workhouses or other near-coercive conditions), or, failing that, to subsistence equivalent to what might have been gleaned from the common.[19] To be sure, there would be disputes about when and how the natural-law requirements are triggered and about what they would mean in particular instances that the natural-law theory could not by itself resolve.[20] But if the theory left balancing the competing claims of natural law and human workmanship open to interpretation and political argument at least at the margins, it also undermined the presumption that whatever the dual-market dynamic produces must supersede competing just claims.[21]

Rethinking Locke's Account

Two principal tasks confront any attempt at a convincing reformulation of Locke's account of the rights and obligations surrounding contemporary work. One involves dealing in a more plausible way than Locke did with the contingencies that carry so much freight in his endorsement of the dual-market dynamic. The second is to replace the natural-law foundations of his account with convincing secular ones, a large task because significant parts of Locke's argument here are less easily severable from his natural-law formulations than is the case with his model of child rearing discussed in Chapter 4. Before turning to these questions, it is useful to explain why—for all its vulnerabilities—Locke's basic outlook fits well with both the governance and opposition dimensions of democratic justice.

On the governance side of the equation, Locke's model is explicitly inclusive in its range and is rooted in the principle of affected interest. Prior to the enclosure of land, no one may be denied access to the common—explicitly said to be given by God to all—or exclude others from its nonexclusive use. Privatization is justified only when it promises all those affected by the change that they will be as well off as if their access to the common had been left undisturbed. Privatization does nothing, however, to extinguish their equal claims. It assumes, rather, that the private regime services those claims better than did the common one. Anyone for whom this turns out not to be so must be entitled to compensatory sustenance from another's plenty or the collective bounty. Locke may be less than satisfying as to just how such compensation should be calibrated and implemented, and democratic justice parts company with his account once those issues come centrally into focus. But a Lockean argument for the continuing existence of the universal constraint is worth holding onto. It shifts the burden of justification to those who would limit the claims of some.

From the opposition standpoint, democratic justice can applaud Locke's linking the justification of the dual-market dynamic to the requirement that it be compatible with what justice requires. There may be good reasons to endorse outcomes that the dynamic generates, but Locke affirms that the status quo may always be opposed, and revised, if it violates the provisos or other natural-law constraints. In the normal course of things this would be pursued through the political process, but there are circumstances in which it might even trigger the right to revolution.[22] Locke's account is generally consistent with the insistence of democratic justice that, to be legitimate, imposed arrangements operate in the interests of those who are forced to accept them, that they be open to all comers rather than the preserve of an insulated subset, and that the costs of exit and external effects be taken into account when evaluating them. Admittedly, for the dual-market dynamic to pass the tests implied by these injunctions, much will need to occur that Locke's sanguine picture of the dual-market dynamic prevented his confronting. Yet the terms of his underlying account are attractive, not least because they emphasize that the dual-market dynamic is not self-justifying. Rather, it must be evaluated in light of the interests of those on whom it is imposed.

EFFICIENCY VERSUS DISTRIBUTION

Locke's appeal to the rights-utility synthesis in justification of the dual-market dynamic runs into difficulties related to both of its components. The utilitarian difficulties, having to do with the distributive impact of appeals to efficiency, are well known and need not long detain us. Defenses of particular economic orders for their propensity to produce greater quantities of wealth than the going alternatives generally gloss over the possibility that they may nonetheless operate to the detriment of some. Locke's account is no exception. His remark that he who encloses an acre of land contributes at least ten times its unenclosed value to "mankind" begins to look dubious once the collective is disaggregated into the individuals who comprise it. Full-blown utilitarians can duck this, either by taking the classical tack and arguing that, whatever the consequences for a given individual, the greatest happiness of the greatest number is the ultimate court of appeal, or the neoclassical tack of ruling out interpersonal comparisons of utility. Both these solutions grate against many sensibilities, and it is not surprising that authors like Locke turn to trickle-down arguments in order to blunt the obvious criticisms. The reality that there is no necessary relation between the quantity of wealth produced and its distribution, however, leaves these arguments perpetually vulnerable to empirical attack. In the face of such phenomena as structural unemployment and regressive redistribution via the market, Locke would be bound to back away from his trickle-down assertions, conceding that the natural-law provisos once again come into play.

Locke never confronted this possibility explicitly, though others—notably

John Roemer—have done so through what might be described as a neo-Lockean lens.[23] Roemer defines exploitation via an opportunity-cost notion. In any economy, a dominated group is described as exploited if there is a feasible alternative arrangement in which its members' lots would improve and the lots of those who remain would worsen were the dominated group to depart for that alternative, taking their fair share of the existing society's assets.[24] Under capitalism the dominated group is imagined to withdraw, taking its members' per capita share of nonhuman alienable property and their own inalienable assets. The question is then asked: would they be better off, and those who remain worse off, than under the status quo? If the answer is yes, they are exploited. Although Roemer does not describe it as such, his thought experiment is Lockean in the sense being explored here: it is designed to equalize "every agent's access to society's inalienable property (non-human means of production) in constructing the hypothetical alternative."[25] Roemer's question is not whether there are mutual gains from trade in wage labor (captured in Joan Robinson's quip to the effect that the one thing worse than being exploited is not being exploited), but rather whether there are people now subject to the dual-market dynamic who would do better if they could depart it for a feasible alternative while retaining their human capital and equal access to existing nonhuman capital assets.

Roemer's test captures what draws people to a Lockean outlook: it embraces self-ownership and endorses individual appropriation, but only up to the point at which this begins to occur at the expense of others. The test encapsulates the rights-utility synthesis without rendering it dependent on the trickle-down hypothesis, yet it is sensitive to the alleged advantages of trickle-down if they really eventuate. A trickle-down defense of the dual-market dynamic can pass muster, but only when it survives the opportunity-cost test. Roemer's formulation has the additional advantage of not relying, as Locke's account implausibly did, on the existence of a precollective condition to which return is in principle possible. The question is not whether the dominated group can, with profit, wind the clock back to an era when everyone lived from the common (which in any case never existed in a pure form). Rather, it is whether a feasible alternative now exists, such that the dominated would be better off withdrawing on the terms Roemer describes. This seems to me the most plausible contemporary rendition of the spirit behind Locke's constraints on the dual-market dynamic, designed to guar-

antee universal fair access to the resources on and with which people work
to produce valuable goods and services.

Roemer's account is more clearly and fully specified than was Locke's, and
partly for that reason it brings the difficulties attending opportunity-cost
conceptions clearly into view. The counterfactual measurement problems
attending any attempt to determine whether the test has been met are immense, not only because of predictable disagreements about what is to count
as a feasible alternative system but also because of the essentially speculative
nature of calculating how a given individual would fare in such a system.
Moreover, even if such calculations could be made, there is no reason to be
confident that they would yield results that Roemer would find congenial,
for the opportunity-cost test need not be egalitarian in effect. Indeed, even
some who might be on the verge of starvation in the present system could
fail the test. Egalitarians like Roemer do not confront these possibilities,
perhaps because they believe that those disadvantaged in the present order
are being taken advantage of by others. Often they are, but even when this
is so they might not do better relying on themselves and a per capita share
of society's present resources in a feasible alternative system.

WORKMANSHIP'S LIMITATIONS

It might be worth trying to respond to the measurement and normative difficulties just mentioned within an opportunity-cost framework, were it not
for more serious failures that become visible once we scrutinize the assumptions about self-ownership at its core. Locke's workmanship ideal is refor-
mulated by Roemer as self-ownership, the idea that individuals are sovereign
over their productive capacities and what flows from them.[26] In Locke's formulation self-ownership is a gift from God, constrained by natural law, and
the normative foundation for all humanly created rights of ownership and
control. In many ways this is an attractive picture, comprising the "rights"
component of the rights-utility synthesis. Yet for a secular formulation of it
to be sustained, the theological accounts of both the gift and the constraints
must be replaced with persuasive alternatives. It is here that the neo-Lockean
outlook runs into terminal, yet revealing, difficulties.

The constraints are perhaps more visibly natural-law-dependent than the
gift of self-ownership; they are rooted in the natural-law injunctions to preserve mankind as well as oneself.[27] Hence the provisos, as well as Locke's

insistence in the *First Treatise*, that just as "*Justice* gives every Man a Title to the product of his honest Industry," so "*Charity* gives every man a Title to so much of another's Plenty, as will keep him from extream want, where he has no means to subsist otherwise."[28] One response to the challenge of secularization is to take Roemer's tack: translate the constraints into a requirement that the disadvantaged be entitled to what they could produce for themselves in a feasible alternative system. The difficulty, as noted, is that even if it could be applied, this test might not even keep them from extreme want. An alternative neo-Lockean solution has been simply to ignore the constraints, either hoping—with Locke—that trickle-down will render them moot, or not minding if it does not. This latter approach is exemplified by such libertarians as Richard Epstein, though it is manifestly un-Lockean in spirit.[29]

Both the Epstein and Roemer solutions in any case skirt the main difficulty: that self-ownership and its attendant incidents are declared by Locke to be gifts from God. What is the secular defense of them? On Locke's account, God gave people the ability to act in a godlike fashion. Their ownership of, and authority over, what they make is rooted in their having done the relevant productive work to create it. Marxists and libertarians endorse this idea. They differ over who "really" does the work of making, whether it is done freely, and whether there are circumstances in which it could be done better or more productively, but they agree on the basic workmanship postulate. Unlike the situation with children, however (where the appropriate secular analogue of the proposition that children are God's property is that they are no one's property), this workmanship ideal of ownership and authority does not fare well once severed from its theological moorings. The central difficulty is that whereas, in Locke's scheme, inequalities flowing from differences in human capacities must be accepted as part of God's design, there is no convincing secular reason either to accept or reject them once divine providence is removed from the picture. This difficulty is compounded by the reality that human capacities to work are partly produced by the work of other humans, a fact that is not easily ignored once our productive capacities are no longer seen as the bounty of a divine beneficence.

Perhaps most obviously vulnerable is the libertarian impulse to assume that the dual-market dynamic will take care of the problem. In effect, this involves "half-secularizing" the Lockean view: embracing something like a natural-law status for self-ownership but rejecting constraints on it as unjustified interference with the natural order. But why should anyone be compelled to accept self-ownership once she no longer believes it to be divinely ordained? Some, such as John Harsanyi, insist on self-ownership as a matter of "sheer natural fact," but this is merely argument by assertion.[30] More commonly the defense is consequentialist: libertarians insist on the trickle-down benefits of a dual-market dynamic in which everyone is sovereign over their capacities and whatever they can get for them. Although, as I note below, such consequentialist reasoning is not entirely without legitimacy, on its own it can be expected to appeal only to those who benefit from it. Some will resist it; to them the libertarian has no convincing response.[31]

The Marxian attitude toward self-ownership is no less problematical. Marx's critique of capitalism embraces self-ownership by its terms; otherwise there would be no basis for his claim that the surplus appropriated by the capitalist rightfully belongs to the worker. Subsequent revisions of the Marxian critique sever the labor theory of value from self-ownership, but they do not reject it.[32] As feminist theorists have pointed out, however, making the wage laborer's self-ownership the point of reference in arguments about exploitation is arbitrary. It ignores the role of a stay-at-home spouse to producing the worker's productive capacity, which is rented to the capitalist and which Marx arbitrarily took to be the worker's "own." Conceding that God does not give us our productive capacities in no way entails that others are obliged to give them to us. From this vantage point, Marx's argument can be turned on a worker's relationship with a spouse to reveal *it* in certain circumstances to be exploitative.[33]

If the use of productive capacities generates entitlements, then tracing the moral reach of a particular productive capacity exercised in the production of a particular nonhuman object or service of value becomes exceedingly complex, arguably impossible even in principle. For the feminist point can itself be generalized: the productive capacities a conventional wife "has" that she expends in her husband's attainment of a professional qualification were no doubt themselves produced partly by the work of others. Parents, perhaps children, Sunday school teachers who drummed into her a particular mixture of the work ethic and conventional family values may all have contributed. If one pushes the idea of productive capacity as the moral basis for entitlement to the limit it seems to point in the direction of a tangled and indecipherable web of overdetermined entitlements, and indeed to reveal a deep tension at the core of the workmanship ideal itself. The claim that we own what we make in virtue of our ownership of our productive capacities undermines the claim that we own our productive capacities, once it is conceded that those capacities are themselves produced partly by the work of others.[34] Yet if we want to employ a variant of the workmanship ideal without pushing it to the limit, and in the absence of a theological limiting device such as Locke's, then the difficulty remains of how to do the pertinent line drawing without inviting charges of moral arbitrariness.

SOCIALIZED CAPACITIES AND FREE CHOICE

Surprisingly, it is liberals, not Marxists, who have seriously explored the possibility of rejecting self-ownership. Rawls and Dworkin both flirt with the argument that, like other resources, human capacities should, for certain purposes, be seen as social goods.[35] This socialization-of-capacities strategy may be thought of as a mirror image of the Marxian one: whereas for Marx nonhuman resources cease to be of independent moral interest, being reducible to the capacities needed to separate them from nature, on this view human capacities cease to be of independent moral interest: they are treated as social resources like any other. Thus Rawls argues forcibly that differences both in natural abilities and in contingencies of upbringing are morally arbitrary factors that should not determine the rewards people receive, usefully rendering the nature/nurture debate beside the point in arguments about social justice.[36] Similarly, Dworkin treats human capacities and external material resources as moral equivalents from the standpoint of distributive justice, arguing that although there may be good reasons for resisting the redistribution of physical and mental resources (insofar as this is technologically feasible), a case might nonetheless be made for compensating those with inferior physical and mental resources for their relative incapacities.[37]

Yet it is notable that both Rawls and Dworkin balk at the implications of the socialization-of-capacities strategy. Rawls explicitly refuses to confront the implications of his account of the moral arbitrariness of differing capacities when he holds that the effectiveness with which people are able to use resources, or choose to use them, is not relevant in deciding how those resources should be distributed. There are two issues here, both of which raise tensions internal to the Rawlsian account. One derives from Amartya Sen's point that if we really want justly to distribute what people of greatly different capacities are enabled to do, then we cannot use Rawlsian primary goods; we need a different metric that takes account of how different people employ capacities and resources.[38] Second, there is the observation made by Cohen, Nagel, Arneson, and others, that different people have different preferences and goals, some more expensive and more difficult to satisfy than others. Rawls's attempt to sidestep this problem by arguing that these are not afflictions but are chosen scarcely meets the objection, because, as Scanlon and others have pointed out, often they are not.[39]

Nor can Dworkin accept the implications of the socialization-of-capacities strategy. He invites us to speculate on how resources might in principle be equalized by use of a hypothetical auction in which all parties begin with the same finite number of bargaining chips.[40] As part of this conceit he argues that human capacities should be considered resources, yet there are two ways in which he dodges the full implications of his own argument. First, he claims that although capacities (his term is "physical and mental powers") are resources and as a consequence legitimate objects of a theory of distributive justice, they should nonetheless be treated differently from "independent material resources." With physical and mental powers, the goal should not be to strive to distribute them justly (which, for Dworkin, means equally). Instead, the problem is construed as one of discovering "how far the ownership of independent external resources should be affected by differences that exist in physical and mental powers, and the response of our theory should speak in that vocabulary."[41] For this reason he argues that people should be compensated by reference to a standard arrived at by our speculations concerning whether and to what extent people would, on average, have insured against the particular handicap or disability or lack of talent, assuming that insurance rates would be set in a competitive market.[42]

Notice that Dworkin supplies no principled argument why physical and mental powers should be treated differently from material resources. The assertion that they "cannot be manipulated or transferred, even so far as technology permits," is not further explained or justified, but because Dworkin has chosen to treat powers as resources an explanation is surely in order.[43] This is so not least because compensation in any amount will sometimes be inadequate to equalize a power or capacity deficiency (as in the case of blindness), as Dworkin elsewhere notes, yet equality of resources is his basic criterion of distributive justice. In such circumstances compensation based on a standard set by a hypothetical insurance auction cannot be said to equalize the resources of two persons, one blind, one sighted.[44] Yet it is not always true, pace Dworkin, that their powers of sight could not be equalized.[45] The state might forcibly transplant one eye from a sighted person to the blind one in order to equalize their resources—or, for that matter, simply blind the sighted person. Less callously and more interestingly, it might invest billions of dollars on research on and development of artificial eyes, financed by a tax on the sighted. If Dworkin is to avoid such unpalatable results, he must supply an argument for why we may said to be entitled to our powers and capacities (and in some sense responsible for having or lacking them) in different (and trumping) ways than we can be said to be entitled to material resources, given his equation of the two.

The second way in which Dworkin refuses to live with the socialization-of-capacities strategy that he otherwise embraces concerns his discussion of how our conception of a person should be distinguished from our conception of her circumstances. Dworkin argues for a view of distributive justice that is "ambition sensitive." He endorses a view of equality by reference to which people "decide what sorts of lives to pursue against a background of information about the actual costs that their choices impose on other people and hence on the total stock of resources that may fairly be used by them." This he tries to achieve by assigning "tastes and ambitions" to the person, and "physical and mental powers" to her "circumstances," arguing that the former are not relevant considerations in deciding how resources should be distributed.[46] In this way he hopes to rescue an island of creative autonomy for the individual agent. Dworkin wants to rescue the kernel of what is intuitively attractive in the workmanship ideal, the idea that when people conceive of and put into practice productive plans, the benefits from the resulting actions should flow back to them. Yet he wants to do this without being swamped by the difficulties of overdetermination that flow from the Rawlsian claim that the distribution of physical and mental powers is morally arbitrary.[47]

Dworkin's strategy fails. The volitions we are able to form, the ambitions it occurs to us to develop—these are greatly influenced, perhaps even determined, by our powers and capacities. To "think big," to "resolve to go for broke," to steel oneself through self-control to perform demanding acts—do these reflect ambition or capacity? When we describe someone as ambitious, are we not describing something more basic to her psychology and constitution than her tastes? There are certainly circumstances in which we would say that lack of confidence is an incapacity that prevents the formation (not just the attainment) of particular ambitions. Different people have different capacities to form different ambitions, and those different capacities must be as morally arbitrary from Dworkin's point of view as any other capacities. Donald Trump is able to develop more far-reaching ambitions than Archie Bunker due at least partly to luck in the genetic pool and in the circumstances of his upbringing.[48] Similar arguments can be made about the different abilities to form (or refrain from forming) different kinds of tastes, whether expensive, compulsive, or both.[49]

With all acquired tastes, experiencing the taste is by definition conditional on the exercise of pertinent capacities. A taste for good beer, or even just for beer, a taste for a particular kind of music, perhaps even for any music—these can be developed only through the exercise of relevant capacities. We would not say of a deaf person that she could have a taste for music of a particular sort, or even a taste for music of any sort (although of course we could intelligibly say that such a person might perhaps wish that she was able to have such a taste). Likewise with beer and someone who had no functioning taste buds or sense of smell. The idea that we form our tastes and ambitions in some way that is independent of our resources and capacities is too whiggish, as would be revealed to anyone who tried to perform a thought experiment in which she was required to decide on her future tastes and ambitions while being kept in ignorance of her powers and capacities. Dworkin's replacement of the resources versus capacities distinction with the ambitions and tastes versus physical and mental powers distinction fails to rescue the Lockean notion of an autonomous agent, of whom rights and responsibilities may legitimately be predicated. Like Rawls, Dworkin fails to provide a convincing secular basis for the rights component of the rights-utility synthesis.

It might be objected that the line of reasoning I have been developing leads too quickly to pure determinism. Surely we should be open to the possibility that some aspects of human action are subject to autonomous choice, and that people might reasonably be held to account for the aspects that fall into that category.[50] This is implicit in G. A. Cohen's argument that "we should compensate for disadvantage beyond a person's control."[51] Cohen has tried to minimize the extent of difficulties involved in delimiting the relevant class that this includes by suggesting that we should not confuse the true claim that our capacities for effort are "influenced" by factors beyond our control with the false claim that those capacities are "determined" by factors beyond our control. Preserving this distinction enables him to say that although not all effort deserves reward, this does not mean that no effort deserves reward. Effort "is partly praiseworthy, partly not." Yet Cohen wisely notes that in practice "we cannot separate the parts." [52]

Conceding this is tantamount to granting that a choice-based view cannot generate a serviceable account of distributive justice. It implies that there is no way for the state to determine which part of a person's decisions are genuinely volitional, as opposed to determined, or how to measure differences in capacities for volitional behavior across persons. Moreover, even if the measurement problems could be solved, the focus on free will has other troubling implications for democratic justice. Most obviously, it suggests that exotic compulsions—such as an addiction to the best available malt liquor— should trump important needs of food and shelter which people might be able to secure for themselves through voluntary action, but only at immense cost. This is to say nothing of the acute moral hazards that should be expected to arise in a regime governed by a principle like Cohen's. To take an obvious case, parents would be given incentives to avoid developing capacities for individual responsibility and autonomous choice in their children, lest they be deprived of compensation to which they would otherwise be entitled. In sum, the difficulties involved in trying to use free will to provide a secular basis for the "rights" component of the rights-utility synthesis are overwhelming. [53]

DEMOCRATIC JUSTICE AND THE DUAL-MARKET DYNAMIC

That self-ownership is so difficult either to defend or to abjure should not be surprising. The Rawlsian moral-arbitrariness argument is decisive, yet one does not have to delve deeply into debates about hypothetical eye transplantation to realize that they lead down a path few will find alluring. This tension reflects a reality that although no persuasive secular defense of the workmanship ideal is available, rejecting it threatens conventional ideas about incentives, responsibility, even identity, and suggests that "givings" may stand in at least as much need of justification as "takings." Most normative political economy proceeds as if the basic question were What to tax?

The lack of a convincing secular defense of the workmanship ideal threatens that What not to tax? might reasonably vie with it for priority.

Democratic justice does not require us to dismiss these fears; rather, it suggests a different perspective on them. Because it recognizes that existing ways of doing things reasonably make a limited claim on our allegiance, democratic justice counsels granting presumptive legitimacy to the dual-market dynamic for many of the conventional reasons. It also advises us, however, to be on the lookout for the ways accepted practices lead to injustice and to refashion them by means of its conditioning constraints. From this point of view, understanding the vulnerability of the conventional defenses of the dual-market dynamic is valuable. On the one hand, the utilitarian benefits are shown to be contingent all the way down. They cannot reasonably be expected to have much pull for those who do not experience tangible advantage from the dynamic's operation. On the other hand, the rights-regarding claims may be judged attractive for a variety of consequentialist reasons, but because they are not divinely ordained, there is no good reason to regard them as sacrosanct. Inevitably they embody arbitrary distributions of capacities and resources that are beyond repair in principle, at least if the expectation is that a just distribution would situate them "beyond" politics. We do better to come to grips with the fact that justice of that kind will never be available, and to shift the focus: away from disputes about who has the more legitimate claim to what is produced, and toward pursuing justice in the power relations surrounding production.

This approach involves repudiating Locke's theological defense of workmanship, as well as the search for alternative secular foundations of it, but there is one notable respect in which it is Lockean in spirit. Locke never thought of rights generated by human workmanship as trumps in the way that libertarians often do, because he saw them as always constrained by other requirements of justice embodied in natural law. Although there are no natural-law constraints from the perspective of democratic justice, by the same token there is no necessary reason to grant primacy to rights generated by human workmanship when they conflict with other justice values. There is bound to be controversy about where they fit into a governing distributive scheme that must cope with multiple demands on scarce resources—from redressing the effects of historical disadvantage, to caring for the sick and elderly, to supporting just causes in other countries. Disagreements about the priorities of competing just claims had to be managed, for Locke, through the political system unless this resulted in "a long train of Abuses, Prevarications, and Artifices, all tending the same way," triggering the right to revolution.[54] Until that concededly illusive threshold was crossed for a great many, even perceived violations of natural law had to be accepted because the individual's right to self-enforcement is given up on entering civil society. Those who dislike the results are free to try to change them through the system, but in the meantime they have to live with them.[55] In these respects Locke's account, like ours, recognizes the priority of politics to arguments about justice.

Work's Significance

The political dimensions of work are rooted in the interaction between its role in meeting human needs under conditions of scarcity and the interdependencies implied in the division of labor. Work in a world of Robinson Crusoes—living by the sweat of their brows on their separate islands—would lack any political dimension.[56] By the same token, the implications of a division of labor in a world of universal superabundance are, for political theorists, little more than counterfactual curiosities.[57] Work's political significance arises out of the human propensity to conjoin necessity with interdependence: that labor is both required for survival and shared in complex ways leads to intermingling power relations with the benefits of cooperation. The possibility of accumulating wealth—sometimes to escape the need to work, sometimes for other reasons—further complicates the story. These facts both trigger the attention of democratic justice and limit its purview. We are preoccupied, that is, with how best to govern the power relations structuring work. Other features of work, though doubtless significant from many points of view, are relevant only to the degree that they affect this.

NECESSITY AND BASIC INTERESTS

Work is integral to vindicating many human interests, but democratic justice is more concerned with its role in some than in others. In this connection it is helpful to draw here on the idea of basic interests developed in Chapter 4, though for somewhat different reasons. In that chapter the focus was on paternalistic judgments about children. Basic interests were contrasted with best interests, in the course of distinguishing those areas within which parents should exercise fiduciary authority from those that are the proper concern of other authorities. Here we are dealing with a circumstance in which all relevant agents are presumed competent judges of their own interests, so that the question of paternalistic judgments does not arise. Yet the idea of basic interests is helpful in getting at the issue of necessity, for it is a feature of basic interests that people are usually constrained to vindicate them. The costs of not doing so are normally high, often intolerably so. Whether for reasons linked to the human constitution, to prevailing social arrangements, or to the ways in which the two interact, there are some things people must do or have so that they may get on with their lives.[58] When their capacity to do or have them is threatened, so are their basic interests. Because many, but not all, of the power relations surrounding work revolve around the possibility of such threats, democratic justice usefully distinguishes circumstances in which they are involved from those in which they are not.[59]

This is not to say that all adults' basic interests are or should be bound up with employment relations. Indeed, substantial costs for democratic justice can be associated with staking the vindication of basic interests on the employment relationship. Among the advantages of the social wage approach defended below are that it limits the financial exposure of firms (which may lack resources to provide effectively for a wide range of workers' basic interests) and that it speaks to the needs of those who are either unemployed or employed in activities, notably domestic labor, that operate outside the money economy.[60] For these reasons, among others, it makes better sense to expand the social wage and limit the direct exposure of firms to responsibility for a relatively narrow class of employees' basic interests.[61]

A word should also be said about my use of the term *usually* in describing basic interests as exhibiting imperative force. By employing it, my aim is to sidestep the philosophically rich but institutionally barren debates concerning exotic compulsions and other esoterica that dominate too much of the distributive justice literature on interpersonal judgments and free will. That this or that person might have an addiction to plovers' eggs needs to be kept in perspective. If people do not generally experience such addictions, we would be allowing the tail to wag the dog if we paid much attention to them in our discussion of the role of necessity in power relations within the firm or the definition of the social wage.[62] Moreover, because my focus is institutional, philosophical questions about what people value, and how to assess and compare their valuations, recede in significance. My defense of robust legal protections for workers within firms when the social wage is low, for instance, assumes that in such circumstances organized workers will press for those things that are needed to vindicate their basic interests (such as job security, disability insurance, and a living wage). This account does not require much in the way of fine-grained knowledge about how they rank these things with respect to one another or to other goods. Indeed, perhaps other things will be more important to them in some circumstances. Clearly these are questions of degree, but it seems safe to assume that, when people lack the things they have to have, they will fight for them first.

THE EMPLOYMENT RELATIONSHIP

Employees within firms are uniquely situated in at least two respects, both linked to exit costs. First, in a world of high capital mobility and permanent less than full employment, it is generally easier for management to replace workers than it is for unemployed workers to find new jobs.[63] This reality is worsened by the fact that workers with seniority, and the various vested benefits that seniority brings, are often less attractive to firms than younger, or temporary, workers. Technological changes and globalization have eroded organized labor's capacity to protect workers to even a greater degree than those who predicted such erosion a generation ago ever imagined.[64] The threat of capital flight keeps the fear of unemployment real throughout the business cycle. What economists describe as workers' high—and, with age, increasing—levels of asset specificity in the employment relationship means that workers have a good deal to lose if they lose their jobs, and that the potential loss increases as they age. Because everyone knows this, workers remain perpetually vulnerable to those who control the firm.

This vulnerability sets workers apart from stockholders, implausibly identified by some commentators as the appropriate repositories of democratic control of the firm.[65] Leaving aside, for now, the agency difficulties that have been identified in the relations between stockholders and managers, stockholders have no incentive to be concerned with employees' interests. Stockholders may or may not constrain managers to maximize profits, or some other good subject to a profitability constraint.[66] But this does nothing to safeguard the interests of workers vis-à-vis managers. On the contrary, to the degree that managers are responsive to stockholders (seeking, in the best case perhaps, to maximize the value of current shareholders' equity), this may well require discounting employees' interests. This is not to say that stockholders' interests are without merit, but they enjoy effective means of protecting them that are not available to employees. Stockholders can diversify portfolios so as to minimize their vulnerability, and they can sell their stock in a firm if they dislike the way in which it is being run. Workers' freedom to leave is seldom analogous.

A second sense in which workers confront high exit costs is rooted in the reality that the human capital cannot easily be separated from its owner, whereas other forms of capital can. This means, as Robin Archer has usefully noted, that workers' persons are subject to managerial authority.[67] If workers dislike coworkers, managers, dress codes, or attendance requirements, or if the work environment is harassing or otherwise oppressive, they must either accept these realities or absorb the often substantial costs of leaving. There is little or no space between their obligations as workers and their persons. Stockholders, by contrast, are no more subject to managers' authority than are the bankers who lend firms money. This is not to deny that they may be subject to risks and constraints that workers might not confront, or that stockholders might be subject to authority relations in other contexts. It is to insist, however, that workers' positions within firms are distinctive in subjecting them personally to employers' authority.

What of managers? They are a heterogeneous group, some of whom are for all practical purposes employees, and some of whom are more like firm owners. Those who are more like employees—such as low-level supervisors and white-collar workers—may be declared to be "management" for legitimate reasons (they exercise managerial responsibility) or for illegitimate ones (to prevent their joining unions). What matters from the standpoint of democratic justice is not the labels but where people stand in the power hierarchies within the firm.[68] To the degree that they are constrained by the necessities and high exit costs just discussed, they are more appropriately thought of as employees; to the extent that they are free of those constraints, they are better conceived of as employers. A high-level manager might be a salaried employee, but so well paid and autonomous within the firm that she confronts few significant exit costs and is insulated, for all practical purposes, from the authority of others within the firm. Indeed, upper managers' control of key information and firm operations may enable them to sustain astronomical salaries and perks at shareholders' expense and to protect themselves with golden parachute provisions in their contracts. Managers of this kind are evidently employees in little more than name. And although they may be lacking in accountability to stockholders, this problem is not serious from the standpoint of democratic justice. Because stockholders are free to diversify risk and preserve cheap exit possibilities if they choose, no substantial cost is incurred to democratic justice by leaving their relations with managers to the market's discipline.

Governing the Firm

Adam Smith was the first modern political economist to draw attention to a systematic power asymmetry within the firm. He traced it to the resource disparity between workers and employers, buttressed by laws forbidding the formation of unions.[69] "We have no acts of parliament against combining to lower the price of work," he observed, but there are "many against combining to raise it." Yet he noted that "masters are always in a sort of tacit, but constant and uniform combination, not to raise the wages of labor above their actual rate"—subsistence. Whereas owners "could generally live a year or two upon the stocks which they have already acquired," most workers cannot subsist without employment longer than a few days or weeks. As a result, although their plight may lead workers to desperate acts of intermittent rage, these are bound to be ineffective: "Partly from the interposition of the civil magistrate, partly from the superior steadiness of the masters, partly from the necessity which the greater part of the workmen are under of submitting for the sake of present subsistence," such "tumultuous combinations" end in "nothing, but the punishment or ruin of the ring-leaders." Accordingly, Smith supported the legalization of trade unions, without which "it is not difficult to foresee which of the two parties, upon all ordinary occasions, have the advantage in the dispute, and force the other into a compliance with their terms."[70]

In the two centuries since Smith wrote, labor movements have been centrally preoccupied with securing public acknowledgment of the power asymmetries within the firm and with sustaining legal recognition both of workers' rights to organize and of concomitant duties on employers to engage in collective bargaining. In the United States the high point in this struggle was the passage of the Wagner Act in 1935, which rested on explicit recognition of "the inequality of bargaining power between employees who do not possess full freedom of association or actual liberty of contract, and employers who are organized in the corporate or other forms of ownership." The act, which institutionalized and protected rights to organize and strike, was intended to redress power disparities by "encouraging the practice and procedure of collective bargaining and by protecting the exercise by workers of full free- dom of association, self-organization, and designation of representatives of their own choosing, for negotiating the terms and conditions of their em- ployment." The act enshrined the right to "self-organization, to form, join, or assist labor organizations, to bargain collectively through representatives of their own choosing, and to engage in concerted activities, for the purpose of collective bargaining or other mutual aid or protection." It also contained affirmative duties on employers to bargain with elected union representa- tives, protections of closed shops, and other collective rights.[71] Whether the Wagner Act was a victory for the labor movement, co-optation of it, or both, continues to be debated, as do the causes and consequences of the act's partial evisceration by legislation in the 1940s and 1950s.[72] Aspects of these issues are touched on below, but my present concern is to explore and build on the Smith-Wagner diagnosis of power asymmetry within the firm.

CONVENTIONAL RESPONSES TO POWER INTERNALITIES AND THE IMPORTANCE OF BURDEN SHIFTING

Even if power externalities did not structure employment relations, demo- cratic justice would prompt questions about the governance of the firm. The conventional firm is hierarchically ordered, both within management and between management and labor. Individual employees typically face hierar- chical arrangements that precede their arrival and survive their departure. The inability of employees, acting individually, to have much impact on this state of affairs gives the Smith-Wagner diagnosis its plausibility, and the response embodied in the Wagner Act makes prima facie sense from the standpoint of democratic justice. Trade unions, protected by a regime of free collective bargaining and the right to strike, public grievance pro- cedures, and independent enforcement tribunals such as the NLRB, might not be sufficient to level the playing field between management and labor, but they can be expected to diminish the angle of incline. Yet the assault on unions that has been under way in many industrial countries since the 1970s must be squarely confronted in developing the argument for democratic justice, because it rests on contentions about tradeoffs between efficiency and participation that call into question the feasibility of democracy's operating as a subordinate good in this context.

The central complaint is one we always find when democracy confronts hierarchies: that the hierarchy in question is essential to the relevant good's provision, and too much democracy will destroy it. Proponents of democratic justice should not dismiss these claims. Rather, they should seek to ensure that there are mechanisms in place to sort the genuine from the spurious among them. Hierarchies within firms might indeed produce efficiency gains, and they might even operate in the interests of employees as some transactions-costs economists claim. But because many of the external effects of hierarchies are unattractive from the standpoint of democratic justice, and because the transactions-costs literature notoriously fails, in any case, to offer an account of the optimal degree or kind of hierarchy within the firm, arguments in support of hierarchical firms are reasonably eyed with skepticism.[73] This skepticism is warranted even before we get to democratic justice's more general reason for worry about hierarchies: their propensity to become diverted from their legitimate purposes and atrophy into systems of domination. This is not to say that proponents of democratic justice should set themselves up as experts in industrial institutional design; the task is not to try to design better firms than those with the relevant insider's wisdom. Rather it is to discover how the power relations among them can be structured so that *they* will seek solutions that are more, rather than less, in keeping with democratic justice. This suggests that burden-shifting requirements are merited, requiring management to justify claims of business necessity when employees dispute them.

Models for burden-shifting devices can be found in American labor law in cases of "disparate treatment" (employment discrimination) and "disparate impact" (when apparently neutral criteria adversely affect certain groups of employees) arising under Title VII of the 1964 Civil Rights Act. Before exploring the possibilities these cases open up, it should be noted that in the United States, unlike many European countries, there is no general burden-shifting requirement of this kind.[74] Employment litigation—like civil litigation generally—requires the complaining party to bear the burden of proof. There are exceptions in the civil service and academic employment. Generally, however, because the employer has the power to set the terms and conditions of employment, this burden will be shouldered by a complaining employee, a union, or some other third party acting on their behalf. Far from shifting burdens to employers, the law in effect confers a procedural advantage on them. In employee discharge cases, for instance, the employee must establish that the discharge was unlawful.[75] If there is no union contract, an employer may discharge workers for any reason that is not explicitly prohibited by law.[76]

The major exception to this rule is arbitration under union contracts, which almost always require "just cause" for discharge. In interpreting these contracts, arbitrators usually require the employer to establish the existence of just cause for discharge. Just-cause provisions thus reverse the presumption that discharge is a legitimate exercise of employer power, eliminating employers' defeasible rights to discharge and vesting employees with defeasible rights not to be discharged.[77] Interestingly, however, the conventional reason given for this reversal is related to the high stakes, for the worker, of losing employment, not to the existence of the contract. As Elkouri and Elkouri summarize the rationale, "Discharge is recognized as the extreme industrial penalty since the employee's job, seniority and other contractual benefits, and reputation are at stake. Because of the seriousness of this penalty, the burden is generally held to be on the employer to prove guilt of wrongdoing, and probably always so where the agreement requires 'just cause' for discharge."[78] That the severity of the penalty, rather than the mere existence of the contract, justifies the burden shifting is underscored by the fact that in union grievances not involving discharge or discipline, arbitrators generally place the burden of proof on the union even when there is a contract.[79]

Given this rationale, it is anomalous that burden shifting in discharge cases requires the existence of a union contract, for the costs to the worker of losing employment are if anything higher where there is no contract.[80] This anomaly is indefensible from the standpoint of democratic justice, because it leaves employers free to act unilaterally against workers when they are most vulnerable. Better are the exceptions to the anomaly that arise under Title VII "disparate treatment" and "disparate impact" defenses. In disparate treatment (employment discrimination) cases, employees claim that employers intentionally discriminated against them based on prohibited classifications. It is an affirmative defense to a disparate-treatment claim that religion, sex, or national origin (but not race) "is a bona fide occupational qualification reasonably necessary to the normal operation of [the] particular business enterprise." [81] The employer bears the considerable burden of meeting this defense of bona fide occupational qualification. [82]

In disparate-impact cases, employers can mount "business necessity" defenses in Title VII actions when plaintiffs challenge apparently neutral employment practices on the grounds that they have a disparate impact on members of a protected class. In the leading disparate-impact case, *Griggs v. Duke Power Co.*, the employer required new employees to be high school graduates and to pass a standardized general intelligence test. [83] These requirements operated to disqualify black applicants at substantially higher rates than whites. The U.S. Supreme Court held that the employer's requirements violated Title VII if they could not be "shown to bear a demonstrable relationship to successful performance of the jobs." In addition to overt discrimination, the act was held to proscribe "practices that are fair in form, but discriminatory in operation. The touchstone is business necessity. If an employment practice which operates to exclude Negroes cannot be shown to be related to job performance, the practice is prohibited." [84] The disparate-impact theory and the business-necessity defenses established in *Griggs* were undermined by subsequent Supreme Court decisions, but Congress codified them into Title VII in its 1991 amendments to Civil Rights Act. [85] Indeed, Congress went further, providing that in a disparate-impact case even where the employer does prove business necessity, employees can still prevail if they demonstrate that there is an alternative employment practice which would achieve the same business ends with less disparate impact. [86] These amendments are very much in the spirit of democratic justice, for they concede the legitimacy of a business-necessity defense while distributing burdens so as to try to ensure that alleged business necessities that conflict with employees' competing claims really are necessary. [87]

Although burden shifting of this kind is needed to keep management honest about claims of business necessity in a civil-litigation system of the American sort, it is not by itself sufficient. Civil service employees are often protected by statutes, ordinances, or rules that prohibit discharge except for cause and that place the burden of proof on the employer.[88] But this will not protect them if those evaluating their claims are beholden to employers. In civil service systems, decision makers are usually appointed by the employing authority, such as the mayor or governor. This invites proemployer bias in varying degrees. Likewise, employees and unions who bring complaints to the NLRB often confront more obstacles that are at least as formidable as the burden of proof. The charging parties will receive a hearing before an administrative law judge only if the NLRB's regional office or general counsel decides to issue an unfair labor practice complaint.[89] No doubt there have been cases where the NLRB dismissed an unfair labor practice charge that would have prevailed before an administrative law judge had the complaint been issued. The decision makers in these civil service and NLRB forums stand in contrast to labor arbitrators in contract disputes. Arbitrators are jointly chosen by the union and the employer, and there is no prima facie reason for suspicion of systematic bias on their part. For that reason, the arbitration model is preferable.

An implication of the preceding discussion is that in the current American system unions and free collective bargaining play doubly important roles from the perspective of democratic justice. First, negotiated contracts are more likely to get to, and be decided by, arbitrators who are not beholden to management. Because the point of burden shifting is, after all, to keep management honest when its claims of business necessity conflict with employees' assertion of their interests, a regime in which independent third parties arbitrate disputed claims is to be preferred to one in which dispute resolution is in the hands of individuals and bodies who have incentives to tilt in the management's direction. Second, although there is some incoherence in the legal rationale that underlies burden shifting as we have seen, most of the time it is triggered by the existence of a union contract.[90] It would be a better world if this were unnecessary. If the Title VII exceptions for disparate treatment and disparate impact became accepted as the general rule, as is the case in many European countries, union contracts might be less important. Given the current reality, however, it is difficult to see a justification for weakening unions. Even in the realm of public employment, it seems that union contracts are needed if the goals of burden shifting are to have a realistic hope of being recognized.

This is not to deny that unions can introduce significant costs from the standpoints of both efficiency and democratic justice. It is to insist, however, that arguing for diminishing those costs is premature so long as the institutional context tilts against labor in ways that undermine burden shifting and the goal it is intended to serve: keeping management honest. Nor do I mean to deny that burden-shifting mechanisms are themselves costly. Dispute resolution takes time and resources away from productive work; as a result, there are obvious efficiency reasons for keeping it to a minimum. This can be achieved by requiring employees to establish a prima facie case before the burden shifts, or by reducing the quantum of proof required to meet management's burden. Specifying the conditions under which such steps can be justified, from the standpoint of democratic justice, requires attending to how serious is the impact on employees of giving management a relatively freer hand. This takes us into the world of power externalities, which I discuss later in this chapter.

ESOPS AND SELF-GOVERNING FIRMS

There is a substantial literature that might be taken to suggest that my discussion so far takes too adversarial a view of industrial relations. On these accounts, arguing for mechanisms that strengthen the relative position of employees is anachronistic. Rather than structure the terms of the conflict in one way or another, management techniques should be geared to eliminating adversarial labor relations. Contributors to this literature identify major inefficiencies in the conventional firm and explore a myriad of alternatives. Sometimes they reject the rigid hierarchies characteristic of large American firms as inappropriate to modern production, pointing instead to the superiority of alternative — usually Japanese — systems that utilize more flexible authority relations, production teams, and fewer intermediate tiers of authority between shop floors and top management.[91] Some commentators go further, contending that conventional divisions between labor and management can be displaced by altering the ownership structure of firms. Here proposals range from employee stock ownership plans (ESOPs) through various types of partnerships, coops, and fully worker-owned firms. Their advocates challenge the neoclassical orthodoxy that hierarchies within firms are efficient, and with it the efficiency-participation tradeoff.[92] On their accounts, limited employee participation is often a source of inefficiency. Particularly in light of the massive decline of union membership in the United

States (from some 37 percent of the workforce in 1953 to less than 12 percent by 1994) that has weakened the relative strength of organized labor, alternative forms of firm organization deserve a look.[93]

Proposals for alternative ways of organizing the firm that are geared solely toward increasing efficiency deal with superordinate goods; they are not our concern. Enhanced worker participation might indeed bring efficiency gains if managers learn through it that workers have pertinent knowledge that had previously been discounted, but when this happens it is a collateral benefit of democratic justice. To the extent that efficiency alone is at issue, democratic justice counsels deferring to insider's wisdom, as disciplined by the burden-shifting requirements already mentioned and the market. It is a different matter when claims are made that alternative systems of organization and ownership can democratize power relations within the firm, for such claims speak to the subordinate good of democratic control. In exploring their potential we are not free to ignore efficiency considerations altogether. But we tend to them only in the context of thinking about democracy as a subordinate good (when enhanced democracy is either efficiency neutral or brings efficiency gains), and considering what to do when it cannot operate in this way (when there really is an efficiency-participation tradeoff). Do ESOPs or other alternative forms of firm ownership offer advances from this point of view?

ESOPs occupy a middle ground between the conventional business and worker-owned firms and coops. The basic idea, developed by an eccentric banker named Louis Kelso in the 1950s, was conceived of as an antidote to both the concentration of wealth and the high entry costs in modern technological production. Acting on the Lockean notion that "the ownership of productive property by an individual or a household must not be allowed to increase beyond the point where it injures others by excluding them from the opportunity to earn a viable income," Kelso argued for the creation of company-funded benefit plans for employees who would agree to invest those plan assets in the company's stock.[94] Hence the ESOP. Some ESOP plans are used as debt instruments, in effect enabling employees to take on debt, backed by the company's collateral, that would otherwise not be available to them. Companies can use the new debt for investment, ideally increasing the value of the employee-owned stock, which workers are free take with them or sell when their employment ends or when the debt for which they have been used as collateral has been repaid. Kelso believed that ESOPs would blur the line between workers and owners in healthy ways and lead to increased worker productivity.

ESOPs grew in popularity in the 1960s and 1970s, particularly after the federal government began subsidizing them through the tax code in 1974.[95] Reports on the numbers of ESOPs and of participating employees vary, but at their height in the late 1980s (when the subsidies were cut back) there were about ten thousand in the United States, accounting for more than eleven and a half million employees.[96] The effects of ESOPs on both productivity and employee income are also debated; the evidence seems to suggest modest gains in both can be realized.[97]

Whatever the numbers of participating employees and the economic effects of their participation, to date ESOPs have done little to alter the power structure within firms because they seldom involve changes in corporate governance. The great majority of private firms with ESOPs do not give employees voting stock, and in public companies (which must pass through full voting stocks for all allocated shares) employees typically own at most 15 to 20 percent of the company's shares, insufficient to have much influence at the board level.[98] The result, one critic has noted, is that "worker ownership has been divorced from any notion of worker control."[99] Given democratic justice's focus on the power dynamics surrounding production rather than incidents of ownership, the ESOP experiment is less than encouraging to date.

In response to these difficulties, some friendly critics of ESOPs have suggested linking government subsidies to the provision of employees' seats on boards of directors, committees for employee relations, health and safety, and dispute resolution, explicit profit-sharing plans, and other mechanisms that will move ESOPs in the direction of more meaningful worker control over time.[100] Such moves would be improvements from the standpoint of democratic justice if they could be implemented, though there are obvious obstacles in a world where the decision to create an ESOP lies exclusively with management. There are, in any case, other relevant difficulties with ESOPs. They seem less than well-conceived as devices for reducing employee vulnerability. From that point of view workers would be better served by being given shares in mutual funds than by having their fortunes tied to their own firm's prosperity.[101] This kind of "pension fund socialism," which offers the obvious advantages of diversification, has in any case been a more effective wealth-spreading device than ESOPs.[102] Assets in uninsured private pension plans have risen steadily since the 1970s, from $504 billion in 1980 to $1,093 billion in 1985, to $1,629 billion in 1990 and $2,356 billion in 1994.[103] ESOP holdings are tiny by comparison. In 1990 Blasi and Kruse put ESOP assets of the top one thousand plans at $47 billion. Other estimates of ESOP-owned equity are notably lower.[104]

Apart from lacking the advantages of diversification, ESOP participation is sharply tilted toward upper management and white-collar workers.[105] The law even permits exclusion of union members from participating in ESOP plans, as well as new and temporary workers, and workers within five years of normal retirement age at time of hire.[106] Owners can use them to help management resist takeovers, sell personal shares at advantageous prices, and get employees to take wage cuts and forgo other benefits and union membership. Indeed, workers can be induced to buy into plans designed to stave off plant closings that—if they fail—leave them even worse off than they would otherwise have been.[107] Thus, despite a few much-discussed success stories, such as Polaroid and Weirton Steel, ESOPs offer few advantages and create new potential difficulties as far as democratic justice is concerned.[108] Unless ESOPs are defended as hybrid organizational forms on the way to something else, we are bound to concur in Weiler's assessment that participants will continue to "experience little change in their daily life on the job, in their relations with their supervisors, and in their influence over the plans of the firm." [109]

COOPS, PARTNERSHIPS, AND WORKER-OWNED FIRMS

If the ESOP movement is underwhelming from the standpoint of democratic justice, what of more far-reaching efforts to reorganize the firm along democratic lines? There is considerable experience and a large literature on this subject, much of it focused on the various forms of employee ownership that prevail in Italy, France, the Mondragon complex in Spain, and on the system of "codetermination" that has prevailed in Germany for much of the postwar period. Although worker ownership and enhanced worker control can go together, our discussion of ESOPs showed that they are conceptually distinct; as a result, it is useful to begin by considering them separately.

Fully worker-owned firms are rare in the industrialized West.[110] At first sight this is anomalous because, as Henry Hansman and others have noted, employee ownership offers a variety of efficiency advantages.[111] High levels of asset specificity in the employment relationship greatly increase the costs, to workers, of changing jobs, producing "lock-in" effects with attendant inefficiencies that could be obviated by employee ownership. Notorious information asymmetries between labor and management contribute to the difficulty, especially in large firms, of monitoring workers; as a result they promote costly opportunism and strategic bargaining. These problems could be reduced, if not eliminated, by removing incentives for workers and management to hide information and take advantage of one another's ignorance. Workers' incentives to behave opportunistically would also be diminished if they were residual claimants on the firm's earnings, as owners are. Add to this the predictable efficiency losses that result from the extensively documented worker alienation in conventional firms, and it seems that there are several mutually reinforcing reasons for supposing that worker-owned firms should be comparatively efficient.[112]

Given these advantages, various explanations have been adduced to account for the relative dearth of worker-owned firms, ranging from the costs of exit, to the difficulties of raising capital, to workers' reputed lack of willingness to bear investment risk.[113] Hansman makes a powerful case, however, that none of the prevailing accounts plausibly explains both the low overall incidence of employee ownership and its prevalence in certain contexts: service industries and sectors dominated by small firms and professional partnerships.[114] He notes that employee-owned firms tend to develop when there are not substantial conflicts of interest among employees, and he argues that the major obstacle to the emergence of employee ownership in most industrial settings—and the main advantage to investor ownership—is linked to the costs of decision making when such conflicts are present. The costs of decision making also explain why the different "patron" groups who transact with firms (employees, investors, consumers, and lenders) seldom share control of them unless this condition is imposed by the state (as in Germany's system of codetermination). Even when there is joint ownership, as with ESOPs, it does not usually extend to joint control. Hansman contends that the reason is that different patron groups bring different interests to the table, and resolving those differences in governance decisions is costly.

A firm's investors share common interests in maximizing the value of their equity; as a result, conflicts among them about the management of the firm are comparatively rare and decision-making costs among them low. Usually they will agree as to what should be done, partly because the costs of shifting investment to the desired firm or industry are also generally low. With a large and diverse workforce in a firm, by contrast, young, healthy workers with few personal responsibilities can be expected to prefer significantly different management decisions from those preferred by aging workers with dependent children and substantial sunk costs in their present jobs. On a host of issues, ranging from vested employment rights, to how much debt the firm should carry, to health insurance and retirement benefits, employees' interests can be expected to differ. Facing high exit costs they will be more likely to rely on "voice"; if they govern the firm, decision-making costs will therefore be high.[115] Their disagreements will continually be manifest, requiring constant renegotiation and compromise. In taxicab companies, plywood coops, law firms, and other professional partnerships, employees have substantially similar interests, often signaled by their interchangeable roles within the firm. Decision-making costs are consequently low in these settings and the efficiency advantages of worker ownership can be realized.[116] Although at first sight Mondragon might be thought to stand as a decisive counterargument to Hansman's thesis, he makes a convincing case that in fact there is not much direct worker control there.[117] Elsewhere, worker ownership that has developed either in whole (as in Italy, France, and the United Kingdom) or in part (as with American ESOPs) in the industrial sector has been heavily subsidized by the state.

Two implications of Hansman's account merit attention from the standpoint of democratic justice. One is that where worker-owned firms, coops, and partnerships do emerge, worrying about their internal governance should not be a high priority. Hansman's argument that in such circumstances participants' interests in firm governance are not intrinsically opposed suggests that the appropriate analogy is to the adult domestic associations discussed in Chapter 5. That is, the state's role should be limited to structuring power externalities in accordance with the principles of democratic justice, leaving the participants to manage the power internalities as they see fit. Enabling statutory schemes (which now exist in most American states) to make worker employee ownership convenient and feasible are in order, as are the usual corporate-law safeguards against fraud and other criminal conduct. The state also takes an appropriate interest in reducing the

costs of exit, to ensure that continued participation in employee-owned entities remains substantially voluntary on all sides. Apart from this issue, it is
best for the participants to design and modify their own regimes of employee
ownership. There is no good reason not to defer to their insider's wisdom.

By the same token, Hansman's argument has a second implication: most
of the time, when employee-ownership does *not* develop, we reasonably assume that conflicts of interest *are* present within the firm that should trigger
more attention from a democratic state. This is not Hansman's concern, because his interest is in the elective affinities between employee ownership
and efficiency. Persuasive as he might be about the nature of this connection, were his argument to be construed as a normative proposal, it would fly
in the face of democratic justice's commitment to the principle of affected
interest. (The limiting illustration of this is Hansman's observation that inefficiencies in market contracting for labor due to the high asset-specificity
of the employment relationship could in principle be resolved, absent laws
against slavery, if the employees were owned by the firm).[118] Because the
failure of employee ownership to emerge is a signal both that there are conflicts of interest within the firm and that one homogeneous subgroup of the
firm's patrons is likely to be in control because this is cheaper than resolving the conflicts, other affected interests can be expected to be discounted
or ignored.

There are at least two reasons to think that ceding control to one patron
group within the firm for the benefits of reduced decision-making costs
brings with it the danger that defensible hierarchy will atrophy into illegitimate domination. Even if one begins by making the heroic assumption
that—as a by-product of advancing its members' interests—the controlling
patron group will act in the best interests of the firm, it can be expected to
do other things as well. Members of the controlling group will be able to engage in opportunistic pursuit of ancillary interests and desires (that have no
bearing on business decisions) as a result of their power monopoly within the
firm. Sexual harassment of employees is a paradigm instance, but there are
many analogous circumstances in which empowering people to make unilateral business decisions provides them with smokescreens for other agendas. Nor need this be entirely cynical. Unaccountable power wielders can
often convince themselves that they need to exercise authority that is in fact
not needed for their legitimate goals. This is why the burden-shifting de-

vices discussed earlier are needed to keep them honest; it would be naïve to suppose that without them opportunistic domination will not occur.

Second, the heroic assumption itself merits scrutiny. Although Hansman's argument requires that the controlling patron group's members mostly agree on particular decisions about firm governance, it does not imply that they will necessarily promote the firm's efficiency. One could imagine a supplementary argument to the effect that firms in which the controlling patron group make decisions to enhance firm efficiency will outcompete firms in which they do not, but it is from obvious that this is so. It might be a characteristic feature of the most internally homogeneous patron groups that they tend to undermine firm efficiency in certain respects, in which case their decisions would be untouched by competition from similarly structured firms. Arguments to the effect that economy-wide investment decisions are destructively geared to the short term, that managers systematically undermine the interests of shareholders, and that buyers loot and destroy profitable firms in certain types of corporate buyouts all rest on assumptions that such systematic divergence between the interests of controlling patron groups and the requirements of firm profitability can prevail. This possibility suggests the wisdom of casting a skeptical eye on the heroic assumption. Perhaps controlling patrons will make efficiency-maximizing choices, perhaps not. Others within the firm, who must bear the externalities of their decisions, thus have a second and more vital reason to keep them honest: they may make decisions that are systematically subversive of the firm's health. Burden-shifting devices, designed to force a degree of public reason giving when policies are in dispute, will not always stop this. But by requiring the controlling group to establish the link between a disputed policy and a legitimate business purpose, at least burden shifting keeps the pressure in the right place.

It might be said that democratic justice ought to take a more ambitious tack here, supporting the view that the state should underwrite—perhaps even mandate—employee-owned firms. If these will not emerge "naturally" in most settings for the reasons Hansman gives, and we have good reasons for doubting the wisdom of ceding unfettered control to the patron group—typically management—that happens to have control, why not argue for legislation requiring employee ownership? Apart from predictable difficulties related to both the efficiency costs of that proposal and the claims of other patron groups who would be excluded by it, this would be unwise for reasons already discussed in connection with ESOPs. Employee ownership increases employees' vulnerability by strengthening the link between their livelihood and the good fortune of their firm. Control is more important than ownership from our point of view, and the history of employee ownership, like that of ESOPs, suggests that massive state efforts geared to rearranging the incidents of ownership would amount, at best, to taking the slow boat to China. In short, democratic justice does not furnish us with reasons to object to state subsidies for experimental forms of employee ownership, nor does it generate good reasons for requiring them.

CODETERMINATION AND "FLEXIBLE SPECIALIZATION"

Turning from ownership to control, the Europeans have the most experience. Since the 1970s, Germany, the Netherlands, Sweden, Norway, Austria, Denmark, and Luxembourg have all passed legislation requiring worker representation on corporate boards. These laws are modeled on the German practice that developed in the coal, iron, and steel industries after the Second World War. Called *Mitbestimmung* ("having a voice"), these laws require an equal representation of workers and shareholders on the board.[119] Because Germany's spectacular postwar industrial growth coincided with the codetermination laws, they are often credited with contributing to a strong economy. Partly for that reason they spread quickly to Sweden (where since 1976 every company with twenty-five or more workers has two employee representatives on the board) and elsewhere.

One limitation of German-style codetermination is that there are usually two boards, "managerial" and "supervisory," and codetermination laws require worker participation only on the latter. In principle this might be argued to make sense from the standpoint of democratic justice, because it is in the supervisory arena that authority is exercised directly over workers and where their voice should be expected to make the most positive difference. In practice, however, supervisory boards tend to meet only three or four times a year, and employee participation is rather limited, at least in the eyes of critics. They charge that the lack of participation on managerial boards prevents workers from having a voice in many strategic and policy decisions that are decisive in shaping the conditions—often even the continuation—of employment.[120] The few empirical studies of codetermination are inconclusive on this point.[121] Freeman and Rogers suggest that works councils and other codetermination mechanisms perform primarily a "voice" function.[122]

This is by no means negligible. Indeed, emphasizing its importance is at the core of much of the literature that criticizes the hierarchical internal labor market of the traditional firm, arguing instead for various forms of team production that bring with it the advantages of flexible specialization.[123] Some, such as Bluestone and Bluestone, would expand the role of employee voice so that workers have a say in every aspect of management as members of "enterprise compacts" that would combine job security with joint commitments to quality and profitability. They hope that these compacts would make workers and managers into an entrepreneurial unit by eliminating the long-standing division of responsibility in American labor-management practice, which reserves to management exclusive decision-making power over product, method, investment, marketing, scheduling, work organization and other factors, except when explicitly covered in the collective-bargaining agreement.[124] Such proposals are often linked to profit-sharing and gain-sharing schemes.[125] These effectively preserve employment on the downside of business cycles by paying below-market wage rates in good times and above-market rates when times are lean.[126] The spirit of all such proposals, like that of ESOPs, is to create a "we're all in the same boat" ethos that minimizes adversary relations within the firm, replacing them with problem-solving teamwork.

Although there is evidence that both profit sharing and enhanced mechanisms for employee participation increase productivity, from the standpoint of democratic justice there are reasons to be skeptical of the enterprise-compact model.[127] Bluestone and Bluestone themselves note that without unions, profit sharing can "breed the temptation to speed up production to an excessive pace or forego reasonable, protective work rules in the drive to reduce costs and make bonus payments more likely."[128] The same is true of enterprise compacts generally. In light of my earlier discussion of Hansman's thesis and conflicts of interest within the firm, one is bound to worry that enterprise compacts threaten to become mechanisms for employee cooptation through what are effectively company unions. The charges of "team Taylorism" and "management by stress" that have accompanied decentralized production teams from the beginning underscore the fact that aligning the perceptions of the group with the goals of the enterprise glosses over the differences of power and interest within it.[129]

Proponents of the "teamwork" and flexible-specialization paradigms tend to resist this reasoning, arguing that section 8(a)(2) of the National Labor Relations Act, which bans company unions, should be repealed in the interests of efficiency and enhanced democratic control.[130] As Barenberg notes, however, there is abundant empirical literature supporting the proposition that the effective team plants are typically unionized operations.[131] In an American context in which it is impossible to insist on a default option in favor of conventional unionization (as works councils in Germany are to some extent), supporting the repeal of section 8(a)(2) seems unwise.[132] Given the obstacles to unionization drives, section 8(a)(2) may often afford workers little real protection. The danger in putting proposals to abandon it on the table is that we will get the repeal without the alternative scheme of governance, ending up with something like the Team Act being pushed by Republicans in Congress in 1995 and 1996.[133]

It might seem anachronistic to defend traditional union protections, given the massive decline in union membership and in the power of organized labor. But we should beware of linking our reflections too closely to the winds of the political moment. Bob Dole's failure in 1996 to get political traction out of attacking "teachers unions" while claiming to support "teachers" may reflect deeper, if latent, prounion sentiment than it is fashionable to acknowledge. Fear of employer reprisal rather than dislike of unions has been documented as a principal cause of the decline in union representation over the past three decades.[134] Polling data in 1991, for instance, revealed that at the same time as 80 percent of the American public believed that employers are likely to fire workers for organizing or engaging in union activities, between 75 and 82 percent believed that unions are "the best instrument" for improving wages and grievance resolution and for enhancing job security.[135] Some 75 percent of workers who have belonged to unions express high absolute levels of satisfaction with their representation.[136] The main decline has been in the private sector and seems to have been driven by well-founded fears of employer reprisal.[137] Whereas in the late 1960s one employer out of twelve (illegally) fired prounion workers in election campaigns preceding NLRB elections and one in two hundred workers voting for unions could anticipate being fired, by 1991 one in three employers were firing prounion workers and one in thirty-six prounion voters could expect to be fired.[138] In such a context, it cannot be surprising, as Barenberg notes, that 70 percent of nonunion workers believe that some employers would penalize or fire prounion workers, and 40 percent believe that their own employers would do so.[139] Weiler and others may well be right to argue that free collective bargaining might be restored to much of the American workplace if this fear could be overcome.[140]

The External Context

Burden shifting helps keep managers honest when they behave in ways that sacrifice democracy to hierarchy. Because legitimate hierarchies have the propensity to atrophy into instruments of domination, managers are appropriately pressured to show that their decisions are necessary to their legitimate goals. Burden shifting helps achieve that result by ensuring that business-necessity arguments are articulated and defended and that serious attention is given to finding ways of pursuing managers' goals that restrict employees' interests no more than necessary.

ADVANTAGES OF A SHIFTING CRITERION

But how much pressure should there be? The answer depends on what is at stake for the parties. Decisions affecting a firm's viability are quite different from those related to managerial convenience, and pursuit of business necessity that threatens a worker's ability to survive must be distinguished from policies that she finds merely disagreeable. To some extent existing law recognizes this. In Title VII disparate-impact cases, we saw that when a business-necessity defense is sustained, employees can still prevail if they show that there is a way for management to achieve its goal with less disparate impact. By the same token, arbitrators have held that when contracts require just cause for termination, this does not deprive management of the right to impose less severe forms of discipline, such as suspensions and warnings, sometimes unilaterally.[141] Policies of this sort indicate an appreciation that costs should not be imposed unnecessarily and that as the stakes go up for the parties, the burdens borne by their adversaries should become heavier.

Arbitration practice is inconsistent in this regard, however. Sometimes the required quantum of proof in discharge cases is the highly demanding "beyond a reasonable doubt" standard of the criminal law, although usually employers are held to lesser burdens. The conventional civil standard of a "preponderance of the evidence" is most common, though "clear and convincing evidence" or "sufficient to convince a reasonable mind of guilt" are also applied.[142] Arbitrators often do recognize that discharge should require a weightier burden than other forms of discipline, as when the proof presented fails to support discharge but they nonetheless judge it sufficient for a lesser penalty.[143] They may also require more substantial showings when the allegations are of criminal misconduct (or for some other reason they carry a stigma of moral turpitude), as well as a demonstration by the employer that the harmful effect of the actions is "reasonably discernible, mere speculation as to adverse effect on the business not sufficing."[144] Thus with the quantum of proof, as with the burden of proof, arbitrators' decisions are often the product of (at least intuitive) calculations of the respective costs of the action and the proposed discipline to the employer and the employee.

It makes sense to regard such a calculation as relevant, though it should not be contingent on the prior existence of a bargaining agreement. Indeed, democratic justice suggests that the terms of bargaining agreements should be limited by law so as to prevent domination. In this regard employment relations differ from the adult domestic relations discussed in Chapter 5. There my argument was that moving toward a regime in which the costs of exit for all parties are both minimized and equalized is realistic and desirable, and that laws regulating adult domestic association should aspire to be no more than efficiency-maximizing default options. Their purpose should be to minimize transactions costs, and within broadly conceived limits, they should be alterable by negotiations of the parties. This argument was developed on the assumption that the relevant external context can be made minimally coercive. People do not have to marry, or to marry in any particular way, and it is reasonable to strive for a world in which they do not have to bear any costs for unorthodox choices.

Work is different, however. Most people must work for others in order to live, a reality that is not going to change in the foreseeable future. Indeed, a plausible design has yet to be developed for an alternative to the dual-market dynamic. In a world constrained by that dynamic, one in which increases in global capital mobility make the Smith-Wagner logic as pertinent as ever, democratic justice cannot commend a regulatory regime designed to facilitate libertarian choices. Rather, the regime should take account of the power externalities attending employment at the same time as it seeks to mitigate them. This suggests the superiority of the kind of system that prevails in Norway, Sweden, Spain, and the United Kingdom, in which the rules regarding termination are set by statute, to the Danish, Israeli, and American systems, where bargaining agreements are the primary source of such rules.[145] There may also be merit to the German hybrid in which major employers and unions (presumed to be more or less equal adversaries) negotiate terms within statutory constraints, and these terms are then enforced as the industry-wide rule.[146]

A SLIDING-QUANTUM RULE?

Focusing on power externalities validates the impulse to treat termination, or the threat of it, differently from other types of industrial conflict, though the weight of the burden should vary with circumstances. At one pole on a continuum of possibilities, surfers' paradise, the state may be thought of as underwriting all basic interests of the population.[147] In principle this could be done directly, through a robust social wage that guarantees sufficient income, health insurance, and retirement benefits to all, or indirectly, by a combination of employer mandates and unemployment insurance. At the continuum's opposite pole, a Dickensian nightmare, there are no such collective provisions. The rule of thumb should be that the closer an actual society is to a surfer's paradise, the lighter should be the quantum of proof that employers must bear in employment litigation, but that the burden should grow as a society approaches a Dickensian nightmare. Such a rule would limit employers' freedom to take advantage of employees' necessity in setting terms and conditions of employment, and it would give employers an interest in the existence of a robust social wage or social safety net. These would diminish employer's costs in industrial litigation and maximize managerial autonomy within the firm. If arbitrators and industrial tribunals could be predicted to act on this rule, corporations would have an interest in supporting social legislation aimed at mitigating the power externalities of employment, a net plus for democratic justice.

Institutionalizing the sliding-quantum rule could be approached in a variety of ways. It could be incorporated into an ambitious legislative program or, in the United States, perhaps even a constitutional protection of basic interests.[148] In that case the rule might be recast by reference to the public-law standards of judicial scrutiny, so that whether minimal, intermediate, or strict scrutiny was deemed appropriate in evaluating threats to basic interests would itself depend on where we were on the continuum.[149] At or near a surfers' paradise, legislation to protect employees might be subject to strict scrutiny, while policies that adversely affected them would be subject to minimal review only. By the same token, moving toward a Dickensian nightmare would increase the costs of industrial litigation to firms. In those circumstances probusiness regulatory regimes would begin to run afoul more stringent forms of judicial scrutiny, while prolabor regimes would be held to less demanding standards. In effect, business and government would have to find an accommodation concerning how they share costs of underwriting the risk that people cannot vindicate their basic interests through the dual-market dynamic. It would make it harder for business and government, collectively, to externalize that cost onto employees at their moment of greatest bargaining vulnerability.

Constitutionalizing industrial relations in this way would, no doubt, have its drawbacks; in any case, such change is not currently in the cards. But an advantage of the sliding-quantum idea is that it can be applied incrementally, starting anywhere. It could operate relatively modestly, for instance, as a criterion for rationalizing application of the various conflicting quanta of proof in discharge litigation already discussed, whether by individual arbitrators engaged in common-law practice, commissions rewriting model arbitration codes, or legislatures acting on a more substantial scale. In federal and confederal systems it could guide the terms on which central authorities offered subordinate units greater relative deregulation and autonomy. In the European Union, for instance, one could imagine the sliding-quantum rule guiding the mix of sticks and carrots employed by Council of Ministers in dealings with member countries. Attacks on social safety nets by national governments would trigger directives that would make more cumbersome the quantum of proof that a business must bear to demonstrate just cause for layoffs. Business interests in the different countries would then stand to gain competitively if their national governments could forestall this result by sustaining social wages and safety nets. Because it is increased flexibility at the plant level that businesses seem, increasingly, to want most, their incentive to support forces protective of the social wage would be strong.[150] In all such circumstances the underlying principle would be the same: decision makers motivated by democratic justice would seek to diminish the extent to which employers or politicians could achieve their goals in ways that prevent people from vindicating their basic interests.

This approach has the further advantage that it can motivate marginal shifts in policy as well as major ones. It might operate, at a minimum, as a defensive barrier, making clear to those who attack the social safety net or shoot down proposals—such as national health-care legislation—designed to expand the social wage, that their politics come with a price. This might seem like a trifling ambition for a political theory, yet the absence of such devices has surely made easier the scorched-earth assault on welfare states that has been under way in many Western countries since the early 1980s. The sliding-quantum rule is, in any case, a principle for all political seasons. As political winds change it might help focus and legitimate substantial expansions of the social wage, perhaps led by the executive branch. Just as the federal government declined to do business with firms that engaged in racial discrimination in the early days of affirmative action, and, indeed, as the first Clinton administration initially declined to do business with firms that employ permanent replacement workers during strikes, so one could imagine an administration withholding contracts from firms that engage in other labor practices that violate basic interests.[151] Although an eventual goal might be a guaranteed basic income for all, it can thus be pursued realistically at the margins of what is politically feasible in a given situation. In short, this is not the kind of principle that sets the best at loggerheads with the good.

Governments, Firms, Unions, and Workers' Basic Interests

That people be able to vindicate their basic interests is more important than hewing to any prescription of just what mix of wages and other resources will make this possible. Familiar considerations about incentives and institutional limitations speak in favor of doing more rather than less through the dual-market dynamic, while the existence of capital-labor power asymmetries and structural unemployment support the view that government should nonetheless be expected to underwrite basic interests. Governments, as we have seen, are thought justified in imposing and sustaining the dual-market dynamic partly because of the promise it holds to people as a mechanism for vindicating their basic interests. In circumstances where it fails to live up to that promise, governments should therefore be obliged to pick up the pieces.

Although government's underwriting obligation should, ideally, have something like a constitutional status, in principle democratic justice is indifferent to what blend of direct social wage provisions (such as a national health-care system) and indirect provisions (such as employer mandates supplemented by a social safety net) is deemed best to meet the underwriting obligation. The point of the sliding-quantum rule is to create pressure for it to be met somehow and thus combat the impulse for all those with the capacity to meet it simply to balk. But I count it an advantage of my proposal that there is more than one way of meeting the obligation. It is compatible with moving toward a world in which conflicts over wages and benefits need not be zero-sum battles between workers and their employers, provided employers are prepared to use resources at their disposal to help see to it that the social wage expands. If, however, in a world governed by the sliding-quantum rule, employers chose instead to pick up a comparatively larger share of the costs of vindicating their employees' basic interests, proponents of democratic justice should not object.

Having said that, there are evident advantages to tilting toward a social-wage approach if it can be institutionalized. In a robust social-wage environment, firms (particularly small firms) would be better off not having to bear the costs of health and retirement benefits for their employees, and they would derive predictable advantages from less demanding applications of the sliding-quantum rule: more managerial flexibility and a relatively freer hand with respect to layoffs. No doubt there are offsetting costs. Increasing the social wage might arguably increase wages, and hence costs, due to the efficiency-wage phenomenon: the gap between actual wages paid and market-clearing wages, which some economists like to think of as a rent paid to employees to reduce the costs of monitoring them. Arguably, more secure workers would become more militant because they would have less to lose and therefore be less fearful of employers. And corporations arguably would bear the costs of financing the social wage through higher corporate taxes, offsetting the benefits described earlier. Although any or all of these is possible in theory, in fact the empirical basis for the efficiency-wage argument appears speculative at best, the European evidence suggests that, if anything, there is an inverse correlation between robust welfare states and industrial militancy, and not every dollar saved in benefits need be spent to finance the social wage.[152] As I note below, there are various ways to finance it, and trying to place the entire burden on corporate shoulders is almost certainly unwise. In short, from a pure cost standpoint, considerations flow in both directions and are probably inconclusive.

The decisive considerations favoring a social-wage approach flow from the disadvantages of a union-centered regime. The more that vindication of basic interests relies on the dual-market dynamic, the more necessary unions are to protect vulnerable workers. If basic interests were not threatened by its operation, we could agree with those who argue for the repeal of section 8(a)(2) of the NLRA, opening the way to the new forms of labor-management cooperation and more creative experimentation in firm governance. This would offer a number of advantages over traditional unions, which, in addition to the reasons that management dislikes them, are less than optimal from the standpoint of democratic justice. Experiments with "mobilizing" and "continuous organizing" models of unionization notwithstanding, unions can be bureaucratic and unresponsive, and they are seldom famous for their internal democracy.[153] Such defects can no doubt be exaggerated, and in any case there is no compelling reason to believe them less curable than the antidemocratic features of the going alternatives. The central difficulty with unions for democratic justice is different. As micro-institutions whose nature requires them to operate first and foremost at the individual firm level, they are not well suited to altering the environment in which they operate.

The relation between the goals of particular unions and the those of the class of actual or possible workers is analogous to that between the goals of individual firms and the class of actual or potential investors. That is, while broadly congruent, these relations are attended by difficulties relating to delegation and monitoring, certain types of conflict of interest, tensions between short-run and long-run objectives, and a variety of collective-action problems. Indeed, some of these difficulties are arguably more serious in the house of labor. There, problems related to delegation, monitoring, and conflicts of interest are less easily shrugged off than in the relations between firms and investors because the costs of exit will be higher for the worker, in the typical case, than for the investor. Tensions between unions' short-

and long-run objectives become manifest when employers offer substantial benefits to current employees in exchange for their mortgaging the bargaining power of future workers. Collective action difficulties arise from the dual role of unions as agents of their local memberships and of employees generally, as when white-collar unions seek to restore wage differentials between their members and blue-collar workers.[154] This can lead to fragmentation and weakening of labor movements, as can the fact that unions are not well positioned to represent the interests of the unemployed. On the contrary, their obligation to advocate the interests of their memberships creates incentives for individual unions to ignore the unemployed in each particular negotiation, even though the existence of a large, vulnerable, unemployed class weakens their bargaining power. Unions do not represent the interests of workers in industries that defy attempts at unionization, not to mention domestic workers who work outside the money economy. To some degree confederations of trade unions and organized labor movements can mitigate and manage these difficulties, but the experience of the 1980s and 1990s throughout the industrialized world reveals them to be more deep-seated than it was once fashionable to believe.

Unions are thus imperfectly suited to their purposes, and they exhibit limitations as agents for the types of evolution in the control of work that proponents of democratic justice should want to see. Nonetheless, in some of the principal cases on record where business has supported expansions of the social wage — during the 1940s and 1950s in Northern Europe and during the New Deal in the United States — it has been in part to escape the pressure that unions were putting on them to provide costly social benefits.[155] Whatever the disadvantages of unions, to date no alternative form of industrial organization has come along that holds out any hope of doing better. In the present context of industrial relations, giving comfort to those who would weaken or get rid of unions for their failure to give optimal representation to workers' interests would be like taking seriously an argument that we should support weakening or abolishing the police on the grounds that they have failed to get rid of crime. For the reasons adduced above, a robust social-wage approach should be preferred to relying on the dual-market dynamic to the extent that we do to vindicate workers' basic interests. But given the inhospitable political climate that expanding the social wage currently confronts, the Smith-Wagner logic remains decisive. It requires defending institutions that pressure those who thrive within the dual-market dynamic, to ensure that their thriving does not come at the expense of the basic interests of those who do not thrive.

Realities and Possibilities

Playing out the principled commitments of democratic justice in the evolving context of industrial relations in the West since the 1970s has brought us to a depressing destination. We seem reduced to arguing for little more than defensive holding actions, to forestall even greater departures from the democratic justice ideal than those that are well under way and seem to be gathering momentum. To some extent this may be an inescapable reality of our times. An increasingly global market is beyond the control of any single player or small group of players, so that attempts at unilateral improvement seem vulnerable to a global "race to the bottom," and any thought of multilateral sanctions risks crippling defection. Yet it is easy to overestimate the inevitability of present arrangements and the obstacles to changing them, as my discussion of evidence concerning latent support for unions indicated. As far as the declining strategic power of organized labor in the West is concerned, it is unclear how much of this is attributable to transnational factors rather than domestic ones. Moreover, there are various actions that Western governments can take, depending on the diagnosis, to ameliorate the problem. These range from supporting global labor standards and the institutions that try to implement them, to negotiating international agreements backed up by the threat of trade sanctions, to redistributive taxation from beneficiaries of the technological revolution to those who have suffered from it, to investment in retraining and reskilling of the unemployed, to public works programs of the sort that helped pull the United States and other Western economies out of the Depression.

Before commenting on these possibilities, it should be said that, in earlier times, arguments about the race to the bottom and the instability of sanctions would have suggested that attempts to abolish slavery, child labor, or apartheid must inevitably fail. History demurred. The campaigns to abolish slavery and child labor in the West were notable successes.[156] The results of the antiapartheid movement seem at variance with conventional wisdom about sanctions.[157] To be sure, these efforts took place over many decades, other favorable factors were involved, and the achievements might be undone in the future. Yet they remind us that human ingenuity can at times subvert, and at times co-opt, self-interest in the service of unlikely goals. In the contemporary world, various coalitions are seeking to restructure the new power externalities of employment. Proponents of democratic justice can learn from their efforts and perhaps explore ways to build on them.

The collapse of the strategic power of organized labor in much of the West seems traceable to two main sources: relative factor-price convergence on a transnational scale, as ever-more-mobile capital seeks out cheap labor markets, and technological changes that have opened a substantial gap—growing since the mid-1970s—between the fortunes of workers whose skills are integral to the information revolution and those whose skills are not.[158] The first results in "social dumping," when the threat of capital flight is used to extract wage and other concessions from unions. The second increases relative inequalities between skilled and unskilled workers in the advanced economies. Because both dynamics lead to the decline of Western manufacturing wages, analysts disagree over the relative importance of trade versus technology as causes. Some, notably Adrian Wood, place the bulk of the blame on increased trade with low-wage manufacturing economies, while his critics point to technological innovation in response to declining productivity in the Western economies after the 1960s. It seems clear that both factors are involved and that they may, indeed, interact, as when corporations engage in "defensive" technological innovation in response to low-wage competition from abroad. Nonetheless, estimates of the trade factor range from its being a relatively minor component to being the predominant cause. Gary Burtless's even-handed survey of empirical studies concludes that trade may account for about half of the decline in U.S. manufacturing wages since the mid-1970s.[159] Because "social dumping" arguments turn on the *threat* to move production to low-wage economies, the numbers may in any case understate the degree to which the decline in Western manufacturing wages is driven by relative price-factor convergence as we have moved to a freer trade regime internationally.[160]

Whatever the relative importance of the different causes, there is no doubt that the combined effects have been devastating to the strategic power of organized labor in many Western economies. In some countries (notably Britain and the United States) the effects are seen in the collapse of union membership and large declines in real wages. In the more corporatist west European economies, unions, and to some extent wages, have survived, but at the price of unemployment levels that have not been seen for decades.[161] Because all agree that the information age is in its infancy and that untapped low-wage labor markets in the ex-Soviet world and China will be massive extensions of what is already available in the rest of Asia and Latin America (not to mention Africa), it is difficult to see how these forces can be resisted. Indeed, the proliferation of international trade agreements since the 1970s seems likely, if anything, to strengthen them.[162]

The scale of these phenomena may be unprecedented, but Western governments have confronted them before. As far as transnational factors are concerned, in the past governments have sometimes shown both the will and the capacity to attach trade sanctions and other penalties to countries that facilitate the social-dumping threat. In the United States, for instance, Congress's 1984 renewal of the Trade Act's provision authorizing the President to grant tariff relief to developing countries excluded any country that "has not taken or is not taking steps to afford internationally recognized worker rights to workers in the country (including any designated zone in the country)." These include the rights of association, organizing, and free collective bargaining, prohibitions on "any form of forced or compulsory labor," minimum age employment requirements, and "acceptable conditions of work with respect to minimum wages, hours of work, and occupational safety and help." Although this is a unilateral United States action, it has an international dimension, because the state department's interpretation of the triggering criteria is based on International Labor Organization conventions.[163] Between 1985 and 1992 thirty-three countries were reviewed under this provision. Nicaragua, Romania, and the Sudan were removed from the program, and Chile, Paraguay, the Central African Republic, Burma, and Liberia were suspended.[164] Similar presidential oversight is required by the 1983 Caribbean Basin Economic Recovery Act and the 1985 congressional reauthorization of the Overseas Private Investment Corporation, which insures investors in less developed countries.[165] Legislation of this kind is to be endorsed from the standpoint of democratic justice, particularly if it can nudge countries in the direction of embracing global minimum labor standards that reflect basic human interests. It might also be wise, for domestic political reasons, to urge earmarking tariffs derived from the enforcement of these laws to compensate workers who are harmed by social dumping.

Such legislation is only as good as the capacity and willingness of the world's most powerful governments to enforce it. The first Clinton administration's rapid about-face on campaign promises to stand up to China on this front revealed the considerable political leverage of forces that resist them. The administration did marginally better with labor side agreements to NAFTA, signed in September 1993.[166] These agreements provide for trade sanctions of up to $20 million (or suspension of equivalent NAFTA trade benefits) for countries that persistently fail to enforce occupational safety and health, child labor, or minimum wage requirements. As Barenberg notes, however, the agreement is limited by the fact that it requires enforcement only of the country's own requirements in this regard, and it contains no sanctions for violations of the country's other labor standards, collective-bargaining laws, or any multilateral labor standards.[167] Proponents of democratic justice should press for more powerful side agreements than this to trade treaties. It is a matter of particular urgency in the United States, where treaties have the force of federal law. Unless such side agreements are put in place, trade treaties can preempt prior state and even federal legislation such as the NLRA.[168] There is thus a substantial danger that hard-won domestic labor standards can be undermined by trade agreements like NAFTA and GATT if they are deemed nontariff barriers to trade, producing "downward harmonization" of domestic standards rather than "upward harmonization" of foreign ones.[169] Comparatively toothless as the NAFTA labor side agreements might be, they are a step in the right direction. Trade agreements ought to pull worse labor standards toward the minimum required by the basic interests criterion; they should not be devices for widening the gap between relatively better labor standards and that criterion.[170]

This logic is sometimes challenged on the grounds that if capital can move to wherever labor costs are lowest unfettered by such constraints, the marginal welfare gain to starving third-world workers will exceed the marginal loss to first-world workers, a net improvement.[171] If the distributive alternatives presented in such examples really were exclusive zero-sum distributive conflicts between first-world and third-world manufacturing workers, or if the living standards of the first-world workers being harmed exceeded the basic interests criterion, such discussions might be worth engaging in.

Neither of these premises is true, however. There are numerous other relevant players, as we have seen, and the levels of poverty at the lower end of the socioeconomic scale in the Western economies make it undeniable that basic interests are at stake there.[172] In this context, it is important to keep the pressure on Western governments to entrench minimum labor standards in national and international laws, whether by constitutional amendments in particular countries, other unilateral requirements, or bilateral and multilateral agreements.[173] From the standpoint of democratic justice, profit maximization may trump other values when basic interests are not threatened. But when its price is their violation, profit maximization should give way.

To date, the most extensive experience, and the most ambitious model, comes from the European Union. The *Community Charter of Basic Social Rights for Workers* was adopted by all member countries except Britain in December 1989, the two hundredth anniversary of the French Universal Declaration of Human Rights. It created a community-wide framework of employment standards, with the prevention of social dumping as one of its explicit goals.[174] The *Agreement on Social Policy*, signed at Maastricht in 1992, is the charter's implementing legislation. Member states are primarily responsible for implementing the agreement in accordance with the EU's governing principle of subsidiarity (whereby the community acts only when set objectives can be more effectively achieved than through action by member states). The agreement is to be backed up, however, by the directive power of the Council of Ministers. It has broad authority to set "minimum requirements for gradual implementation" in the areas of health and safety, working conditions, information and consultation of workers, gender equality of opportunity and "integration of persons excluded from the labor market."[175]

The council first acted on this authority in 1994, issuing a directive on the establishment of European Works Councils for firms employing at least 1,000 workers where 150 or more employees work in two or more member states.[176] It remains to be seen whether these works councils (about 1,300 of which had been created by late 1996) will turn out to strengthen labor as much as the German ones on which they are modeled.[177] But the directive creating them is an important first step in responding to the transnational dimensions of the democratic control of work. More ambitious possibilities under discussion in Europe include requiring firms to incorporate under

EC law as European companies, binding all European corporations (not just cross-border ones) through labor-law directives, mandating choice among a limited menu of industrial relations regimes, and perhaps eventually requiring some Eurowide collective bargaining. Developments of this last kind are clearly a long way off, even in Europe. But in the emerging world of transnational capitalism, the EC as it has evolved to date offers a credible model for managing some of the interactions between work's power internalities and externalities in accordance with the principles of democratic justice.[178]

Although the advantages of anti–social dumping policies will depend on the degree to which the trade-based diagnosis is correct, Wood and Burtless both note that there are also policies that governments can sensibly pursue regardless of how much the pressure on domestic manufacturing is trade based rather than technology based.[179] Redistributive taxation from those who have derived windfalls from the information revolution to those who have been hit hardest by it, publicly sponsored retraining where there are realistic prospects for alternative employment, and public works projects aimed at refurbishing decaying infrastructure while providing employment are the obvious possibilities. Proponents of democratic justice should endorse such policies, provided they are combined with upward pressure on minimum wages so that workers have a realistic chance of vindicating their basic interests within the constraints of the dual-market dynamic. For those who cannot, government's obligation to underwrite their basic interests remains. Although this obligation does not have the natural-law force that Locke believed it did, one is hard pressed to see why anyone should feel, or owe, allegiance to a political order in which this obligation goes unrecognized.

· 7 ·

Life's Ending

LIFE'S ENDING MIRRORS ITS BEGINNING. Whereas children develop from conditions of utter dependence to comparative independence, aging adults lose autonomy as their reliance on others grows. This inverted sequence means that some questions about the elderly arise for democratic justice that parallel those concerning children, although there are also significant differences. Adults know of their impending dependence and can plan for it, at least to a degree. They may be able to put aside resources during their productive years on which to draw later, and they can make their wishes known through various means, while still competent, as to how they wish to be treated if and when their competence dissipates. Also unlike children, adults can participate in democratic policy making about the end of life. They can try to influence the provision of resources that will be guaranteed the elderly through mechanisms such as Social Security and Medicare, as well as the structure of legal protections (against age discrimination, for instance) that the state is obliged to enforce. In these ways, among others, competent adults can participate in shaping the regime that they anticipate will be in place once their competence begins to wane.

The inverted sequence of autonomy and dependence does not free the elderly of every vulnerability that children confront. When advanced age arrives, it can frustrate even the most carefully laid plans. Economic circumstances may change in unexpected ways. Altered demographic conditions or political coalitions can lead to unpredicted shifts in the legal and economic landscape. Changing medical technologies may offer novel possibilities and present new dilemmas, recasting questions about costs and decision making in unanticipated ways. Adult children might turn out, against expectations, to be unable or unwilling to care for aging parents. Because such consequential changes can occur to old people after they have become vulnerably dependent (and hence ill-placed to do much about it), in practice they may turn out to be no less disenfranchised than young children from the standpoint of democratic justice: powerless to participate in, or oppose, decisions that critically affect their interests. This suggests that, distinctive as the condition of the elderly might be, institutional protections may be in order that are in some ways parallel to those required for governing children.

Thinking about democratic justice in death's shadow is challenging, partly because it draws us into realms where power relations are interwoven with intensively experienced matters of personal destiny and some of the most emotionally charged intimacies of which people are capable. True, this scarcely distinguishes life's ending from many aspects of governing children or adult domestic life discussed in earlier chapters, but in some ways the challenges are harder here and the stakes higher. Death's imminence leaves little room to rectify mistakes, or to transform zero-sum conflicts into positive-sum ones; on the contrary, it tends to harden attitudes and close off possibilities. As a result, forced choices can often be stark, leaving little space to reconcile conflicting impulses and responsibilities.

The inescapably unpleasant realities of dying might seem to undermine democratic justice's capacity to operate well as a subordinate good in this area. If there is no good way to die, then there is no superordinate good to be conditioned by our hallmark subordinate constraints. To respond to the circumstances of death and dying in this way would, however, be misguided. People are bound to confront the just management of evils as well as goods, and in any case some ways of dealing with life's ending are better than others. In life's terminal stages, as in other circumstances, we should aspire to move closer to a world in which people can pursue their goals as well as possible, while fostering their participation in relevant collective decisions and preserving their ability to oppose outcomes they reject. Spelling out what this means for governing the elderly is my present task.

Inherited Context

Life expectancy has steadily been increasing in the advanced industrial countries over the past century, but this is only loosely related—if at all—to the creation of a distinct status in the human life cycle called retirement. Until the 1970s much of the increase in life expectancy had to do with diminishing rates of infant mortality, not increased longevity. And at the same time that life spans have been lengthening, the retirement age has been falling, suggesting that a different dynamic is at work.[1]

Sociologists and demographers have looked to a variety of factors to account for the emergence and evolution of retirement, ranging from changing cultural preferences to various postulated effects of modernization. Whatever the underlying forces at work, it seems clear that the proximate causes were tied to the expansion of the dual-market dynamic in the late nineteenth century and the Great Depression in the early twentieth. Business, organized labor, professional groups, and public officials converged on retirement support for different, if partly overlapping, reasons. The demands of corporate efficiency, the pursuit of prosperity's benefits, the desire for security, and consolidation of the emerging regulatory state all played their respective parts. The net effect was to involve government—and increasingly the national government—in underwriting and overseeing retirement.[2]

Neither employers nor state or federal governments had provided pensions during the nineteenth century.[3] In the 1920s and early 1930s the burdens of old-age assistance began to shift from local jurisdictions and private charities, first to the states and then the federal government. The hardship and instability of the Depression gave impetus to the nationalization of old-age support. The federal railroad retirement legislation of the 1930s, for example, moved retirement from the world of collective bargaining to the realm of political action. The old-age provisions of the Social Security Act of 1935 had a similar and more widespread effect.[4]

The political, economic, and institutional forces favoring the creation of retirement were buttressed by market dynamics. Once economists came to believe that some quantity of unemployment is inescapable, a series of interconnected efficiency-based questions were bound to present themselves. Who should work, and for how long? Can public policies be enacted to ensure that people work during their most productive years? If so, is this desirable? What should become of those no longer thought to be sufficiently productive? Economic theorists such as Alfred Marshall had explicitly linked industrial productivity to physical traits that deteriorate, and in 1906 the statistician Frederick Hoffman drew on this reasoning to argue that national productivity would be maximized if the normal workspan ran from ages fifteen to sixty-five.[5] The details of Hoffman's mathematics could be questioned, but his central claim that the appropriate maximand is the productive lifetime dovetailed neatly with the agendas of groups seeking to institutionalize retirement. For unions, the same arguments for changing the ratio of toil to leisure, and for limiting unemployment, that had motivated the campaigns to shorten the working day were naturally extended to this idea. For employers, who had been losing the battle over the working day since the 1880s, relatively less-productive older workers became increasingly costly and retirement correspondingly more attractive. Given the conditions of employment, the attraction of retirement for workers was, no doubt, often self-evident.[6]

The political economy of aging and retirement has taken on a different hue since the 1970s. The postretirement lifespan has been substantially expanded, increasing fiscal pressures on a Social Security system—not to mention the Medicare system of health-care coverage for retired Americans that has been in place since 1965. Scholars divide on the seriousness of the fiscal problems confronting Social Security, but there is little doubt that they will worsen in the next several decades for demographic reasons.[7] Advances in medical technology contribute to the problem as well, both because they help extend life spans of retirees and because their intrinsic expense links Social Security's cost to the more serious fiscal difficulties confronting Medicare. The impulse to take every available measure to save a life is deeply embedded in our culture, partly for good reasons that are explored below. But in a world where the universe of expensive available measures is constantly expanding, this leads to a reality in which a great many resources are spent on people in the last weeks, days, and even hours of life. Inevitably this has produced stress throughout the medical insurance industry and the

Medicare systems, not to mention the Medicaid system for the poor, which has been hit particularly hard.

For a time in the first Clinton administration it appeared that structural reform to address some of these difficulties might be in the cards. The move to a Canadian- or British-style single-payer system was not seriously considered, despite the urging of some commentators, but Clinton's proposed Health Security Act would have required all residents of the United States to participate in some form of health plan that supplied a comprehensive package of benefits.[8] The main elements of the universal package—immunizations for children, standard checkups, and routine medical care—were set out in the legislation, which was eventually to cover dental, vision, and mental health care as well. The universal package would have been regulated by a National Health Board, empowered to include medical treatments it deemed "necessary and appropriate."[9] Grappling with how the National Health Board should determine what to include in the basic package rapidly became an academic question, as significant parts of the medical, insurance, and corporate establishments (some of which had initially seemed favorably disposed to some such plan) financed a successful $50 million public relations and lobbying campaign to derail the legislation.[10] The Clinton effort did accelerate the move toward greater use of health maintenance organizations and more explicit rationing of some procedures by insurers.[11] But most rationing continues to be implicit, and the most egregious ill that the act would have addressed persists: in stark contrast to the other advanced industrial countries, more than forty-one million Americans continue to live without any health insurance at all.[12]

Distributing Resources

Decisions to spend resources generally arise within budget constraints, which can be implicit. When third-party medical payment schemes are criticized on the grounds that neither the provider nor the patient has reason to consider the costs of the procedures they use, for instance, the implication is that the budget constraint is insufficiently explicit. Whether or not the budget constraint is explicit, it is present, however, as this example illustrates. It may show up as lack of adequate resources elsewhere in the health-care system, or as a comparatively high rate of medical inflation as costs are displaced onto unwitting third parties, but when decisions to expend resources are made, they must come from somewhere.

RESOURCE DISTRIBUTION VERSUS MAXIMS OF INDIVIDUAL ACTION

Recognizing this, we can distinguish two types of question for democratic justice: how should decisions be made about what the budget constraints should be, and how should decisions be made within the budget constraints as they exist at any given time? The first type of question is principally about the distributive choices confronting a society for the care of its aging and infirm populations; the second concerns maxims for action within the parameters of the prevailing distributive scheme. The two interact in ways that are partly analogous to the power internalities and the power externalities of the firm discussed in Chapter 6, producing some parallel conclusions that are elaborated below. But it is helpful first to think about them separately.

The confusions that can result from conflating principles of resource distribution with maxims of individual action are well illustrated in Ronald Dworkin's critique of what he describes as the "rescue" principle for distributing medical care. This is the view (often said to be implicit in the Hippocratic oath, which physicians are required to affirm) that it is obligatory to take every possible step to save a life without reference to the cost. Dworkin rejects this principle as "almost wholly useless," despite the fact that it is "so ancient, so intuitively attractive, and so widely supported in political rhetoric." [13] Whatever its appeal in bygone eras, in today's world of continuous innovation in expensive life-prolonging technologies it is a hopelessly expansive criterion. No sane society, he argues, should try to govern decisions about the distribution of health care by the rescue principle "any more than a sane person would organize his life on that principle." [14]

Dworkin is obviously right if the rescue principle is seen as one for distributing resources. Indeed, we can underscore and extend his point by noting that it defies the possibility of consistent application as a distributive device. Even a society that devoted all its tax revenues to life-prolonging medical care could not escape distributive trade-offs among the life-prolonging possibilities for the terminally ill. Should the next marginal tax dollar be spent lengthening the lives of cancer patients or of those with heart disease? Is AIDS research a greater priority than kidney dialysis? Depending on how one interprets the rescue principle, either it seems to counsel that every possible response to forced trade-offs of this kind is illegitimate (thus bordering on the incoherent), or it is silent about those trade-offs.

Dworkin believes that the rescue principle's indeterminacy buttresses his claim about its uselessness, but this is thrown into doubt once we recognize that it is not a distributive principle at all. I noted earlier that a version of the rescue principle is often taken to be embedded in the Hippocratic oath. This provides a clue that the rescue principle is really a maxim of individual conduct. The oath is, after all, part of a code of professional behavior, aimed at physicians, not policy makers. This is not to deem it irrelevant to governmental policy or, by extension, to democratic justice. Governments license physicians and regulate their activities. Enforcing codes of professional behavior is an appropriate part of that licensing and regulation. But it is distinct from questions about the allocation and distribution of health-care resources. The rescue principle is best understood as an admonition to the physician to do everything possible to save and extend life within the prevailing budget constraint, not as a principle about what the budget constraint should be. I make the case below that—thus construed—a version of the rescue principle is defensible not as a categorical imperative but rather as a rebuttable presumption. The focus here is on the budget constraint and its distributive implications. On these subjects Dworkin is right that the rescue principle supplies no helpful counsel.

A WHOLE-LIFE APPROACH

Recall that my discussions of basic interests in earlier chapters were limited neither by age nor by capacity to work. Once the dual-market dynamic prevails, I argued, it makes sense to discern collective responsibilities to guarantee the basic interests of populations subject to the dynamic. This is why governments are obliged to underwrite the basic interests of children and those adults who are unable to vindicate those interests through employment. There is no principled reason to exclude the elderly from this reasoning. The able-bodied elderly who are forced to retire face a form of unemployment that is not relevantly different from that of others who are forced out of work. Those who are unable to work because of incapacity are analogous to the children of poor parents: they lack the resources to survive in an order from which they cannot escape. It is thus time to make explicit what was implicit in my earlier account: that collective underwriting of basic interests should be thought of as extending across the human life span.

It might be objected that the elderly have had an entire lifetime to plan for their impending dependent years. If they fail to save adequately for what is obviously coming, perhaps they should be deemed to have assumed the relevant risks. Notice that nothing in the argument for democratic justice prevents governments from requiring people to save for old age, so long as the compulsory savings rate is not so steep as to undermine their basic interests during their working years.[15] Compulsory saving in this area seems, indeed, to be prudent; otherwise, it will be impossible to avoid the moral hazard that would obviously attend a voluntary system that the state has entrenched obligations to underwrite. Such compulsion is further justifiable because the basic-interests standard does not merely reflect an entitlement. If it did, perhaps it could fairly be waived by risk-embracing individuals. But in democracies, as I have argued, there is also a third-party interest at stake: we reasonably expect others to have the wherewithal to vindicate their own basic interests.

A different objection might emanate from the communitarian feeling that adult children should bear responsibility for their aging parents. On this view, caring for aging parents should not be conceived of as a burden to be foisted onto the state. The communitarian impulse is not entirely without merit in this area, but it is misguided when brought to bear on the subject of resources available to the elderly. In an era when many lower- and middle-income families either have seen real incomes erode or have maintained them only by becoming two-wage-earner families, it is unrealistic in many cases to think that adult children can provide basic income support for their aging parents.[16] Indeed, distributing the financial burden in this way places stress on families that may undermine the supportive interaction between the elderly and their adult children that communitarians would like society to foster. In earlier times, when "stepping down" by the old was a gradual process of declining responsibility and increasing dependence, maintaining them in the framework of the household economy may have made sense. In the contemporary world, when people work, save, and insure as individuals throughout their adult lives, it makes little sense to try to reintroduce them to the household economy as life's ending approaches.[17] Norman Daniels's question, "Am I my parent's keeper?" is thus answered in the negative by democratic justice.[18] Society is collectively responsible for underwriting the basic interests of its members over the course of the life cycle. Beyond this, one's personal ethics or one's upbringing may lead one to discern moral obligations on adult children to their aging parents. But these should not be enforceable by the state.

RETIREMENT AND AGE DISCRIMINATION

Democratic justice generates no right to retire, but nor should it lead us to object to retirement. People might elect to bear a higher savings rate during their working years in order to retire, or to retire earlier rather than later. Likewise with collective decisions to create a retirement status. These might result—as they did, we saw, historically—from a mixture of forces ranging from the desire for leisure, to efficiency considerations, to labor-market dynamics, to outcomes of collective bargaining. Provided the basic interests of retirees are not threatened, democratic justice provides no reasons to regard retirement as illegitimate.

What of the person who abjures retirement? It might be said that partisans of democratic justice should resist mandatory retirement, if only because the presumption of universal inclusion casts suspicion on decisions to withdraw incidents of adulthood from anyone prematurely. This is so, but in a world of less than full employment the question usually posed is not simply whether to deny employment to an elderly person but whether to protect his job at the price of denying a job to someone else potentially in the labor force; it is a question of balancing competing employment claims when all cannot be satisfied. Democratic justice requires that people have, or have the wherewithal to generate, what is needed to vindicate their basic interests. It does not guarantee everyone a job.

Declining to guarantee a job is not, however, the same as prohibiting work by the able-bodied elderly who want to work. A commitment to democratic justice should lead us to reject such prohibition as an unjustified withdrawal of an incident of adulthood before necessity dictates. If people want to work for themselves until they draw their last breath, or if others want to employ them, no one should be able to stop them. In short, we must distinguish compulsory retirement from a particular job or type of job, which will often be justifiable, from compulsory retirement of an individual from all employment on reaching a certain age, which is not.

Some might object that democratic justice would not fall silent if tight labor markets were cited to deny employment to women or minorities, so why treat the elderly differently? Particularly in the United States in recent decades this analogy has been pressed with some success to shield the elderly from age-based employment discrimination.[19] The analogy is faulty, however. Race- and gender-based classifications are appropriately seen as suspect for two reasons that distinguish them from age: they invoke ascriptive characteristics that apply to subsets of the population only, and they single out groups that have historically been subject to domination. Either of these factors would be sufficient to trigger suspicion from a political theory that abjures domination; their joint presence underscores it.

Age-based classifications like retirement have not been associated with a history of discrimination, and they are developmental rather than ascriptive. As the majority Supreme Court opinion put it in *Massachusetts Board of Retirement v. Murgia* in 1976, the elderly, "unlike, say, those who have been discriminated against on the basis of race or national origin, have not experienced 'a history of purposeful unequal treatment' or been subject to unique disabilities on the basis of stereotyped characteristics." The justices went on to note, moreover, that the elderly do not constitute "a 'discrete and insular' group . . . in need of 'extraordinary protection from the majoritarian political process,'" alluding to Justice Stone's standard for special protection in *Carolene Products*, discussed in Chapter 3.[20] Rather, old age "marks a stage that each of us will reach if we live out our normal span."[21]

The logic articulated by the *Murgia* majority admits of exceptions, but they tend to reinforce the general claim that age-based statuses should generally be judged benign. A compulsory-retirement law with a sunset clause thirty years hence, for instance, would invite suspicion from democratic justice because it lacked universal applicability, as would attempts by an age cohort to abolish age-related benefits of which its members had taken advantage (as when the elderly in a jurisdiction organize to cut funds for public education). Age-based classifications might also provoke suspicion if there were reasons for thinking them surrogates for genuinely suspect classifications. A law canceling estate taxes for those who live beyond eighty might be enacted for the racially discriminatory reason that whites, who frequently outlive it, would benefit from it disproportionately to blacks, who typically do not. Age classifications of this sort would rightly trigger suspicion, but only in virtue for the classifications for which age served as proxies.[22]

Granting that age-discrimination is not objectionable as such, it might nonetheless be argued that policies targeting a society's elderly should invite suspicion. One could envisage a fiscally strapped government reneging on obligations to fund Social Security, for instance, as some predict may be in the cards in the United States.[23] The large cohort that entered the workforce during the 1960s will retire in the first two decades of the twenty-first century, placing unprecedented strains on these systems. Because the ratio of retired beneficiaries to employed contributors is growing, the system has become increasingly susceptible to a series of predictable pressures: to increase contribution rates and the retirement age, to tax benefits, and perhaps even "means test" or phase out people above certain income thresholds. Debates over such possibilities are bound to be politically conflictual, but they do not raise issues of principle for democratic justice. If a social insurance system is funded through a "pay as you go" system, demographic bulges are going to have to be managed by borrowing, a smoothing rule, or some kindred budgetary device. Grappling with this may indeed produce coalitions to increase the retirement age or to reduce some benefits. If basic interests are not threatened, such questions should be up for grabs in electoral politics.[24]

Although it is conceivable that a given elderly cohort will be singled out for maltreatment by the rest of the voting population, in practice this seems unlikely, if only because the budgetary pressure grows with the relative size of the retired cohort. More probable is the growth of a well-organized single-issue interest group such as the American Association of Retired Persons (AARP). The danger, in that case, is that the elderly's claims will crowd those of less politically effective groups out of the budget.[25] This is what has been happening for some time to the poor. States generally fix Medicaid budgets before determining eligibility requirements, which are then set as persons living below whatever proportion of the federal poverty level that the budget will bear. By the early 1990s this had led to a reality in which the average income eligibility requirement for Medicaid was less than half the federal poverty level. In real terms this means that a family of three with an income above $5,000 per year typically earns too much to qualify for Medicaid.[26] The eligibility requirements will become still more draconian unless the present system is reformed, because the growth in medical costs continues to outstrip that of the economy and of state budgets.[27] A substantial part of the growth in medical costs results from long-term care for the elderly. In effect, these increased costs are externalized onto the poor who lose Medicaid eligibility. In such circumstances, worrying about the elderly as a potential dominated minority should not be a high priority for democratic justice, and the current American practice in which age is not seen as a suspect classification is warranted.[28]

DIFFICULTIES ATTENDING A WHOLE-LIFE APPROACH

Embracing the whole-life approach raises tricky questions for democratic justice, because life spans of individuals vary, as do those of groups and entire populations. Many factors influence this variation, ranging from genetic luck, to upbringing and occupation, to income and lifestyle, to the incidence of violent crime, to the distributive and regulatory policies of governments—not to mention such exogenous events as wars, diseases, and environmental changes. These and other factors shape a world in which women generally outlive men in most countries, and whites outlive blacks. How should we think about such differences from the standpoint of democratic justice? Should women's relative longevity entitle them to more collectively underwritten resources or fewer? If we say more on the grounds that they live longer, should this commit us to the view that blacks should be entitled to fewer resources than whites on the grounds that they do not live as long? If different logics apply, whence the difference? Should the state perhaps seek to equalize normal life spans across groups? If so, which groups? In short, once we make the human life span the basis for thinking about collective obligations to underwrite basic interests, we are bound to come to grips with the reality that life spans often vary for morally arbitrary reasons.

One set of apparent difficulties can be set aside with the maxim that governments may plan actuarially but must respond individually. The relevant considerations here parallel those discussed in connection with fertility rates in Chapter 4, where indirect forms of regulation were judged obligatory. This is not to affirm every possible actuarial basis for policy making in connection with the human life span. Group classifications that insuring entities are often tempted to use should not pass muster from the standpoint of democratic justice, because they involve targeting vulnerable minorities. But some classifications are acceptable, and within those there will always be variation around the mean. If Social Security is planned on the accurate assumption that on average people will need it for ten years, what of those who outlive the projection? Here governments should, as they typically do now, operate like insurance companies: guarantee full benefits to all clients ex ante, and tax based on actuarial estimates. Those who consume less than average of the insured good ex post in effect subsidize those who require more of it. This has obvious advantages over giving public officials and others with control over resources the power if not of ending life, then of threatening elderly infirm individuals with the loss of vital support. Creating such power over individuals unnecessarily is unwelcome from the standpoint of a presumption against domination.[29] For any individual life the presumption will thus be against ending it unnecessarily. That this rules out compulsory euthanasia is easily derived. What it means in more complex cases of painful terminal illness is taken up below.

Posing the question what should guide government polices affecting the human life span brings more difficult matters into focus. Governments do various things that expand or retard life expectancies. Immunization programs for children are pursued more or less aggressively, or not at all. Healthy living is promoted, or not, by antismoking campaigns, environmental policing, and the regulation of dangerous drugs. More or fewer public resources are invested in life-prolonging technologies and other life-enhancing policies for the elderly. Developments in genetics are likely to increase the plasticity of the human life span further in the future. Governments will have to decide whether to permit them and if so whether to invest in them. This, in turn, will raise questions about how the attendant costs and benefits should be distributed. What light can we shed on such dilemmas?

Democratic justice takes no position on what the optimal life span should be. Its focus, rather, is on how decisions about the life span are made, and how they affect those who are or will be living in the foreseeable future. It instructs us to press for the inclusive feasible participation of those affected by these decisions and to facilitate meaningful opposition from interests that are likely to be affected adversely. It also requires that although governments should be free to decide what their policies concerning longevity should be, these decisions should not enable them to escape their underwriting responsibilities for the basic interests of individuals living within their jurisdictions.

What does this mean in practice? Two constraints suggest themselves, the first having to do with the way policies aimed at altering the human life span are designed and implemented, the second with the rationing of health care. Both leave a great deal up to electoral politics, but both incorporate the notion of basic interests into entrenched limitations on how those politics are played out.

THE LOGIC OF RATCHETING UP

Should policies aimed at expanding the human life span be viewed in the same way as those designed to contract it? At first sight one might be tempted to answer in the affirmative. After all, surely a collective decision to begin a particular immunization program undertaken to extend the average life span in a given population by X years is on a normative par with a decision to end this policy in order to reduce the actuarial expectation by the same amount. There are several reasons to resist this apparent symmetry, however, and to institutionalize a degree of stickiness for policies that might be life-shortening that need not accompany life-lengthening ones. This unpacks into the proposition that although governments are not obliged to enact policies geared to expanding the human life span, such policies, once adopted, ought to be difficult to reverse.[30]

One reason for favoring "ratcheting up" stems from death's finality. Perhaps the day will come when humans can clone from the mummified remains of Egyptian Pharoahs, re-creating them after the style of the dinosaurs in *Jurassic Park*. But in the world we now inhabit the better assumption is that death is final and that what is done to hasten it cannot be undone.[31] Given the limits to our knowledge and the human propensity for fallible judgments, this counsels in favor of making life-shortening policies hard to implement.

A related consideration is that abolishing some particular life-lengthening policy (or adopting a life-shortening one) could run afoul of democratic justice as part of a politics of domination. The policy change might be aimed at a comparatively powerless minority, or, whatever the intention, the impact might fall disproportionately on such a group.[32] True, life-lengthening policies might also (perhaps typically) be disproportionate in their impact, producing windfall longevity gains for groups that are particularly effective—or lucky—in the political process. In such cases, however, the lack of finality leaves open many possibilities: taxing beneficiaries to compensate others, seeking ways to extend comparable benefits to other groups, or—if an appropriate heightened scrutiny requirement is met—reversing the windfall policy. Distributional considerations of this kind reinforce the wisdom of tilting against life-shortening policies and institutionalizing mechanisms that tend to lock in life-lengthening ones.

Third, ratcheting up creates incentives for governments to consider costly implications of life-lengthening policies ex ante; it promotes a logic of looking before you leap. If politicians know that life-lengthening policies are not easily reversible and that they bring with them obligations to underwrite the basic interests of those whose life spans are extended, then they may think twice before adopting the policies. Just as I argued in the area of demographic planning that there is no optimal population size for democratic justice and that the appropriate maximand for government is the proportion of the population whose basic interests can be vindicated, so too in this area. What should matter most for government is not extending or limiting the life span as such but rather ensuring that basic interests can be underwritten for the life spans that are in fact lived. Governments should be free to try to extend actuarial life spans, subject to this quality-of-life constraint. Accordingly, they should know that there will be underwriting costs to extending the human life span. Ratcheting up helps achieve that result.

Ratcheting up offers another advantage: it militates against intergenerational reneging on basic-interest commitments that are specific to particular phases of the life cycle. Just as with parents who begin to oppose public spending on education once their children have completed school, there is the danger that particular cohorts of the elderly may discover incentives to oppose life-lengthening policies from which they have already obtained the relevant advantages. They might derive the life-lengthening benefits, say, of public health campaigns against smoking or vaccination programs early in life, but then organize to defund these programs in favor of cohort-specific benefits or tax breaks for themselves. The more life-expanding policies can be entrenched by ratcheting up mechanisms, the more the whole-life approach will be shielded from erosion by such cohort-based defections with their attendant generational conflicts. Since the whole-life approach has already been shown to be desirable from the standpoint of democratic justice, the possibility of shielding it in this way gives us an additional reason to favor ratcheting up.

THE QUANTITY AND DISTRIBUTION OF HEALTH CARE

There is a degree of artificiality to isolating consideration of how much health care should be provided in a society, at what cost, and to whom, from discussion of policies geared to influencing the human life span. How long people can expect to live is partly a result of the preventive and responsive health care they receive at different points in the life cycle, and the resources available for health care may well be linked to how long people—particularly elderly infirm people—can be expected to live.[33] This is true, but one can still distinguish policies that are concerned with people's health within a given life span that may vary within limits from policies that are concerned with the limits themselves. This suggests that provided we remain cognizant of the interaction between the two and alert to relevant points of contact, we can think about the distribution of health-care resources as a distinct subject.

Democratic justice engages with the distribution of health-care resources through the lens of basic interests. Access to some health-care resources (leaving aside, for now, how many and of what kind) is essential for people to live self-sufficiently for as much of their lives as possible while avoiding unnecessary suffering. This suggests that some health care should be included along with other resources that are underwritten by the state as part of its basic-interests guarantee. These might be provided through a Canadian-style single-payer scheme or through an appropriately reformed version of the system that prevails in the United States, where the state provides essential medical insurance for those who do not get it as a by-product of employment and cannot buy it for themselves. The considerations adduced in Chapter 6 in support of a robust social wage favor the single-payer approach. In principle one might imagine improvements in the protections for the poor in the current American system that would render it acceptable. In practice I argue below that it is difficult to see how such protections can result from majoritarian politics.

But what is the minimum health care that people should be guaranteed, one way or another, to vindicate their basic interests? The central difficulty stems from the fact that however controversial some aspects of basic interests might be, almost everyone would agree that they include the wherewithal essential to survival. It is hard to imagine a more basic interest than survival for most living creatures, and it is correspondingly difficult to entertain the suggestion that there are things essential to a being's survival that do not fall within the ambit of its basic interests. Yet the human capacity to create costly medical resources geared to maintaining human survival, while perhaps not infinite, is exceedingly great. Certainly it is sufficient to outstrip any budget that one could realistically imagine being adopted by an actual democratic legislature. Medical resources that are essential to life-or-death outcomes for billions of people are going to be rationed, implicitly or explicitly, and subordinated to other parts of governments' budgets. If the notion of basic interests is to be helpful in such a context, it is therefore necessary to find ways to rein in its potential demands. To achieve this end it is necessary either to formulate an interpersonal criterion for placing limits on the state's underwriting responsibilities, or, failing that, to come up with a procedure for managing medical rationing decisions that is defensible from the perspective of democratic justice. Ronald Dworkin urges the first course, unsuccessfully. Spelling out the reasons for his failure opens the way to our navigation of the second.

THE PRUDENT INSURANCE MODEL

Dworkin begins from the valid premise that the inherent scarcity of medical resources makes some system of rationing inescapable. To determine what the system should be, he advocates a prudent insurance model by reference to which decisions can be made about the appropriate allocations of public resources "between health and other social needs, and between different patients who each need treatment."[34] To achieve this, he proposes a thought experiment in which we are asked to assume that America is transformed in three ways. First, the distribution of wealth and income is "as fair as it possibly can be." At a minimum this means that everyone's share "would be much closer to the average than is true in America now: the great extremes between rich and poor that mark our economic life now would have largely disappeared." We are to assume, second, widespread state-of-the-art knowledge "about the value and costs and side effects of particular medical procedures," and, third, that there is no information "about how likely any particular person is to contract any particular disease or to suffer any particular kind of accident." Taking these counterfactuals for granted, and assuming also that there is no public health insurance or subsidy of any kind, we are asked to imagine what health-care institutions, practices, and prices the market would generate. Dworkin contends that the results could not be criticized as imprudent or unjust, as this would be a world in which "people have enough resources to buy for themselves the medical care they decide is appropriate."[35]

Dworkin believes that this thought experiment can supply a serviceable criterion for interpersonal judgments about prudent medical insurance. On its basis he speculates that a healthy twenty-five-year-old with average prospects would elect to limit expenditures on health insurance when confronted with market prices. In particular, such a person would forgo costly insurance to be kept alive in a vegetative state in favor of coverage that "would be much better used to enhance his actual, conscious life." Average twenty-five-year-olds would not buy insurance facilitating the current practice in most developed countries in which a large fraction—more than 25 percent of Medicare expenditures in the United States—is spent during the last six months of life. They would opt instead for basic custodial care to maintain dignity and comfort as much as possible in life's terminal phase, while devoting other available resources to sustaining "their earlier, vigorous life." Most people would, however, buy insurance covering "ordinary medical care, hospitalization when necessary, prenatal and child care for their children, and regular checkups and other preventive medicine." Accordingly, Dworkin concludes, a just system of universal health-care insurance should require coverage of this kind (whether through employer mandates, public provision, or some combination), whereas the more expensive insurance that most people would not buy in his hypothetical circumstances should be left to the elective choices of the market.[36]

Dworkin developed his account as part of a supportive commentary on the Clinton administration's ill-starred Health Security Act of 1993. His aim was to buttress the view that it is unjust for millions in America to go without health insurance, a state of affairs that proponents of the act sought, among their other goals, to remedy. Dworkin's suggestion was that the members of the National Health Board envisaged in the legislation should apply his prudent insurance test to determine the contents of the comprehensive benefits package to be made available to all. Conceding that different people might apply the test somewhat differently from him and from one another, he contended that the remedy for this is twofold: include people from all walks of life and stages of the life cycle as well as medical professionals on the board, and use the market as a correcting device. If large numbers of people buy supplementary insurance for a procedure not included in the basic package, this would be a signal that the board had misjudged the public's prudent valuation. In this way the package should be open to continual adjustment in the shadow of observed market behavior.[37]

Dworkin's aspiration — to provide reasoned support for a universally available benefits package — should be endorsed from the standpoint of democratic justice, but his mode of proceeding seems ill-suited to achieving this goal. First, the market correcting device is fatally flawed as an instrument for mitigating errors in the application of the prudent insurance test by the National Health Board. Who is to say that decisions in the actual marketplace will be guided by the prudent insurance model? In the one systematic attempt that has been made to delve into public opinion on the relative value of different medical procedures (undertaken in the course of developing the Oregon plan in the early 1990s), people were revealed not generally to value medical procedures in the manner that Dworkin would deem prudent.[38] Moreover, it is hard to see why Dworkin attaches any normative weight to market behavior in a society that he has already stipulated to be unjust. Because the purchasing decisions people make reflect their budget constraints, what reason is there to think that what they do provides appropriate guidance as to what the comprehensive benefits package ought to include?

Turning to Dworkin's arguments on behalf of the prudent insurance model's merits, he greatly underestimates the likely disagreements about what both prudence and justice require, disagreements that are bound to plague his plan. The least serious difficulty is the one to which he responds: that different board members will apply his test differently. They will also have differing intuitions about what the test should be. Some will object to Dworkin's privileging of a twenty-five-year-old's view on the grounds that perceptions of the value of six months of life fifty years in the future can be predicted to increase as people age. Some will wonder why the "correct" hypothetical ex ante choice is not that of a twenty-one-year-old, or even an eighteen-year-old, ages when people are notoriously more risk-embracing with respect to health and personal safety. Some may doubt that most people of a given age would make the same choices as one another under the same budget constraints. Some will regard Dworkin's framing assumptions about justice as excessively egalitarian, while others will think them insufficiently so—resisting his view that the wealthy should be free to buy private supplementary health insurance.[39]

Upon inspection, then, what remains of Dworkin's proposal is the proposition that health care should be rationed through a legitimate collective process. But what would such a process be? The argument of Chapter 3 suggests the presumptive candidate to be conventional majoritarian decision making, for we are dealing with a circumstance where substantial components of the collective decision in question are competitive rather than cooperative, and there are no obvious reasons to countenance paternalistic decision making. This would be true if the decision in question were to be binding on all the players, but this is seldom even contemplated in American discussions of health-policy reform. The much-debated Oregon plan, for instance, in which "town meetings" were held to set priorities that were taken into account by the legislature in allocating funds, was aimed at nonelderly Medicaid recipients only.[40] Some have suggested that this process conferred legitimacy on the results, particularly because it did make some kind of coverage available to all residents of the state.[41] Dworkin himself praises the Oregon meetings as "valuable sources of information" about the participants' views of prudent insurance decisions. Yet as he notes, the reality was that they were attended by few of the poor, whose health-care priorities were actually being discussed.[42]

Not only were those who must live with the results more or less unrepresented; most of those making the decisions knew that they would never depend on Medicaid. In countries like Britain and Canada, where the great majority of the population use collectively rationed medical services, their participation in majoritarian decision making through the political system lends legitimacy to the resulting policies. By contrast, in Oregon, as Daniels has pointed out, upward of 80 percent of the population is unaffected by the rationing program.[43] The principle of affected interest presumes inclusion of those who are affected by a decision, the presumption being particularly strong when basic interests are at stake. The flip side of this principle is presumptive suspicion of decisions taken by people who will be substantially insulated from the results. This is the situation that Americans confront in health care. Even if the Clinton plan had passed, those with the resources would have been free to buy whatever additional coverage they liked over and above that contained in the comprehensive package.

We are left with a conundrum. The inherent scarcity of medical resources —many of them crucial to human survival—makes some sort of rationing scheme inescapable. In such circumstances majoritarian decision making recommends itself for deciding what medical care should form part of the basic-interests guarantee. Committing the decision to the legislative process runs into difficulties, however, rooted in differing capacities for insulation from the collective mandate. People with the resources to supplement the basic-interests package or to opt out have incentives to ensure that the basic-interests guarantee is minimal, instead protecting themselves from higher tax rates. Those who lack resources to exit will understandably want a more robust guaranteed system. In these circumstances it is necessary to temper majoritarian process with institutional mechanisms to protect the vulnerable.

The rule of thumb that suggests itself is a cousin of the sliding-quantum rule discussed in Chapter 6: deference to the results of the legislative process should vary with the proportion of the population that is actually going to use the publicly funded system. At one pole of what might be described as an impact continuum, imagine a minimal collectively financed system used by almost no one, a world in which people either buy insurance privately or go uninsured. At the other pole would stand a universal single-payer insurance scheme with an immensely high tax on all forms of opting out and supplementation. If such a system were adopted by a democratic legislature, there would be scant prima facie reason to question the legitimacy of trade-offs made in deciding how much medical care to supply or how to ration it. This is not to say that it would provide the best quality of health care in all circumstances, or that it would be free of the inefficiencies that can accompany third-party payment schemes.[44] It is to say, however, that moves away from a universal single-payer system (perhaps to head off such difficulties) toward the impact continuum's opposite pole take us toward a world where the decisions of democratic legislatures become increasingly suspect. This is the case with Medicaid in the United States, which is exclusively a poor people's program.

Whereas the continuum discussed in Chapter 6 (from surfer's paradise to Dickensian nightmare) dealt with the content of collective provision, the impact continuum deals with the issue of who uses it. Its logic suggests that targeted programs like Medicaid should be accompanied by avenues for patients to resist particular rationing decisions. Norman Daniels and James Sabin have argued for the importance of appeal mechanisms in legitimating medical rationing, emphasizing their significance for those who have been excluded from the decision making.[45] This suggestion dovetails neatly with the opposition dimension of democratic justice, which is bound to carry more freight when inclusive decision making fails. We can build on it by arguing that the closer a circumstance is to the Medicaid end of the continuum, the more teeth appeals mechanisms should have. It also suggests that the willingness of courts to review administrative appeals and act on claims that the prevailing coverage violates basic interests should vary with the degree to which plaintiffs are singled out from the rest of the population. Decisions affecting everyone should be comparatively difficult to challenge, but the scrutiny should become more demanding as the exit options multiply.[46]

By the same token, refusing essential treatment for Medicaid patients and the uninsured in the American system should not be an option for healthcare providers. In the same way that firms are more likely to support a robust social wage if the alternative is that they provide its components as part of the wage package, hospitals and health professionals are more likely to get behind universal health insurance if the alternative requires them to absorb the costs of treating those without adequate insurance. Courts, arbitrators, emergency room coordinators, boards of professional ethics, and others with decision-making authority in the relevant circumstances thus act legitimately from the standpoint of democratic justice when they insist that these people be given treatment when they are in need. That this can be expected to add to the fiscal crisis surrounding American health care is not a reason to deny it to them. Granted, point of service is not a good vantage point from which to shape the distributive agenda, and when the democratic process operates to ration health-care resources fairly, neither is it legitimate. But when the democratic process is not doing this, then it is defensible to insist that the most vulnerable should not be made to bear the cost. Hopefully, the time will come when the pressure thus created will help push medical-rationing decisions along the impact continuum to a point where their democratic legitimacy begins to merit respect.

Controlling Decisions

As we turn from decisions about budget constraints to activities within them, democratic justice recommends a two-part principle: preserve elderly people's self-sufficiency as much as possible for as long as possible; and, as self-sufficiency decays, structure the system so that power devolves to those who are most likely to act in the elderly people's interests. This should be intuitively evident from the inclusion presumption. With the elderly as with young children: exclusion demands necessity. Disfranchisement can be justified by incapacity only, and when it occurs great care is in order to protect the interests of the disenfranchised.

ADULT CHILDREN'S ROLES

It might be said that the two-part principle is too simple. Others are affected by the decisions elderly people make, most obviously relatives on whom their costly choices might be imposed. If adult children have to foot the bill for their parents' medical and other basic needs, they clearly have a stake in their parents' behavior and decisions. As for economic costs, I noted earlier that the answer is to minimize the elderly's dependence on their adult children. Whether this is achieved by forced savings during income-producing years, socializing the costs of elderly support, or some combination, it frees the relations between the elderly and their adult children of economic duress. As a result, children need not torture themselves when managing trade-offs between their parents' needs and other demands on their resources. Nor need they worry about the appearance (or reality) of ulterior motives if the time comes when they are called upon to play a role in decision making on behalf of incompetent parents.

Parents can, of course, also impose noneconomic costs on their adult children, most obviously emotional ones. Aging parents can seek to manipulate their offspring with threats of disinheritance, as Locke in effect urged them to do, and they may engage in forms of emotional blackmail that exploit their children's sense of responsibility.[47] The resulting costs can often be substantial, even permanently debilitating, but they are not appropriate objects of governmental concern. Once the resources needed for the vindication of aging adults' basic interests are removed from the equation, the quality of relations between them and their offspring falls into the realm of their best interests, along with their other personal involvements. People may be lonely and miserable in their old age because of the sour quality of their relationships, but this is a risk that they should be deemed to have internalized over the course of their lives. In this respect the dependent old differ from the dependent young. For them, I argue in Chapter 4, there is no room for a doctrine of assumption of risk, and even though government is ill-suited to protect children's best interests, it appropriately retains the role of secondary, or fail-safe, fiduciary. As I argue below, relations between adult children and their aging parents are fiduciary relationships only of a limited and attenuated sort; accordingly, the notion of a fail-safe fiduciary is not called for. We do better to think of relations between adults and their parents as akin to adult domestic relations: government best operates indirectly, to reduce the likelihood of coercion by reducing exit costs. Its goal should be to free people from the possibility of taking advantage of one another's necessity as they pursue their best interests, individually or in common, as they choose.

DISENFRANCHISING THE ELDERLY

Just as children's ages of emancipation vary from activity to activity as their different capacities develop, so too with the "de-emancipation" of the elderly. People may be presumed incompetent to drive a car beyond a certain age (absent their periodic demonstrations to the contrary); this does not mean they should be ineligible to vote. We should think of disenfranchisement as a developmental process, motivated by and linked to the erosion of relevant capacities, ending only in death. Indeed, death itself should be imposed by necessity only. Earlier I argued that although the state should be free, within limits, to seek to alter the actuarial limits of the human life span, it should not be empowered to end individual lives. That argument dovetails neatly with the proposition advanced here: that forcibly ending a life unnecessarily is an extreme form of disenfranchisement which the state should have no authority to undertake. It also suggests opposition to the death penalty.[48]

What of the person who wants death? Here it is customary to distinguish a general proscription of suicide from what Keats described as "easeful death"—an exception to the proscription to prevent unnecessary suffering by the terminally ill, or to minimize their loss of autonomy in decisions about the precise nature of inevitable demise.[49] The proscription might be thought less controversial than the exception, but democratic justice suggests different priorities.

Because democratic justice countenances paternalistic decision making only when people are incompetent, it generates no reason to prohibit a sober decision by a compos mentis adult to commit suicide. This is in line with the reality in most Western countries, where suicide is no longer a crime.[50] One would always want assurances, of course, that the person was not being coerced into the choice, either explicitly or because resources essential to her basic interests were lacking. But it is possible that someone who was not threatened in any of these ways would nonetheless conclude that life is not worth living, either for religious reasons (as with the Heaven's Gate Community in California in March 1997) or for other reasons that seemed compelling. A person might, for instance, be a negative utilitarian impressed by R. N. Smart's observation that immediate suicide offers the best likelihood of minimizing net lifetime suffering.[51] Such convictions are not obviously more absurd than many beliefs people routinely accept in themselves and one another. In any case, democratic justice adopts a political, not metaphysical, stance toward ultimate metaphysical convictions.[52] As a result, while many of us might regard people who act on such beliefs as woefully misguided, there is no defensible reason for government to stop them.

Although compos mentis adults who are bent on suicide cannot fairly be stopped from the standpoint of democratic justice, they may not legitimately take children with them. Children should always be prevented from suicide, or indeed any serious harm to themselves, regardless of their—or their parents'—ultimate metaphysical commitments. Adults are sovereign over their own basic interests and may choose to abrogate them in certain circumstances. The state's role is limited to underwriting those interests and preventing third-party interference with them.[53] But the state is sovereign over children's basic interests and may not permit them to be compromised in service of anyone's ultimate metaphysical commitments. This distinguishes the Heaven's Gate suicide—which, so far as one can tell, was undertaken by consenting adults who were free not to participate—from the suicide-massacre at Jonestown in 1978, where children were included.[54]

If democratic justice bids us to accept the uncoerced considered judgments of healthy adults to end their lives, its suspicious antennae become activated once the elderly infirm are involved. People suffering terminal illnesses, often in great pain, may indeed have justified reasons for wanting to end their lives. The Supreme Court acknowledged a constitutional right to refuse medical treatment or nutrition in the *Cruzan* case in 1990, in effect entrenching the common-law rule that forced medical treatment constitutes a battery.[55] In 1997 the justices unanimously declined to extend this right to physician-assisted suicide.[56] This means that there is a constitutional right for a terminal patient to insist on passive euthanasia, but no such right to active euthanasia. The latter is not ruled out as unconstitutional, however. State governments are free to prohibit it or permit it, though to date only Oregon has followed the latter course.[57]

From the perspective of democratic justice, the freedom of terminally ill people to end their lives should be no different from similar choices by healthy adults. But difficulties present themselves concerning the nature of the choices such individuals make and the contexts in which they typically arise. With respect to the authenticity of choices, it can be hard to know what to make of apparent decisions by the elderly. This is a growing problem because increases in longevity create larger numbers of people who suffer from various forms of dementia such as Alzheimer's disease.[58] Even when they do not suffer from such an affliction, people who know that they are dying often deteriorate mentally, and they can be subject to regimes of medication that cloud their judgments.[59] The situation is further complicated by the reality that in order to end their lives, terminally ill people often need the assistance, whether active or passive, of medical professionals who are licensed by the state. This involves government in the process willy nilly, as Dr. Jack Kevorkian's battles with authorities in Michigan have illustrated. Suspicion naturally arises when the state or its agents play any role in meting out death, suggesting the appropriateness of institutional arrangements that force a good deal of second-guessing and revisiting of decisions to help end life before the patient's wishes can be acted upon.

One logical direction in which to move is precommitment. Concerns about the authenticity of choices by the terminally ill can be allayed by such devices as living wills. Although they are not legal in most European countries, all U.S. states recognize some form of advance directive, in which people can indicate that in certain terminal circumstances they do not wish to be kept alive by medical intervention if they would otherwise die.[60] Appealing as the living will might be, it confronts formidable problems in application. The fact patterns that present themselves will often not have been anticipated in their provisions. In principle, people could construct elaborate "designer" documents spelling out their wishes in various hypothetical circumstances, but life has more imagination than most of us, and there will still be many circumstances that are not covered by such documents unambiguously. Moreover, people change their minds. Diseases and forms of debilitation that a healthy middle-aged person believes would make life not worth living may appear in a different light when that person, some years later, begins to suffer from them. Like conventional wills, living wills are logically similar to unilateral contracts in that they do not bind third parties and can be revoked by the signatory at any time. With incompetent people the conundrum thus becomes: despite the living will, would the person revoke it now, in these new circumstances?

Dworkin takes the view that incompetent people are not competent to retract their consent, so that living wills should be acted upon even in circumstances where a demented person appears content and expresses the wish to go on living. He favors the doctrine of respecting the person's "precedent autonomy." This requires that the earlier, competent, expression of desire trump the current expressed wishes of a patient who has been deemed incompetent.[61] Although there is merit to Dworkin's view that the person's prior competence, character, values, and desires should be taken into account in determining his appropriate treatment in his demented state, this position is unacceptably strong. A demented person may be incapable of withdrawing consent, but that does not mean that he would not retract the living will if he could. Tying incompetent people to prior decisions in such circumstances deprives them of the freedom to oppose. Accordingly, it runs afoul of democratic justice, though it is difficult to see how to do much about it. Most states try to address this problem by making living wills exceedingly easy to revoke. Some go so far as to attach automatic sunset clauses to them, in effect requiring periodic reaffirmation of their provisions as the individual ages.[62] Such provisions are helpful as far as they go, but they do not solve the underlying problem. Institutional mechanisms are needed to get at the question: would the demented person have retracted the living will in these circumstances, were he not demented?

CARETAKERS AS DELEGATES-CUM-FIDUCIARIES

A helpful alternative or supplement to the living will is the durable power of attorney. While still compos mentis, adults can name trusted third parties to make decisions in their stead should this become necessary. The appointed fiduciary is then bound to make decisions that he or she believes the ailing person would have made as the unanticipated circumstances evolve. The caretaker presumably has intimate knowledge of the person in question and would be more likely than anyone else to act as the person would have done. As medical technologies develop, often multiplying unanticipated treatment possibilities, durable powers of attorney may be better devices for giving effect to the dying patient's wishes than the boilerplate "do not resuscitate" provisions of most living wills or more complex instructions that the patient may have tried to craft long before death's imminence. In any case, such documents will often stand in need of interpretation in light of unexpected circumstances; it is better if the interpreter has been chosen by the person on whose behalf she acts.

Those who agree to play this role, or find themselves playing it by default, are not fiduciaries in the same sense as that discussed in connection with governing children. Because children play no role in selecting either their parents or the regime into which they are born, there is no sense in which those with responsibility for their basic and best interests are charged with effectuating their wills. The fiduciary makes his own best judgment as to what course of action will most likely vindicate the charge's interests and acts on that. As the child reaches adulthood in various areas, the fiduciary does not so much take the child's will into account (though a wise fiduciary may often try to do that) as reduce the scope of fiduciary decision making, retreating before the emerging adult's autonomy.

Fiduciary responsibility for the elderly differs by including the idea of delegation. The responsibility is not to act on one's best judgment of what is in the person's interests but rather on one's best judgment of what that person would have decided to do were she not incapacitated.[63] This flows naturally from the hostility of democratic justice to disenfranchising ailing adults sooner or more fully than necessary. It is this impulse that casts the durable power of attorney instrument in an attractive light and suggests that even a person who finds himself in this role without having been appointed by the principal should try to behave as her constructive nominee. At times this will be impossible, and fiduciaries will find themselves forced to act on their own perceptions of the best interests of the elderly people in their care. But as far as possible such fiduciaries should try to act as their agents, not in loco parentis. Whereas Dworkin insists that no fiduciary should ever contradict the instructions in a living will on the grounds that this would constitute "an unacceptable form of moral paternalism," on this view the fiduciary should retract a living will provision if he is convinced that the person would have done so in these circumstances.[64]

In spite of its advantages, durable power of attorney should not go unregulated. The unilateral character of precommitment attends it no less than the living will; as a result, there will always be questions as to whether the incompetent person would continue to want a particular fiduciary in this role in current circumstances. Moreover, it is usually true that the pool of people from which someone might select a nominee (or on whom these responsibilities devolve if none is selected) is small, and it often includes people with whom there are unresolved tensions and possible conflicts of interest. Because the caretaker will normally be a spouse, child, or intimate and trusted associate, it is likely to be someone who bears the emotional and psychological burdens associated with wrenching decisions that must often be made for the chronically sick. The delegate-cum-fiduciary may also be one who stands to inherit assets from the terminally ill person. The knowledge that one's ailing charge will leave a diminished estate if kept alive on costly machines may compound dilemmas as to when the machines should be switched off. Others might suspect one's motives even if they are pure, and, in the emotionally charged world that typically surrounds such decisions, one may have doubts about the reasons for one's own judgments. Perhaps machines will be left on when they should be turned off, for fear of what people may think or in trepidation of one's own subsequent second-guessing.[65]

PHYSICIANS AS DECISION MAKERS

In most advanced countries these decisions are almost never in the sole control of a nominated caretaker or relative. The medical establishment inevitably plays a substantial part in them, usually in the person of a physician who consults with the patient to the extent possible, with the caretaker, and with other relevant kin and close associates. It might be supposed that this presence of the attending physician constrains decisions sufficiently. Physicians are bound by codes of professional conduct, enforced through peer institutions and state licensing mechanisms, not to mention the torts system. They can also be expected to be dispassionate in the sense of lacking a personal stake in the outcome, and hence the appearance of an ulterior motive. This combination of expertise and personal disinterest may make the physician seem like the ideal person to hash out the possibilities with the different players and move the group toward a consensus with which everyone is comfortable.

Democratic justice always cocks a skeptical eyebrow at appeals to consensus; this circumstance is no exception. Although physicians do not bring personal stakes to the table as do family members in these matters, it would be wrong to think that they do not bring stakes. Physicians are subject to pressures from a variety of sources. Obvious among these are the fee schedules of third-party payers (which can promote overtreatment if procedures will be paid for or undertreatment if they will not), opportunity-cost calculations by hospital administrators (who may prefer to allocate resources, at the margin, to maximize revenues), and the incentives to practice defensive medicine (in response to the torts system in the United States). In an ideal world, perhaps, the physician could be relied upon to act solely on the basis of professional judgments and ethics, and no doubt many physicians act in this way today. But institutions should not be designed for the best-case scenario, and it would be naïve not to take such pressures into account when thinking about the institutional constraints that democratic justice should recommend. Enlightened physicians will not always be at the helm.

In the actual world, release from the professional obligation to preserve life should not be up to the physician's discretion. In particular, doctors should be expected to operate on the basis of the rescue principle and required to obtain a release from a disinterested third party—perhaps a probate court judge, perhaps some other independent appointed body—in particular cases when they believe this departure to be warranted. As I argued earlier, this is not to affirm the rescue principle as an appropriate means for distributing health-care resources for a society. Rather, it is best seen as a maxim of professional conduct that loads the dice in a particular way. Thus conceived, the rescue principle, and its implied tilting in favor of life-preserving action, merits support from democratic justice for several inter-locking reasons.

There are, to begin with, the considerations about error and death's ir-revocability already discussed. Although there is no prima facie reason to suppose that errors will more commonly be made in allowing someone to die than in not so doing, action based on the latter judgment is reversible, whereas that based on the former is not.[66] This suggests that there is merit to ensuring that a bright and dispassionate light is focused on the decision be-fore it is acted upon. An authority who is disinterested in both the personal and professional senses can do that, insist that the reasons for the decision be fully articulated and understood by all involved players, that the patient is as cognizant as possible of what is at stake, and that additional medical opinions are not in order. Before releasing the physician from the obligation to act on the rescue principle, that authority should be convinced by the test enunci-ated by Lord Justice Hoffman in the 1993 British case of Anthony Bland, who had been reduced to a permanent vegetative state as a result of a stampede at a soccer stadium four years earlier: "From what we have learned of Anthony Bland from those closest to him, that forced as we are to choose, we think it more likely that in his present state he would choose to die rather than live."[67]

Physicians have roles to play in decisions about the end of life, but the danger to which we must be attuned is that in times of medical extremity people may attribute omniscience to them, rendering them practically om-nipotent in decisions that are "agreed" upon. Democratic justice is not con-stitutionally hostile to expertise; rather, it suggests a need for arrangements that make it possible to use expertise without becoming its hostage. It sug-gests that physicians should have to answer to lay authorities if they seek to utilize their expertise to do anything contrary to the professional impera-tive to preserve life. In contemporary American practice, these matters end up in the courts only if they are contested at the time. Under this proposal all decisions to terminate life support would require third-party approval. It follows that if active euthanasia is permitted (as I suggest below that it should be), it would require similar advance approval. What is objectionable about the Kevorkian phenomenon is not that active euthanasia is carried out but that it is done in secret, often on patients whom Kevorkian barely knows, with no institutional oversight or second-guessing.[68]

Some will argue that turning things over to a judge or some other independent tribunal only pushes the problem a step further back, for whoever makes the authoritative decision brings both professional interests and personal prejudices to the table. On the professional front this objection misses the mark because it is not the physician's professional values that are worrisome. Rather, it is the potential for conflict between those values and the economic and legal context in which the physician must operate that suggests the wisdom of third-party oversight in the American context. To be sure, courts and judges are under fiscal pressure as well, but the potential for conflict between it and the patient's interest is neither so immediate nor so stark. In any case this need not be an institutionally expensive activity. It can generally take place in hospital rooms and may be a good activity to assign to retired judges. As for judges' prejudices, the criticism is also misplaced. Everyone has prejudices. The physician is, however, in a position where his prejudices can all too easily masquerade as his expertise (perhaps even to himself) when those with whom he is dealing are wont to defer to his wisdom at a time of severe personal stress. Using courts affords physicians a measure of protection while limiting the likelihood that their expertise will atrophy into domination.

The mechanism would be activated only if a responsible party sought to facilitate life's ending. The oversight authority could not order euthanasia of any kind over the physician's objection. Similarly, the oversight authority should not have the power to order euthanasia over the objections of the patient's designated lay fiduciary. Because the motivating imperative of the overall scheme is to give effect to what the terminally ill person would have wanted in the circumstances, the supervising authority functions only as a check to ensure that all relevant considerations have been taken into account in the face of death's finality. When physician and designated fiduciary disagree the matter will wind up in court as it does now. Judges should be predisposed in such circumstances to the views of the fiduciary, who is presumed to know what the principal would have chosen. Assessment becomes more difficult when no one has been designated and there is no presumptive course of action. Courts will have to do the best they can to determine what the individual would have wanted on a case-by-case basis.[69]

From this perspective the current constitutional law of euthanasia is only partly defensible. Passive euthanasia must be permitted under *Cruzan*, but states have extensive authority to regulate it. This makes sense from the standpoint of democratic justice, provided the regulations include third-party oversight. It offers the best hope that decisions to end life will not be foisted upon people and that when they cannot tell us, life is permitted to end only when that is what they would have wanted in the circumstances. The dilemmas presented by active euthanasia are not qualitatively different, and it is hard to see a justification for the *Vacco* view that states should be able to force people to stay alive against what we have good reason to believe are their authentic wishes merely because they lack the capacity to do away with themselves. In reversing the Second Circuit Court of Appeals on this point, Justice Rehnquist noted that "when a patient refuses life-sustaining medical treatment, he dies from an underlying fatal disease or pathology; but if a patient ingests lethal medication prescribed by a physician, he is killed by that medication."[70] He thus interpreted *Cruzan* to entrench the right to refuse lifesaving treatment rather than the to commit suicide as such, leaving the space to distinguish it from *Vacco*.

From our point of view here, however, the better course is to recognize that people should generally be free to end their own lives, and to see the difference between passive and active euthanasia as resulting from contingencies regarding the degree to which their maladies incapacitate them.[71] Historically, proscription of suicide stems most recently from the common-law prohibition on the grounds that it deprives the king of the service of one of his subjects and the Lockean view, adapted from Aquinas, that as God's property, human beings are not free to destroy themselves.[72] The former view has no place in a democratic conception of justice, and I argued earlier that appropriate secularization of the latter leads to the proposition that human beings are no one's property. An entrenched right to end one's life gives expression to this idea, provided that the appropriate safeguards are in place. It also gives institutional force to the oppositionalist strand of democratic justice, which values the freedom to say no side by side with the authority of inclusive collective decisions. That the right to end one's life should not include the freedom to get help from a willing third party seems difficult to justify. True, active euthanasia can be abused, but so can passive euthanasia. If a sufficient remedy for abuse of the one is to be sought in the direction of burden shifting and stringent regulation, it is difficult to see why the same is not true of the other.

Some may find it anomalous that a democratic conception of justice should end up endorsing the conclusion that majority decisions should not stop a person from deciding to end his or her life. Indeed, the opinion in *Glucksburg* affirms the view, developed by the Court in its abortion jurisprudence, that states have a legitimate interest in affirming life's value and protecting it if they so decide through their political institutions.[73] Perhaps so, but the central authorizing idea behind inclusive participation on our account is not majority rule. Rather, it is the principle of affected interest, which in this case is served well by subsidiarity. If ever there were an area where local interests should outweigh those of the larger collective, surely it is here. People who seek physician-assisted suicide are typically in great pain that cannot be relieved, victims of terminal illnesses that are excruciating in their slowness. They suffer, often in virtual—if not actual—isolation, with little or no effect on anyone other than their immediate kin. Their stake in the situation is paramount, that of others outside their immediate circle is *de minimus*. Proponents of democratic justice should be greatly concerned that a terminally ill person not be forced or manipulated into the decision to end his or her life, and institutions and codes of professional ethics should be fashioned with those dangers centrally in mind. But when the institutional tilting in life's favor is in place, and we are convinced that death is what the person wants or would want in the circumstances, then it is time to let life's tragedy unfold.

· 8 ·

Deepening Democratic Justice

INDIVIDUALS DIE BUT SOCIETIES PERSIST, with ongoing challenges for democratic justice. Some challenges result from hostility to democracy, most obviously when military coups wipe out representative institutions. Other challenges are due to failed attempts to democratize, as when worker-owned firms do not take root in the economy. Yet other challenges are by-products of partial democratic successes: payment for politicians ends politics as a part-time hobby for the wealthy, but it ushers in new problems surrounding the role of money in political life. Even full-blown democratic successes can present novel questions, as when securing national democracy frees people to focus on the power relations in civil society.[1] And some changes unrelated to the search for democratic justice reorder its agenda. The information revolution and the advent of genetic engineering will reshape power relations in ways we can barely glimpse today. This is not to mention changes that no one yet anticipates. Life has more imagination than we; it will continue to challenge democratic justice so long as human societies endure.

Although the problems change, the basic enterprise remains: to democratize social relations in justice-promoting ways. My aim in this concluding chapter is to take stock of what has been achieved by pursuing this enterprise through the life cycle, to contrast it with the dominant alternative in political theory, and to say something about how it might be developed in other contexts. My semicontextual method limits what can be said of other applications in advance of detailed analysis, but similarities in power patterns will sometimes call for adaptations of arguments developed in this book.

A Distinctive Political Conception of Justice

The argument developed here commits us to promote democracy and justice together. Rather than pour cold water on the popular expectation that this can be done, my motivation has been to try to deliver on it. To that end, I have advanced conceptions of democracy and justice through the life cycle that are intended to be individually satisfying and mutually reinforcing. We should readily grant that there are many conceptions of both ideals that do not meet this dual criterion. That helps narrow the field, because it is vain to suppose that enterprises for social improvement that do not meet it can garner public legitimacy in the medium run. Nor should they, because the popular expectation is warranted. Plausible conceptions of justice and democracy are mutually implicating, as we have seen, even though there are differences between them. The challenge is to find ways of diminishing the resulting tensions, or of managing them as well as possible when they cannot be diminished. Democratic justice is a device to help advance toward this goal. Institutional redesign in a complex and evolving world being what it is, this is an ongoing process. That should not dishearten us. It is part of bequeathing a better world to our children than the one we have inherited.

By its nature a democratic conception of justice is a political one. In some ways it is conceived in a like spirit to Rawls in his "political, not metaphysical" mode, but there are significant differences. Like Rawls, I think that the fact of value pluralism merits considerable weight in any plausible theory of justice. Also like him, I think that this naturally suggests a focus on how decisions are made and limited ambitions for the state in adjudicating among conflicting values in society. But I develop these insights differently than he does. This is partly due to my agreement with Walzer and MacIntyre that an important part of the theory of value is local—my embrace of a role for insider's wisdom. Whereas Rawls constructs a list of primary goods and comes up with a theory about how to distribute them, democratic justice involves ensuring that as people refashion and reproduce their inherited values, this process is democratically conditioned. Hence the concern with mechanisms of participation and opposition, aimed at deepening democracy's subordinate role throughout society. Moreover, whereas Rawls's "political, not metaphysical" stance is advertised as neutral among rational conceptions of the good life, mine is explicitly partial. It is intended to load the dice in favor of goals that can be realized democratically, and to give people incentives to refashion aspirations that cannot. Rawls's political conception is liberal, geared to restricting politics to areas where there is "overlapping consensus." Mine is a democratic conception. It aims at enabling people to live by their values, but always in ways that permit opposition and take due account of the affected interests of others.

Democratic justice presents a different political conception from Rawls's also in taking power relations as its central object of study. Iris Young is right to emphasize that Rawls and his progeny have been blinkered by their focus on distributive questions to too many issues about domination.[2] Just distribution is relevant to democratic justice, but the focus on power prompts distinctive questions about it. We are more centrally concerned than Rawls is with the how than with the what of distributive justice. Who controls whom in distributive struggles and what should be done about it? This differs from asking what the fair way is to divide up goods and services. The different questions involve overlapping concerns, to be sure, because one's access to goods and services affects one's relative power and vulnerability to the power of others. But the questions are different, as is reflected in the contrast between the institutional investigations undertaken in this book and the dearth of attention to such matters in the distributive-justice literature from Rawls to Roemer. My focus on power locates distributive issues in larger concerns about what makes the exercise of power legitimate. With children, for example, although I attended to questions about the distribution of resources, I did this from the perspective of how this affects power relations. Moreover, I was led to consider some questions that are not distributive in the conventional sense at all, such as the limits of parental authority when it conflicts with that of public officials.[3]

Democratic justice also differs from the Rawlsian approach in its more direct engagement with existing institutions and everyday politics. To some degree this reflects the disciplinary perspective of political science rather than philosophy, but it has deeper roots as well. These are buried in method-ology. Rawls's main concern, recently reemphasized, is with what he de-scribes as the basic structure of political institutions.[4] His principles are not meant to apply at the margins to everyday political choices. This preoccu-pation flows naturally out of the social-contract approach. Asking what in-stitutions rational people would agree on were they designing them afresh invites attention to the basic structure. Democratic justice's focus on insti-tutional redesign takes institutions and practices as we find them, subjects them to critical scrutiny through its distinctive lens, and asks how they can be improved as they are reproduced. The lens can be brought to bear wher-ever power relations are involved in human affairs; this does not involve carving out a subset of the social terrain and declaring it to be basic.[5] Resist-ing tabula rasa theorizing leads us to accord greater importance to the world as it actually exists, not least because of the qualified Burkean impulse of democratic justice. Once we grant existing practices some presumptive—but debatable—legitimacy, we inevitably engage with them as they have evolved on the ground.

A significant consequence of this difference is that democratic justice issues in concrete results for actual politics. In Chapter 4 I show how its divided authority regime for governing children speaks to contemporary de-bates about their education, religion, and physical and economic security, spelling out the implications for demographic planning, abortion, and adop-tion policy as well. Likewise with the consensual model of adult domestic life developed in Chapter 5: I explore its consequences for the evolving law of marriage and divorce, and for policies toward such issues as domestic violence, the economic structure of the family, and unorthodox lifestyles. In Chapter 6, I unpack the implications of burden-shifting and the sliding quantum rule for pressing controversies about the ownership and control of the firm, the regulation of work, and the social wage. And in the investiga-tion of democratic justice at life's ending in Chapter 7, I show what majority rule constrained by exit options should mean for the distribution of medi-cal care in the United States today. I also draw out the implications of the delegate-cum-fiduciary model that democratic justice recommends for de-cision making about the elderly infirm, pursuing it into debates about the responsibilities of adult children, the authority of physicians, and the legiti-macy of euthanasia—both passive and active.

So we have a political conception of justice, but a distinctive one. It is democratic rather than liberal, geared to reshaping existing social relations so as to promote inclusion and diminish domination. It tells us that the central focus should be on the power dimensions of human interaction, which we should seek to restructure while interfering as little as possible with the rest of what people aspire to do. It engages directly with existing institutions and practices, unmediated by speculative hypotheticals about the basic structure of a just society that might in principle be designed from scratch. As a result, democratic justice generates concrete recommendations that are designed to advance its cause in contemporary political controversy. It is a political theory that is meant to be useful.

Revisiting the Two Dimensions of Democratic Justice

By tracing the requirements of democratic justice from childhood through adult domestic life, work, old age, dying, and death, we have seen what inclusive participation and loyal opposition can and should mean over the course of the human life cycle in the contemporary United States. It remains to recapitulate my general arguments about them in view of what has been learned thus far. This will shed some glimmerings of light on how they might be deployed elsewhere.

INCLUSIVE PARTICIPATION AND THE FRANCHISE

Whose interests should be included in the governance side of the equation varies with time and circumstance. Economies of smallness and insider's wisdom often counsel moving as far as possible down the ladder of subsidiarity in defining the relevant decision-making demos, but not always. When public goods are involved, when there are great differences in local exit costs, and when accumulated injustices either are products of external action or can be undone only by the state, then it will be necessary to ascend the ladder. This will appear, and will indeed be, vanguardist from more local points of view, even when it is legitimated by democratic decision making farther up the ladder. Those making such decisions higher up will often seem to have, and may sometimes actually have, fewer vital interests at stake than local participants. This means that climbing the ladder should not be done lightly, but not that it should not be done. Decentralization can sometimes be disastrous for democratic justice.

The relevant affected interests are not in any case always local. Especially in today's world, actions and decisions in one part of the globe can be consequential for millions of lives thousands of miles away. Proponents of democratic justice should nonetheless eschew the course urged by those who would have us work for a single world democratic government.[6] Leaving this proposal's lack of realism aside, in many circumstances it should be judged undesirable. Some decisions in far-off places critically affect our most vital interests, others affect us trivially, yet others not at all. Allowing an equal say in a decision to people with greatly differing stakes in the outcome generates pathologies similar to those involving large differences in capacities for exit. This is one reason why the idea of basic interests is an important criterion for delimiting the appropriate decision-making unit in many circumstances. Those whose basic interests are at stake in a particular decision have a stronger claim to inclusion in the demos than those for whom this is not so.

It might be responded that giving weight to basic interests should make us more open to arguments for global democracy than I am suggesting. After all, my discussion of employment relations reveals that workers' basic interests are increasingly hostage to players who are decreasingly answerable within national political institutions, let alone at the firm or local level. This is a good reason, as I argue, for developing devices to limit and counteract the influence of these powerful players, and there are many other areas where institutional innovation is needed to regulate similar kinds of transnational power.[7] The creative way forward in these areas is likely to be through actions that can be taken unilaterally, or at most through regional entities such as the European Union.[8] Trying to get international institutions to promulgate standards of labor practice or to regulate global currency flows is worthwhile, but these institutions have notoriously limited enforcement capacities when they are opposed by both international investors and many national governments.[9] In any event, arguing for such regulation is qualitatively different from advocating world government. Proponents of democratic justice should rather make common cause with those who would disaggregate the traditional incidents of sovereignty, and should reject the view of membership in the demos as an all-or-nothing decision-making trump. The franchise is best defined activity by activity, decision by decision.

Another reason for taking basic interests into account in weighing claims to be included in decision making flows from democratic justice's distinctive focus on power relations. Because people's basic interests include access to the wherewithal for survival, control over them is bound to involve issues of power. This is not to deny that power can be exercised by manipulating forms of necessity that may fall outside the ambit of basic interests. Addicts are the obvious limiting case, and proponents of democratic justice should surely be concerned about their vulnerability to control by others. Normally, however, we regard people as having some meaningful choice over even their strong desires when these are inessential to survival. Compulsion based on necessity is not at stake when people get others to do things by manipulating desires of this sort.

Attention to basic interests is also helpful in distinguishing minorities deserving of protection from majoritarian politics from those that are not. Minorities, such as white South Africans after 1994, may complain that their interests are at risk in democratic politics, and this may indeed be true. But unless they can show their basic interests to be threatened, so that their ability to survive and participate in South African democracy is compromised, then these claims should ring hollow to the ear of democratic justice. Defenders of minority rights tend to forget that there are minorities and minorities, and that democratic movements have often rightly garnered legitimacy by opposing ensconced minority privilege. Democratic justice does not always favor majority rule, as we have seen; in many circumstances subsidiarity considerations and other decision rules protect minority claims. But where majority rule is legitimate, the mere fact of minority status should not be sufficient to limit its reach.

Generalizations of the preceding sort can be adduced, but our journey through the life cycle also reveals that much of settling who should be entitled to decide what is a matter for contextual analysis. Locke's argument that the franchise should be limited by necessity only, for instance, is often a good point of departure, but it has more complex institutional consequences than he perhaps realized. Adults are normally best presumed sovereign over their own decisions, and paternalistic decision making on their behalf is generally not justified. But the possibility of coerced choices leads us to resist the link commonly drawn between antipaternalism and libertarian institutional arrangements. In areas such as employment and adult domestic life, we have seen that the better course lies in underwriting people's individual sovereignty but trying to structure the contexts in which they make decisions so as to minimize the likelihood that they will be coerced. Structural coercion takes different forms in different walks of life. Were these considerations to be pursued into other areas, such as the governance of religious organizations or universities, no doubt different institutional solutions would suggest themselves as best. By the same token, were we to extend the considerations that led to fiduciary arrangements for children and the elderly infirm into other areas where necessity frustrates enfranchisement, such as intergenerational justice and the claims of future generations, no doubt the institutional implications would differ yet again.

Deciding on the appropriate demos for particular decisions is always only part of the story as far the governance side of the equation is concerned. It leaves open the question what the decision rule should be. Here, too, certain general considerations apply, but many choices are dictated by peculiarities of context. Majority rule is more appropriate for competitive interaction and arms-length transactions, whereas unanimity makes more sense for cooperative endeavors and intimate relations. As the exit costs increase for some or all of those affected by decisions, the dangers of minority tyranny begin to attend unanimity rule, and those of majority tyranny begin to attend majority rule. In some circumstances, such as marriage, it makes sense to try to reduce exit costs all around and secure the benefits of unanimity without domination. In the employment context, by contrast, great differences in exit costs between employers and employees will likely persist. Accordingly, decision rules are needed to take account of enduring power disparities.

The answers vary, then, with the facts on the ground and the possibilities of altering them in more felicitous directions. But as democratic justice is pursued through different contexts, the challenge for inclusive participation remains: to come up with decision rules that can reconcile the purposes of different activities with the best possible democratic control of the power relations that structure them.

OPPOSITION AND SUSPICION OF HIERARCHY

The opposition dimension of democratic justice involves comparable mixes of general and contextual considerations. Permissive democratic freedoms of speech, assembly, and organization are generally required for meaningful opposition politics. Yet we saw that they are seldom sufficient, and that on their own they can even have perverse consequences. Given a reality of imperfect decision rules and persisting power disparities, a series of additional measures is needed, derived from our queries about the hierarchies that structure social life. Our interrogatories for probing hierarchies travel well, but, as on the governance side of the equation, the conclusions they generate must be tailored to the context at hand. Although I argue, for instance, that we should generally be skeptical of a robust role for courts in promoting democratic justice, an exception arises with hierarchies, like those over children, that do not easily lend themselves to democratic control. Courts are needed in that context to facilitate parents' roles as secondary or second-guessing fiduciaries of children's basic interests. Somewhat different context-specific reasoning suggest that there is an appropriate role for judges in decisions to terminate life support. We should anticipate that analogous considerations would suggest comparable conclusions in other areas where fiduciary authority is involved. Care for the mentally ill, authority to protect the environment, and responsibility for nonhuman life forms are examples that come to mind.

Reasoning by analogy will be helpful when it captures similarities in patterns of hierarchical authority. This may lead to characteristic ways of thinking about solutions, such as the reliance on altering exit costs and shifting burdens in various applications of the argument developed here. But even when they do travel well, these ideas will have to be applied in ways that defy a great deal of advance specification. Unpacking them plausibly will depend on close-to-the-ground examination of practices as they have evolved, informed appreciation of the available possibilities, and creative adaptation of our opposition injunctions to the activity at hand. And this must be done compatibly with what democratic justice requires on the governance side of the equation.

Endings

Alexis de Tocqueville prefaced his monumental study of *Democracy in America* with a double claim: that the long-term progress of democracy is inevitable and that one of the most pressing tasks for political science is to tame democracy's "wild instincts," lest it run roughshod over the other goods we should rightly value.[10] Both claims were partly correct. Tocqueville was right to think that democracy is an idea with world historical force. It will always appeal, as the natural antidote to exclusion and domination, to those who have been denied a say in the power that is wielded over them. Democracy holds out the hope of righting past wrongs by promoting inclusion and opening up avenues for the expression of legitimate grievance. People's expectations of democracy are often disappointed, but no alternative scheme of governance has been devised that can credibly claim to do better. So it remains an essential part of the battle cry for justice and is likely to do so for as long as injustice persists.

Tocqueville was wrong, however, to think the advance of democracy unstoppable, if not providentially ordained. In his own century it suffered massive setbacks twice throughout Europe. In ours, the blows dealt democracy by fascism and communism should temper triumphalist proclamations that the democratic revolutions since 1989 are moving the world ever closer to a democratic end of history.[11] Partisans of democracy may be greatly heartened by the recent triumphs; they would do well to recognize that these can all too easily be reversed. Most of the fledgling postcommunist regimes are far from being secure democracies. Democracy has broken down before in Latin America; it could do so again.[12] Complacency about a peculiarly democratic African renaissance trades too heavily on the fragile new regimes in southern Africa.[13] We should remember the Algerian and Rwandan possibilities.

Even in the United States, which has thus for escaped totalitarian excess, we have not witnessed the uniform democratic leveling that Tocqueville predicted. To be sure, there have been great advances in promoting inclusion and substantial achievements in ending some of the worst forms of domination. But there have also been setbacks and retrenchments, not to mention exclusionary ideologies that have persisted throughout American history in defiance of the Tocquevillian thesis.[14] Those who value democracy should recognize that there is nothing inevitable about its survival. There will always be forces that stand to lose from democracy's advance. They will oppose it. They will usually be powerful and they will sometimes prevail. But not always. Hence the importance of working to achieve democracy, and to entrench it.

Tocqueville was also partly right about the tensions between democracy and other values. He was right to perceive that these tensions are often real and sometimes inescapable. He was also right to stress the need to "educate democracy; to put, if possible, new life into its beliefs; to purify its mores; to control its actions; gradually to substitute understanding of statecraft for present inexperience and knowledge of its true interests for blind instincts; to adapt government to the needs of time and place; and to modify it as men and circumstances require." [15] Part of what has been attempted here has been an enterprise of educating democracy in Tocqueville's sense. The goal has been to find ways for democracy to coexist with other values, to structure them without stifling them. But there is an additional piece to our enterprise, overlooked in the Tocquevillian worry about democracy's potential to undermine good things. That is its potential to undermine bad things. Important as it is to control democracy's wild instincts by insisting that it operate as a subordinate good, we should not forget that it is a good. Its value derives from the hope it holds out of making the world a more just place. When we impair democracy's capacity to promote inclusion and erode domination, we do not educate—we destroy. A sober appreciation of Tocquevillian anxieties is built into the theory of democratic justice. But so is an equally sober appreciation that the world we have inherited is suffused with injustice. Our purpose is vindicated to the degree that we can do away with the bad without destroying the good, leaving a better world than we found.

Notes

1. Why Democratic Justice?

1. See Robert Dahl and Ian Shapiro, "Impressions from the Soviet Union," *Dissent* (Summer 1991), pp. 342-45.

2. John Dewey, *The Public and Its Problems* (Henry Holt, 1927), pp. 84-85.

3. Rawls is less responsible for the existence of this disjunction than are many of his successors. One of the least discussed features of his argument is the fact that rights of democratic participation are protected by his first principle of justice. Given his lexical ranking, this supplies them with trumping power over many of the subsequent recommendations that flow from his theory, although rights of democratic participation may be substantially limited by other requirements of the first principle. See John Rawls, *A Theory of Justice* (Harvard University Press, 1971), pp. 42-43, 221-34.

4. One exception to this generalization is Amy Gutmann and Dennis Thompson's *Democracy and Disagreement* (Harvard University Press, 1996). They engage with much of the distributive justice literature from the standpoint of democratic theory. However, this occurs principally in the course of defending relatively robust egalitarian preconditions for deliberative democracy as Gutmann and Thompson conceive it. My concern here is the different one of establishing the appropriate place for democratic commitments in plausible arguments about justice. In some respects these enterprises converge on similar concerns for reasons that are spelled out in Chapter 3.

5. Joseph Schumpeter, *Capitalism, Socialism, and Democracy* (Harper, 1942). See also Quentin Skinner, "The empirical theorists of democracy and their critics: A plague on both their houses," *Political Theory*, vol. 1, no. 3 (1973), pp. 287–305.

6. John Dunn, *Western Political Theory in the Face of the Future* (Cambridge University Press, 1979), p. 26.

7. Kenneth Arrow, *Social Choice and Individual Values* (Yale University Press, 1963); William Riker, *Liberalism Against Populism* (Freeman, 1982); and Peter Ordeshook, "Political disequilibrium and scientific inquiry," in Peter Ordeshook and Kenneth Shepsle, eds., *Political Equilibrium* (Kluwer-Nijhoff, 1982), pp. 25–31.

8. In this connection it is notable that the recent turn to contextual justification in much of the methodological writing spawned by Rawls's work has had little impact on the discussion of different substantive principles. The literature seems to proceed on two almost wholly independent tracks; one dealing with different types of justification (Kantian, contextualist, the utility of such devices as reflective equilibrium and hypothetical contract arguments, and so on), the other dealing with different distributive principles (resource-based versus welfarist principles, maximin versus utilitarianism, whether or not liberties should be accorded priority over economic rights, and so on). As an indication of this, notice that virtually none of the literature, by Rawls or others, on his evolving view of justification from *A Theory of Justice* to "Justice as fairness: Political not metaphysical," *Philosophy and Public Affairs*, vol. 14, no. 3, (1985), pp. 223–51, and *Political Liberalism* (Columbia University Press, 1996) deals with the question whether these changes in his views about justification imply any changes in his formulations of the principles of justice.

9. John Locke, *Two Treatises of Government*, ed. Peter Laslett (Cambridge University Press, 1990), II, sec. 23, p. 284; sec. 135, pp. 357–58; and secs. 203–7, pp. 401–4.

10. See Otto von Gierke, *Natural Law and the Theory of Society* (Cambridge University Press, 1934); W. Von Leiden's introduction to Locke's *Essays on the Law of Nature* (Clarendon, 1958); John Dunn, *The Political Thought of John Locke* (Cambridge University Press, 1969); Quentin Skinner, *The Foundations of Modern Political Thought* (Cambridge University Press, 1978); Richard Tuck, *Natural Rights Theories* (Cambridge University Press, 1979); James Tully, *A Discourse Concerning Property* (Cambridge University Press, 1980); Patrick Riley, *Will and Political Legitimacy* (Harvard University Press, 1982), pp. 63–91; and my *The Evolution of Rights in Liberal Theory* (Cambridge University Press, 1986), pp. 23–148.

11. See chapter 3 of Bentham's *Pannomial Fragments*, excerpted in *Selections: A Bentham Reader*, ed. Mary Peter Mack (Pegasus, 1969), pp. 255–57.

12. The combination of Bentham's greatest happiness principle and the principle of diminishing marginal utility seemed to require a radically redistributive state.

If interpersonal comparisons of utility are permitted as Bentham's system required, the principle of diminishing marginal utility mandates redistribution to the point of absolute equality, because by hypothesis wealth taken from the rich and given to the poor adds more utility to the poor than it subtracts from the rich. To avoid this outcome Bentham insisted that the means to achievement of utility are privately produced, and, although he conceded the egalitarian point in principle, he embraced a trickle-down theory of wealth to get him to the conclusion that "practical equality" must fall considerably short of actual equality. See Bentham, "The psychology of economic man" in *Jeremy Bentham's Economic Writings*, vol. 3, pp. 419–54, and *The Theory of Legislation*, ed. C. K. Ogden (Harcourt, Brace, 1931), pp. 109–10. That there is no more agreement on the merits of the trickle-down theory today than there was in the eighteenth century underscores the hopeless character of attempts to found an uncontroversial theory of the nature and limits to the private sphere on such consequentialist considerations. For some of the most recent attempts, see Robert Nozick's argument that market-based systems of appropriation are most efficient in *Anarchy, State, and Utopia* (Basic, 1974), pp. 167–69, 186–87, 191–92, 195, 198–202, 282–83; and Richard Posner's similar argument (on this point) in *The Economics of Justice* (Harvard University Press, 1981), pp. 88–118.

13. John Stuart Mill, *On Liberty* (Hackett, 1978 [1859]), p. 9.
14. On the Supreme Court's move (in interpreting Title VII of the 1964 Civil Rights Act) from *de facto* tests, which required only a showing of discriminatory effects to trigger a remedy, to a *de jure* test, which requires a showing of discriminatory intent, see *Palmer v. Thomson* 403 U.S. 217 (1971), *Griggs v. Duke Power* 401 U.S. 424 (1971), and *Washington v. Davis* 426 U.S. 229 (1976). For the classic defense of strict liability in torts see Guido Calabresi, *The Costs of Accidents: A Legal and Economic Analysis* (Yale University Press, 1970). For a defense of the negligence standard against strict liability, see Posner, *Economics of Justice*, pp. 95–99, 101. This debate in tort law is not new with the advent of interest in strict liability. Even under negligence regimes it is much debated whether establishing a negligent state of mind was necessary to establish negligent conduct, or whether this could be inferred from certain conduct. On the difficulties of interpreting Mill's harm principle generally, see Joel Feinberg, *Social Philosophy* (Prentice Hall, 1973), chapter 2.
15. Consider the differences between Robert Paul Wolff's insistence that respecting Kantian autonomy is inconsistent with any exercise of state authority whatsoever, Nozick's claim that it requires the limited class of privacy rights that libertarians generally endorse, and Rawls's argument that it requires a yet more complex hierarchy of entitlements. Wolff, *In Defense of Anarchism* (Harper, 1970), pp. 12–20, 78–82; Nozick, *Anarchy, State, and Utopia*, pp. 84–117; and Rawls, *A Theory of Justice*, pp. 251–58. Contrast all of these with Kant's assertion that

"welfare does not have any ruling principle, either for the recipient or for the one who provides it, for each individual will define it differently. It depends, in fact, on the will's material aspect, which is empirical and thus incapable of becoming a universal rule." Immanuel Kant, *The Contest of the Faculties*, in *Kant's Political Writings*, ed. H. Reiss (Cambridge University Press, 1970), pp. 183–84.

16. Michael Sandel, *Liberalism and the Limits of Justice* (Cambridge University Press, 1982), pp. 11–14, 183. Generally, see his *Democracy's Discontent: America in Search of a Public Philosophy* (Harvard University Press, 1996).

17. For examples of other romantic communitarian claims, see Robert N. Bellah, Richard Madsen, William Sullivan, and Ann Swidler, *Habits of the Heart* (University of California Press, 1985); and Amitai Etzioni, *The Spirit of Community: Rights, Responsibilities, and the Communitarian Agenda* (Crown, 1993).

18. See Edward Shils, *Tradition* (University of Chicago Press, 1981), pp. 19, 287–330; Lloyd I. Rudolph and Susanne H. Rudolph, *The Modernity of Tradition* (University of Chicago Press, 1967); and Joseph R. Gussfield, *Community* (Blackwell, 1975), pp. 37–39 ff. Those who continue to believe that the Puritan communities of New England provide such models should read George L. Haskins, *Law and Authority in Early Massachusetts* (University Press of America, 1960).

19. G. A. Cohen indicates awareness of the problem when he says that Marxists' confrontation with liberalism "is avoidable only as long as Marxists continue to maintain that abundance will ensure complete compatibility among the interests of differently endowed people, and abundance on the required scale now seems unattainable. A lesser abundance, which enables resolutions of conflicts of interests without coercion, may well be possible." Cohen, "Self-ownership, world-ownership, and equality: Part I," in Frank Lucash, ed., *Justice and Equality Here and Now* (Cornell University Press, 1986), p. 117. But Cohen offers no account of how this might be done, and in his more recent work advocating equalization of "access to advantage" he supplies no account of how and by whom different disadvantages are to be weighted in the event (presumably universal once endemic scarcity is conceded) that equalizing access along some dimension diminishes it along a different one. Cohen, "On the currency of egalitarian justice," *Ethics*, vol. 99, no. 4 (July 1989), pp. 906–44, and "Equality of what? On welfare, goods and capabilities," in Martha Nussbaum and Amartya Sen, eds., *The Quality of Life* (Clarendon, 1993), pp. 9–29. On these issues, see Douglas Rae et al., *Equalities* (Harvard University Press, 1980), pp. 104–29. Even advocates of needs as instruments of social policy making like David Braybrooke concede that the concept breaks down in the face of demands for medical resources (among other areas), although the difficulty is more serious for his theory than Braybrooke imagines. He perceives conflicts between the need for medical care and other needs, noting that in such circumstances choices will have to be made that bring to bear considerations other than that of meeting needs. Braybrooke,

Meeting Needs (Princeton University Press, 1987), pp. 295–306. But he fails to notice that even within the realm of medical care, needs must invariably outstrip resources, so that the problem is not merely one of ranking medical and nonmedical needs but, within the realm of medical resources, deciding how to allocate needed resources to competing claimants.

20. This skepticism of reductionist accounts should not be confused with the view that nothing scientific can be said about politics. It simply means that students of politics must likely accept the reality that human beings and their evolving political environments are too complex to be accounted for by reference to any single set of explanatory variables. See Donald Green and Ian Shapiro, *Pathologies of Rational Choice Theory* (Yale University Press, 1994), and "Pathologies revisited: Reflections on our critics," in Jeffrey Friedman, ed., *The Rational Choice Controversy* (Yale University Press, 1996), pp. 235–76.

21. To be exempted from this generalization are Marx's utopian reflections discussed in the preceding section. The generalization also takes for granted a reading of Plato's *Republic*, not defended here, as geared toward showing the impossibility of a perfectly just social order rather than supplying a blueprint for it. Anyone interested in the vexed debate on what Plato really meant in this regard could do worse than begin with Desmond Lee's introduction to *The Republic* (Penguin, 1955).

22. The most conspicuous example is Bentham, for whom all goods and harms are reducible to a single pleasure-pain calculus. See *A Fragment on Government and An Introduction to the Principles of Morals and Legislation*, ed. Wilfrid Harrison (Blackwell, 1960), p. 125. Nozick also comes close to this view when he assumes that any violation of rights can in principle be fully compensated with money, a notion that separates him from Rawls. See *Anarchy, State, and Utopia*, pp. 54–87, and Rawls, "Social unity and primary goods," in Amartya Sen and Bernard Williams, eds., *Utilitarianism and Beyond* (Cambridge University Press, 1982), pp. 159–85. It is arguable that any proposition in welfare economics that makes use of compensation theory implicitly assumes that all goods are reducible to a single index. See I. M. D. Little, *A Critique of Welfare Economics* (Oxford University Press, 1950), pp. 84–116.

23. Thus Rawls believes that questions about political liberties can in principle be settled before economic questions concerning equality of opportunity and substantive fairness. *A Theory of Justice*, pp. 195–227, 243–50. It is arguable that the lexical ranking device implicitly reintroduces a unitary index. See Kenneth J. Arrow, "Some ordinalist-utilitarian notes on Rawls's theory of justice," *Journal of Philosophy*, vol. 70, no. 9 (1973), pp. 245–63, 254. For Rawls's response, see "Social unity and primary goods," pp. 184–85.

24. Michael Walzer, *Spheres of Justice* (Basic, 1983), pp. 3–20, Alasdair MacIntyre, *After Virtue*, 2d ed. (University of Notre Dame Press, 1984), pp. 181–203.

25. Common targets are Rawls's claim that the difference principle would be chosen in the original position over utilitarianism and the lexical priority he accords to the first principle. In both instances he relies on assumptions about risk that many have resisted. For one telling discussion, see John Harsanyi, "Can the maximin principle serve as a basis for morality? A critique of John Rawls's theory," *American Political Science Review*, vol. 69, no. 2 (1975), pp. 594–606.

26. For the early formulation see *A Theory of Justice*, 154–72; for the more recent contextualization see "Justice as fairness," pp. 223–51, and *Political Liberalism* (Columbia University Press, 1996), pp. 9–11, 133–72.

27. It is sometimes said that one critique of Rawls—that he achieves the agreement of those who accept his intuitions at the price of ensuring the disagreement of those who do not—misses the point of his reflective equilibrium device: that it is intended to get us to look critically at our previously unexamined intuitions. This may be true of some of our intuitions about justice, but it is not true of such empirical assumptions as beliefs about the human propensity toward risk. At no time does Rawls suggest that these can or should be revised as a result of reflective equilibrium; on the contrary, Rawls holds them constant and tries to use them to get people to modify their intuitions about justice.

28. For MacIntyre's account of social practices see *After Virtue*, pp. 187–96. In the chapter on education in *Spheres of Justice*, Walzer treats its purpose as preparing people for democratic citizenship, yet it is unclear how he would respond to someone who disagreed with this, insisting, perhaps, that the goal of education ought to be enlightenment. For more on Walzer's illicit Rawlsian move see Dworkin's "To each his own," a review of *Spheres of Justice* that appeared in the *New York Review of Books* on April 14, 1983, and the exchange between Dworkin and Walzer that appeared there on July 21, 1983. I take up these issues at length in *Political Criticism* (University of California Press, 1990), chapters 3, 5, and 9.

29. By use of the term *foundational* in this context I mean explicitly to refrain from referring to those democratic institutions and distributive mechanisms that Rawls argues would be agreed on in the original position, briefly discussed in *A Theory of Justice* on pages 75–80 and 274–84, and focus instead on the role played by democratic moral commitments in the characterization of the original position itself.

30. See "Justice as fairness." See also *A Theory of Justice*, pp. 387–91, and *Political Liberalism*, pp. 9–11, 133–72.

31. Thus Walzer, in his response to Dworkin's critique of his claim that a more egalitarian distribution of medical care is required by accepted meanings in our culture, insists that his argument is "historical, sociological, contingent. Dworkin wants an entirely different kind of argument, so that one might say at the end, flatly, that a rich society that leaves medical care to the market 'would not be a

just society.' I am in fact disinclined to say that just like that, for it may be the case that the wealth of some particular society ought to be spent on the cure of souls, not of bodies, or on defense, or drama, or education. I don't see how these priorities can be philosophically determined. But that is not to rule out radical criticism, for the actual distribution of salvation, security, and culture is likely to be distorted, has historically been distorted, by wealthy and powerful elites, and it is one of the tasks of moral philosophy (and of social theory too) to explain and condemn the distortions." *New York Review of Books*, July 21, 1983, p. 44.

32. See *Spheres of Justice*, pp. 10–20, and *After Virtue*, pp. 181–203.

33. This state of affairs creates a noteworthy methodological symmetry: as liberal consent theorists move toward contextual justification, their communitarian critics seem to be moving away from it, back in the direction of independent principled argument.

34. Few empirically minded social scientists place as much value on consent and consensus as political philosophers characteristically do. When students of comparative politics confront high levels of agreement in circumstances that they have independent reasons for thinking are based on relations of hierarchy and domination (as in Mexico), they turn to a concept like hegemony to try to explain this. When they discern relatively little of the kinds of conflict they expect in contemporary capitalist countries, they turn to concepts like liberal corporatism to explain the ideological incorporation of the working classes. See Leo Panitch, "The development of corporatism in liberal democracies," *Comparative Political Studies* (April 1977), pp. 61–90. Controversial as such explanations often are, there is no a priori reason for thinking them less likely to be true than to assume, with neither argument nor evidence, that agreement is indicative of fundamental social consensus. On varieties of hegemony in the contemporary world, see Alfred Stepan, *The State in Society: Peru in Comparative Perspective* (Princeton University Press, 1978), pp. 3–113. For philosophical arguments questioning the relevance of agreement to arguments about social justice, see T. M. Scanlon, "The significance of choice," *The Tanner Lectures on Human Values*, Sterling McMurrin, ed., vol. 8 (University of Utah Press, 1988); C. E. Lindblom, *Inquiry and Change* (Yale University Press, 1990); and my argument in *Political Criticism*, chapters 2, 7–9.

35. Rawls, "Justice as fairness," and *Political Liberalism*, pp. 9–11, 133–72; Walzer, *Spheres of Justice*, and "Liberalism and the art of separation," *Political Theory*, vol. 12, no. 3 (1984), pp. 315–30; MacIntyre, *After Virtue*, chapters 2–3; and Jürgen Habermas, *Communication and the Evolution of Society* (Beacon, 1976), and *The Theory of Communicative Action*, vol. 1 (Beacon, 1984), pp. 273–337.

36. Thus Gutmann and Thompson tell us that democratic citizens with moral disagreements "should deliberate with one another, seeking moral agreement when

they can, and maintaining mutual respect when they cannot." Gutmann and Thompson, *Democracy and Disagreement*, pp. 346, 2, 9.

37. Those who bemoan dissensus include many contextualists but also others such as Leo Strauss, especially in *Natural Right and History* (University of Chicago Press, 1953), and Allan Bloom, *The Closing of the American Mind* (Simon and Schuster, 1987).

38. Stephen Holmes, "Gag rules," in Jon Elster and Rune Slagstad, eds., *Constitutionalism and Democracy* (Cambridge University Press, 1988).

39. On what they believed was the relationship between growing social consensus and creeping mediocrity, see Mill, *On Liberty*, pp. 15-71, and Alexis de Tocqueville, *Democracy in America* (Doubleday, 1969), pp. 50-56, 220-26, 246-61. On Big Brotherism the most remarkable statement remains George Orwell's *Nineteen Eighty-Four* (Signet, 1971).

40. Dewey, *The Public and Its Problems*, p. 110.

2. Preliminaries

1. Much of the public-choice literature since Arrow has identified democracy with majority rule or unanimity rule somehow defined. For an overview see Dennis Mueller, *Public Choice II* (Cambridge University Press, 1989), pp. 43-148. The classic account of America's democratic spirit is Tocqueville's *Democracy in America*. For the "defining criteria" approach, see Dahl, "Procedural democracy," in Dahl, *Democracy, Liberty, and Equality* (Norwegian University Press, 1986), pp. 191-225; for the comparative use of the term in the ancient world, see H. D. F. Kitto, *The Greeks* (Pelican, 1973). On the differences between procedural and substantive conceptions of democracy, see Charles Beitz, "Equal opportunity in political representation," in Norman E. Bowie, ed., *Equal Opportunity* (Westview, 1988), pp. 155-74, and Robert Dahl, *Democracy and Its Critics* (Yale University Press, 1989), pp. 163-92. See also John Hart Ely, *Democracy and Distrust* (Harvard University Press, 1980). On democracy as an oppositional ethic see my *Democracy's Place* (Cornell University Press, 1996), chapters 5 and 8. On democracy as republican self-government, see the participatory tradition that begins with Jean-Jacques Rousseau, *The Social Contract* (Pelican, 1972), and finds contemporary expression in such works as Carol Pateman, *Participation and Democratic Theory* (Cambridge University Press, 1970), and Joshua Cohen and Joel Rogers, *On Democracy* (Penguin, 1983). Different variants of the deliberative model are championed in Benjamin Barber, *Strong Democracy* (University of California Press, 1979), and Gutmann and Thompson, *Democracy and Disagreement*. The classic exploration of the costs of deliberation remains James Buchanan and Gordon Tullock, *The Calculus of Consent: Logical Foundations of Constitutional Democracy* (Ann Arbor Paperbacks, 1962).

2. For statements of the conventional academic opposition between democracy and justice, see Adam Przeworski, "Minimalist conception of democracy: A defense," and John Roemer, "Does democracy engender justice?" both in Ian Shapiro and Casiano Hacker-Cordón, eds., *Democracy's Value* (Cambridge University Press, 1999). Philippe van Parijs makes a similar argument in "Justice and democracy: Are they incompatible?" *Journal of Political Philosophy*, vol. 4, no. 2 (1996), pp. 101–17. He insists that where democracy and justice conflict, the former should be sacrificed to the latter. His view is close to mine, however, in that he concedes that one of the standard ways of delegitimating an account of justice is to reveal it to be antidemocratic, and he insists that a defensible conception of justice should include democratic procedures. See especially pp. 109–13.

3. See, for example, Guiseppe Di Palma, *To Craft Democracies: An Essay on Democratic Transitions* (University of California Press, 1990), p. 23, for defense of the view that the democratic ideal should be disengaged "from the idea of social progress" if it is to endure, and Samuel P. Huntington, *The Third Wave: Democratization in the Late Twentieth Century* (University of Oklahoma Press, 1991), pp. 165–69, for the argument that political leaders who sell out their constituents' demands for social justice are more likely to succeed in consolidating democratic institutions than those who do not.

4. Among the entrenched provisions in Article 20 of the German Basic Law are that the Federal Republic of Germany "is a democratic and social Federal state" and that all state authority "emanates from the people" and is exercised "by means of elections and voting and by separate legislative, executive, and judicial organs." Germans are entitled "to resist any person seeking to abolish this constitutional order, should no other remedy be possible." Part 2, Art. 20, sections 1, 2, and 4. For the entrenchment provision, see Part 7, Art. 70, section 3.

5. See my *Democracy's Place*, p. 177.

6. See Iris Marion Young, *Justice and the Politics of Difference* (Princeton University Press, 1990), chapters 2 and 4.

7. Michel Foucault, *The Order of Things* (Routledge, 1974), and *Power/Knowledge* (Harvester, 1980).

8. See Rawls, *A Theory of Justice*, pp. 42–43; 221–34.

9. For my views on philosophical antifoundationalism, see *Political Criticism*, chapters 2, 6, and 7.

10. Rawls, "Fairness to goodness," *Philosophical Review*, vol. 82 (1973), p. 228, "Justice as fairness," pp. 223–26, and *Political Liberalism*, p. 10 ff.

11. Nietzsche is an example of an antifoundationalist who would not find the politics defended here congenial.

12. See Robert Dahl, *After the Revolution* (Yale University Press, 1970), pp. 140–66; Kenneth Keniston, *The Young Radicals* (Harcourt Brace, 1968); Arnold Kaufman, "Participatory democracy: Ten years later," and "Human nature and partici-

patory democracy," in William Connolly, ed., *The Bias of Pluralism* (Lieber-Atherton, 1969), pp. 184-98, 201-212; Pateman, *Participation;* Jane Mansbridge, *Beyond Adversary Democracy* (Basic, 1980); and Michael Walzer, "A day in the life of a socialist citizen," in *Radical Principles* (Basic, 1989), pp. 112-38.

13. My general argument would counsel, however, that when political participation is pursued as a superordinate good, it should be subject to democratic conditioning constraints, as should the pursuit of any other objective that has collective ramifications. This arises in connection with issues having to do with intense preferences, and in particular concerns the difficulty that those willing to invest more time and energy than others in political activities can have disproportionate impacts on the outcome. Elective pursuit of political participation as a superordinate good should be permissible, but not beyond the point at which it undermines democracy's role as a subordinate good for the rest of us. Although I do not explore this issue here, I have made the case elsewhere that democracy should not generally take intensity of preference into account. See my *Democracy's Place*, chapter 2.

14. See Carmen Sirianni, "Participation," mimeo, 1991. Despite his lucid identification of the problem and penetrating criticisms of Barber, Gould, and other participatory democrats, Sirianni fails to break with the way of thinking which assumes that some theory of participation, if only it can be made sufficiently subtle and sophisticated, is the core good to be achieved through democratic politics. See his discussion of first-order, second-order, and metaconsensus, pp. 25-30. For a discussion of the varieties of rule- and act-utilitarianism, see David Lyons, *Forms and Limits of Utilitarianism* (Clarendon, 1965).

15. Two works that do examine education in ways that are largely consistent with the spirit of democratic justice are Katherine McDermott's *Controlling Public Education* (University Press of Kansas, 1999) and Amy Gutmann's *Democratic Education* (Princeton University Press, 1987). I have some disagreements with Gutmann, as noted in *Democracy's Place*, pp. 158-60.

3. The General Argument

1. For conventional statements of the liberal fear of organized power see Judith Shklar, "The liberalism of fear," in Nancy Rosenblum, ed., *Liberalism and the Moral Life* (Harvard University Press, 1989), pp. 21-38, and Stephen Holmes, "The permanent structure of antiliberal thought," ibid., pp. 227-53. For discussions of the threat posed by politics to personal values see Isaiah Berlin, "Two concepts of liberty," in *Four Essays on Liberty* (Oxford University Press, 1969) pp. 118-72, and Patrick Devlin, *The Enforcement of Morals* (Oxford University Press, 1965). The classic statement of principled hostility to political blueprints remains Karl Popper, *The Open Society and its Enemies*, 4th ed. (Princeton University Press, 1963).

2. Barrington Moore, Jr., *Liberal Prospects Under Soviet Socialism: A Comparative Historical Perspective* (Averell Harriman Institute, 1989), p. 25.

3. Nelson Mandela, "Address to court before sentencing," in J. Ayo Langley, ed., *Ideologies of Liberation in Black Africa, 1856–1970* (Rex Collins, 1979), p. 665. On the Chartists, see Dorothy Thompson, *The Chartists* (Temple Smith, 1984). Generally, see Elie Halevy, *The Growth of Philosophic Radicalism* (Kelley, 1972).

4. Mandela, "Address," p. 664.

5. Nor do all liberals agree with one another, any more than all democrats do, over which of these, combinations of these, or combinations of these and other reasons they invoke for adhering to antivanguardist conceptions of the good.

6. For one conventional statement of this view see William Riker, *Liberalism Against Populism* (Waveland Press, 1982). It might be objected that my depiction deals with only a subset of liberalisms. This is conceded, though I would contend that it is an expansive subset, ranging at least from the fears of majority tyranny expressed through the state that can be found in Mill's *On Liberty* and Tocqueville's *Democracy in America*, through the libertarian liberalisms of Riker, Nozick, and Buchanan and Tullock discussed in the text, and the nonlibertarianism antistatism embraced by the Judith Shklar of *Ordinary Vices* (Harvard University Press, 1984).

7. Nozick, *Anarchy, State, and Utopia*, p. 4.

8. See Jules Coleman, "Competition and cooperation," *Ethics*, vol. 98, no. 1, (1987), p. 82 for elaboration of the view that "a scheme of secure property rights is a collective good for those who have it." I take these issues up further in "Three fallacies concerning majorities, minorities, and democratic politics," in John Chapman and Alan Wertheimer, eds., *NOMOS XXXII: Majorities and Minorities* (New York University Press, 1990), pp. 79–125.

9. For extended discussion, see my *Evolution of Rights*, chapters 4–6.

10. Buchanan and Tullock, *Calculus of Consent*, pp. 73–77.

11. Brian Barry, *Political Argument*, 2d ed., (Harvester Wheatsheaf, 1990 [1965]); Douglas W. Rae, "Decision-rules and individual values in constitutional choice," *American Political Science Review*, vol. 63, no. 1 (1969), pp. 40–56; and Michael Taylor, "Proof of a theorem on majority rule," *Behavioral Science*, vol. 14 (May 1969), pp. 228–31. When the number of voters (n) is odd, the optimal decision rule is majority rule, n over two, plus one-half; when n is even, the optimal decision rule is either majority rule (n over two plus one), or majority rule minus one (simply n over two). Generally, see Mueller, *Public Choice II*, pp. 96–111.

12. Even if we accept the contractualist metaphor, the logic of Buchanan and Tullock's defense of unanimity rule breaks down once time and externalities are taken into account. See Rae, "The limits of consensual decision," *American Political Science Review*, vol. 69, no. 4 (1975), pp. 1270–94.

13. It might appear that no-fault divorce destroys the marriage contract qua contract entirely, because it is terminable at the will of either party. But such a conclusion ignores the fact that conventional unanimity rule operates in marriages unless and until they reach the point of dissolution. It also conflates the grounds for divorce with the terms of divorce, matters I take up in Chapter 5. Notice also that many countries, and some American states, that embrace some form of no-fault divorce do not go all the way with it. Instead they insist that the court find that "irretrievable breakdown" has occurred, for which purpose the judge may take various factors, including the wishes of both parties, into account. See Mary Ann Glendon, *Abortion and Divorce in Western Law* (Harvard University Press, 1987), pp. 64-81.

14. See Robert Dahl, *A Preface to Economic Democracy* (University of California Press, 1985), pp. 111-35.

15. See Elaine Spitz, *Majority Rule* (Chatham, 1984), pp. 135-215.

16. See Andrew Duff, ed., *Subsidiarity Within the European Community* (Federal Trust, 1993), and Kees Van Kersbergen and B. Verbeek, "The politics of subsidiarity in the European Union," *Journal of Common Market Studies*, vol. 32, no. 2 (June 1994), pp. 215-37.

17. See James Scott, *Seeing Like a State: How Certain Schemes to Improve the Human Condition Have Failed* (Yale University Press, 1998).

18. I argue for this proposition at length in *Political Criticism*, pp. 252-61.

19. The $50 million figure is reported by Tim Rinne, "The rise and fall of single-payer health care in Nebraska," *Action for Universal Health Care*, vol. 3, no. 10 (May 1995), pp. 4-5. See also Tom Hamburger and Theodore R. Marmor, "Dead on arrival: Why Washington's power elites won't consider single payer health reform," *Washington Monthly* (September 1993), pp. 27-32.

20. This is a result of the blank check that the United States Supreme Court has given those who have large amounts of money, or the capacity to raise it, to shape the terms of public debate since 1976. In *Buckley v. Valeo* 424 U.S. 1 (1976) the Court held, *inter alia*, that although Congress may regulate financial contributions to political parties or candidates, it cannot otherwise regulate private expenditures on political speech, which latter are protected by the First Amendment. For all practical purposes the *Buckley* rule makes it impossible to limit privately funded political advertising.

21. Most liberals take the basic unit of the nation-state for granted, treating it as a kind of Lockean voluntary association writ large, as has often been pointed out in criticism of Rawls. See *A Theory of Justice*, pp. 371-82, and his "Law of peoples," *Critical Inquiry*, vol. 20 (Autumn, 1993), pp. 36-68. No doubt this is often a consequence of the liberal proclivity for thinking in contractualist terms. The exception is Bruce Ackerman in *Social Justice in the Liberal State* (Yale University Press, 1980), pp. 69-103, 256-57, 375. For an illustration of the com-

munitarian view of membership as the basic trumping good, see Walzer, *Spheres of Justice*, pp. 29, 31–63.

22. My contention that the causally based view is more defensible than the going alternatives is compatible with a number of recent arguments whose purpose is to decenter membership-based sovereignty as the decisive determinant of participation and to replace it with systems of overlapping jurisdiction in which different groups of persons are seen as sovereign over different classes of decisions. See Thomas Pogge, "Cosmopolitanism and sovereignty," *Ethics*, vol. 103 (October 1992), pp. 48–75; Alexander Wendt, "Collective identity-formation and the international state," *American Political Science Review*, vol. 88, no. 2 (June 1994), pp. 384–96; and William Antholis, "Liberal democratic theory and the transformation of sovereignty," Ph.D. diss., Yale University, 1993.

23. Moore, *Liberal Prospects*, p. 8. On the origins of the idea of loyal opposition see Archibald S. Foord, *His Majesty's Opposition, 1714–1830* (Oxford University Press, 1964).

24. Long before the advent of the modern literature on public choice, Schumpeter had exposed the logical flaws in the Rousseauist idea of a general will, concluding that "though a common will or public opinion of some sort may still be said to emerge from the infinitely complex jumble of individual and group-wise situation, volitions, influences, actions and reactions of the 'democratic process,' the result lacks not only rational unity but also rational sanction." Schumpeter, *Capitalism, Socialism, and Democracy*, p. 253. For an even earlier critique along these lines, see Walter Lippmann, *The Phantom Public* (Harcourt Brace, 1925).

25. See Robert Dahl, *Polyarchy: Participation and Opposition* (Yale University Press, 1971), and Huntington, *Third Wave*, pp. 6–7.

26. Stone focused his attention on "statutes directed at particular religious . . . or racial minorities" and circumstances that tend "seriously to curtail the operation of those political processes ordinarily to be relied upon to protect minorities." *United States v. Carolene Products Co.*, 304 U.S. 144 (1938), 152*n*4.

27. John Hart Ely, *Democracy and Distrust* (Harvard University Press, 1980). Ely described his argument as purely procedural, designed to repair defects of democratic process; but as critics have pointed out and the discussion below makes clear, it is obviously a substantive argument. See Rogers M. Smith, *Liberalism and American Constitutional Law* (Harvard University Press, 1985), pp. 89–91, 170–74.

28. Charles Beitz, "Equal opportunity in political representation," in Norman E. Bowie, ed., *Equal Opportunity* (Westview, 1988), pp. 155–74. It should not be thought that *Carolene Products* logic is the exclusive preserve of the political left. For instance, Riker and Weingast employ it to criticize taxation of property: "What protection is there against members of today's majority from providing

private, redistributive benefits to themselves under the guise of public purposes and at the expense of some minority of owners and the efficiency of production? Why is the abridgement of some minority's economic rights less troubling than an abridgement of the political rights of minorities?" William H. Riker and Barry R. Weingast, "Constitutional regulation of legislative choice: The political consequences of judicial deference to legislatures," *Virginia Law Review*, vol. 74, no. 2 (March 1988), pp. 378–79.

29. Beitz, "Equal opportunity," p. 168.

30. For discussion of additional weaknesses in the *Carolene Products* approach, see Bruce Ackerman, "Beyond *Carolene Products*," *Harvard Law Review*, vol. 98, no. 4 (February 1985), pp. 713–46.

31. The quixotic political commitments that follow from the injunction to overthrow all hierarchy everywhere have been explored in Roberto Unger's three-volume *Politics* (Cambridge University Press, 1987). For criticism of his argument, see my "Constructing politics," *Political Theory*, vol. 17, no. 3 (August 1989), pp. 475–82.

32. *Wisconsin v. Yoder* 406 U.S. 205 (1972). From the standpoint of democratic justice *Yoder* was thus wrongly decided, although it would have been a more difficult case had the parents pressed their best understandings of their children's interests rather than their own.

33. This is not to say that all polygamous regimes fare equally poorly from the standpoint of democratic justice. See Chapter 5.

34. The Oneida perfectionists, founded in 1848 in Oneida, New York, by John Henry Noyes, rejected all forms of private property and extended their belief in community property to community property in persons. Like the Mormon polygamists, they were persecuted by the state, eventually abandoning their commitment to complex marriage in 1879. See Carol Weisbrod, "On the breakup of Oneida," *Connecticut Law Review*, vol. 14, no. 4 (Summer 1982), pp. 717–32. In fact, the community was run in an authoritarian manner by Noyes, who indulged himself in the sexual initiation of many young girls and decided unilaterally who could marry. This suggests that the community would have been suspect on a number of grounds from the standpoint of democratic justice. See Spenser Klaw, *Without Sin* (Allen Lane, 1993).

35. Rawls, *A Theory of Justice*, pp. 42–45, 61–65, 82–89, 151–61.

36. It is not difficult to demonstrate the existence of contradictory imperatives flowing from Rawls's lexical rankings. See T. M. Scanlon, "Rawls's theory of justice," in Norman Daniels, ed., *Reading Rawls* (Blackwell, 1975), pp. 169–205; H. L. A. Hart, "Rawls on liberty and its priority," ibid., pp. 230–52; and Benjamin Barber, "Justifying justice: Problems of psychology, politics and measurement in Rawls," ibid., pp. 292–318.

37. This is the view defended in Richard Arneson and Ian Shapiro, "Democracy and

religious freedom: A critique of *Wisconsin v. Yoder*," in Ian Shapiro and Russell Hardin, eds., *NOMOS XXXVIII: Political Order* (New York University Press, 1996) pp. 365–411.

38. The Supreme Court thus reached a defensible result from the standpoint of the democratic justice in *Bob Jones University v. United States*, when it held that the federal government may legitimately deny tax-exempt status to institutions that would otherwise qualify but which engage in racial discrimination. 461 U.S. 574 (1983).

39. To some even this approach will sound like opening the way for dangerously radical interference with freedom of religious worship. But reflection on our current laws concerning racially exclusionary organizations, and on the distinctions we comfortably draw between religions and cults and between education and brainwashing, should reveal that we routinely make many judgments of this kind, however implicitly.

40. Robert Dahl has argued that analogous skepticism is in order toward claims that democratic control of nuclear arsenals and development interferes with their efficient deployment. See *Controlling Nuclear Weapons: Democracy Versus Guardianship* (Syracuse University Press, 1985), pp. 33–51.

41. On citizen juries, see Ned Crosby et al., "Citizens' jury on the at-risk children of greater New Haven: The research report," 1994. On deliberative polls, see James Fishkin, *Democracy and Deliberation: New Directions for Democratic Reform* (Yale University Press, 1991).

42. Giovanni Sartori, *The Theory of Democracy Revisited* (Chatham, 1987), vol. 1, pp. 119–20.

43. Citizen juries must confront the difficulty that whoever sets the agenda may exert disproportionate influence on the outcome, but this is a difficulty that every decision-making procedure must confront. It is not the weakness in democratic theory that they are intended to resolve, though proponents of citizen juries, like proponents of other decision-making mechanisms, need to be concerned about it.

44. See Herbert Alexander, *Financing Politics: Money, Elections, and Political Reform* (Congressional Quarterly Press, 1976), and Frank J. Sorauf, *Inside Campaign Finance* (Yale University Press, 1992).

45. In this connection a small but not insignificant victory was achieved for democracy in March 1990 in *Austin v. Michigan State Chamber of Commerce*, 110 S.Ct. 1391, when the Supreme Court cut back on the *Buckley v. Valeo* rule, holding that some corporate expenditures on political speech may be regulated. As for term limits, there is considerable scholarly debate about how bad the incumbency problem is and whether term limits would solve the problem of the ossification of power in professional hands. They might, for example, lead to a net transfer

of power from politicians to bureaucrats, as Morris Fiorina suggests in *Divided Government* (Macmillan, 1992), pp. 53–59.

46. John Dewey, "Democratic ends need democratic methods for their realization," *New Leader* 22 (October 21, 1939), reprinted in John Dewey, *The Political Writings*, ed. Debra Morris and Ian Shapiro (Hackett, 1993), p. 206.

47. See Jennifer Hochschild, *The New American Dilemma: Liberal Democracy and School Desegregation* (Yale University Press, 1984). The subject of which intervening institutions are the best is taken up at the end of this chapter.

48. Katherine McDermott thus identifies a double failing for democracy in Connecticut's public schools when she discovers intense local participation in fiscal matters but widespread indifference on most other matters, even when schools and local school boards try to foster greater community involvement. *Controlling Public Education*, chapters 3–4.

49. "A pure public good has two salient characteristics: jointness of supply, and the impossibility or inefficiency of excluding others from its consumption, once it has been supplied by some members of the community." Mueller, *Public Choice II*, p. 11.

50. Adam Przeworski, *Democracy and the Market* (Cambridge University Press, 1991), pp. 183–84. See also Janos Kornai, *The Road to a Free Economy: Shifting from a Socialist System* (W. W. Norton, 1990); Jeffrey Sachs, "The transformation of Eastern Europe: The case of Poland," The Frank E. Seidman Lecture, Rhodes College, Memphis, Tenn., September 26, 1991; Boris Pleskovic and Jeffrey Sachs, "Political independence and economic reform in Slovenia," in Oliver Blanchard, Kenneth Froot, and Jeffrey Sachs, eds., *The Transition in Eastern Europe* (University of Chicago Press, 1994), vol. I, pp. 191–220.

51. Since the early 1990s, evidence has begun to accumulate suggesting that shock therapy is less effective than gradual market reforms that can garner legitimacy over time. See Mitchell Orenstein, "Out of the red," Ph.D. diss., Yale University, 1997, and his "Lawlessness from above and below: Economic radicalism and political institutions," *SAIS Review* (Winter–Spring 1998), pp. 35–50. The discovery that shock therapy does not work has caused many commentators, including Przeworski, to back away from it—a salutary illustration of dangers of being seduced by confidently pressed technocratic arguments. See Adam Przeworski, et al., *Sustainable Democracy* (Cambridge University Press, 1995), pp. 91–106.

52. Przeworski, *Democracy and the Market*, pp. 183–84.

53. On the collapse of the roundtable negotiations and the emergence of an elite pact between the National Party and ANC leaderships, see my *Democracy's Place*, chapter 7.

54. The constitution requires that any member of parliament who ceases to be a member of his or her political party also ceases to be a member of parliament,

to be replaced by someone else from the party's parliamentary list. This provision obviously strengthens the hands of party leaderships. As for bribes, all civil service jobs and salaries were guaranteed for at least five years following the transition, and in the last weeks before the election President De Klerk transferred some three million acres of land to Zulu king Goodwill Zwelitini in order to prevent their falling under the control of the new national government following the April 1994 elections. *New York Times*, May 24, 1994.

55. These categories are supposed to be linked both to the importance of the right in question and to the magnitude of the injustice to which ameliorative policies are addressed, although American courts do not always consistently adhere to this principle. In affirmative action, for instance, with a few exceptions that have not been followed, the Court has insisted on strict scrutiny of all race classifications, though since *Craig v. Boren* 429 U.S. 190 (1976), gender classifications have been subject to intermediate scrutiny only, producing the anomaly that affirmative action designed to benefit women is less suspect than that to benefit blacks. Generally, see Laurence H. Tribe, *American Constitutional Law*, 2d ed. (Foundation, 1988), pp. 251–75.

56. On the changing law of marital rape in the United States, see Diana E. H. Russell, *Rape in Marriage*, 2d ed. (Indiana University Press, 1990), and Rebecca M. Ryan, "The sex right: A legal history of the marital rape exception," *Law and Social Inquiry*, vol. 20, no. 4 (Fall 1995), pp. 941–1001. On the English evolution of the marital rape exception, see P. M. Bromley and N. V. Lowe, *Family Law*, 7th ed. (Butterworths, 1987), pp. 109–12.

57. For discussion of the extent and effects of these policies, see Margaret Kiloh, "South Africa: Democracy delayed," in David Potter, David Goldblatt, Margaret Kiloh, and Pal Lewis, eds., *Democratization* (Blackwell, 1997), pp. 295–99.

58. Walzer, *Spheres of Justice*, pp. 3–30.

59. Robert A. Burt, *The Constitution in Conflict* (Harvard University Press, 1992), p. 29.

60. *Brown v. Board of Education I* 347 U.S. 483 (1954).

61. *Brown v. Board of Education II* 349 U.S. 294 (1955).

62. Burt, *Constitution in Conflict*, pp. 271–310.

63. Ruth Bader Ginsburg, "Speaking in a judicial voice," Madison Lecture, New York University Law School, March 9, 1993, mimeo., pp. 30–38. See also "Nomination of Ruth Bader Ginsburg to be an associate justice of the United States Supreme Court: Report together with additional views," *Exec. Report.* 103-6-93-1 United States Senate.

64. *Roe v. Wade* 410 U.S. 113 (1973).

65. Ginsburg, Madison Lecture, p. 32.

66. Burt, *Constitution in Conflict*, p. 348.

67. Ibid., pp. 349–52. The Ginsburg-Burt approach was finally adopted by the Su-

preme Court in *Planned Parenthood of Pennsylvania v. Casey* 112 S.Ct. 2791 (1992). By affirming the existence of a woman's fundamental constitutional right to an abortion, recognizing the legitimacy of the state's interest in potential life, and insisting that states may not pursue the vindication of that interest in a manner that is unduly burdensome to women, the Court set some basic parameters within which legislatures must now fashion regulations that govern abortion. The *Casey* dissenters are right to point out that there will be a degree of unpredictability and confusion as different regulatory regimes are enacted in different states and tested through the courts. 112 S.Ct. 2791, at 2866 (1992). On views of adjudication that encourage efficiency and clarity above all else this will appear to be a reprehensible invitation to further litigation. On the Ginsburg-Burt view, however, that *Casey* invites litigation may be a cost worth paying. It places the burden of coming up with modes of regulating abortion that are not unduly burdensome on democratically elected legislatures and forces them to do this in the knowledge that the statutes they enact will be tested through the courts and thrown out if they are found wanting. I take these issues up further in my introduction to *Abortion: The Supreme Court Decisions* (Hackett, 1995), pp. 1–23.

68. *Dred Scott v. Sandford* 60 U.S. 393 (1856), *In re Civil Rights Cases*, 109 U.S. 3 (1883), and *Lochner v. New York* 198 U.S. 45 (1905).

69. From an address to the Philosophical Union of the University of California in November 1918, reprinted in Dewey, *Political Writings*, p. 44.

4. Governing Children

1. In 1996, 68 percent of American children were reported as living with both parents and 24 percent with a mother only (9 percent divorced, 6 percent married spouse absent, 9 percent never married, and 1 percent widowed). Four percent were reported as living with the father only and 4 percent with neither parent. *Statistical Abstract of the United States* (United States Department of Commerce, 1997), p. 66.

2. See Laurence Houlgate, *The Child and the State* (Johns Hopkins University Press, 1980), pp. 23–24; Barry Nicholas, *An Introduction to Roman Law* (Oxford University Press, 1962), p. 66; and Olimpiad Ioffe, *Roman Law* (University of Connecticut School of Law Press, 1987), pp. 30–36.

3. Houlgate, *The Child and the State*, p. 23, and Harold Goldstein, "Child labor in America's history," *Children Today*, vol. 5 (1976), p. 30.

4. On parental obligations see Mary Ann Mason, *From Father's Property to Children's Rights: The History of Child Custody in the United States* (Columbia University Press, 1994), pp. 7–10.

5. See Nancy Folbre, *Who Pays for the Kids: Gender and the Structure of Constraint*

(Routledge, 1994), pp. 174–75, and Ray Marshall and Marc Tucker, *Thinking for a Living: Work, Skills, and the Future of the American Economy* (Basic, 1992), pp. 166–72.

6. See Jacques Donzelot, *The Policing of Families* (Pantheon, 1979), and Christopher Lasch, "Life in the therapeutic state," *The New York Review of Books* (June 12, 1980), pp. 24–31. The emergence of a therapeutic state was not entirely the product of conscious design. For instance, Folbre notes that much late nineteenth- and early twentieth-century child-labor legislation was enacted partly at the behest of adult men who sought protection from low-wage competition. *Who Pays for the Kids*, p. 174.

7. See Laura Nader, "The vertical slice: Hierarchies and children," in Gerald Britan and Ronald Cohen, eds., *Hierarchy and Society* (Institute for the Study of Human Issues, 1980), p. 33. See also Mason, *From Father's Property to Children's Rights*.

8. On the general expansion of the federal government's administrative capacities in the nineteenth century, see Stephen Skowronek, *Building a New American State: The Expansion of National Administrative Capacities, 1877–1920* (Cambridge University Press, 1982).

9. For instance, the juvenile justice system was founded on the notion that children should be protected from the harshness of the criminal law. In practice, children often found themselves with fewer protections than adult criminal defendants. The power exercised over them may have been couched in therapeutic metaphors, but it was power nonetheless. Hence Andrew Polsky's description of the juvenile justice system as occupying "a shadowy ground between legal tribunal and social agency." *The Rise of the Therapeutic State* (Princeton University Press, 1991), p. 66. See also Anthony M. Platt, *The Child Savers: The Invention of Delinquency* (University of Chicago Press, 1977).

10. The Massachusetts Stubborn Child Law was taken almost verbatim from Deuteronomy 21:20–21. See John R. Sutton, "Stubborn children: Law and the socialization of deviance in the Puritan colonies," *Family Law Quarterly*, vol. 15, no. 1 (Spring 1981), pp. 31–63. For a general account of the mutually reinforcing character of church, state, and family hierarchies in colonial New England, see George L. Haskins, *Law and Authority in Early Massachusetts: A Study in Tradition and Design* (Archon, 1968).

11. Though much of this went on at the state rather than the federal level. See Richard Morgan, *The Supreme Court and Religion* (Free Press, 1974).

12. *Pierce v. Society of Sisters* 268 U.S. 510 (1925).

13. *State* and *parent* are terms that connote unitary actors; this can be misleading. Parents can disagree with one another over how to raise children, sometimes in ways that cannot be resolved, and state authority over children is divided both because of the constitutional separation of powers and because of federal divi-

sions among national, state, and local institutions. These complexities are taken up below; suffice it to note here that they are subsidiary to the dual-regime system that they complicate, and it is this dual-regime system that structures the main contours of adult-child relations today.

14. Parents, too, may often have made no conscious decision to have children, but this is not necessarily so and in any case a doctrine of assumption-of-risk may reasonably be thought to accompany procreative activity.

15. For the view that it is a defect of family practice that we have different ages of emancipation for different purposes, see Houlgate, *Child and the State*, pp. 3–4.

16. See Philippe Ariès, *Centuries of Childhood* (Vintage, 1962), and Norbert Elias, *The Civilizing Process: The History of Manners* (Urizen, 1978).

17. This point is usefully emphasized by Peter Schrag, who notes that much contemporary complaining about the American public schools misses the fact that until recently its aspirations were less than universal. "The great school sell-off," *The American Prospect*, no. 12 (Winter 1993), p. 36.

18. This is not to prejudge the debate on deskilling. It may be that certain occupations in high-technology service economies—checkout clerks in supermarkets—no longer require people even to be literate or numerate, so that minimal preparation is required of them. The pertinent point here is that if a certain class of persons is not to be selected for these occupations at birth or some other morally arbitrary way, everyone will need to have the resources, training, and opportunities to discover and develop capacities that can best support their aspirations. I am here following Sen's useful lead in thinking of an opportunity-based society as one in which "shortfall" inequality is minimized—that is, one in which everyone comes as close as possible to achieving his or her potential. Amartya Sen, *Inequality Reexamined* (Russell Sage Foundation and Harvard University Press, 1992), pp. 90–93.

19. By the same token, as I argue in Chapter 7, the elderly should not be excluded from decision making that significantly affects their interests unless and until incapacity makes exclusion unavoidable.

20. *Compact Edition of the Oxford English Dictionary* (Oxford University Press, 1971), vol. 1, p. 992.

21. A. S. Neill, *Summerhill: A Radical Approach to Childrearing* (Hart, 1961). See also Howard Cohen, *Equal Rights for Children* (Littlefield, Adams, 1980); John Harris, "The political status of children," in Keith Graham, ed., *Contemporary Political Philosophy* (Cambridge University Press, 1982); Richard Lindley, "Teenagers and other children," in Geoffrey Scare, ed., *Children, Parents, and Politics* (Cambridge University Press, 1989); Ann Palmeri, "Childhood's end: Toward the liberation of children," in William Aiken and Hugh LaFollette, eds., *Whose Child? Children's Rights, Parental Authority, and State Power* (Littlefield, Adams, 1980); Bob Franklin, *The Rights of Children* (Blackwell, 1986). For a useful critique of this lit-

erature see Laura M. Purdy's *In Their Best Interest? The Case Against Equal Rights for Children* (Cornell University Press, 1992).

22. There is curious respect in which the dependent-subjects view overlaps with the miniature-adults picture: by assuming that children are transformed overnight from a condition of utter dependence, not to say servitude, to one of complete liberation, the dependent-subjects view also appears to ignore, or underplay the significance of, any developmental dimension to childhood.

23. See Jean Piaget, *Six Psychological Essays* (Vintage, 1978), and Purdy, *In Their Best Interest?* pp. 10, 87–123.

24. See Douglas W. Rae, "Small tyrannies of place," in Ian Shapiro and Casiano Hacker-Cordón, eds., *Democracy's Edges* (Cambridge University Press, 1999).

25. For a discussion of the dearth of theoretical literature in this area, see Carl E. Schneider, "The next step: Definition, generalization, and theory in American family law," *Journal of Law Reform*, vol. 18, no. 4 (Summer 1985), pp. 1039–59.

26. See Patrick Riley, *Will and Political Legitimacy* (Harvard University Press, 1982), pp. 63–91.

27. Tully, *A Discourse Concerning Property*, pp. 109–10, 121.

28. Locke, *Two Treatises*, I, sec. 50, p.176.

29. Ibid., I, sec. 53, p. 178.

30. Ibid., I, sec. 54, pp. 179–80, Locke's italics.

31. Though even in this hypothetical eventuality Locke resists the absolutist case by arguing that "every one who gives another any thing, has not always thereby a Right to take it away again" (ibid., vol. I, sec. 52, p. 178) and observing that because the woman "hath an equal share, if not greater" in nourishing a child, the creationist theory in any case does not justify paternal absolutism. Ibid., I, sec. 55, p. 180. See also II, secs. 52–53, pp. 303–4.

32. Ibid., I, sec. 53, p. 179.

33. Ibid., II, sec. 56, p. 305.

34. Ibid., II, sec. 55, p. 304, Locke's italics.

35. Ibid., II, sec. 69, pp. 313–14, Locke's italics.

36. Ibid., II, sec. 72, p. 315.

37. Ibid., II, sec. 69, p. 313.

38. Ibid., II, sec. 65, p. 311, Locke's italics.

39. For a useful secular exploration of some of the absurdities that can be shown to result from taking making-based ownership rights over children seriously, see Susan Okin, *Justice, Gender, and the Family* (Basic, 1989), pp. 74–88.

40. Nozick, *Anarchy, State, and Utopia*, pp. 287–89.

41. I have argued elsewhere that the difficulties are general and fatal. See *Democracy's Place*, chapter 3.

42. At bottom, Locke's justification presumably rests partly on the dual require-

ment of natural law: that each person preserve himself and that "when his own Preservation comes not in competition," that each person ought "as much as he can, to preserve the rest of Mankind, and may not unless it be to do Justice on an Offender, take away, or impair the life, or what tends to the Preservation of the Life, the Liberty, Health, Limb or Goods of another." *Two Treatises*, II, sec. 7, p. 271. There is, however, a more specific obligation that falls on parents, because God made them "Instruments in his great design of Continuing the Race of Mankind, and the occasions of Life to their Children." Consequently, he "laid on them an obligation to nourish, preserve, and bring up their Off-spring." Ibid., II, sec. 66, p. 311. Because Locke was primarily concerned with the limits of parental authority, he never considered the interesting question whether natural law creates an obligation on the part of able adults to become parents as part of their responsibility to preserve mankind. I maintain below that there is no such obligation, because it seems to be in the nature of adult-child nurturance that an unwilling parent cannot be an effective parent. This is not to say that nonparents should be immune from the costs of producing the next generation (which they may bear indirectly via tax subsidies for child-rearing parents). This is distinct from the question, also taken up below, whether those who produce children may absolve themselves from financial responsibility for their offspring during their dependent years.

43. It might be suggested that the parent-child relationship should be seen as a constructive contract. To see how unattractive this approach is, consider the appropriate response of a court or adoption agency to prospective adoptive parents who propose the following contract: they undertake to expend unusually large quantities of resources on the child's upbringing, which, in return, will subsequently obligate the child to the parent in certain unusual respects. No doubt the proposed transaction, which carries with it the whiff of indentured servitude, will affront many moral sensibilities about the unconditional character of parental commitment. Why such commitment should be both expected and encouraged to be unconditional is taken up below.

44. Rejecting the idea of a constructive contract between parents and children does not mean that people may not be required to care for the dependent old. As I argue in Chapter 7, we might legitimately be taxed for this purpose, whether this is understood as a collective decision to aid others or a system of forced saving, such as social security, whereby we are required to put some resources aside during our productive years to provide for ourselves when we can no longer be productive and would otherwise become dependent on others.

45. Locke, *Two Treatises*, II, sec. 13, p. 275, Locke's italics.

46. Ibid., II, sec. 96, p. 332, Locke's italics.

47. Ibid., II, sec. 96, p. 332. The majority may choose to retain all powers of government, thereby creating a "perfect" democracy. Alternatively, it may delegate

some or all of its powers, creating various "forms of commonwealth," such as oligarchies or elective or hereditary monarchies. But the majority never relinquishes its "Supream Power," which comes into play when delegated power either expires or is abused. Ibid., II, sec. 132, p. 354.

48. Ibid., II, secs. 208–9, p. 404.

49. Ibid., II, secs. 202–10, pp. 400–405.

50. Locke's strong commitment to majority rule has, indeed, been criticized as insufficiently protective of minority rights, and it is true that there is no necessary place in Locke's scheme for such countermajoritarian institutions as the American judiciary. See Willmoore Kendall, *John Locke and the Doctrine of Majority Rule* (University of Illinois Press, 1965). Whether courts protect individual rights more effectively than majority rule is an empirical question that, Robert Dahl reminds us, has not been decisively settled. See *A Preface to Democratic Theory* (University of Chicago Press, 1956), pp. 105–12, and *Democracy and Its Critics*, pp. 188–92.

51. Note, parenthetically, that the logic of Locke's argument for majority rule does not hold in that context. It turns on the (tacit) consent of all adults who remain in a country to be parties to the social contract that legitimates majority rule. Whatever the general difficulties of Locke's discussion of tacit consent, it certainly cannot apply to dependent children, who, by definition, are incapable of consenting or, for that matter, of leaving. On the much debated subject of Locke's view of tacit consent, see Paul Russell, "Locke on express and tacit consent: Misinterpretations and inconsistencies," *Political Theory*, vol. 14, no. 2 (1986), pp. 291–306.

52. On this subject, see Richard Ashcraft, *Revolutionary Politics and Locke's Two Treatises of Government* (Princeton University Press, 1986), especially pp. 521–89.

53. See Thomas Hobbes, *Leviathan*, ed. Richard Tuck (Cambridge University Press, 1991 [1651]), pp. 127–28. In the nineteenth century this view was forcefully stated by John Austin, who insisted—by reference to Article V of the Constitution—that the indivisible sovereignty of the United States rests in two-thirds of the House and the Senate acting in concert with three-quarters of the state legislatures. *The Province of Jurisprudence Determined*, ed. Wilfred E. Rumble (Cambridge University Press, 1995 [1832]), pp. 209–10. From a different perspective Marx scoffed at the idea that power could be divided, insisting that government is neither more nor less than the epiphenomenal reflection of ruling-class interests, so that in a capitalist society government is the "executive committee" of the bourgeoisie. See Marx and Engels's "Manifesto of the Communist Party," in Robert C. Tucker, ed., *The Marx-Engels Reader* (Norton, 1978), p. 475. In the twentieth century the elite theorists are best known for insisting on what Gaetano Mosca referred to as the "iron law of oligarchy": that no matter what the formal political structure, a single elite will always have effective power.

The Ruling Class (McGraw-Hill, 1939 [1896]). See also Robert Michels, *Political Parties* (Dover Publications, 1959 [1915]), and C. Wright Mills, *The Power Elite* (Oxford University Press, 1956).

54. For the canonical statement of how ambition can be channeled to counter-act ambition in a divided authority regime, see Federalist no. 51, *The Federalist Papers*, ed. Clinton Rossiter (New American Library, 1961), p. 322. Generally, see Gordon S. Wood, *The Creation of the American Republic, 1776-1789* (Norton, 1969).

55. See the transcript of President Clinton's speech entitled "We heard America shouting" in the *New York Times* (January 26, 1995).

56. As brilliantly portrayed in Martin Gilbert's *Churchill: A Life* (Heinemann, 1991), pp. 4-17.

57. Richard H. Brodhead, "Sparing the rod," in *Cultures of Letters* (University of Chicago Press, 1993), p. 19.

58. Though no doubt these may be involved as well.

59. Stephen Wizner, "The child and the states: Adversaries in the juvenile justice system," *Columbia Human Rights Law Review*, vol. 4 (1972), pp. 389-99.

60. Notice that this point applies to separation-of-powers arguments generally. The United States federal courts have no armies or police forces to back up their views when they clash with those of the keepers of executive authority. Instead, courts rely on their institutional legitimacy, backed up by public reason giving and justification, to get others to respect their authority. Considerations of this sort suggest that one can overstate the worries arising from the power asymmetries between parents and public officials, though they do not render these worries groundless. For a revealing discussion of judicial worrying on this score in the context of the *Brown* school desegregation litigation, see Richard Kluger's *Simple Justice* (Knopf, 1976).

61. As Charles Black points out in *Structure and Relationship in Constitutional Law* (Ox Bow, 1985), despite all the academic discussion of institutional separation of powers in the United States, the great majority of federal court involvement actually has to do with federalism and supremacy-clause questions.

62. The idea of lexical ranking requires that in the case of conflict, an imperative that is more highly ranked trump the imperative that is less highly ranked. See Rawls, *A Theory of Justice*, pp. 42-45, 61-65, 82-89, 151-61.

63. They also have other options, as Kukathas has noted in connection with the 1987 *Mozert* litigation (where Christian fundamentalist parents objected to readers that implicitly challenged gender stereotypes on the grounds that this conflicted with their religious values. *Mozert v. Hawkins Cty. Bd. Of Ed.*, 827 F. 2d 1058 (6th Circuit, 1987).) Such parents can move to a different local community or send their children to religious schools where books that they find more agreeable are used. See Chadran Kukathas, "Cultural toleration," in Ian Shapiro and Will

Kymlicka, eds., *NOMOS XXXIX: Ethnicity and Group Rights* (New York University Press, 1997), pp. 95–96. Such parents would likely lose (as the parents in *Mozert* did) by an intermediate-scrutiny test, because the avowed purpose of the reading curriculum was to encourage the making of critical judgments, a goal that was seen as important in promoting the values of democratic citizenship. The fundamentalist parents resisted this goal, but I argue below that it falls squarely within the purview of children's basic interests, for which the state is ultimately responsible. Because the terms of the fundamentalists' argument conceded that the policy was substantially related to the objective (which they disliked), it is difficult to see how they could prevail had the proposed test been applied.

64. See note 50.

65. There are powerful reasons, however, having to do with the nature of adult domestic commitments, for the state to avoid trying to force couples to stay together against the wishes of either party. Combining that reasoning with the present argument suggests support for a presumption in favor of joint custody at divorce, whenever this can be made to work.

66. Locke, *Two Treatises*, II, sec. 55, p. 180. It should be evident that my argument here for the presumption that two parents are better than one entails nothing about the conventional two-parent family. It is compatible with gay parents serving as child rearers, as well as a variety of communal child-rearing arrangements. Some states have begun to recognize such parenting arrangements as legitimate. See, for example, the coverage of New Jersey and New York litigation described in the *New York Times* (October 28, 1995, and November 3, 1995). On same-sex adoptions generally, see Frederick W. Bozett, ed., *Gay and Lesbian Parents* (Praeger, 1987), and the symposium "Defining family: Gays, lesbians, and the meaning of family," in *William and Mary Bill of Rights Journal* (Summer 1994).

67. In *Beyond the Best Interests of the Child* (Free Press, 1973), pp. 40–42, 115 ff., Joseph Goldstein et al. stress the importance of minimal state interference in the functioning of family life: "At best and at most, law can provide a new opportunity for the relationship between a child and an adult to unfold free of coercive meddling by the state." In *Before the Best Interests of the Child* (Free Press, 1979), pp. 62, 75, the same authors emphasize even further their belief that the state should carry a heavy burden of proof to justify intervention; only a parent's certifiable insanity or conviction of a sexual offense—in other words, only a threat of severe bodily injury—justifies a neglect proceeding.

68. It thus supplies helpful tools to debunk claims of biological parents that they have a "right" to retrieve "their" children from adoptive parents because of a change of heart. See the account of the Baby Jessica case (in which the Supreme Court decided for the biological father) in the *New York Times* (August 8, 1993).

69. For criticism of the Goldstein, Freud, and Solnit proposals see Martha Garrison, "Why terminate parental rights," *Stanford Law Review*, vol. 35 (1983), 432-74. For studies that show that decreased parental conflict, not continuity, is the most important factor in healthy adjustment to divorce, see Robert E. Emery, "Interparental conflict and the children of discord and divorce," *Psychological Bulletin*, no. 35 (1982), pp. 310-13, and Edith S. Ellison, "Issues concerning parental harmony and children's psychosocial adjustment," *American Journal of Orthopsychiatry*, vol. 53, no. 1 (1983). Still other research shows that children are better off when they continue their relationship with both parents (in contrast to Goldstein, Freud, and Solnit's advocating complete control by the psychological parent); see Judith Wallerstein and Joan Berlin Kelly, *Surviving the Breakup: How Children and Parents Handle Divorce* (Basic, 1980), p. 215.

70. Goldstein et al. are concerned with the particular problem of awarding custody at divorce or breakup of the family for other reasons. My criticism of them in the context of this specific issue is that courts should not be in the business of trying to decide which (between a divorcing couple or contending "birth" and "adoptive" parents) would make the best parents. In such dispute democratic justice affirms that the court's first responsibility is to insist on the placement in which the child's basic interests are most likely to be protected, and, as Mary Ann Glendon has argued, that maintenance of the essential resources needed for that purpose trumps conflicts between spouses over marital property. Mary Ann Glendon, *Abortion and Divorce in Western Law* (Harvard University Press, 1987), pp. 94-101. If more than one placement is acceptable from the standpoint of protecting basic interests, then other considerations come into play. Democratic justice does not help us choose among them. But it does suggest that courts would not be justified in preferring one parent over another if, in the court's judgment, one would do a better job of vindicating the child's best interests (say, because the other has bohemian values).

71. For discussion of this in connection with Rawls, see my *Evolution of Rights*, pp. 204-70.

72. On hierarchies of more and less controversial arguments about human interests, see Len Doyal and Ian Gough, *A Theory of Human Need* (Macmillan, 1991), and David Braybrooke, *Meeting Needs* (Princeton University Press, 1987).

73. See Sen's *Inequality Reexamined* (Harvard University Press, 1992), pp. 75-84.

74. Ibid., pp. 39-55.

75. This argument does not refer to the permanently sick or disabled. These groups may not be able to avoid being a net drain, and appropriately society does not penalize them.

76. See, for example, Charles Murray, *Losing Ground* (Basic, 1984), and Christopher Jencks's critique of it, "Losing Ground," *New York Review of Books* (May 9, 1985), pp. 41-49.

77. It should be emphasized that the structure of opportunities is as important as the development of human capital for the vindication of basic interests. This tends to be lost sight of in debates about skills development and job training. In the bottom half of the U.S. economy, for instance, it now seems clear that the shortage of predictable, reasonably paid employment is such that no amount of training or skills development will solve the problem. See Gordon C. Lafer, "Job training as political diversion: The false promise of JTPA," Ph.D. diss., Yale University, 1995. A related issue, pointed out to me by Clarissa Hayward, is that what basic interests require in one context may contradict what they require in another. Developing the capacities needed to survive in a gang-dominated urban ghetto, for instance, may diminish the odds of surviving in the larger culture. To the extent that tensions of this kind prevail, they reflect the failures to offer some children contexts of local survival that are compatible with the larger society's opportunity-structure. This should not, however, be seen as a failure of the argument for democratic justice. Rather, it is a failure of government to create an environment in which all citizens can vindicate their basic interests.

78. This claim should not be confused with the view that children should be indoctrinated into mindless acceptance of democratic values. By its terms democratic justice requires critical thinking about all institutional arrangements, including those it recommends. Prevailing ways of doing things can almost always be improved upon, and the possibilities for such improvement vary with changing circumstances, technological developments, human ingenuity, and other factors. Human knowledge is, in any case, corrigible, so that what democratic justice is thought to recommend in a particular circumstance might turn out to rest on inadequate understanding or faulty premises. This congenital state of affairs is part of what was invoked to justify democratic justice, in Chapters 1–3, against those who believe that they have the key to the universe, human perfectibility, or both. Consequently I would reject as unpersuasive any claim to the effect that requiring that people be taught to value democratic justice amounts to indoctrinating them. The defense of democratic justice, to reiterate, is "political, not metaphysical," and part of what is intended to make it attractive is its hostility to dogmatism and openness to critical thinking. Those who insist that this is itself a dogma are right in a trivial sense only.

79. Thomas C. Schelling, *The Strategy of Conflict* (Harvard University Press, 1960), chapters 2, 5, and 7.

80. Przeworski, *Democracy and the Market*, pp. 19–34.

81. See my *Democracy's Place*, chapter 4.

82. Concerning elite beliefs in democracy, see Huntington, *The Third Wave*, pp. 36–37. For the political culture argument, see Robert Putnam et al., *Making Democracy Work* (Princeton University Press, 1993), especially chapter 4, pp. 83–120. For an empirical study that suggests that no single variable is decisive,

see Dirk Berg-Schlosser and Gisèle De Meur, "Conditions of democracy in interwar Europe: A Boolean test of major hypotheses," *Comparative Politics*, vol. 26, no. 3 (April 1994), pp. 253–80. For an analysis that suggests that some aspects of political culture matter more than others for sustaining democracy, see Edward N. Muller and Mitchell A. Seligson, "Civic culture and democracy: The question of causal relationships," *American Political Science Review*, vol. 88, no. 3 (September 1994), pp. 635–52.

83. If A is opposed to B on issue 1 but knows that in the future he is likely to be allied with B in opposition to C on issue 2, then A has an incentive to moderate his present conflict with B as much as possible and cultivate him as a future ally. If, on the other hand, A and B know that they are likely to be on opposite sides of the fence on every issue, then there are no incentives favoring moderation, and if one of them expects always to be in the minority he has no self-interested reason to be committed to a democratic order. The pluralists generalized this, arguing that only when cleavages are pluralistic or cross-cutting will a democratic order be stable. See Nicholas R. Miller, "Pluralism and social choice," *American Political Science Review*, vol. 77, no. 3 (1983), pp. 734–47.

84. Hence the critique of consociationalism as a response to what are thought to be single-cleavaged societies, often on the basis of scanty evidence, that they may actually produce the malady to which they are supposed to respond. See *Democracy's Place*, chapter 6, and Ian Shapiro and Courtney Jung, "South African democracy revisited: A reply to Koelble and Reynolds," *Politics and Society*, vol. 24, no. 3 (September 1996), pp. 237–47.

85. This suggests that Wollheim's paradox—which turns on the possibility of tension between what an individual wants and how he ought to view that preference in the event that he does not prevail through procedures of democratic decision that he accepts as legitimate—should be thought of more as a problem of political socialization than as a philosophical paradox. See Richard Wollheim, "A paradox in the theory of democracy," *Philosophy, Politics, and Society*, 2d series, ed. Peter Laslett and W. G. Runciman (Blackwell, 1962), pp. 71–87.

86. Hobbes, *Leviathan*, pp. 39, 469.

87. It is sometimes alleged or implied that endemic disagreement about the human good is the parochial product of modern secular pluralism and that it could be avoided if we could reinvigorate natural law or re-create "traditional" society. Arguments of this sort can appear plausible only to those who know little of the large disagreements that have prevailed within and among natural-law traditions on this question, or about the conflicts that have beset societies that nostalgic hindsight leads some political theorists to characterize as "traditional." See my *Political Criticism*, pp. 113–18, 141–49.

88. In distinguishing best from basic interests, I do not suggest that the former are subjectively identified while the latter are objective, or that it is possible to make

interpersonal judgments about basic interests only. In rearing children it is inevitable that third parties make judgments about their interests until they are able to make their own decisions. Democratic justice counsels that this point should not be delayed unnecessarily, but in the meantime interpersonal (and paternalistic) judgments about both types of interest have to be made. The question is who makes the relevant paternalistic judgments.

89. See Valerie Lee and Anthony Bryk, "Science or policy argument? A review of the quantitative evidence in Chubb and Moe's 'Politics, Markets and America's Schools,'" in Edith Rasell and Richard Rothstein, eds., *School Choice: Examining the Evidence* (Economic Policy Institute, 1993). For a summary of the existing empirical evidence and the conclusion that "a careful effort to separate anecdote from evidence suggests that we know very little at all," see Jeffrey R. Henig, *Rethinking School Choice: Limits of the Market Metaphor* (Princeton University Press, 1994), pp. 117.

90. Some voucher schemes (e.g., those proposed by John E. Chubb and Terry Moe in *Politics, Markets, and America's Schools* [Brookings, 1990], and John E. Coons and Stephen D. Sugarman in *Education by Choice: The Case for Family Control* [University of California Press, 1978]) propose that vouchers be used within the public schools system, effectively abandoning designated school districts by requiring public schools to compete with one another for children. Similar objections can be raised to such schemes, however. Assuming that they raise the average quality of public schools (which has yet to be demonstrated empirically), the parents of some children will lack the time and resources to drive them across town to a better school, and some schools—because of the environments in which they find themselves—will find it impossible to compete. The children who have no choice but to remain in these schools will suffer as vouchers are spent elsewhere and these schools become increasingly starved for funds. It may be, as some contend, that these children are not being any better served by the existing system. Even so, the worry about vouchers remains that this reality of neglect will become reinforced by a new structure of incentives and so become even more difficult to tackle than it is now.

91. See Marjorie R. Freiman, "Unequal and inadequate protection under the law: State child-abuse statutes," *George Washington Law Review*, vol. 50 (1982), pp. 243–74.

92. For a survey of American law and political activism on this question, see Janna C. Merrick, "When a child dies: Christian Science healing and the law," paper presented at the 1994 meeting of the American Political Science Association, New York City, September 1994.

93. For a discussion of appropriate line drawing in the rearing of Amish children, see Richard Arneson and Ian Shapiro, "Democratic autonomy and religious freedom: A critique of *Wisconsin v. Yoder*," in Ian Shapiro and Russell Hardin,

eds., *NOMOS XXXVIII: Political Order* (New York University Press, 1996), pp. 365–411.

94. See Amartya Sen, "Population: Delusion and reality," in *New York Review of Books*, vol. 41, no. 15 (September 22, 1994), pp. 62–72.

95. As Charles Murray's critics have noted, if having children were a response on the part of the poor to perverse incentives created by Aid to Families with Dependent Children (AFDC) and related benefits that were abolished in the 1996 Welfare Reform Bill, then it is difficult to account for the steady increase in the numbers of children born into poverty since the early 1970s, when the real value of such benefits has been stagnant or declining. See Michael B. Katz, *The Undeserving Poor: From the War on Poverty to the War on Welfare* (Pantheon, 1989), pp. 151–56. Murray's response (in support of which he cites no evidence) has only to be stated for its absurdity to be plain: "In the late 1970s, social scientists knew that the real value of the welfare benefit was declining, but the young woman in the street probably did not." Charles Murray, "Does welfare bring more babies?" *The Public Interest* (Spring 1994), p. 25.

96. See *World Resources, 1990–91*, report by the World Resources Institute and International Institute for Environment and Development, pp. 256–66, and Paul Kennedy, *Preparing for the Twenty-First Century* (Random House, 1993), pp. 339–43. Note, further, that the United States Congress's decision to turn many of these questions over to the states in 1995 [H.R. 2491 and S. 1357], signed by President Clinton in the runup to the 1996 elections, should be expected to make things worse. A predictable consequence of "ending welfare as we know it" via this devolution is that in order to avoid becoming magnets for the poor and to export them instead, states will face powerful new incentives to compete with their neighbors for having the most punitive systems. Furthermore, because most poor children live in inner cities, while most state legislatures are controlled by suburban voters, the federal government's decision to turn welfare over to the states will likely further exacerbate the fiscal crises of American cities.

97. It might be said that the same result could be achieved by random assignment of children to parents, so why prefer the "morally arbitrary" accidents of birth? Such a proposal has only to be stated for its lack of attractiveness to be evident. In any case, even a lottery system would have to be administered by public officials, increasing their authority unnecessarily in the domain of best interests. Moreover, it is difficult to see what would be gained, even in principle, for children are in fact distributed by the lottery of birth.

98. It should be noted parenthetically that even if it could be implemented, such a principle would not produce equality of outcome.

99. See Rawls, *A Theory of Justice*, pp. 90–95, 395–99; Amartya Sen, "Equality of what?" *The Tanner Lectures on Human Values*, ed. Sterling M. McMurrin (University of Utah Press, 1980), pp. 197–220; Amartya Sen, "Well-being, agency,

and freedom," *Journal of Philosophy*, vol. 82, no. 4 (April 1985), pp. 169–221; and Ronald Dworkin, "What is equality?" part 2, "Equality of resources," *Philosophy and Public Affairs*, vol. 10, no. 4 (Fall 1981), pp. 283–345.

100. This claim can be overstated for the sorts of reason that James Scott points out in *Weapons of the Weak* (Yale University Press, 1985)—namely, that states might lack the resources to get recalcitrant parents to comply with their demands. For instance, for decades before the *Wisconsin v. Yoder* litigation public officials had made sporadic attempts to get the Amish to send their children to accredited high schools, usually giving up in the face of such tactics as starting children late, keeping them back in eighth grade unnecessarily, and so on. See Donald B. Kraybill, *The Riddle of Amish Culture* (Johns Hopkins University Press, 1989), p. 137. Generally, in regimes—such as the American one—where in practice a great deal of responsibility for basic interests is delegated to parents, public officials may simply lack the information and other resources needed to do much about parental malevolence or failure. This is, notoriously, the case with violence and sexual abuse, which often comes to light only when it is too late for government to do anything about it.

101. In one respect it is artificial to call it a dual-regime system, for I have already recognized courts as playing a quasi-independent role in conflicts between other public officials and parents.

102. Joshua Cohen and Joel Rogers, "Secondary associations and democratic governance," *Politics and Society*, vol. 20, no. 4 (December 1992), pp. 391–472. For a concrete illustration, see Senator John Ashcroft's proposal that would allow states to contract directly with religion-based charities for the delivery of social services to the poor. William Raspberry, "Personalizing welfare," *Washington Post* (May 29, 1995).

103. See the transcript of Mayor Giuliani's speech in the *New York Times* (August 15, 1995).

104. The preceding logic could be turned against governments as well, on the grounds that they have no particular reasons to be concerned about noncitizens. This is conceded, but scarcely amounts to a reason to make the problem worse.

105. In particular, they opined that education beyond age fourteen substantially increased the likelihood that children would decide to leave the Amish community. See Arneson and Shapiro, "Democratic autonomy and religious freedom," pp. 368–72.

106. It might be said that this argument establishes too much because the state has Metternichian incentives to create pliant, obedient citizens above all else. This is true; but recall that here we are concerned with devolving parental authority, and that in any case by my account the state should be concerned, on the civic front, only with developing essential capacities for political participation, not with what Metternich would have regarded as "good citizens."

107. See Herbert Gans, *The War Against the Poor: The Underclass and Antipoverty Policy* (Basic, 1995).

108. This is transparently evident in the debate on welfare benefits and out-of-wedlock births, where politicians routinely advocate punitive measures aimed at poor mothers. See William Bennett's proposal that women who have children out of wedlock lose all welfare and AFDC benefits. *USA Today Magazine*, vol. 123, no. 2594 (November 1994), p. 14. Those who traffic in such proposals ignore the fact that female-headed families have, on average, slightly fewer children than married-couple families. Clifford M. Johnson et. al, *Child Poverty in America* (Children's Defense Fund, 1991), p. 12. Nor are such proposals the exclusive preserve of Republicans. William Galston, political theorist and domestic-policy spokesman for the Clinton administration, has advocated comparable proposals to use the tax code and other implements at government's disposal to increase the costs of divorce and out-of-wedlock births. He believes that government's goal should be to promote "neotraditional" families consisting of "stably married parents" on the grounds that this is in children's best interests. William Galston, "Home alone: What our policy makers should know about our children," *New Republic* (December 2, 1991), p. 43. Galston passes over the fact that, as Iris Marion Young has noted, the effects of divorce and single parenthood on child development are ambiguous, partly because these are so difficult to distinguish empirically from other factors, such as hostility in the home and poverty. Iris Marion Young, "Mothers, citizenship, and independence: A critique of pure family values," *Ethics*, 105 (April 1995), pp. 535-56.

109. I take the right to abortion to be defensible on several other grounds. For discussion of the possibilities, see my introduction to *Abortion: The Supreme Court Decisions* (Hackett, 1995), pp. 1-23.

110. It might be said that democratic justice provides no grounds to criticize incest or sexual abuse, for sexual mores fall within the realm of best interests, but this is not so without qualification. Laws prohibiting sex with children are an appropriate part of the state's protection of children's basic interests because the scars from it so compromise their ability to become normal adults. See David Finkelhor, *Child Sexual Abuse: New Theory and Research* (Free Press, 1984), and John Briere and Marsha Runtz, "Post-sexual abuse trauma: Data and implications for clinical practice," *Journal of Interpersonal Violence*, vol. 2, no. 4 (1987), pp. 367-69. Beyond this, it is part of the definition of fiduciary authority (and part of what makes it attractive from the standpoint of democratic justice) that fiduciaries are expected to act in the interests of their charges. An adult who engages in sex with a child is, by contrast, seeking his or her own sexual gratification and making use of the child for that purpose. The behavior is thus objectionable from the standpoint of democratic justice, regardless of other considerations that might also lead us to object to it. Other aspects of sexual mores may also fall within the

domain of basic interests. For instance, with the emergence of a life-threatening virus such as AIDS, unprotected sexual activity becomes a public health problem. This reasonably triggers action by government to educate sexually active teens about the risks and get them to limit dangerous sexual behavior, whether parents object to this or not.

111. Data taken from Johnson et. al., *Child Poverty in America*, pp. 11–20; Sheila B. Kamerman and Alfred Kahn, *Starting Right: How America Neglects Its Youngest Children and What We Can Do About It* (Oxford University Press, 1995), pp. 30–31; and Lawrence Mishel, Jared Bernstein, and John Schmitt, eds., *The State of Working America, 1996–7* (Economic Policy Institute, 1996), pp. 298, 312.

112. See K. McCurdy and D. Daro, *Current Trends in Child Abuse Reporting and Fatalities*, Report of the National Center on Child-Abuse Prevention Research, Chicago, 1992; and "National child-abuse and neglect data system," working paper no. 1, 1992 summary data component, National Center on Child Abuse and Neglect, Washington, D.C., 1992.

113. *1995 Index of Social Health: Monitoring the Well-being of the Nation*, Fordham Institute for Innovation in Social Policy, Tarrytown, N.Y., 1995, p. 6.

114. *The State of America's Children Yearbook, 1994* (Children's Defense Fund, 1994), p. 15.

115. *Kids Count Data Book, 1993* (Center for the Study of Social Policy, 1993), p. 21.

116. *Kids Count Data Book, 1995* (Annie Casey Foundation, 1995), p. 11.

117. Ibid., p. 11.

118. E. Zigler, C. S. Piotrkowski, and R. Collins, "Health services in Head Start," *American Review of Public Health*, vol. 15 (1994), p. 516.

119. Amy Gutmann, *Democratic Education*, p. 147.

120. Ibid., p. 273. Other estimates are considerably higher. See, for instance, Carmen St. John Hunter and David Harman, *Adult Literacy in the United States: A Report to the Ford Foundation* (McGraw-Hill, 1979), who contend that 40 percent of the population in the United States (some 65 million) are functionally illiterate.

121. See Henig, *Rethinking School Choice*, pp. 26–52.

122. *Kids Count Data Book, 1993*, p. 21; *Kids Count Data Book, 1995*, p. 18.

123. *Kids Count Data Book, 1993*, p. 21.

124. *Kids Count Data Book, 1995*, p. 18. The effects of fewer resources for children at the bottom of the heap are compounded by tracking. See Jeannie Oakes, *Keeping Track: How Schools Structure Inequality* (Yale University Press, 1985), and Jeannie Oakes and Gretchen Guiton, "Matchmaking: The dynamics of high school tracking decisions," *American Education Research Journal*, vol. 32, no. 1 (1995), pp. 3–33.

125. See Nancy Folbre, "Children as public goods," *AEA Papers and Proceedings*,

vol. 84, no. 2 (May 1994), pp. 86-90, and Marshall and Tucker, *Thinking for a Living*, pp. 109-27.

126. The commission recommended a $1,000 refundable child tax credit for all children through age eighteen, partly to be funded by eliminating the personal exemption for dependent children. *Beyond Rhetoric: A New American Agenda for Children and Families* (National Commission on Children, 1991), p. 18.

127. Assuming the cost of acceptable all-day care for preschool children to be $4,800 per child per year, Barbara Bergman calculates that the cost of providing the lowest 20 percent in income (principally those who live in poverty) with free care and the next-lowest 40 percent with partially subsidized all-day care would be about $36 billion a year. Prorated calculations for before- and after-school care of children between 5 and 12 to the same income groups on the same basis would add another $39 billion, producing an annual cost in 1994 dollars of $75 billion. Barbara R. Bergman, "Curing child poverty in the United States," *AEA Papers and Proceedings*, vol. 84, no. 2 (May 1994), pp. 76-80. This calculation ignores the increased tax revenues and other externalities that would presumably result from the increased employment of working mothers. For discussion of other targeted policies that could be aimed at children in the first three years of life (where they are likely to produce the most benefit), see Kamerman and Kahn, *Starting Right*, chapters 7 and 8.

128. See Trudi J. Renwick and Barbara R. Bergman, "A budget-based definition of poverty with an application to single-parent families," *Journal of Human Resources*, vol. 28, no. 1 (Winter 1993), pp. 1-24. The basic needs budget (BNB) of children includes minimally essential food, housing, clothing, health care, child care, and transportation if the parent or parents work. Even on this minimal definition, they calculate that a minority of single mothers already holding jobs in the United States earn enough to finance a BNB for a family of three. In the area of child abandonment, federal policies, such as the 1975 Child Support Enforcement Act and the 1988 Family Support Act, have done little to help, principally because child support continues to be critically reliant on a patchwork of state laws and enforcement of absent-parent responsibilities through private litigation. Irwin Garfinkel makes a powerful case that child support can be assured only if government pays what is needed to move a child above the poverty line directly to the custodial parent, and itself takes on the responsibility of either recovering the absent parent's contribution or paying for it through the tax system. How much parents, absent and present, should be required to contribute to their children's needs is a subject for debate. But unless the state guarantees the benefit to the child, it will be forced to internalize the cost; for this no justification can be given. Garfinkel recommends a percentage-of-income standard that depends on the gross income of the nonresident parent and the number of children to be supported: 17 percent for the first child, rising to 25, 29, 31, and 34 per-

cent, respectively, for two, three, four and five children. Aspects of his scheme for income recovery from absent parents have been implemented in Wisconsin and New York, though the "advance" assured benefit for children has not been implemented in the United States. Variants of it have, however, been in force in Scandinavia for decades, and more recently have been adopted in Germany, Austria, France, and parts of Switzerland. Garfinkel, *Assuring Child Support: An Extension of Social Security* (Russell Sage Foundation, 1992), pp. 45, 106-7.

129. Amitai Etzioni, *The Spirit of Community: Rights, Responsibilities, and the Communitarian Agenda* (Crown, 1993), pp. 54-56, 77.

130. Howard Fineman, "The virtuecrats," *Newsweek* (June 13, 1994), pp. 31-36.

5. Consenting Adults

1. See Okin, *Justice, Gender, and the Family*, pp. 134-69.

2. *Bowers v. Hardwick*, 106 S.Ct. 2841 (1986). The Defense of Marriage Act, P.L. 104-199, was signed into law by President Clinton in September 1996.

3. On the structure of marriage in colonial New England, see Laurel Ulrich, *Good Wives: Image and Reality in the Lives of Women in Northern New England, 1650–1750* (Random House, 1982). On the generally hierarchical character of colonial society see George Haskins, *Law and Authority in Early Massachusetts* (Archon, 1960). On the extent of the original chattel status of wives at common law, see Catherine O'Donovan, "Wife sale and desertion as alternatives to judicial marriage dissolution," in John Ekelaar and Sanford Katz, eds., *The Resolution of Family Conflict* (Butterworths, 1984), pp. 41-51.

4. See Linda Kerber, *Women of the Republic: Intellect and Ideology in Revolutionary America* (University of North Carolina Press, 1980), and "The paradox of women's citizenship in the early republic: The case of *Martin v. Massachusetts, 1805*," *American Historical Review*, vol. 97 (April 1992), pp. 349-78. For a useful history of American marriage, see Stephen Mintz and Susan Kellogg, *Domestic Revolutions: A Social History of American Family Life* (Free Press, 1988), pp. 3-187. On the political and legal exclusion of women from American public life through the late nineteenth century, see Rogers M. Smith, *Civic Ideals* (Yale University Press, 1997), pp. 58-69, 110-13, 146-47, 167-68, 185-86, 208-13, 230-35, 284-85, 293-95, 311-16, 337-42, 385-90, 401-2, 453-59, 465-68.

5. To say that patriarchal assumptions were widely accepted in the dominant culture is not to say that women or children were utterly subjugated and powerless; often they were not. Social hierarchies usually breed resistance, no matter how subtle or indirect. The story of American women's response to most forms of patriarchy confirms this generalization. See Ulrich, *Good Wives*. Generally see James Scott, *Domination and the Arts of Resistance* (Yale University Press, 1990).

6. Daniel Patrick Moynihan, *The Negro Family: The Case for National Action* (Office of Policy Planning and Research, U.S. Department of Labor, August 1965), p. 6.

7. Martha Minow, "The free exercise of families," Harvard Law School, mimeo; Constance Sorrentino, "The changing family in international perspective," *Monthly Labor Review*, vol. 41 (March 1990); *General Household Survey, 1986*, Office of Population Censuses and Surveys (Washington, D.C.); *Statistical Abstract of the United States, 1990*, U.S. Bureau of the Census (Washington, D.C., 1990), pp. 43–54, 86–89; *Statistical Abstract of the United States, 1997*, U.S. Department of Commerce (Washington, D.C., 1997), p. 403; Arland Thornton, "Cohabitation and marriage in the 1980s," *Demography*, vol. 25, no. 4 (November 1988), pp. 497–508; Mintz and Kellogg, *Domestic Revolutions*, pp. 217–35.

8. Prominent among the suggested remedial measures was that black men should be encouraged to join the military, "because it is an utterly masculine world." Given the strains of the "disorganized and matrifocal life in which so many Negroes come of age," Moynihan insisted, "the Armed Forces are a dramatic and desperately needed change: a world away from women, a world run by strong men of unquestioned authority, where discipline, if harsh, is nonetheless orderly and predictable." Only by adopting measures of this kind, he argued, could the "pathology of the disturbed group" of blacks be broken. Moynihan, *The Negro Family*, pp. 1, 29–46.

9. See Oscar Lewis, "The culture of poverty," in *Anthropological Essays* (Random House, 1970).

10. For the initial reaction to the Moynihan Report see Lee Rainwater and William Yancey, *The Moynihan Report and the Politics of Controversy* (MIT Press, 1967), and Christopher Lasch's discussion in *Haven in a Heartless World* (Basic, 1977), pp. 157–63. For early critics of Lewis, see Eleanor Leacock, ed., *The Culture of Poverty: A Critique* (Simon and Shuster, 1971), and Charles Valentine, *Culture and Poverty: Critique and Counter-Proposals* (University of Chicago Press, 1968). For Wilson's argument, see William Julius Wilson, *The Truly Disadvantaged* (University of Chicago Press, 1987), and William Julius Wilson, "Studying inner-city dislocations: The challenge of public agenda research," *American Sociological Review*, vol. 56 (February 1991), pp. 1–14. For criticism of Wilson's views as elitist and aspiring to "social engineering," see Adolph Reed Jr., "The liberal technocrat," *The Nation* (February 6, 1988), pp. 167–70.

11. Carole Pateman, *The Sexual Contract* (Stanford University Press, 1988), p. 187.

12. Leonore Weitzman, *The Marriage Contract: Spouses, Lovers, and the Law* (Free Press, 1981), p. 338. More features of it are now alterable than when Weitzman wrote. Most important, as I discuss below, whereas agreements in contemplation of divorce were then regarded as void, many features of such agreements are now enforceable in most American states.

13. Donzelot, *The Policing of Families*, Lasch, "Life in the therapeutic state." On

the effects of the therapeutic state on children, see also my discussion in Chapter 4.

14. Lasch, "Life in the therapeutic state," p. 30.

15. Michel Foucault, *The History of Sexuality* (Pantheon, 1978), *The Birth of the Clinic* (Pantheon, 1973), and *Discipline and Punish* (Pantheon, 1977).

16. Of course it is not only those who are subjugated by patriarchal marriage who might object. John Stuart Mill, who likened becoming a wife to becoming a slave, drew up a statement with Harriet Taylor two months before their marriage in 1851 in which Mill repudiated all legal powers he would acquire as a husband that in any way compromised her equal freedom. As Pateman points out in *The Sexual Contract* (p. 161) — and as Mill was aware — this was unenforceable. He was one of many who have argued, as we surely must, against relying on the benevolence of individual husbands not to take advantage of patriarchal powers. See Mill, "The subjection of women," in J. S. Mill and H. Taylor Mill, *Essays on Sex Equality* (University of Chicago Press, 1970), pp. 158–65.

17. Some will dispute the claim that the marriage status is not a public good on normative grounds. My argument in Chapter 3 requires, however, that something be a public good in the technical sense, requiring both joint supply and nonexcludability before the public goods exception to the presumption against vanguardism is triggered. I doubt that it could be argued convincingly that marriage must be jointly supplied in the sense that clean air must. Certainly nonexcludability does not hold here — as proponents of gay marriage, among others, can point out almost everywhere except in Hawaii.

18. One might agree that the general public lacks a strong interest in how any particular marriage is governed, yet insist that children living with a married or cohabiting couple have a substantial interest in the nature of their relationship. This is true, but because children do not vote, different means are needed to protect their interests — as described in Chapter 4. It should also be noted that many of those who object to "designer" marriage by reference to "what about the children?" arguments will doubtless also resist as too subversive of the integrity of "the family" my claim (in Chapter 4) that the state has a role in protecting children's basic interests. The fact that such critics try to have it both ways indicates what they really want: that the heavy hand of the state should impose the particular view of the family that they find agreeable, and no other. But no principled defense of having it both ways is available. In a world with multiple conceptions of the best domestic arrangements, accommodation has to be made between one's own views of what is best and what others can legitimately be forced to accept.

19. Okin, *Justice, Gender, and the Family*, pp. 134–69. On gender differences in labor-force participation and wages see Claudia Goldin, "The gender gap in historical perspective," in Peter Kilby, ed., *Quantity and Quiddity* (Wesleyan University

Press, 1987), pp. 135–68, and Claudia Goldin, *Understanding the Gender Gap* (Oxford University Press, 1990), pp. 58–118. On the disvaluing of domestic labor, see Nancy Folbre, "Exploitation comes home," *Cambridge Journal of Economics*, vol. 6 (1982), pp. 317–29. On the effects of economic differences outside the family on the power relations between men and women in the family, see Philip Blumstein and Pepper Schwartz, *American Couples* (Morrow, 1983).

20. Okin, *Justice, Gender, and the Family*, pp. 170–86.

21. "Given the enormous significance our society attaches to money and earnings, we should insist that the earnings be recognized as equally earned by the two persons. To call on Walzer's language, we should do this in order to help prevent the inequality of family members in the sphere of wage work invade their domestic sphere." Okin, *Justice, Gender, and the Family*, p. 182.

22. I leave aside the difficulty that not everyone is a wage earner who has a paycheck that can be equally divided. Some people own and run businesses, others sell ideas. Okin's scheme would presumably require public officials to redistribute appropriate amounts of income and other assets to spouses in these types of circumstance as well, lest the system be vitiated by an additional class bias problem deriving from its being applied to wage earners only. It is far from obvious what the appropriate redistributive criteria and modes of enforcement would be in these types of circumstance.

23. Okin, *Justice, Gender, and the Family*, p. 67.

24. Ibid., pp. 89–109, 173.

25. Rawls, *A Theory of Justice*, p. 154. For discussion of these assumptions see my *Evolution of Rights*, pp. 210–34.

26. I skirt the additional difficulties that would be generated were one to take the unemployed into account.

27. By the same token, the domestic worker whose spouse earned a wage worth more than double the value of domestic work would be exploiting the wage-earning spouse on Okin's proposal.

28. Some might also say said that mandatory wage splitting is worth defending on purely pragmatic grounds. For instance, when the political cards are heavily stacked against alternatives like a comparatively robust social wage or a refundable tax credit for homemaking, then Okin's proposal might begin to look like an attractive alternative to the status quo. The difficulty with that line of thinking, and the reason I do not pursue it here, is that the same antistatist forces that resist expanding the social wage or subsidizing behavior deemed socially desirable must surely be predicted to resist mandatory wage splitting.

29. See William N. Eskridge, Jr., *The Case for Same-Sex Marriage: From Sexual Liberty to Civilized Government* (Free Press, 1996), pp. 1–13, 66–70.

30. For discussion of antimiscegenation statutes and criticism of them, culminating in the Supreme Court's decision, in *Loving v. Virginia*, 388 U.S. 1 (1967),

that laws against interracial marriage are unconstitutional, see Tribe, *American Constitutional Law*, pp. 1475–81.

31. In 1988 sodomy (defined to include oral sex) between consenting adults remained illegal in twenty-six states, but all private sexual acts between consenting adults had been declared legal in twenty-five states. Hayden Curry and Denis Clifford, *A Legal Guide for Lesbian and Gay Couples*, 5th ed. (Nolo, 1988), pp. 2.8, 2.9. *Bowers v. Hardwick*, 106 S.Ct. 2841 (1986) stands as a continuing barrier to liberalization in this area. In this decision the Supreme Court held that a Georgia statute criminalizing sodomy was not unconstitutional. This means that opposition to such statutes must take one of three forms: federal legislation (which may or may not be unconstitutional for states'-rights reasons), new legislation at the state level, or challenge in state courts by appeal to state constitutions. Little headway was made on any of these fronts in the decade following *Bowers*, so that in 1995 sodomy remained illegal in at least 20 states. Eskridge, *The Case for Same-Sex Marriage*, p. 135. Hawaii's decision to recognize same-sex marriage in 1996 prompted Congress to enact the Defense of Marriage Act (P.L. 104-199) in September of that year, prohibiting the federal government from recognizing same-sex marriages and enabling states to refuse to recognize them when performed in other states as well.

32. *Reynolds v. New York* 98 U.S. 145 (1878). *Reynolds* also mentions the protection of children, which will not be pursued further here. Following the argument of Chapter 4, before the state's fiduciary responsibility ought to be triggered it would have to be shown that raising children in a polygamous household threatens their basic interests. If the sense in which protecting children merely concerns their exposure to heterodox sexual mores, this falls in the category of their best interests—the purview of parents, not public officials.

33. R. H. Coase, "The problem of social cost," *Journal of Law and Economics*, vol. 3 (October 1960), pp. 1–44.

34. The principal cases rejecting the old presumption that agreements in contemplation of divorce should be regarded as void as against public policy are *Hudson v. Hudson* 350 P.2d 596 (1960); *Posner v. Posner*, 233 So. 2d 381 (1970); and *In re Marriage of Newman* 653 P.2d 728 (Colo. 1982). Generally, see J. Thomas Oldham, "Premarital contracts are now enforceable, unless . . ." *Houston Law Review*, vol. 21, no. 4 (July 1984), pp. 757–88; Twila L. Perry, "Dissolution planning in family law: A critique of current analyses and a look toward the future," *Family Law Quarterly*, vol. 24, no. 1 (Spring 1990), pp. 77–125; Weitzman, *Marriage Contract*, pp. 335–457; and Judith T. Younger, "Perspectives on antenuptial agreements," *Rutgers Law Review*, vol. 40 (1989), pp. 1059–91. See also the Uniform Premarital Agreement Act (which is considerably more permissive in what it suggests should be enforced than most states will allow), reprinted in the *Baylor Law Review*, vol. 42 (Fall 1990), pp. 866–74.

35. See Okin, "Economic equality after divorce: 'Equal rights or special benefits?' " *Dissent* (Summer 1991), pp. 383–87.

36. Recall that democratic justice does not rest on an appeal to neutrality. Rather, it rests on the claim that in a world in which neutrality is unavailable, regimes that facilitate self-governance while limiting possibilities for domination are to be preferred.

37. See Pateman, *Sexual Contract*, p. 8.

38. Ibid., pp. 154–88.

39. Ibid., p. 3.

40. Ibid., p. 43.

41. Ibid., pp. 223–29.

42. It is perhaps instructive that Pateman cautions feminists who argue for appropriating the idea of contract for their own purposes that although Marx had to adopt the idea of individual self-ownership in order to formulate his critique of capitalism, he could not "have called for the abolition of wage labour and capitalism, or what, in older socialist terminology, is called wage slavery, if he had not also rejected this view of individuals and the corollary that freedom is contract and ownership." Ibid., pp. 13–14. Trenchant as Marx's critique of capitalism is, his brief remarks on communism as a society of free producers, in which people would contribute on the basis of ability and be rewarded on the basis of need, are less than compelling as a feasible path forward. See my discussion in *Democracy's Place*, pp. 53–78.

43. Lasch, *Haven in a Heartless World*, pp. 134–41.

44. The fact of this decline is uncontroversial, but the extent of it is in dispute. Weitzman's claim that, following divorce, men's living standards rise by 42 percent while those of women fall by 73 percent is not sustained by the data she presents in *The Divorce Revolution*, pp. 4–97, 323–43. Reanalyzing the data, Richard Peterson concludes that the relevant figures to be a 10 percent improvement for men and a 27 percent decline for women. His results are more in line with other studies, which have found an average decline of between 13 and 35 percent for women, suggesting that the rise of no-fault has not increased the economic costs of divorce for women significantly. This may reflect the ease with which divorce had become available before the no-fault revolution. Richard R. Peterson, "A re-evaluation of the economic consequences of divorce," *American Sociological Review*, vol. 61, no. 3 (June 1996), pp. 528–36.

45. No-fault divorce was not conceived as a leveling device historically. The principal argument adduced in its support was that the traditional fault standards had been so corrupted by the practice of parties and the courts (which had routinely come to pretend that it had been met when a divorce was desired) that it had effectively been abandoned. See Deborah Rhode, *Justice and Gender* (Harvard

University Press, 1989), pp. 147–48. Just why this began and took on momentum in the early 1970s is unclear.

46. This would be the converse of traditional Jewish practice, which gave the husband the unilateral right to initiate divorce. The biblical basis for this was Deuteronomy 24:1–2. See Roderick Phillips, *Putting Asunder: A History of Divorce in Western Society* (Cambridge University Press, 1988), pp. 19–20, and David Werner Amram, *The Jewish Law of Divorce According to Bible and Talmud* (Hermon, 1968), pp. 54–77.

47. Tenured employment is the limiting case here: no one complains about the indentured servitude of universities or federal courts, but they surely would if professors or judges were similarly bound.

48. Estimates of the number of physically abusive marriages in the United States range from two million to six million. See Chris Raymond, "Campaign alerts physicians to identify, assist victims of domestic violence," *Journal of the American Medical Association*, vol. 261, no. 7 (February 17, 1989), pp. 963–64. Rates of arrest and conviction for domestic violence are notoriously difficult to determine. One yearlong study of a large metropolitan South Florida sheriff's department in 1991 revealed that only 28.8 percent of domestic violence cases and 37.4 percent of aggravated battery cases ended in arrests, and that arrested women in domestic disputes were more than twice as likely as men to be charged with serious crimes. Sherry Bourg and Harley Stock, "A review of domestic violence arrest statistics in a police department using a pro-arrest policy: Are pro-arrest policies enough?" *Journal of Family Violence*, vol. 9, no. 2 (June 1994), pp. 177–89. For a general account of the attitude that domestic violence is not a crime—prevalent before the 1980s and still likely to be in circulation to some extent—see G. A. Goolkasian, *Confronting Domestic Violence: The Role of Criminal Court Judges* (National Institute of Justice, 1986).

49. *Reynolds v. New York* 98 U.S. 145, 167 (1878). The distinction between belief and practice on which the court based its decision is widely believed by commentators to be neither sustainable nor consistent with the court's First Amendment jurisprudence. See Penelope W. Saltzman, "*Potter v. Murray:* Another interpretation of polygamy and the First Amendment," *Utah Law Review*, vol. 86, no. 2 (1968), pp. 345–71, and Edwin Firmage, "Religion and the law: The Mormon experience in the nineteenth century," *Cardozo Law Review*, vol. 12 (February–March 1991), pp. 765–803.

50. Elizabeth Joseph, "My husband's nine wives," *New York Times*, May 23, 1991, and "Polygamists emerge from secrecy seeking not just peace but respect," *New York Times*, April 9, 1991.

51. Curiously, one of the ways in which American courts have limited the reach of *Reynolds* is by holding that the decision does not apply among Indians, on the grounds that their practice of plural marriage is enshrined in tribal law. *See Hal-*

lowell v. Commons, 210 F 793, 800 (8th Cir. 1914), *Compo v. Jackson Iron Co.*, 50 Mich. 578, 16 N.W. 295, 296 (1883), *Ortley v. Ross*, 78 Neb. 339, 110 N.W. 982, 983 (1907). From the standpoint of democratic justice, that plural marriage is enshrined in Indian tribal law makes it prima facie more rather than less suspect than were this not the case.

52. Corollaries of this were that the wife often could not be held liable by third parties, whereas the husband could be liable for many of the wife's tortious and criminal actions, as well as for her breaches of contract. By the same token, often the wife could not be a plaintiff in a civil action unless her husband was also joined as a party. Bromley and Lowe, *Family Law*, pp. 102–47.

53. For discussion of this legislation see the American Bar Foundation's *Guide to Family Law: The Complete and Easy Guide to the Laws of Marriage, Parenthood, Separation, and Divorce* (Random House, 1996), pp. 146–47.

54. Certain characteristic difficulties can arise concerning frivolous lawsuits and the possibilities of defrauding third parties such as insurance companies. But the experience of jurisdictions that have abolished the doctrine suggests that both of these may have been overrated, and mechanisms are evolving to deal with them. See Carl Tobias, "Interspousal tort immunity in America," *Georgia Law Review*, vol. 23 (1989), pp. 359–478.

55. This claim is consistent with many theories of the nature and purposes of criminal law, for it requires only that we treat prenuptial agreements like other kinds of contracts when thinking about the appropriate limits to contracting around criminal liability. It is not consistent with every possible view of the criminal law, however. On Richard Posner's account, for instance, criminal law is not seen as qualitatively different from other branches of law. Criminal sanctions arise only because of inefficiencies attending the securing of certain rights through a private-law regime. See Richard Posner, "An economic theory of the criminal law," *Columbia Law Review*, vol. 85, no. 6 (October 1985), pp. 1193–1232. Posner concedes that there are points at which this theory breaks down (notably having to do with victimless crimes and certain crimes of violence, which defy his efficiency calculus). Leaving its intrinsic plausibility as an account of the genesis of the criminal law aside, Posner's economic theory is likely to affront many intuitions about means of limiting criminal liability. It implies, for instance, that people might insure against criminal conviction or waive criminal liability by contract (as when *x* allows *y* to kill him in return for a payment by *y* into *x*'s estate). These implications are among the many reasons for skepticism of Posner's view. For other reasons, see my "Richard Posner's praxis," *Ohio State Law Journal*, vol. 48, no. 4 (December 1987), pp. 999–1047.

56. As in the criminal area, affirming this view does not require a full theory of the nature of tort law. The argument requires only that whatever theory of criminal tort law we affirm, it be applied in the domestic domain as elsewhere.

57. The same reasoning suggests that noncriminal torts should be modifiable by contract in the domestic domain as they are outside it, and that people should be free to insure against noncriminal tort liability within marriage (assuming such insurance were to become available), just as they can insure outside of it.

58. See note 48.

59. Battered women's syndrome has commonly been observed to include "learned helplessness" and a paradoxical attachment to the abusive partner, as well as other traumas. See M. A. Douglas, "The battered woman syndrome," in Daniel J. Sonkin, ed., *Domestic Violence on Trial: Psychological and Legal Dimensions of Family Violence* (Springer, 1987), pp. 39–54, and Donald G. Dutton and Susan Painter, "The battered woman syndrome: Effects of severe and intermittent abuse," *American Journal of Orthopsychiatry*, vol. 63, no. 4 (October 1993), pp. 614–22.

60. For many women divorce means falling into or close to poverty. One 1989 study showed that in the first five years after divorce, 26.1 percent of women experience poverty. 10.2 percent of married women were found to be poor before divorce and 12.3 percent near-poor. Three to four years after divorce the respective figures were 17.8 percent and 24.9 percent. Leslie A. Morgan, "Economic well-being following marriage termination: A comparison of divorced and widowed women," *Journal of Family Issues*, vol. 10, no. 1 (March 1989), pp. 86–101.

61. See note 48.

62. Several studies have shown that arrest is effective in reducing spousal abuse. See L. Sherman and Richard Berk, "The specific deterrent effects of arrest for domestic assault," *American Sociological Review*, vol. 49, no. 2 (April 1984), pp. 261–72; Richard Berk and P. Newton, "Does arrest really deter wife battery?" *American Sociological Review*, vol. 50, no. 2 (April 1985), pp. 253–62; and Richard Berk, Alec Campbell, Ruth Klap, and Bruce Western, "The deterrent effects of arrests in incidents of domestic violence: A Bayseian analysis of four field experiments," *American Sociological Review*, vol. 57, no. 5 (October 1992), pp. 698–708.

63. See Chapter 4, note 108.

64. This is an independent reason for favoring the comparatively robust social wage defended in the industrial context in Chapter 6.

65. See Chapter 4, notes 69–70 and accompanying text.

66. Ibid.

67. H. H. Clark, *The Law of Domestic Relations in the United States*, 2d ed. (West, 1988), p. 589.

68. See Ira Ellman, Paul Kurtz, and Katherine Bartlett, *Family Law* (Michie, 1991), pp. 265–66.

69. In *Orr v. Orr* 440 U.S. 268 (1979) the Supreme Court held that statutes that make alimony payable by husbands but not by wives violate the equal-protection clause of the Fourteenth Amendment. No longer may alimony be awarded by

reference to gender-based categories; awards must follow, and be justified by reference to, particularized inquiries into the needs of the parties.

70. See Bromley and Lowe, *Family Law*, pp. 103–47; Clark, *Law of Domestic Relations*, pp. 589–616; and Ellman, Kurtz, and Bartlett, *Family Law*, pp. 265–91.

71. This was not always so. Until the passage of the Uniform Marriage and Divorce Act in 1970 (which became the model for most statutes subsequently adopted) courts in common-law jurisdictions had usually allocated the property of divorcing spouses to the party who held title or had made financial contributions to the purchase of the asset. Rhode, *Justice and Gender*, p. 148.

72. In practice the regimes are not as different as one might think. Many common-law states have passed statutes defining "marital property" and differentiating it from "separate property," permitting courts to divide the former in ways that are similar to what goes on in community-property states. In other common-law states courts are permitted to distribute all the property owned by either spouse regardless of how it was acquired, and in a few states the statutes are so brief that the courts can proceed more or less as they please. The difference between equal and equitable division is also often less significant than might be thought, for equal divisions are modified for equitable reasons, and some notion of equality often plays a part in what courts in common-law states choose to regard as equitable. Clark, *Law of Domestic Relations*, pp. 590–91.

73. See Bruce Ackerman, "Neo-Federalism?" in Jon Elster and Rune Slagstad, eds., *Constitutionalism and Democracy* (Cambridge University Press, 1988), pp. 153–93.

74. See note 44.

75. *O'Brien v. O'Brien* 66 N.Y. 2d 576 (1985).

76. Saying that courts should take domestic labor into account and that income-producing diplomas may be regarded as marital property is quite unlike Okin's wage-splitting proposal, it should be noted, for two reasons. First, it involves the state in the distribution of marital assets only when there is no alternative—that is, when the marriage is breaking down and the parties cannot reach agreement about division. Second, although it tells the court to work with an expansive conception of marital property and to take domestic labor into account, it does not enunciate a distributive rule; instead, it leaves the court considerable latitude to decide, taking these factors into account, what equity or equality requires.

77. It should be noted that *O'Brien* was an unusual case. The trend in the prevailing law outside New York is not to treat degrees and diplomas as marital property. See Leslie Burns and Gregg Grauer, "Human capital as marital property," *Hofstra Law Review*, vol. 19 (1991), pp. 499–541, and Ellman, Kurtz, and Bartlett, *Family Law*, pp. 321–29. On the treatment of business goodwill see ibid., pp. 305–20, and on changing status of pensions as marital property, see Clark, *Law of Domestic Relations*, pp. 610–16.

78. On the implications of prenuptial agreements for child rearing, see Kenneth H.

Ernstoff, "Forcing rites on children: Can prenuptial agreements stipulate a child's religious upbringing?" *Family Advocate*, vol. 6 (Winter 1984), pp. 13–15. For a comparative look, see Susan Brown, "The enforcement of marital contracts in the United States, Great Britain, France, and Quebec," *Boston College International and Comparative Law Review*, vol. 6, no. 2 (1983), pp. 475–507.

79. For a discussion of the advantages and disadvantages of these different rules, see Younger, "Perspectives on antenuptial agreements," pp. 1073–79.

80. For a defense of the value of prenuptial agreements that goes further than mine, see Weitzman, *Marriage Contract*, pp. 227–55.

81. Some might sense a tension in the argument at this point, because the system of default institutions does not permit the state to intervene in much of the ongoing daily business of domestic life. In my discussion of Okin's wage-splitting proposal I suggested that we have good reasons to maintain that the state should not force adherence to any particular economic structure of domestic relations, and since then I have argued that so long as certain minimal requirements are met the state should generally keep out. How, then, can I consistently claim that courts may become involved in the daily management of the fine points of domestic life as a by-product of enforcing prenuptial agreements? Any tension here is merely apparent, however. By making a legally enforceable agreement which either party can litigate, the parties are themselves inviting the state to enforce certain standards of conduct and distributions of resources that they themselves have chosen. For this reason, although the state may be intervening in their lives more than would be the case had there been no prenuptial agreement, this is only because they have elected that it should do so.

82. These are not the only special privileges that have attached to the marital status. The common-law doctrine of "coercion," for instance, absolved the wife from criminal liability for many crimes committed in the presence of her husband, on the grounds that he was presumed to have coerced her into committing the criminal act. This and related defunct special-privilege doctrines, all of which derived from the suspension of the wife's legal identity during marriage, will not concern us. For more on them, see R. Perkins and R. Boyce, *Criminal Law* (Foundation, 1982), pp. 1018–27.

83. See Susan Demidovich, "Loss of consortium: Should marriage be retained as a prerequisite," *Cincinnati Law Review*, vol. 52 (1983), pp. 842–60.

84. Deborah Rhode, *Justice and Gender*, p. 251.

85. For discussion of the evolving law of spousal testimonial privilege, see Graham Lilly, *Evidence*, 2d ed. (West, 1987), and Marc Murphy, "Partners in crime: An examination of the privilege against adverse spousal testimony," *Journal of Family Law*, vol. 22 (1983–84), pp. 713–35.

86. Although many federal, state, and local benefits and protections continue to be denied to partners in unorthodox unions, this is not the universal rule. Homo-

sexuals have made some progress in New York, winning a landmark decision in *Braschi v. Stahl Associates* 74 N.Y. 2d 201 (1989), when the New York Court of Appeals held that a homosexual male couple is entitled to the same benefits as married couples under state rent-control laws. The court endorsed the use of such actuarial criteria as degree of emotional commitment and interdependence, interwoven social and financial life, and longevity and exclusivity of cohabitation, rather than the status of marriage, to determine eligibility for protection. By the 1990s many local and state governments had enacted "domestic partnership legislation" concerning health benefits, sick leave, and bereavement leave, and similar measures were under consideration in other cities and states. Insurance companies in Massachusetts, Washington, D.C., and Pennsylvania had begun underwriting "domestic partner" health insurance policies employing similar actuarial criteria. See Lambda Legal Defense Fund's *Domestic Partnership: Issues and Legislation* (New York, 1990) and Lewis Becker, "Recognition of domestic partnerships by governmental entities and private employers," *National Journal of Sexual Orientation Law*, vol. 1, no. 1 (1997), pp. 91-104.

87. For analogous reasons, the tax code should not be used to promote a particular type of marital or domestic-partnership form. If tax exemptions are available to married couples, the same exemptions should apply to unorthodox couples and to the unmarried. Whatever system of tax exemptions is in effect to compensate parents for the costs of child rearing, this should be unaffected by whether or not those parents are married, unconventionally married, or unmarried.

6. Controlling Work

1. Issues of child labor are best examined through the lens of Chapter 4. Virtual slave labor in countries like China is obviously unjust from the standpoint of democratic justice and is not further discussed here.

2. Statistics on the size of the public sector (which exclude military personnel) taken from *OECD Public Management Developments: Update 1995* (OECD, 1995), and on total workforce size from *OECD Quarterly Labor Force Statistics, 1995* (OECD, 1995).

3. See *World Development Report, 1996: From Plan to Market* (World Bank / Oxford University Press, 1996), pp. 14-15.

4. On the early origins of markets generally, see Alan Macfarlane, *The Origins of English Individualism: The Family, Property and Social Transition* (Blackwell, 1978). The classic, if disputed, accounts of the sixteenth-century origins of capitalist market relations in labor are Karl Marx, *Grundrisse: Foundations of the Critique of Political Economy* (Penguin, 1973), pp. 277-80, and *Capital*, vol. 1 (Penguin, 1976), pp. 455-700; Max Weber, *Economy and Society* (University of California Press, 1978), pp. 199-211, 237-41; and Max Weber, *The Theory of Social and Economic Organization* (Oxford University Press, 1974), pp. 258-80. For helpful surveys

of these debates see Maurice Dobb, *Studies in the Development of Capitalism* (Routledge, 1946), as well as the first three chapters of Macfarlane's *Origins*.

5. Adam Smith, *An Inquiry into the Nature and Causes of the Wealth of Nations* (Modern Library, 1937), pp. 4–5.

6. *Human capital:* Gary S. Becker, "The economic way of looking at behavior," *Journal of Political Economy*, vol. 101, no. 3 (July 1993), pp. 385–409.

7. Ronald M. Mason, *Participatory and Workplace Democracy* (Southern Illinois University Press, 1982), p. 102.

8. On work's sociological dimensions, see Kai Erikson and Steven Vallas, eds., *The Nature of Work: Sociological Perspectives* (Yale University Press, 1990), and Jon Elster, *The Cement of Society* (Cambridge University Press, 1989).

9. "Men . . . begin to distinguish themselves from animals as soon as they produce their means of subsistence. As individuals express their life, so they are. What they are, therefore, coincides with their production, both of what they produce and with how they produce. The nature of individuals thus depends on the material conditions determining their production." Karl Marx and Frederick Engels, *The German Ideology*, part 1 (International Publishers, 1970), p. 42.

10. Locke minimizes the independent contribution of resources by arguing that the world that has been given us in common is God's "waste" and insisting that "labour makes the far greater part," although he is famously vague about the precise relative contributions of labor and nature. Locke, *Two Treatises*, II, secs. 25–51, pp. 285–302.

11. Ibid., II, sec. 27, p. 288.

12. Ibid., II, sec. 6, pp. 270–71. For extended discussion see my *Evolution of Rights in Liberal Theory*, chapter 3.

13. Tully, *Discourse*, pp. 109–10, 121.

14. There is also some evidence that Locke believed workers' productivity to be influenced by mercantile workhouse discipline. See Tully, "Governing conduct," in E. Leites, ed., *Conscience and Casuistry in Early Modern Europe* (Cambridge University Press, 1988), pp. 12–71.

15. Locke, *Two Treatises*, II, sec. 28, pp. 288–89, sec. 85, p. 322.

16. Ibid., II, sec. 37, p. 294.

17. Locke believed that money, in addition to being impervious to physical decay, made possible the comparatively more productive use of natural resources through trade and productive work. See Richard Ashcraft, *Locke's Two Treatises of Government* (Allen and Unwin, 1987), pp. 123–50, and *Revolutionary Politics*, pp. 270–85.

18. That is, I agree with Tully in thinking Macpherson was mistaken to interpret Locke as meaning that the natural-law provisos could ever be "transcended." See my discussion in *Evolution of Rights*, pp. 23–27, 67–79.

19. On the role of the provisos in the theory of individual appropriation, see Locke,

Two Treatises, II, sec. 27, pp. 287–88, and on the requirements of charity ibid., I, sec. 42, p. 170, and II, sec. 93, p. 328. There are other indications that Locke regarded the system of positive rights as constrained by natural law. For instance, he insisted that there are limits in wartime to the reparations a conqueror could legitimately demand, having to do with the subsistence rights of the wives and children of defeated soldiers. Ibid., II, sec. 182, pp. 389–90.

20. As Ashcraft has shown with respect to eighteenth-century English debates about poor relief, the scope of what subsistence requires could be expanded and pressed into the service of a radical Lockean critique of the claims of capital. See Richard Ashcraft, "Lockean ideas, poverty, and the development of liberal political theory," in John Brewer and Susan Staves, eds., *Early Modern Conceptions of Property* (Routledge, 1995), pp. 43–61.

21. On the hierarchical priority of Locke's natural-law requirements, see Ashcraft, *Locke's Two Treatises*, pp. 123–50.

22. Locke, *Two Treatises*, II, secs. 223–25, pp. 414–15.

23. John Roemer, "Exploitation, alternatives and socialism," in *Egalitarian Perspectives: Essays in Philosophical Economics* (Cambridge University Press, 1994), pp. 15–36. Roemer thinks of himself as a Marxist, not a neo-Lockean. I will not here take up the question whether the opportunity-cost (my term, not his) notion of exploitation he defends in this essay is analytically equivalent to the Marxian idea of exploitation, as he asserts.

24. Ibid., pp. 17–18. Unfortunately, he does not define *dominated*.

25. Ibid., p. 24.

26. Here I skirt the measurement issue that divides neoclassical theorists from Marxists, namely whether "flows" should be measured by reference to the market value of the productive capacity in question or the market value of what is produced by its use. Both groups embrace self-ownership, the former applying it via marginalist price theory, the latter via various classical and neo-Marxist definitions of exploitation.

27. Locke, *Two Treatises*, II, sec. 7, p. 271.

28. Locke, *Two Treatises*, I, sec. 42, p. 170.

29. See Richard Epstein, *Takings: Private Property and the Power of Eminent Domain* (Harvard University Press, 1985). For discussion of the violence Epstein does to Locke's argument, see Rogers M. Smith, " 'Don't look back, something might be gaining on you': The dilemmas of constitutional neoconservatives," *American Bar Foundation Research Journal*, vol. 1987, no. 1 (Winter 1987), pp. 281–310.

30. John Harsanyi, "Democracy, equality, and popular consent," in Ian Shapiro and Grant Reeher, eds., *Power, Inequality, and Democratic Politics* (Westview, 1988), p. 279.

31. As is perhaps best illustrated by Nozick's tortured failures of logic concerning his "independents." See my *Evolution of Rights*, chapter 4.

32. See my *Democracy's Place*, pp. 58–63.

33. See Nancy Folbre, "Exploitation comes home: A critique of the Marxian theory of family labor," *Cambridge Journal of Economics*, vol. 6, no. 4 (1982), pp. 317–29.

34. In recent years American courts have begun to recognize how complex this can be in divorce settlements. See pages 137–39.

35. As Cohen notes, in this respect liberals like Rawls and Dworkin should be judged to the left of Marxists. "Self-ownership, world ownership, and equality: Part I," in Frank Lucash, ed., *Justice and Equality Here and Now* (Cornell University Press, 1986), pp. 113–15. Cohen is himself a partial exception to this generalization. See his explorations of the idea of "joint ownership" in G. A. Cohen, *Self-Ownership, Freedom, and Equality* (Cambridge University Press, 1995), pp. 14–15, 83–84, 93–106, 111–15.

36. See Rawls, *A Theory of Justice*, pp. 12, 15, 72–73, 101–3, 507–11.

37. Ibid., pp. 12, 18–19, 137–38, 172, 200, and Ronald Dworkin "What is equality?" part 1, "Equality of welfare," *Philosophy and Public Affairs*, vol. 10, no. 3 (Summer 1981), pp. 300–301.

38. See Sen, "Equality of what?" pp. 212–20, and "Well-being, agency, and freedom," pp. 185–221.

39. Rawls's most explicit statement of the view that people must be regarded as responsible for their preferences can be found in "Social unity and primary goods," in Amartya Sen and Bernard Williams, eds., *Utilitarianism and Beyond* (Cambridge University Press, 1982), pp. 168–69. For discussion of the tensions between this claim and the argument that differences in capacity are arbitrary, which Rawls defends most fully in *A Theory of Justice* (pp. 101–4), see Thomas Scanlon, "Equality of resources and equality of welfare: A forced marriage?" *Ethics*, vol. 97, no. 1 (1986), pp. 116–17, and "The significance of choice," *The Tanner Lectures on Human Values*, vol. 8 (University of Utah Press, 1988), pp. 192–201; Richard Arneson, "Property rights in persons," *Social Philosophy and Policy*, vol. 9, no. 1 (Winter 1992), pp. 201–30, "Primary goods reconsidered," *Nous*, vol. 24 (1990), pp. 429–54, and "Equality and equal opportunity for welfare," *Philosophical Studies*, vol. 56, no. 1 (May 1989), pp. 77–93; and Cohen, "Equality of what?"

40. Dworkin, "What is equality?" part 2, "Equality of resources," *Philosophy and Public Affairs*, vol. 10, no. 4 (Fall 1981), pp. 283–345.

41. Ibid., pp. 300–301.

42. As a result, insuring against the possibility of not having an extremely rare skill would be far more expensive than insuring against the possibility of not having a widely shared capacity, such as sight. In this way Dworkin hopes to come up with a theory of equality of resources that does not itself make implicit judgments about welfare and avoids the "slavery of the talented" problem that any theory

that permits compensation for differences in capacities must confront. Ibid., pp. 292-304.

43. Ibid., p. 301.

44. See ibid., p. 300, where Dworkin asserts in opposition to the idea that there can be a view of "normal" human powers that no amount of initial compensation could make someone born blind or mentally incompetent equal in physical or mental resources with someone taken to be "normal" in these ways.

45. "Someone who is born with a serious handicap faces his life with what we concede to be fewer resources, just on that account, than others do. This justifies compensation, under a scheme devoted to equality of resources, and though the hypothetical insurance market does not right the balance—*nothing can*—it seeks to remedy one aspect of the resulting unfairness." Ibid., p. 302, italics added.

46. Ibid., pp. 311, 288, 302.

47. Ibid., pp. 311-13.

48. I should not be understood here to be saying that people always have the capacities to achieve their ambitions, or even that we cannot develop ambitions that we know we cannot achieve, although I suspect that sustained analysis would reveal part of the difference between an ambition and a fantasy to reside in the fact that the former is generally a spur to action in a way that the latter need not be. Here I intend only to establish that it is not credible to believe that our ambitions are developed independently of our capacities, which Dworkin's categorial distinction requires.

49. Dworkin is aware of this, but considers only a case in which a person might have an incapacitating obsession that he wishes he did not have. Dworkin deals with this by arguing that such cravings may be thought of as handicaps and thus handled via his hypothetical insurance scheme. "What is equality?" part 2, pp. 302-3 ff. But this is to sidestep the point being made here, which is that the obsession may itself incapacitate a person from forming the relevant second-order desire to make Dworkin's hypothetical insurance solution work. Are we to say of an alcoholic whose affliction is so severe that he cannot even form the desire not to be an alcoholic that his preference for alcohol results from his taste rather than his incapacity? I think not.

50. John Roemer has made the argument to me in correspondence.

51. Cohen, "On the currency of egalitarian justice," p. 922.

52. Cohen, "Equality of what?" pp. 14-15. Once it is conceded that the very decision to choose to expend effort is influenced by factors that are conceded to be morally arbitrary, one suspects that the difficulty becomes one of principle rather than practicality; certainly Cohen offers no account of how that component of effort meriting reward might in principle be singled out.

53. Some have taken the view that Kant's categorical imperative can provide a secular foundation for the "rights" component of workmanship. I will not repeat

the arguments I have made elsewhere to the effect that this notion is so under-determined empirically that it yields no particular conclusions in the field of normative political economy. See *Evolution of Rights in Liberal Theory*, pp. 161–64, 242–46, 264–66.

54. Locke *Two Treatises*, II, sec. 225, p. 415.

55. Ibid., II, secs. 226–33, pp. 415–20.

56. Assuming, of course, that none had his Man Friday.

57. Not surprisingly, Marx and Engels described such a world as one in which the state withers away and "the government of persons is replaced by the admin-istration of things." Frederick Engels, *Socialism: Utopian and Scientific*, in Karl Marx and Frederick Engels, *Selected Works* (Progress Publishers, 1969), vol. 3, p. 147. See also their *Manifesto of the Communist Party*, ibid., vol. 1, p. 127; Engels, "On authority," ibid., vol. 2, p. 378; and Marx, *Critique of the Gotha Program*, ibid., vol. 3, pp. 18–19. As noted in Chapter 1, superabundance is inherently unattainable.

58. What counts as a basic interest is to some degree socially and historically con-ditioned. In the realm of education, for instance, if the larger economy is fully marketized, then the imperative to develop a marketable stock of human capi-tal will—for a given individual—for all practical purposes be inescapable, even though in other circumstances this might not have been so.

59. Notice that this claim about necessity is agnostic with respect to whether the imperatives on which people must act are "natural" features of the human con-dition or "socially constructed." Whether the imperatives on which people must act are alterable—and if so, by whom and at what cost to whom—are important issues that play a role in the following discussion. But it is a common misconception to believe that questions about the alterability of the human condition depend on views about social construction. The degree to which things are alter-able may not vary with the extent to which they are socially constructed at all. Many features of the natural world, ranging from the temperature of our bath-water to the genetic structure of our beings, can be altered by conscious human design. As the advent of genetic engineering indicates, those features of human life that are alterable may themselves change, so that what has to be accepted as given in one era may become subject to human modification in another. Socially constructed phenomena, by contrast, often defy all efforts at conscious human control. Markets are human constructions, yet we may be unable to regulate them so as to operate at full employment without inflation. Ethnic hatred might concededly be learned behavior, yet we may have no idea how to prevent its being reproduced in the next generation. It is a mistake to leap from the idea of social construction to that of alterability; at best, the two are contingently related.

60. By the same token, there may be circumstances in which the state lacks the rele-

vant mix of financial and institutional resources to provide many components of a social wage needed to vindicate basic interests, but it could induce corporations to provide some of them. I think particularly here of countries like contemporary South Africa, which has almost 40 percent unemployment in many regions, chronically inadequate basic education and medical care for the majority, a collapsed currency and depleted capital reserves, and a political capacity to tax that is not remotely equal to the demands it confronts. In such conditions it might be appropriate for the state to offer corporations a mix of incentives and penalties to induce them build and run local hospitals and schools for their workers and families. Although, for reasons elaborated later in this chapter, this is a less than ideal approach to vindicating basic interests of a population, when the situation is so bad, and no feasible alternative is on the horizon, loading even these basic interests onto the employment relationship may be defensible.

61. By focusing on the imperatives that people are constrained to satisfy, I do not mean to suggest that people always value them more highly than other activities. People might resent the constraining effects of many basic interests (on themselves or on others); they might find them irksome or mundane. One could, indeed, imagine a person reasonably concluding that a life in which one can do no more than act on such imperatives is not worth living.

62. This is not to deny that how to cope with expensive addictions should figure prominently in a discussion of the collective health care provision.

63. See Lester C. Thurow, *The Future of Capitalism: How Today's Economic Forces Shape Tomorrow's World* (Morrow, 1996), pp. 26–29.

64. On the effects of global trade on wages and employment, see Adrian Wood, *North-South Trade, Employment, and Inequality: Changing Fortunes in a Skill-Driven World* (Clarendon, 1994). For a review of literature that points to factors other than trade, principally technology, see Gary Burtless, "International trade and the rise of earnings inequality," *Journal of Economic Literature*, vol. 33 (June 1995), pp. 800–816.

65. "In fact there *is* democracy in the typical capitalist firm; it is just that investors of capital do the voting rather than workers. Converting to worker ownership means not only enfranchising the workers but also *dis*enfranchising the firm's investors." Henry Hansman, *The Ownership of Enterprise* (Harvard University Press, 1996), p. 43.

66. Candidates commonly discussed by economists include maximizing sales, capital, and managers' and own compensation subject to a profitability constraint, or maximizing the probability that profits will remain above a given threshold. For an overview, see David Kreps, *A Course in Economic Theory* (Princeton University Press, 1990), pp. 724–41.

67. Robin Archer, *Economic Democracy: The Politics of Feasible Socialism* (Clarendon Press, 1995), pp. 47–48.

68. For the same reason, whether the employment relationship is in the public or private sector is of no particular concern from the standpoint of democratic justice (although the strategic possibilities for advancing democratic justice may be different in public- and private-sector employment).

69. The Combination Acts of 1799 and 1800 replaced the patchwork of eighteenth-century legislation banning combinations in particular trades with comprehensive laws outlawing strikes and trade unions throughout Great Britain. Contrary to basic principles of English law, the acts compelled workers to testify against themselves and contained draconian penalties, forcing unions to go underground or maintain their existence as friendly societies. The acts were repealed in 1824. See Mary Davis, *Comrade or Brother: A History of the British Labour Movement, 1789–1951* (Pluto, 1993), pp. 27–28, 36.

70. Smith, *Wealth of Nations*, pp. 66–67.

71. Quotations from the Wagner Act taken from the *Legislative History of the National Labor Relations Act, 1935*, vol. 2 (National Labor Relations Board, 1959), secs. 1, 7, 8, arts. 1–5, pp. 3270–74. Legal protection of trade unions was secured when the Supreme Court upheld the Wagner Act in 1937, declaring that employees "have as clear a right to organize and select their representatives for lawful purposes as the [company] has to organize its business and select its own officers and agents." *NLRB v. Jones & Laughlin Steel Corp.* 301 U.S. 1 (1937), p. 323.

72. On the passage of the Wagner Act see Michael Goldfield, "Worker insurgency, radical organization, and New Deal labor legislation," *American Political Science Review*, vol. 83, no. 4 (December 1989), pp. 1257–82, and the exchange between Goldfield, Theda Skocpol, and Kenneth Feingold, "Explaining New Deal labor policy," *American Political Science Review*, vol. 84, no. 4 (December 1990), pp. 1299–1315, as well as David Plotke, "The Wagner Act, again: Politics and labor, 1935–37," *Studies in American Political Development*, vol. 3, ed. Karen Orren and Stephen Skowronek (Yale University Press, 1989). On the cutting back of its provisions in the 1947 Taft-Hartley Act and the 1959 Landrum-Griffin Amendments, see Julius Getman and Bertrand Pogrebin, *Labor Relations: The Basic Processes, Law, and Practice* (Foundation, 1988), pp. 1–4.

73. For an useful review essay of the transactions-costs literature on the firm, see Oliver Hart, "Contractual freedom in corporate law: An economist's perspective on the theory of the firm," *Columbia Law Review*, vol. 89 (November 1989), pp. 1757–75.

74. Because the European practice is to recognize that workers have an equity interest in their jobs, placing substantial burdens on employers who would terminate employment seems normal. See Gary Murg and John Fox, *Labor Relations Law: Canada, Mexico, and Western Europe* (Practicing Law Institute, 1978), vol. 1, p. 4, and Roger Blanpain and Tdashi Hanami, eds., *Employment Security: Law and Practice in . . . the European Communities* (Peeters, 1994), pp. 13–39. When dis-

missal is at stake, some European countries, notably Germany, Norway, and Sweden, go so far as to require employment to be maintained until the case is resolved. Blenk, *European Labour Courts*, p. 49.

75. This is the rule in cases under Title VII of the 1964 Civil Rights Act. *St. Mary's Honor Center v. Hicks* 509 U.S. 502, 113 S.Ct. 2742 (1993); *Texas Dep't of Community Affairs v. Burdine* 405 U.S. 248 (1981).

76. Although the burden of proof usually falls on the employee in discharge cases and employment disputes generally, there are situations in which some burden shifts to the employer. In employment discrimination cases, once an employee makes out a prima facie case of discrimination (usually by showing that he or she is a member of a protected class and was treated less favorably than someone who is not a member of said class), the employer has the burden of production: it must "articulate" some legitimate, nondiscriminatory reason for firing or otherwise acting against the employee. *Texas Dep't. of Com'nity Affairs v. Burdine*, 450 U.S. 248 (1981); *McDonnell Douglas Corp. v. Green*, 411 U.S. 792 (1973). This burden-shifting framework, developed in cases under Title VII of the 1964 Civil Rights Act, has also been applied under the Age Discrimination in Employment Act and the Reconstruction-era Civil Rights Acts. *O'Connor v. Consolidated Coin Caterers Corp.*, 116 S. Ct. 1307, 1310 (1996). The shifted burden is not onerous, however. Under the *Burdine-McDonnell Douglas* doctrine, even once the employee has made out a prima facie case, the employer need not prove that it acted for a nondiscriminatory reason; it merely has to articulate such a reason. *Burdine*, 420 U.S. at 253.

77. This is not to be confused with the separate matter of economic layoffs. Employers are not generally required to prove cause for layoffs, although union contracts usually stipulate certain requirements, such as that layoffs be in reverse order of seniority.

78. Frank Elkouri and Edna Asper Elkouri, *How Arbitration Works*, 4th ed. (Bureau of National Affairs, 1985), p. 661.

79. Ibid.

80. Indeed, there is no necessary link between just-cause provisions and burden shifting. In 1991 the National Conference of Commissioners on Uniform State Laws approved the Model Employment Termination Act (META), intended to reform state common law on the employer's right to discharge. *Uniform Laws Annotated* (West Publishing, 1996), pp. 78–81. Section 3 of META prohibits the discharge of covered employees except for "good cause," but a complainant employee must shoulder the burden of proving that the termination was without good cause. META sec. 6(e).

81. 42 U.S.C. sec. 2000e-2(e)(1).

82. *Automobile Workers v. Johnson Controls*, 499 U.S. 187, 200–201 (1991).

83. 401 U.S. 424 (1971).

84. *Griggs*, 401 U.S. at 431.

85. The 1991 amendment provides that when a plaintiff demonstrates disparate impact, the employer has the burden of proving "that the challenged practice is job related for the position in question and consistent with business necessity." 42 U.S.C. sec. 2000e-2(k)(1)(A)(i). This amendment overturned in part the Supreme Court's decision in *Ward's Cove Packing Co. v. Antonio*, 490 U.S. 642 (1989). In *Ward's Cove* the Court had held that once a disparate impact is established, the employer has only the burden of production to articulate a business justification; the plaintiff was then required to prove that the practice does not have a business justification. The 1991 amendment thus returned the burden to the employer in a business-necessity defense, where it should be.

86. U.S.C. sec. 2000e-2(k)(1)(A)(ii), sec. 2000e-2(k)(1)(C).

87. The 1991 Civil Rights Act also sets forth comparable rules for "dual motive" cases, which arise where the employee succeeds in proving that an employer's adverse action toward him or her was taken for a prohibited motivation, but the employer argues that there was also a legitimate, nondiscriminatory reason for the adverse action. In these cases the burden shifts to the employer to prove that it would have taken the adverse action even in the absence of the prohibited motivation. See *NLRB v. Transportation Management Corp.*, 462 U.S. 393 (1983), where the prohibited motivation was antiunion discrimination, and *Mt. Healthy City Board of Education v. Doyle*, 429 U.S. 274 (1977), which involved discharge of an employee in violation of First Amendment rights. In 1989 the Supreme Court had limited its impact, holding that if the employer carried its burden of proving that it would have taken the action absent the prohibited motive, this would constitute an affirmative defense, relieving the employer of liability. *Price Waterhouse v. Hopkins* 490 U.S. 228 (1989), at 246. Congress responded in the 1991 Civil Rights Act by providing that the employer's proof in a dual-motive case could not absolve it of liability. It could only limit the relief available to the plaintiff to declaratory and injunctive relief and attorney's fees. This means that if the employer proves that it would have taken the adverse action in the absence of a prohibited motive, a Title VII plaintiff can obtain attorney's fees but not back pay or reinstatement. 41 U.S.C. sec. 2000e-2(m) and 2000e-5(g)(2)(B). This requirement, which goes further than the mere burden shifting in the discrimination and disparate-impact cases, is defensible as a device to give employers incentives to avoid discriminatory behavior in dual-motive circumstances.

88. This allocation of burdens is explicable by analogy to employees under a union contract, giving employees a defeasible right not to be discharged. Some civil service systems view the employer as the plaintiff, bringing charges against the employee that have to be proved. They may permit employers to suspend employees unilaterally without pay, but not to discharge them until the charges have been proved.

89. "The Board's General Counsel has unreviewable discretion to refuse to institute an unfair labor practice complaint." *Vaca v. Sipes*, 386 U.S. 171, 182 (1967).

90. This incoherence, which depends on requiring the existence of a union contract to burden-shift on the one hand, and giving as the reason the high costs of job loss to the worker on the other, is more fully explored in connection with my discussion of variations in the appropriate quantum of proof.

91. See Joanne Yates, *Control Through Communications* (Johns Hopkins University Press, 1989), and Thurow, *Future of Capitalism*, pp. 79–82.

92. For helpful surveys of the neoclassical account of firms as sets of profit-maximizing production possibilities, as well as weaknesses in the neoclassical view pointed out in the literatures on managerial theories of the firm, principal-agent theory, transactions-costs economics, and contract theory, see Kreps, *A Course in Microeconomic Theory*, pp. 723–70.

93. On the decline in union membership, see Mark Barenberg, "Democracy and domination in the law of workplace cooperation: From bureaucratic to flexible production," *Columbia Law Review*, vol. 94, no. 3 (April 1994), p. 758.

94. Lewis Kelso and Mortimer Adler, *The Capitalist Manifesto* (Random House, 1958), p. 68.

95. The first legislative provision for ESOP tax incentives was in the 1973 Regional Rail Reorganization Act. General use of the ESOP was provided for in section 407(d)(6) of the 1974 Employee Retirement and Income Security Act (ERISA).

96. Corey Rosen, "Employee ownership: Performance, prospects, and promise," in Corey Rosen and Karen Young, eds., *Understanding Employee Ownership* (ILR, 1991), p. 20. Blasi and Kruse come up with an estimate of 10.8 million workers covered by "employee ownership plans" in 1989. Their figure is based partly on estimates from the National Center for Employee Ownership and includes pensions, 401(k) plans, and profit-sharing plans that hold employer stock, stock options, and the like. Joseph Raphael Blasi and Douglas Lynn Kruse, *The New Owners: The Mass Emergence of Employee Ownership in Public Companies and What It Means to American Business* (Harper Business, 1991), pp. 8–28.

97. Rosen, "Employee ownership," pp. 24–35.

98. Ibid., pp. 32–33. See also William Smith, "The ESOP revolution: Will it increase employee involvement?" *SAM Advanced Management Journal*, vol. 57, no. 3 (June 22, 1992), p. 14.

99. Joseph Blasi, *Employee Ownership: Revolution or Ripoff?* (Ballinger, 1988), p. 240. See also Robert Dahl, *A Preface to Economic Democracy* (University of California Press, 1985), pp. 92–93.

100. See David I. Levine, "Public policy implications of imperfections in the market for worker participation," *Economic and Industrial Democracy*, vol. 13 (1992), pp. 183–206, and David Ellerman, *The Democratic Worker-Owned Firm: A New Model for East and West* (Unwin Hyman, 1990), pp. 115–16.

101. See Paul Weiler, *Governing the Workplace: The Future of Labor and Employment Law* (Harvard University Press, 1990), pp. 172–73.

102. "Pension fund socialism" is Peter F. Drucker's term in *The Unseen Revolution: How Pension Fund Socialism Came to America* (Harper and Row, 1976).

103. *Statistical Abstract of the United States, 1995* (U.S. Government Printing Office, 1995), p. 535. This excludes insured private pension funds, which held $172 billion in 1980, $393 billion in 1985, $784 billion in 1990, and $1,123 billion in 1994, as well as additional holdings in state and local government pension funds. These latter stood at $197 billion in 1980, $399 billion in 1985, $820 billion in 1990, and $1,223 billion in 1994. Ibid.

104. Blasi and Kruse, *New Owners*, p. 23. In 1987 it was estimated that nearly nine thousand companies had adopted ESOP plans, which combined to hold some $19 billion of stock in trust for some eight million participating employees. See *The Employee Ownership Report* (National Center for Employee Ownership, September–October 1988), p. 1. Weiler notes, in *Governing the Workplace*, pp. 169–70, that during the 1980s the vast majority of ESOP plans took the form of tax credit ESOPs under which the federal government in effect gave American corporations roughly a dollar in tax savings in order to create $1.25 of stock ownership for employees. Once Congress became aware of the dimensions of this tax break, it was repealed as part of the general 1986 Tax Reform Act, leaving the classic ESOPs (leveraged or not) as main instruments for promoting employee ownership. According to Blasi, by 1983 these were responsible for about $3.86 billion in assets (about 0.03 percent of all assets and 0.18 percent of all corporate stock) owned for the benefit of about a million workers (less than 1 percent of the workforce) at the cost to the federal government of about $1.5 billion in tax subsidies. Blasi, *Employee Ownership*, pp. 117–18.

105. Weiler, *Governing the Workplace*, p. 171.

106. A plan can completely exclude members of a collective bargaining unit provided the union has the option to bargain directly for employee ownership on behalf of its members, whether or not any actual bargaining on this subject occurs. Blasi, *Employee Ownership*, p. 41. On other exclusions see Weiler, *Governing the Workplace*, pp. 170–71, and Blasi, *Employee Ownership*, pp. 41–42.

107. See *Employee Stock Ownership Plans: Benefits and Costs of ESOP Tax Incentives for Broadening Stock Ownership* (U.S. General Accounting Office, 1986), pp. 20–32, and Weiler, *Governing the Workplace*, pp. 171–73.

108. In 1988 Polaroid's management created an ESOP to block a hostile takeover. The company purchased ten million shares (about 20 percent) of its stock, designating them for employees. They reduced wages by 5 percent to pay for the repurchase and canceled the company's 401(k) plan. Shares were to be released to employees twice a year, with all shares to be fully allocated by 1998. Employees enjoy voting rights of whatever stock they own, as well as one representative

on the sixteen-member board of directors. The Weirton Steel Company of Weirton, West Virginia, established an ESOP in 1984 to help employees buy a steel mill that was scheduled for closure. Employees took a 20 percent pay cut, agreed to a six-year wage freeze in return for a five-year allocation of the company's shares to the employees and three representatives (all union officials) on the thirteen-member board. In 1989 the employees opted to restructure their ownership by taking the company partly public, and by 1992 some 22 percent of its shares were publicly traded. For more details see Smith, "The ESOP revolution," p. 14; Blasi, *Employee Ownership*, pp. 212-16; Barry Bluestone and Irving Bluestone, *Negotiating the Future: A Labor Perspective on American Business* (Basic, 1992), pp. 110-12; and Ellerman, *Democratic Worker-Owned Firm*, p. 115.

109. Weiler, *Governing the Workplace*, pp. 171-72.

110. For instance, the *Directory of Workers' Enterprises in North America* (ICA Group, 1991) lists 154 worker-owned cooperatives with 6,545 members; 106 democratically managed ESOPs with 84,110 employees; and 143 ESOPs with 87,225 employees where workers own a majority of the company's stock. Fewer than 100,000 employees are listed as working at an employee-owned firm of any type. For data from outside North America, see Hansman, *Ownership of Enterprise*, 67-68.

111. Hansman, *Ownership of Enterprise*, pp. 66-88. See also David Levine and Laura D'Andrea Tyson, "Participation, productivity, and the firm's environment," in Alan Binder, ed., *Paying for Productivity* (Brookings, 1990), pp. 183-243.

112. Hansman, *Ownership of Enterprise*, pp. 66-74.

113. John Bonin, Derek Jones, and Louis Putterman, "Theoretical and empirical studies of producer cooperatives: Will ever the twain meet?" *Journal of Economic Literature*, vol. 31 (September 1993), pp. 1290-1320, conclude that the "weight of the theoretical reasoning and evidence surveyed convinces us that the explanation of the relative scarcity of coops lies in the nexus between decision-making and financial support" (p. 1316). Mark J. Roe, "A political theory of American corporate finance," *Columbia Law Review*, vol. 91 (1991), pp. 10-21, argues that suboptimal arrangements (such as investor ownership) have triumphed because of the political power of key interest groups, comparable to the historical study of the driving out of efficient alternatives offered by Charles Sable and Jonathan Zeitlin in "Historical alternatives to mass production: Politics, markets, and technology in nineteenth-century mass production," *Past and Present*, no. 108 (1986), pp. 133-76. Harvey Leibenstein blames the high entry costs of altering established practices in *Inside the Firm: The Inefficiencies of Hierarchy* (Harvard University Press, 1987), as do Jon Elster (who also cites adverse selection and free rider problems) in "From here to there; or if cooperative ownership is so desirable, why are there so few cooperatives?" *Social Philosophy and Policy*, vol. 6

(1989), pp. 93–124, and Louis Putterman in "Some behavioral perspectives on the dominance of hierarchical over democratic forms of enterprise," *Journal of Economic Behavior and Organization*, vol. 3 (1982), pp. 139–60.

114. Hansman points out that, contra Alchian and Demsetz's oft-repeated claim in "Production, information costs, and economic organization," *American Economic Review*, vol. 62, no. 5 (December 1972), pp. 777–95, worker ownership does not tend to emerge in circumstances in which employees are unusually hard to monitor. Nor does employee ownership correlate well with employee lock-in; on the contrary, employee owners tend to be unusually mobile (*Ownership of Enterprise*, pp. 70–71). Large firms with substantial hierarchy and division of labor between management and the rest of the labor force also tend not to be employee owned, despite its potential advantages in reducing opportunism and strategic bargaining. Rather, worker-owned firms tend to be in industries in which there are comparatively few information asymmetries and hierarchies are lacking (ibid., pp. 91–92). Nor does the argument about the difficulty of raising capital square with the evidence that employee-owned firms are common in capital-intensive industries and with the willingness of employee owners in such firms to bear substantial amounts of risk (ibid., pp. 75–77).

115. Albert O. Hirschmann, *Exit, Voice, and Loyalty* (Harvard University Press, 1970).

116. Further evidence of this is the fact that employee ownership used to prevail in craft professions such as shoemaking and barrel making, but this independence disappeared as these tasks began to be performed in large firms with significant divisions of labor. The recent evolution of the medical practice in the direction of the HMO and the emergence in law firms of cadres of permanent associates who never become partners appears, similarly, to be undermining full employee ownership in those contexts. Hansman, *Ownership of Enterprise*, pp. 94–97.

117. Direct employee participation at Mondragon is limited to annual meetings and large elections for nine-member supervisory boards of directors for staggered four-year terms. These boards in turn appoint managers for (minimum four-year) terms who can be removed only for cause. There are "social councils" elected by local constituencies within each firm, but they are "voice" mechanisms only. Firms within the system must adopt wage structures within the narrow range established by the Mondragon system's central bank, and 90 percent of net earnings after wages are paid must be retained for investment in capital accounts. These and other financial restrictions are imposed on the cooperative units by a "contract of association" with the central bank, which is not alterable by the unit's workers or management. Ibid., pp. 98–103.

118. Ibid., pp. 33–34.

119. The possibility of deadlock is avoided because the chairman, appointed by the shareholders, gets a second vote in the event of a tie.

120. See Ronald M. Mason, *Participatory and Workplace Democracy: A Theoretical Development in the Critique of Liberalism* (Southern Illinois University Press, 1982), p. 163.

121. See Alan Hyde, "Endangered species," *Columbia Law Review*, vol. 91, no. 2 (March 1991), pp. 456–72, for this complaint. See also John Addison, Kornelius Kraft, and Joachim Wagner, "German works councils and firm performance," in Bruce E. Kaufman and Morris M. Kleiner, eds., *Employee Representation: Alternatives and Future Directions* (Industrial Relations Research Association, 1993), pp. 305–38, which examines fifty German firms but fails to find much evidence that works councils have either a positive or a negative effect on productivity.

122. Richard B. Freeman and Joel Rogers, "Who speaks for us? Employee representation in a nonunion labor market," in Kaufman and Kleiner, *Employee Representation*, pp. 49–55. The works councils may, however, have contributed indirectly to the power of German trade unions, which have made strategic use of them that was not anticipated by their designers. See Wolfgang Streek, "Codetermination: After four decades," in *Social Institutions and Economic Performance* (Sage, 1992), pp. 137–68.

123. The term *flexible specialization* first achieved prominence with Michael J. Piore and Charles Sable in *The Second Industrial Divide: Possibilities for Prosperity* (Basic, 1984), who argued that large hierarchical firms are for a variety of reasons being replaced by smaller and more efficient types of firm. For a useful and sympathetic survey of the resulting literature (which is linked to a variety of real-world movements, including "quality of work life" [QWL], "total quality management" [TQM], "lean production," and "self-managing teams"), see Barenberg, "Democracy and domination," pp. 884–90.

124. Bluestone and Bluestone, *Negotiating the Future*. For discussion of James Meade's seminal work on capital-labor partnerships, see Anthony Atkinson, *Alternatives to Capitalism: The Economics of Partnership* (St. Martin's, 1993). See also D. M. Nuti, "Alternative employment and pay systems," in Samuel Bowles, Herbert Gintis, and Bo Gustaffson, eds., *Markets and Democracy: Participation, Accountability, and Efficiency* (Cambridge University Press, 1993), and D. M. Nuti, "On traditional cooperatives and James Meade's labor-capital discriminating partnerships," in Derek C. Jones and Jan Svejnar, eds., *Advances in the Economic Analysis of Participatory and Labor-Managed Firms*, vol. 4 (JAI Press, 1992), pp. 1–26.

125. Gain sharing differs from profit sharing in being directly linked to improvements in productivity or the costs of production.

126. See Martin Weitzman, *The Share Economy* (Harvard University Press, 1984). Profit-sharing systems are self-adjusting through pay, rather than through the number of workers employed. Lincoln-Electric, a manufacturer of arc-welding equipment, has long been noted for its use of profit-sharing and piece rates to maintain stable employment. Gain sharing has sometimes been implemented

as an explicit part of employment-stabilization plans. See the case study of the Scanlon plan at Xaloy, Inc., a firm producing specialized metal piping. Steven E. Markham, K. Dow Scott, and Walter G. Cox Jr., "The evolutionary development of a Scanlon plan," *Compensation and Benefits Review*, vol. 24 (March 1992), pp. 50–56. Weitzman's profit-sharing plan has been called "taxation without representation" because he assumes that workers will not acquire managerial control under profit sharing and therefore will not acquire the power to restrict hiring. See John P. Bonin, "The share economy: Taxation without representation," in Derek C. Jones and Jan Svejnar, eds., *Advances in the Economic Analysis of Participatory and Labor-Managed Firms*, vol. 3 (JAI Press, 1988), pp. 185–200.

127. On the productivity effects of profit sharing, see Martin Weitzman and Douglas Kruse, *Profit-sharing and Productivity* (Brookings, 1990), pp. 138–39. On the productivity effects of increased worker participation in management, see Weiler, *Governing the Workplace*, pp. 172–73, and Rosen, "Employee ownership," pp. 29–35.

128. Bluestone and Bluestone, *Negotiating the Future*, p. 217.

129. See Stephen Wood, "The cooperative labor strategy in the U.S. auto industry," *Economics and Industrial Democracy*, vol. 7 (1986), pp. 415–47, and Mike Parker and Jane Slaughter, *Choosing Sides: Unions and the Team Concept* (South End, 1988), chapter 3, pp. 16–29.

130. *E. I. Du Pont de Nemours & Co.*, 311 NLRB 88 (1993) and *Electromation, Inc.*, 309 NLRB 990 (1992) interpret section 8(a)(2) of the NLRA, which prohibits employers from "dominat[ing] or intefer[ing] with the formation or administration of any labor organization or contribut[ing] financial or other support to it." 29 U.S.C. sec. 158(a)(2) (1988). The act defines "labor organization" sufficiently broadly to include "any ongoing employee entity," even if informal and bearing no resemblance to an independent labor union. Barenberg, "Democracy and domination," p. 760. Since *General Foods Corp.*, 231 NLRB 1232 (1977), employers have been permitted to establish "participatory" work teams that lack "representative" team leaders, probably (as Barenberg notes on p. 761) in violation of the act, section 2(5) of which explicitly includes participatory entities within the meaning of "labor organization." He notes that in practice team production does involve elected or rotating team leaders, who serve representative liaison functions with the rest of the firm, in effect violating even the *General Foods* exception.

131. Barenberg, "Democracy and domination," p. 889. See also pp. 888, 921–26.

132. Ibid., pp. 932–33, 960–61. Barenberg's ideal scheme is one in which employees would be free to choose nonunion and company union options by vote, but the default option would be a conventional independent union. Defensible as that might be, it is the opposite of present reality, in which the default option is no union and unionization is difficult and costly to achieve.

133. The Team Act (1996) HR743 proposed, in part, to modify the NLRA "to make clear that U.S. businesses can establish, without the presence of a labor union, workplace groups consisting of both labor and management to address productivity, quality control and safety." Amendments proposed by Democrats—that employees in such groups be elected by fellow employees, and that the groups' range of authority be limited—were rejected. *Congressional Quarterly*, September 30, 1995, pp. 3009, 3028, and May 11, 1996, p. 1278. In late 1996 the Team Act had passed both houses, but, following a veto threat from the Clinton administration, Republicans detached it from the minimum wage bill, to which it had been attached, in the runup to the 1996 elections.

134. Paul C. Weiler, "Hard times for unions: Challenging times for scholars," *University of Chicago Law Review*, vol. 59, (1991), p. 1030.

135. Fingerhut and Powers, *National Labor Poll*, 1991 (cited in Barenberg, "Democracy and domination," p. 932). A 1988 Gallup poll showed that 69 percent of workers identified labor unions as "good for the nation as a whole," 75 percent described them as the best instrument to increase wages and enhance job security, 82 percent thought the same about grievance resolution, and 81 percent supported the right to unionize. The same poll showed that most workers (mistakenly) believed that 45 percent of the American workforce is unionized. Gallup Poll, *Public Opinion and Knowledge Concerning the Labor Movement* (1988). The picture that emerges from more recent polling is broadly compatible with these findings, supporting a dominant perception of unions as a necessary evil. Fifty-five percent of Americans polled in 1995 believed that union leaders are more interested in promoting their personal interests than helping their members (Time/CNN Yankelovich Partners Inc. Poll, August 1995, Roper Public Opinion Online, accession no. 0242067), and some 62 percent placed at least some blame on unions for job losses (New York Times Poll, December 1995, Roper Public Opinion Online, accession no. 0256213). Nonetheless, some 68 percent of the American public continued to believe that labor unions are still needed (Time/CNN Yankelovich Partners Inc. Poll, September 1995, Roper Public Opinion Online, accession no. 0242066), and in June 1996 some 62 percent registered approval of labor unions (Newsweek Poll, June 1996, Princeton Survey Research Associates, Roper Public Opinion Online, accession no. 0256213).

136. See Richard Freeman and James L. Medoff, *What Do Unions Do?* (Basic, 1984), pp. 143–45.

137. In the U.S. public sector, where workers do not face aggressive antiunion campaigns, they unionize at European rates (about 37 percent in 1991), even though the public-sector union wage premium is lower than in the private sector. Barenberg, "Democracy and domination," p. 931, and H. Gregg Lewis, "Union/ nonunion wage gaps in the public sector," in Richard B. Freeman and Casey Ichniowski, eds., *When Public Sectors Unionize* (University of Chicago Press, 1988),

pp. 169–94. Generally, there appears to be no evidence that employer resistance to unionization is related to industry levels of economic rents available to share with workers. See John M. Abowd and Henry Farber, "Product market competition, union organizing activity, and employer resistance," (National Bureau of Economic Research Working Paper no. 3353, 1990). See also Richard Freeman and Morris Kleiner, "Employer behavior in the face of union organization drives," *Industrial and Labor Relations Review*, vol. 43, no. 4 (April 1990), pp. 360–64, and Richard Freeman and Joel Rogers, "Worker representation and participation survey: First report on findings," in Paula Voos, ed. *Employee Voice*, Proceedings of the Forty-Seventh Annual Meeting of the Industrial Relations Research Organization (Washington, D.C., 1995), pp. 432, 345.

138. Weiler, "Hard times for unions," p. 1027.

139. Barenberg, "Democracy and domination," p. 931.

140. Paul Weiler, "Promises to keep: Securing workers' rights to self-organization under the NLRA," *Harvard Law Review*, vol. 96 (1983), p. 1777. For his own proposal for unions supplemented by "employee participation committees" in nonunion firms, see *Governing the Workplace*, pp. 284–89. For other evidence that the oft-proclaimed demise of the American labor movement is exaggerated, see Marie Gottschalk, "Flexible futures: Labor, business, and the retrenchment of the American welfare state," Ph.D. diss., Yale University, 1997.

141. Elkouri and Elkouri, *How Arbitration Works*, p. 653.

142. Ibid., p. 662.

143. Ibid.

144. Ibid., pp. 662–63, 657.

145. Blenk, *European Labor Courts*, pp. 47–82.

146. Ibid., 47–54, 58–61. See also Kathleen Thelen, *Union of Parts; Labor Politics in Postwar Germany* (Cornell University Press, 1991), pp. 40–42.

147. The term *surfers' paradise* derives from the debate over whether surfers should be paid, raised by Philippe van Parijs's defense of a universal basic income in *Real Freedom for All* (Oxford University Press, 1995). See the symposium about his argument in *The Good Society*, vol. 6, no. 2 (Spring 1996), pp. 38–51.

148. Some U.S. state constitutions contain provisions guaranteeing a basic minimum. For instance, Article 17 of the New York State Constitution requires the provision of assistance to the needy, which courts have held to create an entitlement to public assistance to those defined as needy, although the legislature retains discretion to define *needy*. *Tucker v. Toia* 371 N.E. 2d 499, 452 (N.Y. 1977). On the turn to organizing and litigation in support of welfare guarantees at the state level in the face of growing hostility in Congress and the federal courts, see Barbara Sard, "The role of courts in welfare reform," *Clearinghouse Review* (August–September 1988), pp. 367–88. For a proposal for federal constitutional reform, see "A call for economic justice," Draft Labor Party Program as adopted

in Cleveland, Ohio, September 1996, which calls for a constitutional amendment to guarantee a "living wage."

149. See the discussion of standards of review in American constitutional law in Chapter 3, p. 56.

150. See Jonas Poutousson and Peter Swenson, "Labor markets, production strategies, and wage bargaining institutions: The Swedish employer offensive in comparative perspective," *Comparative Political Studies*, vol. 29, no. 2 (April 1996), pp. 223–51, and Kathleen Thelen, "The changing character of industrial relations in contemporary Europe," in Peter Hall and Peter Lange, eds., *The New European Political Economy* (Cambridge University Press, forthcoming).

151. On the affirmative-action front, Franklin D. Roosevelt first issued executive orders linking federal contracts to the avoidance of racial discrimination through his Committee on Fair Employment Practice in 1941 and 1942. The first executive order with real teeth was issued by the Kennedy administration in 1961; it required federal contractors to "take affirmative action to ensure" that individuals not suffer racial discrimination. Hugh D. Graham, *The Civil Rights Era: Origins and Development of National Policy* (Oxford University Press, 1990), pp. 8–14; Herman Belz, *Equality Transformed: A Quarter-Century of Affirmative Action* (Transaction, 1991), pp. 18–19. In September 1996, the Clinton administration gave up on its policy of refusing to do business with firms that hire permanent strike replacements by declining to request Supreme Court review of an adverse decision by the D.C. Circuit Court of Appeals concerning the legality of the administration's March 1995 executive order. *The Reuter Business Report* (September 9, 1996).

152. On the efficiency-wage argument, see Howard Botwinick, *Persistent Inequalities: Wage Disparities Under Capitalist Competition* (Princeton University Press, 1992), pp. 56–60, and Daniel Raff and Lawrence Summers, "Did Henry Ford pay efficiency wages?" *Journal of Labor Economics*, vol. 5, no. 4, part 2 (1987), pp. S57–S86. On the correlation between robust welfare states and industrial militancy, see Walter Korpi and Michael Shalev, "Strikes, industrial relations and class conflict in capitalist societies," *British Journal of Sociology*, vol. 30, no. 2 (June 1979), pp. 164–87; Alessandro Pizzorno, "Political exchange and collective identity in industrial conflict," in Colin Crouch and Alessandro Pizzorno, eds., *The Resurgence of Class Conflict in Western Europe Since 1968* (Holmes and Meier, 1978), vol. 2, pp. 277–98; Douglas Hibbs, "On the political economy of long-run trends in strike activity," *British Journal of Political Science*, vol. 8, part 2 (April 1978), pp. 153–75; and David Cameron, "Social democracy, corporatism, labor quiescence, and the representation of economic interest in advanced capitalist society," in John Goldthorpe, ed., *Order and Conflict in Contemporary Capitalism* (Clarendon Press, 1984), pp. 143–78.

153. See Barenberg, "Democracy and domination," p. 926.

154. See Peter Swenson, "Labor and the limits of the welfare state: The politics of intraclass conflict and cross-class alliances in Sweden and West Germany," *Comparative Politics*, vol. 24, no. 4 (July 1991), pp. 379–99.

155. See Peter Swenson, "Bringing capital back in, or social democracy reconsidered," *World Politics*, vol. 43, no. 4 (July 1991), pp. 513–44, on Denmark and Sweden, as well as his forthcoming work on the New Deal in the United States.

156. On the mobilization to end slavery in the British Empire, see Seymour Drescher, *Capitalism and Antislavery: British Mobilization in Comparative Perspective* (Oxford University Press, 1986), pp. 67–110, and on Britain's eventual use of unilateral force to achieve it, see Howard Temperley, *British Antislavery, 1833–1870* (University of South Carolina Press, 1972), pp. 168–83. On the campaign to abolish child labor in Britain, see Alec Fyfe, *Child Labour* (Polity, 1989); Pamela Horn, *Children's Work and Welfare, 1780s to 1880s* (Macmillan, 1994); Gary Anderson and Robert Tollison, "A rent-seeking explanation of the British Factory Acts," in David Colander, ed. *Neoclassical Political Economy* (Ballinger, 1984), pp. 187–204; and Clark Nardinelli, *Child Labor and the Industrial Revolution* (Indiana University Press, 1990), especially chapters 5–7, which describe the alliance between labor and other reform groups, as well as exogenous changes, that reduced business opposition to the Factory Acts. For the French story, see Lee Shai Weissbach, *Child Labor Reform in Nineteenth-Century France* (Louisiana State University Press, 1989). In the United States, as in Britain, the campaign for child-labor regulation was led by humanitarian reformers and labor leaders, passing a patchwork of state legislation in the nineteenth century. Attempts at federal legislation (such as the Keating-Owen bill passed in 1916) were struck down as unconstitutional during the *Lochner* era in decisions such as *Hammer v. Daggenhart*, 247 U.S. 251 (1918), prompting unsuccessful attempts to enact a child-labor amendment to the Constitution.

157. For the conventional wisdom, somewhat qualified, see Gary Clyde Hufbauer, Jeffrey J. Schott, and Kimberly Ann Elliott, *Economic Sanctions Reconsidered* (Institute for International Economics, 1990), 2 vols.; and Robin Renwick, *Economic Sanctions*, Harvard Studies in International Affairs, no. 45 (Harvard Center for International Affairs, 1981). For arguments and evidence contrary to the conventional wisdom, see M. S. Daoudi and M. S. Dajani, *Economic Sanctions: Ideals and Experience* (Routledge, 1983), and David A. Baldwin, *Economic Statecraft* (Princeton University Press, 1995). For a discussion that deals specifically with South Africa, see Lance Compa and Tashia Hinchliffe-Darricarrere, "Enforcing international labor rights through corporate codes of conduct," *Columbia Journal of Transnational Law*, vol. 33 (1995), pp. 663–89.

158. *Relative factor-price convergence* is Adrian Wood's term, signaling his rejection of global price-factor equalization, which relied on the Heckscher-Ohlin equilib-

rium model of international trade. Wood, *North-South Trade, Employment, and Inequality*, pp. 28-30.

159. Burtless, "International trade," p. 813.

160. World Bank statistics reveal that tariff barriers on manufactured goods entering developed countries fell from a 40 percent average in the late 1940s to less than 7 percent by the end of the 1970s. Wood, *North-South Trade, Employment, and Inequality*, p. 173.

161. Streek, "Codetermination," pp. 159-68; Wood, *North-South Trade, Employment and Inequality*, pp. 149-50 ff; Burtless, "International trade," p. 812.

162. Bilateral, regional, and global trade agreements in the 1980s and 1990s have produced more than thirty regional trading blocs in the world economy. Vincent Cable and David Henderson, eds., *Trade Blocs? The Future of Regional Integration* (Brookings, 1994), p. 1.

163. The International Labor Organization was set up in 1919 to begin creating a multilateral regime protecting basic labor rights. For a thoughtful discussion of attempts in United States legislation to increase its enforcement through unilateral linkage of trade benefits to abiding by ILO provisions, see Harlan Mandel, "In pursuit of the missing link: International worker rights and international trade?" *Columbia Journal of Transnational Law*, vol. 27 (1989), pp. 443-82.

164. Mark Barenberg, "Federalism and American labor law: Toward a critical mapping of the 'social dumping' question," in Ingolf Pernice, ed., *Harmonization of Legislation in Federal Systems* (Nomos Verlagsgesellschaft, 1996), p. 106.

165. Ibid., pp. 106-7.

166. This is the North American Agreement on Labor Cooperation. For a summary and (rather sanguine) early assessment, see Joaquin F. Otero, "The North American Agreement on Labor Cooperation: An assessment of its first year's implementation," *Columbia Journal of Transnational Law*, vol. 33 (1995), pp. 637-62.

167. Barenberg, "Federalism and American labor law," p. 107.

168. Though not, of course, constitutional requirements—another reason to support constitutionalizing basic interest provisions.

169. Conrad Weiler, "GATT, NAFTA, and state and local powers," *Intergovernmental Perspective*, vol. 20, no. 1 (Fall 1993-Winter 1994), pp. 38-41. Among the more pressing issues in this regard in late 1996 was GATT. At the end of the Uruguay round of talks, the Clinton administration proposed continuing negotiations toward minimum global labor and environmental standards, enforceable by a new World Trade Organization, at the Singapore round in 1996-97. Barenberg, "Federalism and American labor law," p. 105. The labor piece of this appeared in late 1996 to have been dropped in subcommittees, however. (Barenberg, in conversation.)

170. For a helpful summary of six possible strategies governments can pursue, see

Mark Barenberg, "Law and labor in the new global economy," *Columbia Journal of Transnational Law*, vol. 33, no. 3 (1995), pp. 445–55.

171. For a canvassing of these views, see Barenberg, "Federalism and American labor law," pp. 112–18.

172. In the United States there were 29.3 million (13 percent) in poverty in 1980, rising to 33.6 million (13.5 percent) in 1990, 35.7 million (14.2 percent) in 1991, 36.9 million in (14.5 percent) in 1992, and 39.2 million (15.1 percent) in 1993. *Statistical Abstract of the United States*, 115th ed. (Department of Commerce, 1995), p. 482. In 1996 the European Community published data indicating that on average 14.3 percent of households in Europe live in poverty, about 52 million people. *Social Portrait of Europe* (Office for Official Publications of the European Community, 1996), p. 212.

173. On attempts to institutionalize global standards, see Steve Charnovitz, "Promoting higher labor standards," *Washington Quarterly*, vol. 13, no. 3 (Summer 1995), pp. 167–87.

174. See Roger Blanpain, *Labor Law and Industrial Relations of the European Community* (Kluwer Law and Taxation Publishers, 1991), chapter 4.

175. *Agreement on Social Policy Concluded Between the Member States of the European Community with the Exception of the United Kingdom of Great Britain and Northern Ireland* (Maastricht, February 7, 1992), article 2.

176. "Council Directive 94/45/EC of 22 September 1994 on the establishment of a European Works Council or a procedure in Community-scale undertakings and Community-scale groups of undertakings for the purposes of informing and consulting employees," Brussels, Commission of the European Communities, 1994 OJ L 254 (September 30, 1994).

177. For the story of how the German works councils, conceived initially to limit union power, actually helped strengthen it, see Thelen, *Union of Parts*, pp. 63–83. As Peter Swenson has pointed out to me in conversation, there is some doubt as to whether this could occur with the European Works Councils as presently constituted, because the 1994 directive contains no arbitration requirement. For a relatively optimistic early assessment of the European Works Councils, see Lowell Turner, "The Europeanization of labor: Structure before action," *European Journal of Industrial Relations* (November 1996), pp. 325–44.

178. Recognizing the significant role for the council is not to deny that its democratic accountability should be enhanced. Exploring this subject would take us too far afield. Suffice it to say that although reducing the "democratic deficit" in Europe is an important goal, this does not obviously mean strengthening the power of national parliaments.

179. Wood, *North-South Trade, Employment, and Inequality*, pp. 346–94; Burtless, "International trade and earnings inequality," p. 315.

7. Life's Ending

1. See Alex Inkeles and Chikakao Usui, "Retirement patterns in cross-national perspective," in David Kertzer and K. Warner Schaie, eds., *Age Structuring in Comparative Perspective* (Lawrence Erlbaum, 1989), pp. 227-61, 239; and David W. E. Smith, *Human Longevity* (Oxford University Press, 1993), pp. 13-14.

2. William Graebner, *A History of Retirement: The Meaning and Function of an American Institution, 1885-1978* (Yale University Press, 1980), pp. 10-17.

3. See Carole Haber, *Beyond Sixty-Five: The Dilemmas of Old Age in America's Past* (Cambridge University Press, 1983). A significant exception to the generalization in the text is the case of Civil War veterans, who received generous disability benefits for themselves and their dependents from the federal government, and pensions as well after 1890. By 1900 nearly a million veterans were receiving pensions that generally amounted to about a third of the average wage. Maris Vinovskis, "Stepping down in former times: The view from colonial and 19th-century America," in Kertzer and Schaie, *Age Structuring in Comparative Perspective*, pp. 221-22.

4. Graebner, *A History of Retirement*, pp. 14-15. On the British history, see Chris Phillipson, *Capitalism and the Construction of Old Age* (Macmillan, 1981), pp. 16-38.

5. Frederick L. Hoffman, "The physical and mental aspects of labor and industry," *Annals of the American Academy of Political and Social Science*, vol. 27 (May 1906), p. 3.

6. See Karl Mayer and David Featherman, "Methodological problems in cross-national research on retirement," in Kertzer and Schaie, *Age Structuring in Comparative Perspective*, p. 266.

7. Compare Peter Peterson's alarmist account in *Will America Grow Up Before It Grows Old?* (Random House, 1996) with the more sober assessment by Jerry Mashaw and Theodore Marmor, "The great Social Security scare," *American Prospect*, no. 29 (November-December 1996), pp. 30-37.

8. It was anticipated that most insurers would offer a variety of more expansive packages as well at escalating premiums. For an endorsement of a single-payer system, see Theodore R. Marmor, *Understanding Health Care Reform* (Yale University Press, 1994), pp. 179-94.

9. For a helpful summary of the main provisions in the legislation, see Ronald Dworkin, "Will Clinton's plan be fair?" *New York Review of Books* (January 13, 1994), pp. 20-25.

10. See Chapter 3, note 19. No doubt other factors—ranging from the structural deficit inherited from the Reagan years to the political ineptitude of the novice Clinton administration—played their respective parts. See Theda Skocpol, *Boomerang: Health Care Reform and the Turn Against Government* (Norton, 1997),

and Jacob Hacker, *The Road to Nowhere: The Genesis of President Clinton's Plan for Health Security* (Princeton University Press, 1997), for accounts of the failure.

11. For a powerful argument to the effect that further privatization of health-care insurance is unlikely to diminish the injustices that currently attend its provision, see Allen Buchanan, "Privatization and just healthcare," *Bioethics*, vol. 9, nos. 3–4 (1995), pp. 220–39.

12. In 1994 Marmor reported that Canada, France, and Germany provided universal insurance coverage at a cost of between 8 and 9.5 percent of GNP. Britain, Japan, and Australia provided it for between 6 and 8 percent of GNP. The United States, which then spent 12 percent of GNP on health care, had thirty-seven million uninsured (including ten million children, six million unemployed and five million part-time workers); it ranked below all other OECD countries for levels of infant mortality and life expectancy. *Understanding Health Care Reform*, pp. 2–3, 184. By mid-1997 the uninsured had exceeded forty-one million, and Medicare spending alone spending stood at $196 billion a year—the largest component, at 12.2 percent, of the federal budget after defense and Social Security, and 14 percent of GDP. Expenditures were expected to grow to $312 billion by 2002, and the Republican Congress was planning to increase age-eligibility for Medicare to sixty-seven while retaining a retirement age of sixty-five, in effect threatening to create a new tier of elderly uninsured. See "Will anyone dare touch Medicare?" *Economist* (June 28, 1997), pp. 53–54.

13. Dworkin, "Will Clinton's plan be fair?" p. 22. The qualifier "almost wholly" reflects the fact that one implication of the rescue principle garners Dworkin's approval: that medical rationing should not be based on money.

14. Ibid., p. 22.

15. A caveat should be added to the effect that the rate of forced savings should not be so steep as to undermine people's ability to discharge any delegated responsibilities they may have to provide for the basic interests of their children.

16. For evidence that the decline in lower- and middle-class real family incomes (defined as the bottom 60 percent) was partly cushioned in the 1980s, and to a lesser extent in the 1990s, by the increase in two-earner families, see Lawrence Mishel, Jared Bernstein, and John Schmitt, *The State of Working America, 1996–97* (Economic Policy Institute, 1997), pp. 74–98.

17. Those who believe that returning to the days when the elderly were cared for within the household economy would improve their lot idealize the past. For an illuminating corrective they should read Andrejs Plakans, "Stepping down in former times: A comparative assessment of 'retirement' in traditional Europe," in Kertzer and Schaie, *Age Structuring in Comparative Perspective*, pp. 175–95.

18. Norman Daniels, *Am I My Parent's Keeper?* (Oxford University Press, 1988).

19. See Peter Schuck, "The graying of the civil rights law: The Age Discrimination Act of 1975," *Yale Law Journal*, vol. 89, no. 1 (1979), pp. 27–93.

20. See also my discussion in *Democracy's Place*, pp. 30-42.

21. *Massachusetts Board of Retirement v. Murgia*, 427 U.S. 307, 312 (1976). For an extended philosophical defense of the developmental view, see Daniels, *Am I My Parent's Keeper?* pp. 3-20, 83-95.

22. This is not to say that legislatures should be unable to legislate against age discrimination, only that age-based statuses should not be presumed suspect regardless of what legislatures do.

23. See Peterson, *Will America Grow Up?* pp. 31-49.

24. This is not to deny the existence of issues of principle about treatment of the elderly for democratic justice; important matters having to do with longevity, medical care, and termination of life are taken up below. It is merely to say that because democratic justice seeks to entrench basic interest protections over the course of the lifetime, it takes no position on distributive conflicts among age cohorts that are by-products of accounting schemes and demographics. For similar reasons democratic justice is silent on whether retirement systems should be centralized (as with Social Security), decentralized (as with employment pensions and individually managed retirement instruments), or some combination. These are matters for policy debate and trial and error.

25. Data on age cohorts and poverty in the United States are consistent with this possibility. As I note in Chapter 4, since the 1960s the proportion of the elderly in poverty has been declining, while that of children has been increasing. On the political efficacy of the AARP, see Schuck, "Graying of the civil rights law," pp. 39-42.

26. Judith Rooks, "Let's admit we ration health care—then set priorities," *American Journal of Nursing* (June 1990), p. 41.

27. Marmor, *Understanding Health Care Reform*, p. 103; "Will anyone dare touch Medicare?"

28. See Schuck, "Graying of the civil rights law," pp. 63-65, for a summary of the standards for review of age classification in constitutional interpretation and as set out in the 1975 Age Discrimination Act. For a review of more recent case law, which continues to affirm that age is not a suspect classification, see David M. O'Brien, *Constitutional Law and Politics*, 3d ed. (Norton, 1997), chapter 12.

29. This is a fortunate result in light of Anthony Trollope's brilliant exploration in his novel *The Fixed Period* (Penguin, 1993) of the perverse consequences that should be anticipated if the state had the power to end individual lives once the life span deemed legitimate had been used up.

30. This could be accomplished in various ways. Life-contracting policies might be subjected to heightened judicial scrutiny, or, in a system lacking judicial review, they might be required to garner supermajorities or unusual bicameral support. My present focus is on the principle rather than the mechanism.

31. This is not to mention the questions of personal identity that are in any case unresolved by cloning.

32. I leave aside what the test should be de facto or de jure.

33. I sidestep the debate as to whether increases in longevity have been accompanied by an increase or decrease in the quality of life of the elderly. James F. Fries argues that increased life expectancy for older Americans has been accompanied by improved health. See his "Aging, natural death, and the compression of morbidity," *New England Journal of Medicine*, vol. 303 (1980), pp. 130–35, and "The compression of morbidity: Near or far?" *Millbank Memorial Fund Quarterly*, vol. 67 (1989), pp. 208–32. For the contrary view, see E. M. Gruenberg, "The failure of success," *Millbank Memorial Fund Quarterly*, vol. 55 (1977), pp. 3–34, and M. Kramer, "The rising pandemic of mental disorders and associated chronic diseases and disabilities," *Acta Psychiatrica Scandanavica*, no. 285 (1980), pp. 382–97. For a more mixed account, see Kenneth G. Manton, "Changing concepts of morbidity and mortality in the elderly population," *Millbank Memorial Fund Quarterly*, vol. 60 (1982), pp. 183–244, and Kenneth G. Manton, Eric Stallard, and Larry Corder, "Changes in morbidity and chronic disability in the U.S. elderly population: Evidence from 1982, 1984, and 1989 national long-term care surveys," *Journal of Gerontology* series B, vol. 50 (1955), pp. S194–S204.

34. Dworkin, "Will Clinton's plan be fair?" p. 22.

35. Ibid., pp. 22–23.

36. Ibid., pp. 23–24. For a more general defense of this approach, see also Dworkin's "What is equality?" part 2, "Equality of resources."

37. Dworkin, "Will Clinton's plan be fair?" p. 24.

38. Initial attempts by the Oregon Health Services Commission (OHSC) to rank procedures prudentially by cost-effectiveness so as to maximize "quality-adjusted life years" produced a storm of public protest because it ended up ranking many relatively minor medical procedures above lifesaving procedures. See David C. Hadorn, "Setting health care priorities in Oregon: Cost-effectiveness meets the rule of rescue," *Journal of the American Medical Association*, vol. 26, no. 17 (May 1, 1991), pp. 2218–25.

39. Dworkin's discussion of how the members of the National Health Board would utilize the prudent insurance model is uncharacteristically imprecise. Here I interpret his position to be that the different board members—selected from different walks of life and points in the life cycle—should appeal to their intuitions about how a prudent twenty-five-year-old would insure in a just society if he had perfect information about available medical technologies and no knowledge of the ills to befall him in the future. It could be that what Dworkin means to say is that the different members should simply apply their own intuitions about prudent medical insurance. This would save him from my objections, but as the

price of rendering his model irrelevant to their deliberations. That being the case, what reason would there be to propose the model?

40. In 1990, forty-seven community meetings were held across the state, attended by about one thousand people in total. They were asked to rank categories of treatment by importance and articulate the values that guided their decisions. Taking this data into account, the OSHC eventually produced a ranked list of more than seven hundred conditions and appropriate treatments. The state legislature then used the list as a yardstick to appropriate Medicaid funds. The Oregon plan was intended to expand Medicaid eligibility from 68 percent of those at the federal poverty level to 100 percent and to finance the increased cost by prudent rationing of procedures. Although Oregon did end up expanding coverage to some 126,000 additional citizens by February 1997, much of this was actually achieved by appropriation of new funds by the legislature rather than from savings generated by the explicit rationing. This suggests that as a device for focusing attention on the medical needs of the poor and achieving expanded coverage, processes like the Oregon plan may be advantageous. As a means of achieving collective rationing, however, the benefits are less obvious. See Norman Daniels, "Is the Oregon rationing plan fair?" *Journal of the American Medical Association*, vol. 265, no. 17 (May 1, 1991), pp. 2232-35; Jim Montague, "Why rationing was right for Oregon," *Hospitals and Health Networks* (February 5, 1997), pp. 64-66; and Lawrence Jacobs, Theodore Marmor, and Jonathan Oberlander, "The Oregon health plan and the political paradox of rationing: What advocates and critics have claimed and what Oregon did," mimeo, Yale University, 1998.

41. For defenses of the Oregon process, see Michael Garland and Romana Hasnaid, "Community responsibility and the development of Oregon's health priorities," *Business and Professional Ethics Journal*, vol. 9, nos. 3-4 (1991), pp. 182-99; Leonard Fleck, "The Oregon medical experiment: Is it just enough?" *Business and Professional Ethics Journal*, vol. 9, nos. 3-4 (1991), pp. 201-17; and Montague, "Why rationing was right for Oregon." For a critical assessment of its effects in limiting poor people's access to health care, see Bruce Vladeck, "Unhealthy rations," *American Prospect* (Summer 1991), p. 101.

42. Dworkin, "Will Clinton's plan be fair?" p. 24. Daniels reports that the meetings were attended predominantly by "college educated, relatively well off, and white" audiences, half of which consisted of health professionals. Only 9.4 percent of the attendees were uninsured (compared with 16 percent of the state's population at the time), and Medicaid recipients (the only direct representatives of poor children) were underrepresented by half. "Is the Oregon rationing plan fair?" p. 2234.

43. Daniels, "Is the Oregon rationing plan fair?" pp. 2233-34.

44. See Rooks, "Let's admit we ration health care," p. 41.

45. Norman Daniels and James Sabin, "Limits to health care: Fair procedures, democratic deliberation, and the legitimacy problem for insurers," mimeo, 1997.

46. This is not to favor "judicial legislation." Beyond the general considerations disfavoring extensive judicial activism discussed in Chapter 3, courts evidently lack relevant medical expertise in this area. Courts could, however, play a role as an escape valve in a process like the Oregon one, by declaring the coverage agreed to by the legislature to be insufficient in light of the deliberative process that preceded it and remanding it back to the legislature for further consideration.

47. Locke, *Two Treatises*, II, sec. 72, pp. 314–15. This assumes that private inheritance is legitimate. This large subject is not taken up here; suffice it to say that from the standpoint of democratic justice, the right to bequeath is justifiable, if at all, on consequentialist grounds (such as providing the incentive to work) only. That intergenerational transfers of wealth should be prime candidates for heavily progressive taxation seems an easy call to me, though the extent to which it should be relied upon as against other forms of taxation is a matter for electoral politics.

48. Some will say that the same logic should commit us to opposing abortion as well. In fact, the parallel argument does not hold. Whereas it is uncontroversial that putting someone to death involves terminating his life, the question when human life begins is part of what is at issue in the abortion debate.

49. See Sissela Bok, "Easeful death: From Keats to Kevorkian," *Harvard Medical Alumni Bulletin*, vol. 70 (Winter 1997), pp. 16–19.

50. Ronald Dworkin, *Life's Dominion: An Argument About Abortion, Euthanasia, and Individual Freedom* (Vintage, 1993), p. 183.

51. R. N. Smart, "Negative utilitarianism," *Mind*, vol. 67 (1958), pp. 542–43. Those who dismiss such thinking as one of the sillinesses of utilitarianism might be interested to learn that the early Christian Circumcelliones were noted for practicing suicide to eliminate the risk that they would sin and suffer eternal damnation as a result. It was thought particularly good to provoke an infidel to martyr you or to adopt austerities that would lead to your death, but in the last resort other means were acceptable. See G. Steven Neeley, *The Constitutional Right to Suicide: A Legal and Philosophical Examination* (Peter Lang, 1994), p. 40.

52. Accordingly, we need not engage the many arguments, religious and secular, that have been made for and against the permissibility of suicide. For a useful history of the subject, see Neeley, *Constitutional Right to Suicide*.

53. It might be said that suicide is a more thoroughgoing compromise of a person's basic interests than selling oneself into slavery or indentured servitude, which I argue—in Chapter 5—is ruled out by democratic justice. The difference, however, is that he who sells himself into slavery or indentured servitude places himself in the power of another, whereas he who commits suicide does not. Needless to say, it would be a different matter if the decision to commit

suicide was accompanied by a contract to sell organs or some other power-laden third-party involvement.

54. Not to mention the fact that some of the adult deaths at Jonestown were murders. See Kenneth Wooden, *The Children of Jonestown* (McGraw-Hill, 1981).

55. *Cruzan v. Director, Missouri Dep't of Health*, 497 U.S. 261 (1990).

56. In *Washington et al. v. Glucksburg et al.*, 138 L. Ed 2d 772 (1997), they rejected a due-process argument for this extension, and in *Vacco et al. v. Quill et al.*, 138 L. Ed 2d 834 (1997), they were no more impressed by an equal-protection appeal to the *Cruzan* logic.

57. On Oregon's legalization of physician-assisted suicide for terminally ill adults in 1994, see Linda Greenhouse, "Before the court, the sanctity of life and death," *New York Times* (January 5, 1997), Week in Review section.

58. See Dworkin, *Life's Dominion*, pp. 218–20.

59. See Elisabeth Kübler-Ross, *On Death and Dying* (Macmillan, 1969), and Herbert Hendin, "Physician-assisted suicide: What next?" *Responsive Community*, vol. 7, no. 4 (Fall 1997), pp. 21–34.

60. The idea to provide a legal basis for living wills in the United States was first proposed by Luis Kutner in "Due process of euthanasia: The living will, a proposal," *Indiana Law Journal*, vol. 44 (1969), pp. 539–85. Courts and state legislatures first addressed the issue in the mid-1970s, when California enacted the Natural Death Act, providing the foundation for subsequent legislation in other states. In most states living wills are effective only to refuse extraordinary life prolonging care (such as artificial respiration or circulation and cardiopulmonary resuscitation) when there is no real prospect for improvement or cure. Whether nutrition can also be withheld via instructions in a living will varies from state to state. See Christopher Condie, "Comparison of the living will statutes in fifty states," *Journal of Contemporary Law*, vol. 14, no. 1 (1988), pp. 105–29.

61. Dworkin, *Life's Dominion*, p. 228.

62. Except for Arkansas and Connecticut, every state allows revocation of a living will at any time. Georgia allows revocation "by any means." California and Idaho have five-year sunset clauses, and Georgia provides for a seven-year time limit. Condie, "Comparison of living wills," pp. 116–19.

63. Some might contend that there is a parallel with children here in that the best guide, when trying to decide what is in a child's interest, is to take the decision that one believes the child will thank you for as a mature adult. This could be said to be a constructive attempt to give ex ante effect to the child's mature will. Although this is a defensible view of how best to make decisions for children, there may well be others. In any case, the parallel is partial only, because the fiduciary is instrumental in shaping the child's values and preferences, and hence the adult who the fiduciary hopes will one day thank her. Fiduciaries for the elderly must take their values and preferences as given.

64. Dworkin, *Life's Dominion*, p. 231.

65. For a review of evidence suggesting that this occurs on a significant scale, see Dworkin, *Life's Dominion*, pp. 182–83.

66. Dworkin is unimpressed by appeals to the possibility of error in arguments for making euthanasia difficult, countering that not ending a life that should be ended harms the patient just as ending a life that should not be ended does. *Life's Dominion*, pp. 196–97. This argument is unconvincing. One can concede his point that keeping someone alive in certain circumstances may do him significant harm yet still believe that it is better to err on the side of life because decisions to end it are irrevocable whereas decisions not to end it are not.

67. *Airedale NHS Trust (Respondents) v. Bland*, House of Lords, Judgment, February 4, 1993.

68. Physicians might complain that the proposed oversight infringes on their professional autonomy. In fact, it offers valuable protection of it. If a patient's kin disagree with one another as to what should be done, if they experience subsequent changes of heart, if they decide later that they were manipulated into making a decision that they have come to regret, or if some new relevant player who was not consulted emerges after the fact, the physician will be grateful for a larger institutional context through which the decision has been approved. Even Jack Kevorkian might agree that an appropriately regulated process would be superior to the activity in which he engages in the back of his Volkswagen van.

69. This happened in the 1991 case of Joseph Finelli described by Dworkin in *Life's Dominion*, pp. 232–33. In the course of a heart transplant, Finelli had suffered severe brain damage, which reduced him to the mental condition of a six-month-old. He had executed neither a living will nor a durable power of attorney. The hospital in which he had the operation performed, and which had cared for him for many years, sought to take him off immune-suppressing medicine that he needed to prevent rejection of his transplanted heart. The expectation was that this would lead to his death. His adamantly opposed family took the matter to court. The judge appointed a guardian, who came to the view that if Finelli could decide for himself he would prefer to be dead. The judge took the family's side, however, refusing to order termination of the medication. The right thing to do is unclear in this case because a fiduciary had not been designated by Finelli. Arguably, the judge took the correct action from the perspective of democratic justice, assuming that the hospital had a financial interest at stake and the court-appointed guardian had not known Finelli. But one cannot have a great deal of confidence in this judgment. This type of outcome underscores the value of the durable power of attorney.

70. *Vacco v. Quill*, 138 L. Ed 2d (1997), at 842. The decision reversed 80 F. 3d 716.

71. For a sensitive investigation of these contingencies, see Gerald Dworkin, "The nature of medicine," mimeo, 1997.

72. Locke, *Two Treatises*, II, sec. 23, p. 284; sec. 135, p. 357. On the king's prerogative, see Neeley, *Constitutional Right to Suicide*, pp. 47–49.

73. See my *Abortion*, pp. 1–23, and *Washington v. Glucksburg* 138 L. Ed 2d (1997), at 793–97.

8. Deepening Democratic Justice

1. We should endorse Przeworski's contention that those who dismiss minimalist Schumpeterian democracy have not seriously confronted what life is like without it, but not his inference that we should therefore reject more robust conceptions. Adam Przeworski, "Minimalist conception of democracy: A defense," in Ian Shapiro and Casiano Hacker-Cordón, eds., *Democracy's Value* (Cambridge University Press, 1999). When democratic national institutions are lacking, it is always important to work for them. But when they are established, and people discover how many consequential power relations structuring everyday life they do not affect, then it makes sense to refocus the lens on those undemocratic power relations. Does this mean democratic national institutions should lead the list of democratic priorities? Often, but not always. Sometimes democratic forces are too weak to prevail in authoritarian national politics, yet able to achieve some successes in civil society that can have positive spin-offs for national democratization over time. For discussion of this possibility in the case of Egypt, see Bruce Rutherford, "Can an Islamic group aid democratization?" in John Chapman and Ian Shapiro, eds., *NOMOS XXXV: Democratic Community* (New York University Press, 1993).

2. Iris Young, *Justice and the Politics of Difference* (Princeton University Press, 1990), pp. 15–65.

3. Questions about the division of authority are distributive in the sense that they deal with the distribution of power, but this is evidently a different sense of distribution than that which informs the distributive-justice literature.

4. See *Political Liberalism*, pp. 257–88. For his earlier discussions see *A Theory of Justice*, pp. 7–11.

5. Accordingly, we are able to sidestep debates about what should be seen as part of the basic structure. See Susan Okin's critique of Rawls for excluding the family from it in *Justice, Gender, and the Family*, pp. 93–97.

6. See Kai Nielsen, "World government, security, and global justice," in Steven Luper-Foy, ed., *Problems of International Justice* (Westview, 1988), pp. 263–82.

7. George Soros is surely right that ways should be sought to regulate the activities of international currency speculators and hedge fund managers. They often control resources well in excess of the foreign-exchange reserve of governments, so that their speculative activities can lead currencies to collapse and undermine the policies of elected governments. George Soros, *The Crisis of Global Capitalism* (Perseus, 1998), pp. 175–94.

8. For a useful discussion of transnational forms of regulation in the absence of global political institutions, focused on financial services, international criminal cartels, and dual-use goods (which can be converted from civilian to offensive military use), see Wolfgang Reinicke, *Global Public Policy* (Brookings, 1998).

9. See Elmar Altvater, "The democratic order, economic globalization, and ecological restrictions: On the relation of material and formal democracy," in Shapiro and Cordón, *Democracy's Edges*.

10. Alexis de Tocqueville, *Democracy in America*, ed. J. P. Mayer (Doubleday, 1969), pp. 12–13.

11. See Francis Fukuyama, *The End of History and the Last Man* (Free Press, 1992).

12. See Juan Linz, *The Breakdown of Democratic Regimes: Crisis, Breakdown, and Reequilibration* (Johns Hopkins University Press, 1978), and Juan Linz and Alfred Stepan, eds., *The Breakdown of Democratic Regimes: Latin America* (Johns Hopkins University Press, 1978).

13. See Thabo Mbeki, "Africa will surprise the world again," speech to the United Nations in Tokyo, reported in *Business Day* (Johannesburg, South Africa), April 14, 1998.

14. See Smith, *Civic Ideals*.

15. Tocqueville, *Democracy in America*, p. 12.

Index

278–79*n*30; and interspousal tort immunity, 131, 282*n*54; libertarian considerations on, 122–24; libertarianism's limits on, 124–26; Mill on, 277*n*16; and no-fault divorce, 33, 252*n*13; and obstacles to exit, 129–31; patriarchy's legacy regarding, 111–15; physical abuse in, 129, 131, 132–33, 281*n*48, 283*n*62; polygamy, 27, 44, 112, 123, 130, 254*n*34, 279*n*32, 281*n*49, 281–82*n*51; prenuptial agreements, 58, 124, 139–40, 279*n*34; privacy of spousal communications, 141–42; as public good, 277*n*17; rape in, 57, 113, 116, 131, 257*n*56; reform of marriage status, 115–22; single-sex marriage, 111, 122–23, 277*n*17, 279*n*31, 286*n*86; special privileges of, 140–42, 285–86*nn*86–87; and spousal liability, 131–32, 282*n*52, 285*n*82; state's role in, 116, 277*n*18; statistics on, 112; and tax code, 140, 141, 286*n*87; and unanimity rule, 33; and wage splitting between husbands and wives, 117–22, 278*nn*21–22, 278*nn*27–28, 284*n*76, 285*n*81; wife's employment outside of home, 112; women's property rights in, 57, 113, 121, 136, 284*nn*71–72. *See also* Divorce; Family; Parent-child relations

Marriage of Newman, In re, 279*n*34
Married Women's Property Acts, 113, 121
Marshall, Alfred, 199
Marx, Karl, 8, 10, 146, 154, 155, 245*n*21, 263*n*53, 280*n*42, 286*n*4, 287*n*9, 291*n*57
Marxism, 22, 34, 153, 154, 244*n*19, 288*n*23, 288*n*26
Mashaw, Jerry, 308*n*7
Massachusetts Board of Retirement v. Murgia, 205, 310*n*21
Massachusetts Stubborn Child Law, 259*n*10
McDermott, Katherine, 250*n*15, 256*n*48
McDonnell Douglas Corp. v. Green, 294*n*76
Means-ends dichotomies, 53
"Means testing," 206
Medicaid, 200, 206–7, 215, 216, 217, 312*n*40, 312*n*42
Medical care. *See* Health care
Medical technologies, 26, 28, 106, 197, 311*n*39
Medicare, 196, 199, 200, 309*n*12

Membership-based sovereignty, 38–39, 252–53*n*21, 253*n*22
META. *See* Model Employment Termination Act (META)
Metarules and metaprinciples, 45–46
Metternich, Klemens von, 271*n*106
Military, 48, 49, 276*n*8
Mill, John Stuart, 7, 243*n*14, 248*n*39, 251*n*6, 277*n*16
Miller, Nicholas R., 268*n*83
"Minimal" scrutiny, 56
Minorities: domination of, by democratic processes, 41, 253*n*26, 253–54*n*28; and high school graduation, 107; and infant mortality rates, 106; and low-birth-weight children, 106; Moynihan Report on blacks, 104, 112, 113, 276*n*8, 276*n*10; poverty of, 105–6; tyranny of, 33, 237; white South Africans, 236
Mintz, Stephen, 275*n*4
Mithestimmung ("having a voice"), 179
Model Employment Termination Act (META), 294*n*80
Moe, Terry, 269*n*90
Mondragon, 176, 299*n*117
Moore, Barrington, 30, 39
Mormons, 45, 123, 130, 254*n*34
Mosca, Gaetano, 263*n*53
Mt. Healthy City Board of Education v. Doyle, 295*n*87
Moynihan Report, 104, 112, 113, 276*n*8, 276*n*10
Mozert v. Hawkins Cty. Bd. of Ed., 264–65*n*63
Mueller, Dennis, 248*n*1
Muller, Edward N., 268*n*82
Murray, Charles, 113, 270*n*95

Nader, Laura, 66
NAFTA, 193
National Conference of Commissioners on Uniform State Laws, 294*n*80
National Labor Relations Act (NLRA), 181, 188, 193, 301*n*130, 302*n*133
National Labor Relations Board (NLRB), 166–67, 170, 181, 296*n*89
Nation-state, 252*n*21